RELUCTANT
REBELS

CIVIL WAR AMERICA   Gary W. Gallagher, editor

The Confederates Who Joined the Army after 1861

RELUCTANT
REBELS

KENNETH W. NOE

THE UNIVERSITY OF NORTH CAROLINA PRESS   Chapel Hill

Designed by Courtney Leigh Baker and set in Arno Pro with Rockwell Display by Keystone Typesetting, Inc. Manufactured in the United States of America. The paper in this book meets the guidelines for permanence and durability of the Committee on Production Guidelines for Book Longevity of the Council on Library Resources. The University of North Carolina Press has been a member of the Green Press Initiative since 2003.

ISBN 978-0-8078-3377-3

A portion of this work appeared previously, in somewhat different form, as "'Alabama, We Will Fight for Thee': The Initial Motivations of Later-Enlisting Confederates," *Alabama Review* 62 (July 2009): 163–89, and is reprinted here with permission.

Book club edition

FOR NANCY, AS ALWAYS

CONTENTS

ILLUSTRATIONS

ACKNOWLEDGMENTS

In November of 2002, three dozen Civil War historians gathered in Washington at the Library of Congress for a symposium entitled "The Civil War and American Memory." Earlier, organizer Gary Gallagher had asked me to help comment on Joseph Glatthaar's presentation, "Why They Fought: Soldiers and Civilians of the Civil War Era." Scholarly commentary usually involves pointing out the flaws in a presentation, as well as the strengths, and suggesting areas for improvement. When Joe Glatthaar's paper arrived in the mail, however, I faced an uncomfortable and unfamiliar situation. It simply was too good to pick apart. With clarity and style he had neatly summarized a half-decade of scholarship on why Civil War soldiers enlisted and fought, and succinctly offered his own conclusions as well. Faced with the embarrassment of having nothing to say, I nearly gave up, until I realized that there indeed were flaws after all, not with the excellent essay, but rather with the literature as a whole. Studies of Civil War soldiers, I later nervously contended that chilly November afternoon in the nation's capital, clearly favored the men who had enlisted at the beginning of the war and battled as long as they could in the so-called fighting regiments. Where were the conscripts? I asked. Where were the deserters? Where were the men who broke and ran away? Where were the garrison troops and backwater outfits? For that matter, where were the reluctant Rebels, the men who waited months or years before enlisting? Scholars and general readers alike would never truly understand the full range of the soldier experience, I suggested, until all those men found their historians too. When the session ended, fellow panelists Catherine Clinton and Anne Sarah Rubin, as well as David Eicher, offered support and encouragement for my ideas. And so this book was conceived.

Over the last eight years, many more people have helped me turn that fleeting idea born of intellectual desperation into reality. Like all historians, I owe great debts to the archivists who preserve and generously make available the documents upon which we depend. While every last one deserves personal thanks for fetching me yet another folder, I must point especially to Dwayne Cox of Auburn University's Special Collections; Norwood Kerr and Debbie Pendleton of the Alabama Department of Archives and History; Teresa M. Burk of Emory University; Germain J. Bienvenu of Louisiana State University's Special Collections; Jay Richiuso of the Tennessee State Library and Archives; Kristy Dixon of the W. S. Hoole Special Collections Library, University of Alabama; Anne Prichard of Special Collections, University of Arkansas; Brian Cuthell and Henry Fulmer of the Caroliniana Library, University of South Carolina; Geoffrey Stark of the University of Arkansas Libraries; and Toni Carter-Dean, Graham Dozier, Lee Shepard, Greg Stoner, and Tyler Young, all of the Virginia Historical Society (although Toni has since moved on to join us at Auburn). Clinton Bagley of the Mississippi Department of Archives and History not only identified a source I otherwise would have missed, but took me to lunch at the home base of the Sweet Potato Queens. As usual, Art Bergeron and Richard Sommers of the U.S. Army Military History Institute were tremendous resources during my sojourns at Carlisle Barracks. My greatest archival hero, however, remains the admirable young student employee at Duke who brought me collections for parts of three days while tottering about on her crutches.

Beyond the archives, Daryl Black, Peter Carmichael, Tony Carey, Ruth Crocker, Harriet Amos Doss, Mark Franklin, Guy Hubbs, and George Rable happily provided feedback and suggestions for additional research. Harriet also pointed me to Alan Pitts and his noteworthy thesis on Alabama soldiers. Identifying what soldiers were or were not later enlisters sometimes proved a trying task, but one that was made somewhat easier thanks to the timely and knowledgeable assistance of Keith Bohannon, Bill Carraway, Jim Gabel, Richard Lowe, George Martin, Joseph A. Matheson Jr., Jim Martin, Greg Miller, Alan Pitts, Gary Smith, O. Lee Sturkey, and Scott Treadway. Evan Nooe tracked down confirmations for me at the University of South Carolina. My friend and former colleague Rafe Blaufarb connected me with Jonathan Sheppard of Florida State University, who photocopied material I needed at a time when I could not travel.

As the book neared completion, Pat Brady and Shirley Spears, as well as Auburn colleagues Cate Giustino and Abby Swingen, gave me opportunities to try out my ideas on otherwise unwitting audiences. I did the same with my parting shot as president of the Alabama Historical Association. Portions of that address, later published in the *Alabama Review*, are to be found here with permission from editors Bill Trimble and Carey Cauthen. I also am grateful to Craig Wilkie of the University Press of Kentucky for granting me permission to include in this work a section of text that appeared previously in the edited collection *Sister States, Enemy States*, edited by Kent Dollar, Larry Whiteaker, and Calvin Dickinson.

More than ever, research is an expensive as well as time-consuming effort. Thus I am most appreciative of Nelson Lankford and Paul Levengood of the Virginia Historical Society, who awarded me an Andrew W. Mellon Research Fellowship that made my time in Richmond both productive and affordable. Throughout the project, I also was supported with research funding provided by Ralph B. Draughon Jr. and the late Caroline Marshall Draughon through Auburn University's Draughon Chair in Southern History. At crucial moments Auburn Department of History chairs Bill Trimble and Tony Carey provided additional support and time away from the classroom. And that I didn't need to travel more than I did is in part a tribute to Pambanisha King's efficient interlibrary loan office across campus.

It has been a great pleasure to work at last with the University of North Carolina Press, and to join the legion of published scholars publically indebted in print to David Perry. Series editor Gary Gallagher has been a much-appreciated supporter throughout the project, and indeed throughout my career. Bill Blair also provided wise and welcome suggestions as a reader for the press. Among others in Chapel Hill I also thank Liz Gray, Ron Maner, and Zach Read. Any errors that remain, of course, are mine alone.

I researched and wrote much of this book during a difficult few years shaped by health problems and the stress that came along for the ride. It is difficult to imagine ever completing it without the care I received from Dr. Julie Harper and the unwavering counsel of Golden Jenkins. I also am blessed with good friends who helped carry my burden and keep me going through the toughest of times: Scott Billingsley, David Carter, Don Cole, Cita Cook, Charles Israel, Joe McCall, Tim Thornton, and John Walsh.

Most of all, I once again thank my family for their constant love and support. In the spirit of transparency, I probably should note that my father, Ken, my grandfather Jesse, and his brother Bennie were all later enlisters or conscripts in more recent conflicts, yet all three went on to courageously risk their lives for their country. None of them shirked. When this project began, my son Jesse was a high school student, and now here he is, a young man graduating from college with honors and going off into the family business. But thanks be to God, my wife, Nancy, remains where I always can count on her to be, still right by my side. No father could possibly be prouder, nor any husband more richly blessed. I do admit that we occasionally still debate the proper length of my endnotes, and sadly she appears to have gleefully won this round.

RELUCTANT
REBELS

We are a band of brothers and native to the soil,

Fighting for the property we gained by honest toil;

And when our rights were threatened, the cry rose near and far,

Hurrah! for the Bonnie Blue Flag that bears a single star.

—HARRY MCCARTHY, "The Bonnie Blue Flag"[1]

INTRODUCTION

WHAT THEY DID NOT FIGHT FOR

At 4:30 A.M. on April 12, 1861, an explosion of powder, fire, and shells announced the Confederate attack on Fort Sumter and the beginning of the American Civil War. Thirty-four hours later, the Stars and Stripes came down in surrender. When word of the bombardment reached Washington, Abraham Lincoln called 75,000 state militiamen into federal service for a period of ninety days in order to suppress the Southern rebellion. Every non-Confederate state received a quota to fill. The men of the free states responded to Lincoln's call for troops with fervor. "War fever" swept the North; most states met and exceeded their quotas within days as eager would-be soldiers overwhelmed state authorities. Flags flapped in the wind, bands played incessantly, ministers preached love of country, and young women showered recruits with affection as they marched away in uneven, unpracticed cadence.

In the Confederacy, Southerners too rushed to their brand new colors with enthusiasm if not outright joy.[2] "The wave of the secession tide struck us in full career," *London Times* correspondent William Howard Russell wrote from Goldsboro, North Carolina, on April 16. "The station, the hotels, the street through which the rail ran was filled with an excited mob all carrying arms, with signs here and there of a desire to get up some kind of uniform—flushed faces, wild eyes, screaming mouths, hurrahing for 'Jeff Davis' and 'the Southern Confederacy'. . . . Here was the true revolutionary fervor in full sway. The men hectored, swore, cheered, and slapped each other on the backs; the women, in their best, waved handkerchiefs, and flung down garlands from windows. All was noise, dust, and patriotism."[3]

For days, as he continued his journey into the Confederacy, Russell watched the tableau repeated again and again. "Confederate flags and sentiments greeted us everywhere," he wrote from eastern North Carolina. "Men and women repeated the national cry; at every station militia men and volunteers were waiting for the train, and the everlasting word 'Sumter' ran through all the conversation in the cars. . . . Farmers in blue jackets, and yellow braid and facings, handed round their swords to be admired by the company." In Charleston he found "crowds of armed men singing and promenading in the streets. . . . Secession is the fashion here. Young ladies sing for it; old ladies pray for it; young men are dying to fight for it; old men are ready to demonstrate it."[4]

But not all of them, as it turned out, answered the stirring call of "The Bonnie Blue Flag." Indeed while Russell assumed that every able-bodied man in the Confederacy was racing to the recruiting office even as his train car whizzed by, cold statistics paint a starkly different picture. Fifteen percent of all of the men who would eventually serve the Confederacy during the war, roughly 120,000 soldiers, would enter the army unwillingly as conscripts, civilians forced into their gray uniforms against their will beginning in the spring of 1862. Almost another 9 percent, 70,000 men, arrived in camp as substitutes who had enlisted tardily for the money given to them by other Confederates who wanted out of the war. Finally, an additional 180,000 others—22.5 percent of all Confederate soldiers—resisted the siren call of glory in 1861 long enough that they only enlisted later on in the war, after 1861.[5] With an occasional nod to the conscripts and substitutes, this volume explores the reasons that compelled most of those "later enlisters" in the final group to stay at home initially only to join up later on, as well as the factors that kept them in the ranks and emboldened them in combat once irregularly clad in butternut or gray.

THE VOLUMINOUS LITERATURE on Civil War soldiers has largely slighted these reluctant Rebels. Yet a brief survey of that historiography is instructive, if only for the context it provides. Bell Wiley's pioneering work on Billy Yank and Johnny Reb, now over a half-century old and shaped by what was then the recent experience of the Second World War, emphasized interlocking combinations of social and cultural factors in explaining why Civil War soldiers flocked to the colors. Many Johnny Rebs enlisted, he maintained, because they hated Yankee insults and especially Northerners' constant criticism of slavery and the South, not to mention the North's apparent willingness to destroy Southern society as they knew it through the coercion of forced abolition. Others bowed to peer and family pressure or community expectations, all of which swirled together in the pomp of colors and martial music William Howard Russell described. The thrill of the moment, a taste for excitement and adventure, a desire to prove courage and manhood before a short war ended, and sometimes even the need of a regular paycheck proved equally important to some.

What drove relatively few Confederates to the colors, Wiley added, were ideas, ideological tenets of democracy, republican politics, or conceptions of liberty. Beyond a vague sense of patriotism, the Southerners he affectionately described were even less politically ideological than their Federal foes, who for that matter worried relatively little about high-flown ideas either. Wiley concluded that Confederate recruits, like their counterparts north of the Mason-Dixon line, reacted more than they reasoned.[6]

Wiley's conclusions proved powerful and durable enough to dominate scholarship for over three decades. Only in the 1980s did a new generation of historians, influenced by the Vietnam War, the domestic struggle for civil rights, and the so-called new social history with its "bottom-up" approach, again take up the topic of Civil War soldier motivations. Most of them, however, initially continued to stress sociocultural causes and deemphasize political ideology just as Wiley had done. They did however utilize different approaches. At one end of the spectrum, Wiley's student James I. Robertson offered a similarly argued "supplement" to his mentor's original volumes based on newly discovered sources. Quite different in conception was Michael Barton's content analysis of published soldier letters and diaries, a book clearly influenced by both quantitative history and works of the French postmodernist Michel Foucault. Barton's real concerns were not soldier motivation, but sectional conceptions of the characteristics that made soldiers "good men." Accordingly, he focused on so-called core values of personal achievement, morality, progress, and especially self-control. While Barton argued that expressions of patriotism mattered as well, in the end he essentially joined Wiley in dismissing them as nonideological "psychosocial" values. Impetuous, verbose, and concerned with "gallantry," Confederates and especially the officers, according to Barton, cared relatively little about abstract notions of freedom and democracy.[7]

In a more influential and ultimately controversial work based on traditional scholarship, Gerald Linderman similarly depicted the soldiers of 1861 and 1862 as nonideological. The men he described were products of an Age of Romanticism, aching to prove themselves in the dramatic crucible of war. Linderman identified expressed qualities comparable to Barton's—duty, godliness, honor, knightliness, manliness—but in the end concluded that all were only facets of the one essential true core value, courage. Men joined the army selfishly to prove their individual bravery, for only in the ultimate test of battle could they establish that they were not unmanly cowards. More recently, Paul Christopher Anderson, Stephen Berry, Kenneth Greenberg, and Larry Logue in various degrees have modified and extended this twist on the Wiley interpretation by placing the demands of honor and especially masculinity ever closer to center stage. Berry, for example, still emphasizes the notion of battlefield as testing ground, but what really mattered to recruits, he adds, was establishing their manhood and importance in the eyes of the women they loved.[8] "Men joined the army to fight for cause, comrades, and country," he agreed, "and they gave fealty to these motives in their public remarks. But privately they were fighting, as they always had, for women and eminence."[9]

The new sociocultural interpreters, however, faced increasing challenges. Taking a boldly different tack, Reid Mitchell provided a transitional consideration that gave more credit to the power of patriotism and especially the nation's revolutionary heritage while still emphasizing combinations of family, community, and personal concerns. Mitchell's Confederates enlisted to defend their homes from expected Northern invaders they perceived as fanatics and savages, protect Southern culture and society, maintain economic opportunity, and honorably defend hearth and home. More than anything else, they joined their local companies to maintain slavery and white supremacy, the twin ideological foundations of their economic and social worlds.[10]

A bevy of recent scholars followed and extended Mitchell's path to a more broadly defined political interpretation that elevated liberty and slavery as the twin keystones of Confederate soldier motivation. To be sure, none dismissed entirely the now-familiar list of social factors. Writing of Confederates, for example, James McPherson especially stressed *rage militaire*, that mixture of flag-waving and furor that gripped Southern men after Fort Sumter. Desires for adventure, concerns regarding honor and masculinity, and defense of home, he conceded, did matter. But ultimately, he continued, all were secondary to political ideology. Confederate soldiers enlisted to fight for slavery and liberty, with the latter seen and defined through the ideological lens of the American Revolution and its republican rhetoric as the polar opposite of slavery. To bow to Northern "subjugation" not only would mean dishonorable unmanliness but, worse, slavery in another guise, a virtual enslavement of whites by former African American slaves and their Northern allies.[11]

Some scholars went even farther. Randall Jimerson identified the determination to protect slavery from Northern attack as the "one basic premise" that connected the rhetorical dots of rights, liberty, masculinity, and defense of home. "Southerners," he wrote, "anticipated an attack on slavery that would eventually result in destruction of their property rights, emancipation, and disruption of race relations. . . . Liberty itself would be overthrown." When Southerners spoke of defending liberty, in other words, what they really meant was defending slavery and the slave society that both slaveholding and nonslaveholding whites inhabited. David Williams, while maintaining that preachers and wealthy Southerners essentially bamboozled young white men into service, agreed that slavery and racism drove even poor whites to arms.[12] Chandra Manning has most expanded the McPherson interpretation, asserting that most Confederate recruits understood that the war was really about preserving slavery. In her estimation, talk of honor and masculinity really meant controlling blacks as well as white dependents. Liberty for Southerners was "the unobstructed pursuit of material prospects for white men and their families," a definition that meant maintaining slavery as both a source of labor and a leveler of white society. Patriotism too could not escape the reach of chattel bondage, for Southerners defined it as loyalty to a government that would assist their families through slavery's preservation. "It is patronizing and insulting to

Confederate soldiers," she asserts, "to pretend that they did not understand the war as a battle for slavery when they so plainly described it as exactly that. There is no way to understand the war from a Confederate perspective . . . without understanding why white nonslaveholding men would believe that the preservation of slavery justified a fight."[13]

As the sesquicentennial of the war approaches, the ideological school holds the historiographical field, at least for the moment. Yet in truth, whether one sides with Wiley and the others who stress social and cultural pressures over ideas and causes, or aligns with those in a growing phalanx who argue for the primacy of ideology and slavery, the basic list of factors involving the many individual decisions to fight seemingly remains firmly established, with only the weighting of components differing among scholars. Much of the remaining historical debate over soldier motivations in fact devolves rather quickly into semantics, often revolving around little more than individual historians' different definitions of the words "ideology" and "patriotism," and their views of the relationship between the two. If simple expressions of patriotism and support for slavery comprise parts of a real ideology, as McPherson maintains, then Civil War soldiers were ideological. But if one follows Wiley's contention that vague statements about God and country meant nothing of the kind, then they fought less for ideals than for more basic reasons. The soldiers' letters and expressions remain constant regardless.

The continuing bifurcated debate over "what they fought for" as it has been waged unfortunately also has obscured and diverted related questions and perspectives that in the end would provide a more rounded view of the whole. If men fought "for cause and comrades," for honor and masculinity, or simply for or against slavery, how do we explain the actions of the many men, half of all soldiers according to McPherson, who routinely avoided battle or deserted entirely? What of their ideology, their beliefs about slavery?[14] Or what about the substitutes and draftees? And what of the later enlisters? Hatred, a taste for adventure, local pressures, pomp, packages containing women's undergarments designed to shame the recipient, the demands of honor and masculinity, the legacy of the Founding Fathers, patriotism however defined, white supremacy, the determination to hold on to slaves—the simple fact is that none of the familiar factors were enough to convince them to join the army in 1861.[15] Either those initial factors were not as strong as historians have surmised, or more likely another counter menu of even more powerful factors compelled those men temporarily at least to remain civilians. Yet those men and causes largely remain ignored in the pertinent literature. In nearly every case the standard scholarly approach has been to lump all soldiers either in one military melting pot or else two labeled "blue" and "gray," in spite of when they enlisted. Either way, the voices of the earliest and most ardent dominate.[16]

The end result is a voluminous literature on "Civil War soldiers" that is in actuality only a detailed study of the most motivated men who enlisted in the first year or so of the war, those one logically would assume to be most likely to fight for a cause. Others are ignored or else shunted aside. Bell Wiley devoted only a few single pages here and there to conscripts, hesitant recruits, and older men, lumping them in with other "exceptional" or "random" types, such as the foreign born, disguised women, and African American body servants. His emphasis was on the young men who enlisted at the war's opening salvoes. Linderman likewise paid attention only to "the volunteers of 1861–62, those who fought the great battles of the east and of Sherman's campaign, who arrived early and tried to fight the war to its end."[17] McPherson, too, openly focused on the initial waves of recruits, while honestly indicating his aversion to reluctant soldiers, "sneaks" and "skulkers." Accordingly, he skewed his samples "toward those who volunteered in 1861–62" so that they contained "disproportionately few draftees, substitutes, or those Union soldiers who enlisted in 1863–64 for large bounties." His definition of "sneaks," moreover, is in retrospect comparatively wide, including men who "seemed to melt away when the lead started flying. . . . Some deserted for good. Some really were sick much of the time. Others got what combat soldiers called 'bombproof' jobs a safe distance behind the lines—headquarters clerk, quartermaster sergeant, wagon-train guard, teamster, hospital attendant, and the like. Even the best regiments contained their quota of sneaks." As for the Confederate army specifically, he states unequivocally that "the prototypical unwilling soldier . . . was a nonslaveholding Southern married farmer with small children who was drafted in 1862 or enlisted only to avoid being drafted." Moreover, "the soldiers who felt this way furnished a disproportionate number of deserters and skulkers—according to the letters of highly motivated soldiers. They may have been right." Yet in the end, McPherson like the others, was not interested in reluctant soldiers enough to find out for sure.[18]

To be fair, one cannot not criticize scholars too much for this lacuna in the literature of soldiers, for as it turns out there is a practical problem in pursuing such men. Most recent historians, again following a path broken by Wiley, wisely have shied away from memoirs and histories written after the war, assuming that changing perspectives and new events of the postwar era shaped much of what these contained. While that still leaves a wealth of contemporary letters and diaries overall, surprisingly few later-enlisting Confederates wrote during the war. They were especially silent about their decisions not to enlist in 1861. For some later enlistees, the answer nonetheless is obvious: about a quarter of those sampled here simply were too young to join the army after Fort Sumter without official sanction or parental permission, which sometimes came only reluctantly. University of Alabama student Robert Webb Banks, to cite one example, was eighteen in 1862. For a year he had pressured his family for permission to enlist. In the spring he wrote his parents again that "the country needs my services, and has adopted a measure to secure them," referring to the new conscription law. "Why not allow me to go with your blessing," he pleaded, ". . . rather than be compelled to let me go. . . . I know that having always cherished the idea of my being an educated man . . . it is hard for you to entertain the thought of having your fondest dreams nipped in the bud; but then you remember the times have changed a great deal within the last few years."[19]

As to the others, most of their wartime letters went to parents or wives fully aware of what had led their sons or husbands to initially overcome war fever. Further discourse was unnecessary at best and perhaps painful at worst. The result is a simple but unfortunate dearth of open explanation. Among the 320 men sampled for this volume, only eight, two of them youths and six over the age of twenty, specifically mentioned their reasons for not enlisting after Fort Sumter. At best, eight voices can only offer clues, not definitive answers. The suggestions at least are tantalizing. Alabama lawyer James Washington Inzer, a delegate to his state's secession convention, came down with malaria after the war began.[20] Employed as a civilian at an armory after the conflict began, Virginian B. Wylie Scott admitted that he delayed entering the ranks until 1862 because he "prefered going to war with my friends." When they enlisted in 1862, so did he.[21] Two others more or less fit McPherson's description of "skulkers who did their best to avoid combat." Nineteen-year-old W. H. Franklin went to work at a "gun factory," commenting to his brother in February 1862 that "I can hardly stand it but I will do the best I can for I know that it is better than being in the army."[22] And M. C. Hart, a Louisiana militiaman who served only briefly and apparently unwillingly in national service when Confederate commanders assumed control over his unit, explained his decision not to enlist simply if somewhat cryptically when he wrote, "I felt it my duty to stay at home as long as I could."[23]

But as Joseph Glatthaar has noted in his examination of Lee's "soldiers of '62," the demands of home delayed more men. Richard Henry Brooks wanted to enlist in 1861 but bowed to his wife's opposition. Thirty-two-year-old North Carolinian J. M. Davidson was the brother of a congressman and a cousin to Governor Zebulon Vance. Although motivated by patriotism and a desire for Southern independence, Davidson spent the war's first year as a sutler instead of a soldier to please his beloved and frail wife Julia, who "told me that she did not know how she could give me up."[24] Like Davidson, twenty-nine-year-old Mississippian William L. Nugent spent 1861 out of uniform but associated with the army in the role of civilian inspector general. He too wrestled with his decision. Nugent hated Yankees as well as any Southerner, feared the consequences of abolition, and in the years to come would write frequently about liberty and independence. Yet initially for him there was a greater consideration still, his religious faith. "There is a kind of vindictive spirit that impels me to want to engage in the service of my Country right away," he confessed to his wife in August. "I feel that I would like to shoot a yankee, and yet I know that this would not be in harmony with the Spirit of Christianity, that teaches us to love our enemies & do good to them that despitefully use us and entreat us." For Nugent, enlisting meant finding a way to reconcile his faith with his patriotism.[25]

Age, camaraderie, Christian duty, and the greater demands of home— these, then, were at least some of the motivating factors that inoculated men against the war fever of 1861. Yet all of these men ultimately ended up voluntarily enlisting in Confederate gray later in the war. Did they enlist only to become "sneaks and skulkers?" Or furnish most of the Confederacy's deserters? Does McPherson's definition—"nonslaveholding Southern married farmer with small children who . . . enlisted only to avoid being drafted"—hold true? In trying to understand why men did not fight initially but did enlist later, the historian must emulate the detective. Having observed the scene and found a few initial clues, one must move on to a more in-depth analysis of the available evidence in order to understand what they did not fight for as well as what did propel them into the ranks at last.

The thematic chapters that follow offer several interlocking explanations. Part I concerns and ultimately questions the ideological argument that men rallied to the colors, in Harry McCarthy's stirring words in "The Bonnie Blue Flag," over their rights. Chapter One maintains that as a group, late-enlisting Confederates were less ideological politically than the men who went before them. While a few vociferous examples to the contrary existed, most of them wrote little or nothing about Confederate nationalism, much less their revolutionary forebears, liberty, subjugation, or states' rights, all words and concepts that are commonly found in the letters of 1861 enlistees. Nor were they much concerned with conceptions of honor and duty. That relative lack of interest in politics seems to have retarded enlistments in the war's first year, especially in the Upper South. The one exception was slavery, which was just as important to later enlisters as to the earliest firebrands. As discussed in Chapter Two, ardent proslavery advocates admittedly were as rare among them as the soldiers of 1861, but the percentage of slave owners and their sons among the later men actually was comparable to the regional average, undermining the assertions of some scholars that the war had become "a rich man's war and poor man's fight." Later-enlisting Confederates as a group, men from the cotton states especially, and most of all those who benefitted from slave labor personally, openly accepted slavery as natural and desirable. They particularly opposed emancipation. In contrast, only three men in the sample spoke out against what they saw as a war to preserve slavery for Southern aristocrats.

Part II focuses on the notion frequently offered as a counterpoint to the ideological explanation, that Confederates simply enlisted to defend their homes. By and large, they did, but the reality is more complex than that simple, traditional assertion implies. Chapter Three examines the symbolic and real roles that women and families played in motivating later-enlisting Confederates. For many late enlisters and especially youths, romance and ideals of southern womanhood, a different kind of "ideology," provided a tangible reason to fight. Older, married men meanwhile determined to protect both their loved ones and their hard-won property. As the war strained family relationships, the survival of their economic prospects increasingly concerned later-enlisting soldiers in the field. In other words, their fight was as much about the "property gained through honest toil" as it was safeguarding the home folks.

Chapter Four again considers later enlisters' attitudes toward their families and lands, but from a different perspective, as potential targets of Union soldiers and freed African American allies. Many men in 1861 had expected an easy gentleman's war between combatants, a brief conflict that would spare civilian lives and property. When the war instead evolved into something more brutal, a contest involving widespread foraging and property destruction as well as freedom and perhaps even equality for the slaves, the sheer hatred white Southerners developed for the invaders induced many of them to fight at last. This motive proved especially strong in a Lower South just confronting incursions in 1862. New Confederate enrollment and conscription policies also played a role in enlistment, but Chapter Five maintains that the draft, bounties, and substitution played a smaller and more subtle role in motivating later-enlisting Confederates than previous scholars have assumed. Moreover, enlistment for money needs not to be judged as a character flaw, but rather understood as another response to the Southern man's imperative to defend home and hearth.

All together, Parts I and II deal with factors that both induced men to enlist and then sustained them while in service. In the final part of the book, the narrative turns decisively more to the latter. Religion proved one major factor in maintaining the morale of later-enlisting Confederates, as did camaraderie. They are the subjects of Chapters Six and Seven respectively. In both cases, the power of home again remained surprisingly strong. Later enlisters' enduring, individual religious connections to kin and home kept many of them going but simultaneously undermined group fellowship. Their practices especially retarded their participation in the legendary Confederate revivals, suggesting that historians must look beyond those dramatic events for a better, more nuanced understanding of Confederate piety.

Home ties also complicated primary group cohesion. Comrades were likely to be other men from home, notably relatives and neighbors, leaving many men unable or unwilling to forge new ties with soldiers they did not know before the war. Such localist attitudes undermined to an extent the development of both unit pride and esprit de corps, qualities notably lacking among later enlisters. The final chapters deal with the question of military effectiveness, both in camp and on the battlefield. Later enlisters grew weary of the war and ached to return home, yet there is no real evidence that they were more likely to shirk, run, or refuse to fight. Instead, most of the men discussed here tried to be good soldiers. They fought and died when called upon to do so. Ultimately health and age, rather than will, most stood in the way of those many bands of brothers.

READERS SHOULD BE AWARE that certain methodological considerations are followed throughout the narrative. First, for the sake of comparison as well as utility, this study borrows from the increasingly standard model introduced to Civil War studies by James McPherson, which was drawn in turn from the work of military historian John Lynn. Noting both the major logistical problems and questionable leadership that otherwise hobbled the successful French Army du Nord of the early revolutionary period, Lynn proposed that the army's battlefield victories really grew instead out of its "combat effectiveness." Utilizing a sophisticated model to understand combat effectiveness, Lynn maintained that all soldiers historically fight for three "interests": coercion, remuneration, or "normative factors" that otherwise motivate men to win the praise of their comrades and community. In the heady days of the French Revolution just as in the Civil War, soldiers largely served not because they wanted to avoid physical punishment or expected to enrich themselves with pillaged booty. Instead, they came to value the "national sociopolitical system, the military unit, and the primary group" enough to overcome fear and the desire for self-preservation. Each institution in turn played a role in creating high morale. The wider community shaped attitudes and reinforced morale through demonstrations of support. The military ideally indoctrinated and molded citizens into soldiers, building in the process confidence, pride, and technical expertise. Finally, the successful "primary group"—the small group of soldiers who bonded into a pseudo-family and who supported each other without hesitation—created tight building blocks that together made up a victorious force. Motivation, as well as interest and primary-group cohesion, comprise combat effectiveness in Lynn's model. Factors that spurred enlistment, or at least led men to go along with being drafted, comprised *initial motivation*. The factors that kept commitment and morale high once in service apart from the battlefield are termed *sustaining motivation*. *Combat motivation* finally enabled men to overcome obvious self-interest to risk life and limb in battle. Lynn's framework, whether explicitly noted or simply assumed, has particularly shaped the work of those who stress the centrality of ideology. It is also important in this study.[26]

In contrast, the reader should note, I depart from McPherson's otherwise model study by routinely identifying the soldiers I cite. He maintained that "few of them were famous people, and to scatter hundreds of different names over these pages would overwhelm and confuse the reader." It is a fair argument. But at the same time, Reid Mitchell has written eloquently about how Civil War soldiers feared becoming automatons, nameless, faceless, forgotten cogs in the war machine. At the risk of confusing the reader, I determined not to add to soldiers' namelessness or anonymity.[27]

Like most of those historians who have gone before me, I use no post-1865 essays, memoirs, or regimental histories as primary sources. Every source utilized here was written no later than the summer after Appomattox, before Federal occupation, Reconstruction, Redemption, and the aging of veterans. Nonetheless, like the samples used by previous scholars, what follows still cannot comprise a true random sample along the lines of a modern opinion poll. A truly random and representative sample of men long dead is impossible this side of heaven. Only a rough approximation based on extant sources is possible. For the sake of comparison, I originally planned to utilize the surviving wartime documents of 400 later-enlisting Confederates in creating that sample, given that McPherson examined 429 Confederates in his study and Manning 477. Unfortunately, whether due to lower rates of literacy, the increasingly fragile and much-condemned Confederate postal system and its ersatz substitutes, postwar issues, the flaws inherent in modern archival cataloging systems, or most likely a combination of all the above, building such a sample of later-enlisting Confederate soldiers proved surprisingly impossible. Accordingly, Table 1 in the Appendix contains information on 320 later-enlisting Confederates examined for this volume, *later enlisters* specifically defined as men who joined the army no earlier than January 1862, when a new round of legislation, enlistments, inducements, and company creation brought a surge of new men into the Southern Confederacy's military.

Using such sources is not as simple as it initially looks. As Joseph Glatthaar recently noted, anyone can cherry-pick qualitative information from Civil War letters and diaries in order to produce almost any desired finding. Indeed, such politicized practices are lamentably frequent.[28] One way to overcome that temptation is simply to count and categorize rigorously and systematically, which I have done here. As John Lynn himself maintained, "an analysis of this revolution in personnel ought to be both quantitative and qualitative."[29] Yet there are even pitfalls involved in using the statistics that result. Some soldiers are represented by over a hundred letters each, while others left only one to posterity. Small collections and randomly saved letters drive down any percentages across the board and most likely distort reality, but in the end I thought it nonetheless crucial to include the barely literate along with the fluent and verbose, else this become yet another study of white Southern elites. That discrepancy, however, makes the measurements or statistical analyses that follow only suggestive at best for the entire population. Readers thus should not regard them as anything more than guideposts erected for the sake of comparison from soldier to soldier or chapter to chapter within the current volume.

Those caveats aside, the numbers do reveal much from the outset. Take the issue of rank. Knowing a soldier's status is important when judging his knowledge of events and thus his writings. Privates, sergeants, and colonels all experienced the war differently. While researching I particularly tried to avoid men who began the war with a rank above captain, concerned that the views of that presumably powerful minority might skew the sample. In the end, of the 320 soldiers in the sample, I ultimately was able to identify ranks for 289 of them, using clues within collections, available unit rosters, and the National Park Service's online Civil War Soldiers and Sailors System. Often the ranks varied over time, of course, as men rose in stature or, in a few cases, were conversely busted in rank. At the time they first entered the army, the lion's share of the sampled men identified by rank, 207 (71 percent), enlisted as privates. There also were 12 corporals, 27 sergeants, 27 lieutenants, and 6 captains. Out of those same soldiers, 172 (60 percent) ended their military experience still at the rank of private; but at that juncture there also were 9 corporals, 27 sergeants, 39 lieutenants, 24 captains, a lieutenant colonel, and a colonel. Clearly some men moved up the chain of command throughout the conflict. In addition to men holding traditional ranks, the sample includes three chaplains, three surgeons, an adjutant, an artificer, a commissary, and a ward master. The voices of privates thus dominate this study just as they did the army's actual rank and file; but noncommissioned officers form a healthy minority, just as they did in the war, while enough commissioned officers are included to represent their views. When a soldier's rank at a given moment was murky, I automatically honored postwar practice and defaulted in the text to the highest rank obtained.[30]

Age is another crucial factor when studying later enlisters. Their ages ran the gamut, but collectively later enlisters were slightly older than the average 1861 enlistee in his early twenties. Two distinct cohorts appear in the pages that follow. James McPherson notes that almost 40 percent of Civil War soldiers were aged twenty-one or younger at enlistment. In contrast, of the 244 sampled late enlisters whose ages can be identified in the census or elsewhere, barely a quarter of them (60 men, or 24.6 percent) were youths aged twenty or younger in 1862. In contrast, just over three-quarters (184 men, or 75.4 percent) of the total identified were over the age of twenty. The mean age of all the men in the sample in 1862 was twenty-five and a half, the median age barely twenty-six, and the modal average age nineteen. Counted differently, fifty-nine men were in their teens in 1862, ninety-seven were in their twenties, seventy-one were in their thirties, fourteen were in their forties, and one was in his fifties. Two soldiers, John J. Mendenhall and W. H. Rucker, were in their sixties when they enlisted. As a group, in short, later enlisters were older than their veteran comrades at the time of enlistment.[31]

When broken down further, the statistics not surprisingly demonstrate that officers tended to be older still than enlisted men. Among men whose ages could be identified, those who entered the army as officers had a mean age in 1862 of thirty-one, a median age of thirty, and modal ages of thirty and thirty-three. Enlisted men who rose through the ranks to officer status tended to be slightly younger, with mean and median ages of twenty-eight and modal ages of twenty-three and twenty-nine. Men who served in the ranks throughout the war were slightly younger still, with a mean average age of twenty-nine and a median age of twenty-six, but a modal age of nineteen.

Almost exactly half of the 210 men whose marital status can be determined were married (106), making later enlisters as a population more likely to be married than Confederate soldiers as a whole. Comparably, the numbers of men who were heads of households (111, 53 percent) were only slightly greater than those of dependents (99, 47 percent). Of the 209 men in the sample whose realty appeared in the census, 135 (65 percent) were from within landowning householder families, while 74 (35 percent) were not. Of course, assuming, as most Southern historians do, that most of the men not found in the census also owned no land, the number of nonlandowning men in the sample theoretically could rise as high as 58 percent.[32]

The mean average landowner or landowner's son in the census possessed $9,037 worth of real property in 1860, but that figure frankly is grossly misleading due to the skewing presence of several wealthy planters and their sons. The mother of James and Samuel Pickens, for example, owned realty valued at $209,600. The median real landowning was a more modest $1,500, and the modal average was $1,000. When one adds in the seventy-four men who owned no realty property in 1860, those figures fall to a mean of $5,837, a median average of $600, and a modal average of zero. Percentages relating to personal property were similar. Out of the same 209 soldiers in the census, 21 desperately poor men or their parents owned no personal property, but an additional 188 men or their parents did. Among personal property owners and their dependents alone, the mean average value of personal property in 1860 was $14,689, but again, the presence of a few wealthy men such as the Pickens boys skews the reality enough to make that figure suspect. More illustrative is the median personal property figure of $2,000. In regard to modal averages, eight men owned $200 worth of personal property, while another eight owned $300 worth of personal property. When one factors in the men who owned nothing, the figures fall to a mean of $13,072, a median of $1,500, and a mode of zero.

As they were older, officers also were wealthier. Men who served throughout the war as officers and who can be found in the census owned a mean average of $12,316 worth of real property in 1860. The median average was $1,000, but the modal average was zero. Additionally, they owned a mean average of $10,988 of personal property, a median of $3,010, and a mode of zero. Enlisted men who rose to officer's rank during the war owned significantly less property, suggesting that they had achieved their ranks in part due to merit rather than prewar status. The average officer in that group owned a mean average of only $3,455 worth of realty. The median was $500 and the modal average zero. As for personal property, they again lagged behind, with a mean average holding of $10,988, a median of $2,242, and modal averages of $2,242 and $5,000. Still, merit was not everything. Soldiers who rose through the ranks still were more prosperous than most of those soldiers who remained as enlisted men. The privates, corporals, and sergeants found in the census owned a mean average of $6,560 worth of real property, but a median average of $400 and a modal average of zero. In regard to personal property, the mean average was $6,327, the median average $1,000, and the modal average zero. Here again, the presence of a few wealthy privates skews the means.

In the South, the census taker included slaves as personal property. Of the 209 men in the sample who also can be located in the census, 92 (43 percent) were slave owners themselves or came from slave-owning families, as shown in Table 3. Of the eighty-five who could be matched to rank, seventeen (20 percent) entered the army as officers, another eleven (13 percent) rose to hold officer's rank, and two-thirds of them (fifty-seven men, or 67 percent) remained in the ranks throughout the war. Taken together in sum, these figures regarding wealth demonstrate that despite specific contrary examples, economic class still mattered within the army chain of command; but it counted for less as the war dragged on. Moreover, there were plenty of slave owners in the ranks.

I was able to identify occupations for about two-thirds of the sampled soldiers (216 men, 67.5 percent). Of that group, eighty-one (37.5 percent) were either landowning farmers or the sons of landowners. An additional man referred to himself as a tenant; another was an overseer; and fifteen men identified themselves to the census taker as laborers. Thirty-three soldiers (15 percent) called themselves "farmers" but seemed to own no land, denoting them probably as tenants. Together, just over half of the identified men (61 percent) can be identified conclusively as involved somehow in farming, almost exactly what Bell Wiley found for Confederate soldiers as a whole. The realities of the census, however, suggest that most of the 105 soldiers who could not be identified in the census at all were either tenants, laborers, or transients. Thus perhaps as many as 74 percent of the total sample worked the land in some capacity.[33]

Almost half of the men who listed an occupation were not farmers or planters. Fifty-one (24 percent) were professional men, with teachers, clerks, merchants, and doctors leading the way. Four were clergymen and three were attorneys. Another seventeen men (8 percent) were skilled workers, notably blacksmiths and painters. Using Wiley's sample, McPherson notably identified only 12.2 percent of the men in his sample as professionals and white-collar workers of various stripes, while the 1860 census found only 13.3 percent of Southern men in that category. On the other hand, they found almost twice as many skilled laborers (14.1 percent). Taken as a group, in other words, and acknowledging possible differences in determining categorical status, nonfarming later enlisters in the sample were almost twice as likely to be established professional men in various white-collar occupations, but half again as likely to be skilled laborers as compared to both the entire Confederate army and the white male population as a whole.[34]

When broken down by rank, moreover, a pattern emerges. If up to three-quarters of the men in the total sample toiled the land before the war, only about a third of men identified as officers did. Of the twenty-eight men who could be found in the census and identified as officers throughout the war, twelve professional men (43 percent) slightly predominated over ten landowning farmers (36 percent). In addition there were two probable tenants and three craftsmen: a carpenter, a freighter, and a ginwright. One listed no occupation. Men who rose from the ranks were even more likely to come from the nonfarming professional classes, with ten professionals (42 percent) outnumbering seven landowning farmers (29 percent), two tenants, two former students, one former laborer, and two skilled workers (a carpenter and a harness maker). Taken together, twenty-two men who ended their wartime service as officers (42 percent) came from the white-collar professional class, while only seventeen (33 percent) were landowning farmers. The most represented profession was business, with four merchants and another four clerks.[35]

As Table 2 in the Appendix demonstrates, the sample is not perfect. Men from the states of Alabama and North Carolina are overrepresented in the sample, while soldiers who hailed from Tennessee as well as the border slave states are underrepresented. Members of slave-owning families seem at first glance overrepresented; 93 (46 percent) of the 201 men who can be identified conclusively were slave owners or the sons of slave owners. Yet again, 104 sampled men do not appear in the census at all. While several factors can account for the former group missing the census taker, poverty, then as now, was the major determinant. Thus it is more likely that the slaveholders represent a smaller overall percentage of the men sampled, possibly as few as 30 percent but more likely just a bit higher, as it was in the Confederacy as a whole.

These basic statistics in sum suggest that assumptions such as McPherson's description of the "prototypical" later enlister as "a nonslaveholding Southern married farmer with small children" must be reevaluated. Many were older men to be sure, but a quarter of them were youths. Half of late-enlisting Confederates were unmarried, while a quarter of them (especially officers) did not work the land. Contrary to conventional wisdom, many of them, even men in the ranks, also owned slaves. While they were not always so different than other soldiers—and those similarities as well as differences will be delineated in the pages that follow—later-enlisting Confederates ultimately defy simple stereotyping and must be met on their own ground. Doing so offers a fuller portrait of them and all Confederate soldiers.

PART I

"WHEN OUR RIGHTS WERE THREATENED"

1

DUTY, HONOR, COUNTRY

"PATRIOTISM IS A FINE WORD FOR HISTORIANS"

Only seventeen when the Civil War began, Harden P. Cochrane spent the first year of the war safely at home in Tuscaloosa, Alabama, a student at the local university. In March 1862, however, he and several other members of the University Cadet Corps marched away from their campus to help train new recruits at Camp Winn. His assignment was to help drill Company E of the new 28th Alabama Infantry. Just after the Battle of Shiloh, and only a few days before the regiment left its camp of instruction for the new front at Corinth, Cochrane witnessed a significant moment in the short life of the new regiment. On the night of April 11, the new soldiers of the 28th Alabama gathered outside the hotel at Shelby Springs to serenade their regimental colonel. The men were in high spirits, convinced that their army had won a

Colors of the 28th Alabama Infantry, painted by the noted artist Nicola Marschall and later captured at Orchard Knob in November 1863. Photograph courtesy Alabama Department of Archives and History, Montgomery, Catalogue No. 86.3945.1.

victory at Pittsburgh Landing. When they demanded a speech, however, the colonel abruptly refused to say anything, handing the duty instead to the regimental adjutant. His oratory fell flat, and the mood soured even more when the commander of a nearby regiment rose to warn the men that contrary to the initial reports they had heard, the Confederates actually had been *"slightly whipped"* at Shiloh.[1]

Such an acknowledgment of defeat, however qualified, rankled the recruits. They now raucously demanded that Company E's Capt. H. A. M. Henderson speak to them. Despite being ill, the former Methodist minister stood and gave the men the stem-winding oratory they clearly wanted and perhaps needed on the eve of their deployment to the front. He began by announcing that he "had a different opinion from that of some who had expressed theirs before." He had not despaired of victory, he assured his men, for "he did not believe we could be whipped. . . . he did not believe there was a man in the whole regiment so debased as would not fight, and, if needs be, die for his country." When the Southern states had seceded, he went on, all had agreed that the Confederacy "would be *exterminated* before it would submit, and that he would rather see our rivulets crimson with blood and every spot in our fair South from Shiloh to the Gulf of Mexico a soldier's sepulchre." But that would not happen, he added. Indeed, echoing William Shakespeare's Henry V on St. Crispin's Day, Henderson promised that "when we had gained our independence each man who had participated in the obtaining of it would be respected and loved by their wives, children, friends, and neighbors, be respected by all that knew them and on the other hand those who were killed would live in the mind of those who knew them and their names would be handed down by tradition to posterity." Overcome with emotion, Henderson's company broke into song, promising, "Oh, Alabama, we will fight for thee."[2]

Harden Cochrane ultimately did not follow the 28th Alabama into Gen. Braxton Bragg's army, but he did not return to school either. Soon after the night of speeches and song he enlisted as a private in the newly formed 2nd Alabama Cavalry. Writing home from that regiment's camp that fall, however, he still remembered Henderson's words and similar expositions, as he assured his reader that "we are whipping the enemy and driving them from our sunny South and before long I think the trumpet of Peace, Freedom, and Independence will be sounded and we will return to our happy homes in peace."[3]

MEN SUCH AS Captain Henderson and Private Cochrane were not alone among later enlisters in using words such as "country," "freedom," "submission," and "independence" to explain their decision to join Confederate ranks. Others couched their decision to enlist with words and phrases that reflected at least a simple patriotism if not a more developed political ideology. John Dooley, the twenty-year-old son of one of Richmond's wealthiest and most influential Irish families, was one. When the war began, his father became a company commander in the 1st Virginia. For reasons that remain unclear, the devoutly Catholic son remained in Washington of all places until the following year, continuing his studies at Georgetown College. The months in Lincoln's capital proved difficult, for at one point he lashed out against the city's politicians and the North in general for unleashing "this diabolical alternative upon our native land." In the spring, as Union forces approached his hometown of Richmond, Dooley finally went south and enlisted as a private in his father's regiment.[4]

Dooley was not the only soldier who averred that he enlisted at least in part to defend his "native land." Sixty-one (19.1 percent) of the 320 later-enlisting soldiers in the sample at least in part explained their initial decision to fight for the Confederacy in ideological language. Thirty-eight of them, 11.8 percent of the total, specifically mentioned their "country" at least once. Gary Gallagher has maintained that such statements, except when they explicitly refer to a state, comprise evidence of nationalism, "collective loyalties transcending state and locality." On Gallagher's scale, even one mention counts as evidence of nationalist sentiments.[5] Not all scholars would agree, of course. Indeed, for many decades historians have debated Confederate nationalism. One school of thought regards it as either limited to a few elites or else denies its existence entirely. Paul Escott's pathbreaking work acknowledged that while Jefferson Davis became over the course of the war a nationalist who put the needs of the entire Confederacy ahead of states and localities, he was ultimately an exception to a general rule. Indeed his inability to stir up Confederate national unity became the root cause of the nascent country's defeat. Committed to states' rights and distrustful of Davis's centralizing policies, politicians at the local and state levels constantly threw up roadblocks to filling and feeding the ranks beyond their own constituents. Masters too resisted and held back their slaves from vital war work, while the Southern yeomanry increasingly resented and resisted the proverbial "rich man's war, poor man's fight" policies of conscription and impressment. Confederate nationalism, in the end, stunted and withered on the vine, unable to overcome localism, racial divisions, and class tensions.

Echoing Escott, other scholars reaffirmed and indeed extended the primacy of self-interest, extreme localism, and class while stressing the concurrent absence of nonelite nationalism.[6] Although their definition of "nationalism" differs somewhat, the four authors of *Why the South Lost the Civil War* likewise maintained that the new Confederacy as a whole lacked "a feeling of oneness, that almost mystical sense of nationhood. . . . The Confederate nation was created on paper, not in the hearts and minds of its would-be citizens." Too attached to their American past and allegedly guilt ridden over establishing a nation to protect slavery, Southerners never developed that emotional feeling of being Confederates instead of Macon Countians, Alabamians, or Americans. The book's authors famously pointed in particular to Paraguay, which between 1864 and 1870 fielded a proportionally larger army and eventually lost over half of its total population during a bitter war with three powerful neighbors. The Confederates' devotion to their country and resulting war effort seemed "feeble in comparison."[7]

Other historians, however, interpreted the evidence differently. Over a half-century ago, David Potter stimulated such revisionist thoughts when he warned his fellow historians that blanket dismissals of the existence of Confederate nationalism could be dangerously presentist, rooted in a modern reluctance to give much credit to a nationalism rooted in slavery.[8] Potter's observations about what Gallagher later termed an "aroma of moral disapprobation" ultimately prodded several scholars to reexamine the question. They concluded that by 1860 many white Southerners indeed believed themselves to be a separate people who required a nation of their own. Emory Thomas, for example, forcefully maintained that Confederates after 1861 followed increasingly revolutionary economic, military, and political trajectories that together produced a true sense of nationhood among most white Confederates by the summer of 1863, although in the end it could not withstand the battlefield reverses that followed.[9] Drew Gilpin Faust meanwhile offered a significant new consideration of the subject that depicted white Confederates as consciously and successfully acting to construct the unique national culture they knew they required, a "commentary upon itself," that would both present the new nation's best face to the world and "build a consensus at home, to secure a foundation of popular support for a new nation." Steeped in the imagery of the French Revolution and especially the American War of Independence—which Confederates widely appropriated as their own protohistory—the main tenets of Confederate nationalism according to Faust were Christianity, republican virtue, slavery, and racial solidarity. The Confederate nation belonged to white Southerners, God's new chosen people, who were to fulfill His divine will through a pure republican government that had jettisoned the corrupting excesses of mid-nineteenth-century Jacksonian democracy.[10] George Rable's examination of the Confederate government reached similar conclusions about nationalism's relationship to Christian thought and classical republicanism while stressing the latter. Anne Sarah Rubin's recent work, reminiscent in many ways of Faust's in its emphasis on popular culture, Revolutionary motifs, chosen peoples, and proslavery ideology, offers the boldest assertion yet that Confederate nationalism not only was real but was felt deeply, widely, and quickly by a majority of whites. Indeed, it was durable enough to survive the actual collapse of the government in 1865.[11]

Not surprisingly, many historians of Civil War soldiers also have weighed in on the question of nationalism and its relationship to enlistment and subsequent military service. Those who stress social and cultural factors admit that patriotism played a role but minimize its importance. Stephen Berry, for example, suggests that public pronouncements of cause and country actually masked deeper, more private issues. In contrast, many of those who point to ideological motives highlight nationalistic expressions. Reid Mitchell viewed patriotism as a spur to enlistment and especially a sustaining motivator,[12] while James McPherson especially stressed soldiers' love of country, noting that two-thirds of the men in his sample at some point indicated patriotic reasons for service, with men from slaveholding families twice as likely to express patriotic sentiments as nonslaveholding Johnny Rebs. Confederate nationalism was a reality, with "roots several decades back in the antebellum ideology of Southern distinctiveness. Thus it seemed natural for many Confederate soldiers to express a patriotic allegiance to 'my country.'"[13]

Gary Gallagher, Peter Carmichael, and Aaron Sheehan-Dean likewise emphasize strong nationalist sentiments among Confederate soldiers. Carmichael finds nationalism especially among young, college-educated officers from the slaveholding class, while Sheehan-Dean describes a Confederate nationalism that developed among all ranks beginning in 1862. Gallagher adds that service across the South and with men from other states tended to increase nationalism among men in uniform as the war progressed. For most white Confederate civilians and men stationed beyond the Old Dominion, Robert E. Lee's Army of Northern Virginia became the symbol and hope of an independent Confederacy.[14]

The evidence compiled for this study, however, suggests that, in contrast, relatively few *later-enlisting* Confederates ever became nationalists to any degree. Only ten examples among youth—17 percent of all those identified as age twenty or younger—occur in the sample, and they are generally limited to the simplest expressions of patriotism and "country," the sorts of brief, rhetorical statements that Bell Wiley dismissed altogether as cant. For example, writing from Vicksburg in May 1862, seventeen-year-old planter's son Pvt. Willie Sivley of the 3rd Mississippi tried to persuade his sister that a cousin should join him in his company, for "he can't do more for his country any where else than here, he will be fighting for his country and home too."[15] Likewise, a young Texan, Sgt. Thomas Smith, a former resident of Illinois, wrote in his diary on July 4, 1862, that "the Confederate States of America will ere soon show to the nations of the world that they are an independent nation." Smith later copied into his diary a poem which began: "Better to die on the Battle Plain / To die for our native land."[16]

As the war progressed, love of country continued to serve as a sustaining motivator for this handful of youthful soldiers. During the summer of 1863, North Carolina Capt. J. F. Coghill lamented the death of a friend "in the cause of his beloved country."[17] Sgt. Abraham Jones of the 5th North Carolina Cavalry, recently captured and exchanged, wrote his parents in August 1863 that "we held a meeting day before yesterday & passed resolutions condemning the course of the Raleigh Standard, progress, & other disloyal papers & citizens in the state. . . . I hope it will have some effect on the cowardly men at home, who don't know war is & who had rather see their country's rights trampled in the dust than take up arms." Three weeks later he confided that he would prefer to go into winter quarters back in North Carolina, but added that he was "perfectly willing to remain here, if we are of more service to the country than we would be there."[18]

The call of duty to country had less appeal still to older men. Twenty-eight sampled later-enlisting Confederates over the age of twenty, 15.2 percent of that cohort, referred to their country at some point in their letters. A select few stood out in their fervor. Sgt. John Price Thurman, a West Tennessee farmer who enlisted in Nathan Bedford Forrest's 3rd Tennessee Cavalry early in 1862 at the age of thirty-one, stressed nationalism from the beginning. On the way to join his company after enlistment, he wrote his wife from Memphis that "it becomes the duty of every Patriot to make any sacrifice that our country demands." After he arrived in camp, he sent home another missive in which he maintained that serving his nation was "an endorsement of my principals as a free man."[19] A month later, after the Battle of Shiloh, Thurman's patriotism still burned brightly. Admitting his homesickness, he added that "I feel at the same time that I have a high duty to perform here and if needs be must sacrefice eny other consideration and for my God my country my wife & my children all to give even my life as a ransom to . . . our country from disgrace and insults as a people." And two years later the veteran trooper praised the kinfolk who "have stood by our country in her woes, toils & hardships, fighting on & ever will yet win for her a glorious independence."[20]

Like Thurman, Pvt. William Ross Stilwell of the 53rd Georgia wrote eloquently and frequently of his patriotism. A twenty-three-year-old harness maker before the war, Stilwell rushed with his unit to the Virginia front just before the Seven Days Battles. "I don't know when I may be killed," he wrote his wife after his baptism of fire, "it may be in a few days and it may never be, but I expect to try to die like a brave man fighting for the right of his country." A week later, he again affirmed that "my duty to my country demands my service and I must obey."[21] Stilwell's regiment went on to fight at Antietam and took heavy casualties there. Among them was "old man Guest" who "was a brave man and a good soldier and died in the defense of the rights of his country." As new campaigns approached, Stilwell continued to tell his spouse that "duty to you, duty to my country, and duty to God demands that I should act my part and if I fall, I want to fall in the discharge of duty and that foremost among the foemen." After the Gettysburg campaign, while serving as a courier for his brigade commander, he again wrote that "I feel that I will die in a just cause if I die it will be in defense of my country and the liberty of my people." From Petersburg in July 1864 Stilwell told his wife that if Federal forces reached his home in Henry County, Georgia, she was to "tell them that I breath the air of a true patriot fighting for my God, my country, my religion, my wife, and dear children. Should they insult you it will only cause me to strike the harder blows for all that is near and dear to man."[22]

Sgt. Maj. Marion Hill Fitzpatrick was a third older later-enlisting Confederate who wrote about his country, although not as often as Stilwell or Thurman. A Georgian like Stilwell, he enlisted in the 45th Georgia in the summer of 1862, at the age of twenty-seven. In September 1862, he wrote his wife that illness and hunger to the contrary, he had tried "to bear up cheerfully and do my whole duty to my country. . . . I have never regretted coming to the war and I feel proud that I have been of some service to my Country." The following spring, he asked her to "not grieve for me, even if I should fall, but remember me as one dieing to save his country." Six months later, after the Gettysburg summer, he looked forward to a day "when peace will have spread her balmy wings o'er the Suny South and Liberty shall have perched herself firmly on our banner and we shall be a free, independent and happy people."[23]

Still, despite a voluminous correspondence with his wife, Fitzpatrick mentioned his country on only four occasions. Pvt. James Michael Barr and Sgt. John Crittenden both did so three times each. Crittenden, a schoolteacher and planter's son-in-law, joined the 34th Alabama in March 1862. "I am in the path of duty," he explained to his wife. Two years later, he remained among those Confederates willing to "yield up our lives a Sacrifice to our country."[24] A prosperous thirty-four-year-old South Carolina slave owner, Barr enlisted more reluctantly in early 1863, and only after revisions to the Conscription Act cost him the exemption he had held as a major in the militia. Yet writing from the coast, where he served in the 5th South Carolina Cavalry, Barr asserted in March that "I came here to try to be of service to my Country and shall never try to get off unless I prove unfit for duty." Six months later, he contemplated the military reverses of the year and concluded that "if we only, as a nation, would put our trust in God as we should, I don't think the time would be long before we could have peace." A few weeks later, he added that "when our Country calls we must obey."[25]

There is another later-enlisting Confederate included in the sample who wrote frequently of his nation, although he did so in a manner far different from the others. Alabama-born Edwin Fay was a Harvard graduate and a thirty-year-old teacher when he enlisted as a sergeant in 1862. Bell Wiley suspected that Fay joined the army only to avoid conscription, while Gerald Linderman suggests that he donned Confederate gray to impress his young wife, a former student. Certainly, his subsequent attempts to escape the army with a teacher's exemption bear out his lack of enthusiasm for military service. Allegedly willing to die "in my Country's cause" in June 1862, a few weeks after his enlistment, Fay nonetheless added that "I hold that my first duty is to my family, my country is secondary," a theme he frequently repeated in subsequent letters. "Patriotism . . . is a fine word for historians, novelists and Big Gen'ls," he lectured his wife the following month, "when they have done some fighting and expect to have to do some more."[26]

Such sentiments obviously displeased Sarah Fay, a staunchly loyal Confederate. By September 1862, their argument over patriotism and the Confederate nation had grown bitter, with Edwin now referring derisively to "your country." A year later the sniping had not abated. Thoroughly disgusted with what he saw as an ever more tyrannical government in Richmond—it held him to the terms of his enlistment—Fay told his wife that her beloved government would be as "corrupt" as the one in Washington within five years. "I assure you that *spoken* patriotism is cheap," he intoned, ". . . if patriots at home knew what it was to be a soldier they would cease talking about patriotism. Patriotism is only a word embodying some ill defined idea of something, I fear *patriots* know not what. I tell you all the romance of patriotism consists in words which thrill the feelings for a time and is mistaken for something real." He added in October 1863, "Curse the country and the govt too! If it destroys my happiness what advantage is it to me. I am selfish I acknowledge and lay but small claim to what is called patriotism."[27]

Fay to be sure was an exception, yet in his own sour way he too saw the Confederacy as a nation worth writing about, if not one particularly worth fighting for. As for the others, two crucial points are worth considering. First, as discussed in later chapters, patriotism was hardly their only motivator, but instead part of a more complicated whole. Thurman's anger over Federal depredations sustained his will to fight, just as did Stilwell's faith and love of family. Barr meanwhile worried about keeping his slaves. Conceptions of liberty and independence played roles as well, as discussed below. Beyond that is the larger fact that the five older patriot soldiers, as well as Fay, simply spilled more ink about country and cause than did any of the other twenty-three who mentioned it. The expressions of nationalism coming from that majority were infrequent and brief. Here one must be careful, of course. During the war, letters often were never delivered. Others were lost over time. We cannot know for sure what men thought when only a handful of their letters survive. What did they talk about on the march, or around the campfire at night? Yet given the only available evidence available, one must conclude that nationalism was not a major factor to most later-enlisting soldiers. Thus, Pvt. S. W. Farrow of the 19th Texas mentioned his country in only two of his fifty-six letters, and all the others did so only once. With obvious affection for their new nation to be sure, but also almost in rote passing as well, they at one point referred to their willingness to do their duty to "my country," "our country," "our bleeding country," "the whole country," "our infant confederacy," "our little confederacy," "a glorious nation," "our once-happy and prosperous land," and "the South," even when it meant hardships and absence from home.[28]

Other words and phrases apparently much beloved by 1861 recruits are all but absent in the record for later enlisters. James McPherson found mentions of "the altar of my country" so typical that he gave that name to a chapter, yet the phrase only appears twice in the writings of later enlisters, once in a stirring jeremiad written by the 2nd Georgia's Pvt. Charles Terrill, a Canadian-born substitute who moved to Georgia from Boston only in 1857.[29] If brief statements scattered through diaries and letters about "my country" do indicate real nationalism, one must conclude nonetheless that nationalism was a relatively minor motivator for the men who joined the gray-clad army beginning in 1862. Moreover, nationalists were not equally distributed but rather were more likely to come from the Deep South; over half of those expressing nationalism in the sample came from three states— Georgia (nine), Alabama (seven), and Texas (five). At best, nationalism can help account only for the service of little more than 10 percent of late enlisters, and only then in tandem with other motivators. The soldiers of 1861 simply were stronger and more committed nationalists than those who came after them.

NATIONALISM AND DISCUSSIONS of independence are closely related, but the emphasis was slightly different on the latter. Any distinct group of people theoretically could produce a country or comprise a nation, but for Americans the specific word *independence* immediately called to mind the historic legacy of their revolution against Great Britain. Historians have differed on the impact of that legacy in motivating soldiers to fight. Bell Wiley passed over entirely the impact of the American Revolution in his earlier study of Johnny Rebs, and in but a single page briefly pointed to it as an initial motivator for the more politically motivated Billy Yank. Scholars who echoed the Wiley interpretation followed suit and minimized the importance of Revolutionary rhetoric and ideals.[30] It took Reid Mitchell to move the War of Independence toward the center stage of Civil War soldier historiography. He observed that "the Civil War proved curiously filled with echoes of the American Revolution. The patriotic past and the Biblical past were the two great historical memories by which Americans measured their present." Men on both sides thus initially proved eager to claim the mantle of true Revolutionary heirs while damning their foes as un-American. They embraced Revolutionary imagery, celebrated Washington's Birthday and the Fourth of July, sang patriotic songs, and routinely proclaimed their true cause as freedom. For newly minted Confederates, Mitchell continues, that "freedom" meant the right to pursue economic advancement through African-American slavery, just as so many Founding Fathers had done.[31]

Those scholars who increasingly stressed ideology as a central motivator likewise considered the impact of the War of Independence to be significant. Randall Jimerson maintained that in part Northern recruits enlisted to preserve the liberty and independence given to them by heroic past generations, and they considered it a duty to pass those virtues on to future Americans as well as to the rest of the globe. But Confederates also joined the army to protect the Revolutionary gifts of self-government and constitutional liberty, and they justified their decisions with repeated references to the Founding Fathers' noble stand against British tyranny. Where they differed was on the role of the Federal government: Northerners saw it as a protector of liberty; Southerners considered it a threat. For Confederates, moreover, the obvious and familiar counterpoint to liberty was slavery, and no middle ground could exist. They would be free men in an independent Confederacy, or "slaves" to the abolitionists in the old Union.[32]

James McPherson significantly amplified on this theme. "The patriotism of Civil War soldiers," he maintained, "existed in a specific historical context. Americans of every Civil War generation revered their Revolutionary forebears. Every schoolboy and schoolgirl knew how they had fought against the odds to forge a new republic conceived in liberty. Northerners and Southerners alike believed themselves custodians of the legacy of 1776." For Southerners, "liberty" meant resistance to the political and social "slavery" that would follow emancipation of the slaves, or as they called it in shorthand, "subjugation." Confederates adopted Revolutionary rhetoric and the legacy of the Founding Fathers to resist that subjugation. Like their forebears in 1776, they became in their own eyes latter-day patriots resisting a tyrannical empire intent on depriving them of liberty. Ironically, like their Union counterparts, they embraced the celebrations and the abstract but powerful symbols of that past conflict: "country, flag, Constitution, liberty and legacy of the Revolution." As the war dragged on, those symbols and that rhetoric became even more important as sustaining and combat motivators. Many Johnny Rebs maintained their morale by reminding themselves and others of the defeats Americans endured at the hands of the British before achieving final victory.[33]

After McPherson's central work appeared, other scholars affirmed and expanded upon these assertions to the point that they are now historical gospel. Elisabeth Lauterbach Laskin maintained that men in the Army of Northern Virginia fought for independence, to avoid "subjugation," and to preserve slavery and white superiority. Both Chandra Manning and Armstead Robinson highlighted the place of slavery in the Southern definition of liberty, while Anne Sarah Rubin saw the new Confederacy as a nation created and initially interpreted entirely within the South's conception of the Revolution, both as a blueprint for and justification of secession. Confederates in their own words were not dismembering but rather rescuing the vision of the Founding Fathers from the perversions of Puritanical Yankee and abolition fanatics, while at the same time consciously downplaying the importance of slavery in the new founding. Indeed, the founders of the Confederacy saw themselves as the better Americans, and so had no compunction about appropriating the symbols of the American past or proclaiming the constitutionality of their actions. Southern Unionists thus easily became "Tories," immigrant Union soldiers were "Hessians," and George Washington emerged as the new country's leading icon, appearing both on the Confederacy's Great Seal and on its stamps. For a time, Confederates also could explain away military defeats given the many defeats Washington endured before victory at Yorktown. As Gary Gallagher pointed out, contemporary interpretations of the Revolution in the field both helped enshrine Robert E. Lee as the Confederacy's new Washington figure and created a climate at the end of the war that permitted discussions of whether the Confederates should embrace guerrilla tactics.[34]

Given the major importance assigned to the iconography and ideals of the Revolution by the ideological school of historians, it is thus both surprising and telling to find that only 9 of the 320 sampled later-enlisting soldiers referred directly to the American Revolution. One, already noted, was the youthful Texan patriot Sgt. Thomas Smith, who utilized imagery of the Revolution when he composed his journal entry for "the glorious 4th! Yes Glorious to us as much as the North. . . . the day on which the independence of our Forefathers was declared and thus I trust we will also soon celebrate the day in which *our* independence is declared."[35] Alabamian Pvt. Samuel Pickens and Georgian Pvt. William Ross Stilwell both meanwhile wondered how the Yankees could celebrate Washington's Birthday. "Strange to think that they would celebrate the birthday of the father of rebellion," Stilwell wrote.[36]

Likewise, the strongly patriotic John Thurman expressed his devotion to "(Our Country) bequeathed to us by our *fathers*."[37] James Michael Barr wrote his young wife in September 1862 that "our forefathers fought for the privileges they enjoyed, and the time is now here for us to fight for our liberty."[38] Drawing a similar comparison was Arkansas artillery captain Thomas J. Key, a former newspaper editor and fervent proslavery crusader who had served in the notorious Lecompton Constitutional Convention while living in Kansas. Key enlisted as a private after the Battle of Shiloh before rising to the rank of captain. In a letter written in January 1864, he mentioned in passing that he had been reading a book on "the first revolution" and had concluded that his Federal enemies reminded him of the British. Alabamian Pvt. John S. Tucker made a similar observation.[39] Two other men referred to the celebrated suffering of the Revolutionary soldier. Pvt. G. H. Burns, drum major of the 34th Georgia's regimental band, wrote his wife from Tennessee in August 1862 that "this begins to remind me of Revolution times we are under going hardships almost more than we can bear for our rights our wives our babes."[40] Later in the war, Chaplain Francis Milton Kennedy of the 28th North Carolina, noting the bitterly cold November of 1863, wrote in his diary that "the scenes of suffering at Valley Forge in the old revolution which are so historically famous, are surpassed in the present war."[41]

Other examples of Revolutionary rhetoric are just as sparse in the writings of later enlisters. Only twenty-nine soldiers, 9.1 percent of the total sample, specifically mentioned the word "independence" at all. Three were youths, while three-quarters represented the Lower South states that first instigated secession. Sgt. Pharis Shearer, for example, enrolled in the 45th Mississippi to pursue "our fight for independence."[42] The son of a wealthy planter, former United States Treasury Department official, and Confederate bureaucrat, Joseph Joyner of the 7th North Carolina left school and enlisted reluctantly as a private in 1862. Once he had seen combat, however, he expressed a determination to fight on "to the bitter end or achieve our independence."[43] The remaining twenty-seven soldiers were hardly more prone to refer to independence as one of their motivators. The Pickens brothers of Alabama, by far the wealthiest men among those surveyed, each mentioned independence three times in their diaries. Pvt. William Ross Stilwell mentioned it three times as well in his 127 surviving letters. Just after the Battle of Antietam, he wrote his wife Molly, "I think our independence ought to be worth a great deal for it cost enough." A month later, he expressed his determination to fight on. "We must have our independence," he maintained, "if not our way, we must have it another." The following summer, Stilwell again averred that he was fighting for Confederate independence.[44]

In his voluminous correspondence, Pvt. James Michael Barr twice commented that he and his comrades were fighting for independence, as did Sgt. Maj. Marion Hill Fitzpatrick. The other seventeen mentioned independence only once each. Ten of the twenty-five who wrote of independence did so in 1862, in what might be ranked as initial motivation, while an additional eight did so in 1863, six in 1864, and two in February 1865. A closer examination suggests that the bitter winter of 1863–64, after the defeats at Gettysburg and Vicksburg, particularly evoked sustaining thoughts of the Revolution and war, but the soldier's comments simply are too brief and too few to be definitive.[45]

By the same token, only sixteen soldiers, four age twenty or younger and the balance older men, specifically condemned "tyranny." Two-thirds of them again hailed from the cotton states. Among the youths, former Washington resident John Dooley heaped scorn upon Lincoln's "dastardly government,"[46] while Sgt. Abraham Jones of the 5th North Carolina Cavalry condemned "Yankee tyranny."[47] Sgt. Edwin Fay, Lt. William L. Nugent, and Alabamian Pvt. E. W. Treadwell among the older men attacked Union "despotism" as well.[48] As the war ended, Texan Lt. Lee Faulkner lamented the Confederacy's apparent defeat at the hands of "the greatest tirants on earth."[49]

A few not surprisingly focused on the president himself. In August 1862, Alabama private John W. Cotton assured his wife that "if I get killed just say I dyed in a good cause ould abe lincon and his cabinet could not daunt me now."[50] That statement was mild, however, when compared to the abuse that ensued once Lincoln issued the Emancipation Proclamation. In the months that followed the provisional and especially the final version of the bill, a handful of late enlisters seethed. Thomas Key and Edwin Fay, both prosperous older men and proslavery advocates, condemned Lincoln the Emancipator as an abolitionist and dictator.[51] "Lyncoln has issued his E. proclamation seting the negros free and arming them for the fight," a humbler man, Pvt. G. W. Burns wrote, "how will our union men south fix it up now it is also stated that he has called out three hundred thousand more men to carry on this unholy war let them come we will meet them."[52] Chaplain Marcus DeWitt of the 8th Tennessee condemned "Lincoln's despotic acts,"[53] while young Cpl. J. F. Coghill of the 23rd North Carolina affirmed that "I had rather live under the emperor of France than old Lincon."[54] "Old Abe is very stiffnecked," attorney and Mississippi cavalryman Lt. William L. Nugent explained in September 1863, "and will prolong the war to ensure his reelection to office."[55] To Sgt. Pharis Shearer, Lincoln was simply "King Abe the II."[56]

Lincoln's reelection in November 1864 brought forth a new round of condemnation. Missouri sharpshooter Lt. James T. Wallace recorded in his diary that "we know now what to depend on we have them to whip or be whipped or be overpowered and ground down by the iron heel of war and oppression this must nerve us anew to strike for Liberty and Independence: *amen*." Pvt. Grant Taylor of the 40th Alabama meanwhile wrote his wife, "it is reported here that old Lincoln is elected again. If so we may look for nothing short of freedom or subjugation."[57]

And what of "subjugation," the word James McPherson found so ubiquitous in the writings of average soldiers? Only seventeen soldiers in the sample (5.3 percent), roughly representing Lower South and Upper South evenly, joined Taylor in decrying it. Four did so in the immediate wake of their enlistment, suggesting that for them subjugation was an important initial motivator. "We may be a ruined people but never subjugated," Capt. R. H. Lee wrote from camp. "Before submission let us all die—carry desolation over the land."[58] Six more sounded the same note after the unsuccessful campaigns of the summer of 1863 when subjugation seemed a more realistic threat. Cpl. J. F. Coghill of the 23rd North Carolina asserted that Lincoln "said nothing but the restoration of the union or our subjugation will cause peace."[59] Lt. William L. Nugent meanwhile wished from Tupelo that "*Uncl. Sam* would recognize his nephew and give us peace. I do not desire a reconstruction & a hollow truce, a servile place in the family of nations and to eat the bread of dependence while I am denied all the privileges of a freeman." It would be better to become the colony of a European power, he averred, rather than be subjugated by abolitionists who would deprive Southern whites of their slaves and make the South "a barren waste and a desolate place."[60]

Three additional soldiers, all now veterans, decried subjugation during the long, bloody summer of 1864. Pvt. Willie Sivley swore that he "had rather see my coffin to night than be subjugated & have to live under old Abe's rules."[61] Again, William Nugent was the most adamant, declaring from Atlanta in August 1864 that the South "may expect nothing but vassalage and slavery all our lives. Our rights and privileges will be totally destroyed and military governors and yankee judges will govern us, while our lands will be parcelled out among a horde of foreign adventurers and mercenary soldiers. This is a fate to which we can never submit."[62] Finally, at the beginning of 1865, young Pvt. Erastus Willis of the 3rd South Carolina wrote home that while many men in his regiment opposed the arming of slaves as soldiers, he found it preferable to "subjugation."[63]

Surprisingly, given the traditional, central place occupied by "states' rights" in the postwar canon of the Lost Cause, references to rights and liberties were scarce. Only 7 soldiers among the sample of 320 men spoke of defending their liberties, while only 5 additional men wrote of fighting for their rights. And again, many of the same names appear: James Michael Barr, J. F. Coghill, Thomas Key, William P. Head. Indeed, twenty-four of the men who discussed nationalism also are among those who discussed liberty or rights, independence or subjugation. The conclusion is inescapable.

Irrespective of army or theater, only a handful of late-enlisting soldiers fervently and vocally supported an independent Confederacy that protected the rights and liberties deeded to them by the Founding Fathers. Only 19 percent of the sample overall spoke even occasionally in the language of political ideas, a subset that largely contained men from the cotton states that had birthed the Confederacy. In other words, the ideological concerns that motivated the recruits of 1861 do not seem to have stirred most later recruits and were especially easy to resist in the Upper South. Again, the nature of the available evidence assuredly underrepresents and perhaps even distorts the reality of soldiers' motivations, yet given the only sources at hand, the numbers remain striking. Hardly more than one of ten were nationalists using the most generous definition. Fewer still concerned themselves with the vision of the Founding Fathers, and only a mere handful said anything about "subjugation" or the old shibboleth of "states' rights." One well might surmise that the later recruit's hesitancy to enlist after Fort Sumter can be traced at least in part to his relative lack of the kind of militant patriotism and nationalism that energized the initial waves of recruits, especially in those states that left the Union more reluctantly after Fort Sumter. The majority simply were not men who worried enough about the political rhetoric of Southern rights and Yankee domination to go to war at its onset.[64]

BY MARCH OF 1862, two of the Reverend Drury Lacy's sons already had taken up the fight. Before long, the sixty-year-old North Carolinian and former college president would follow them, assuming the role of chaplain to the 47th North Carolina. Lacy's middle son, William, however, nineteen years of age, remained a seminarian at Hampden-Sydney College. There he studied under the tutelage of the noted Presbyterian theologian Dr. Robert Dabney.[65] Neither Drury Lacy nor Dabney wanted the young man to enlist; Dabney wanted Willie Lacy to wait until he was licensed to preach, and then go to the army as a chaplain. Around the beginning of the month, however, the younger Lacy defied them both and joined the elite Rockbridge Artillery as a private "after long and anxious thought and prayer." It was necessary to move quickly to avoid conscription, he explained, and so he had acted without consulting his parents. The threat of the draft did partially convince Lacy to act, as did the pressure of peers who were coming to the same decision. But, he admitted, there was one thing more. "After long meditation," he wrote, "I could not shake off the conviction that it was my duty to volunteer even though it was against the advice of my professors."[66]

"Duty, Honor, Country": so reads the motto of the United States Military Academy. The three concepts were intrinsically linked in the American mind by the 1860s. Gerald Linderman not surprisingly maintains that duty was another central initial and sustaining motivator of Civil War soldiers and especially officers. Although they usually did not define the object of that duty, many spoke of feeling its effect on their decision to fight. Reid Mitchell and James McPherson agreed and cited duty as a crucial combat motivator as well, especially for Union soldiers, with Mitchell adding that Confederates' conflicting duties to family and cause ultimately undermined the Southern war effort.[67] As with politics, however, only a handful of the later-enlisting Confederates in the sample, fourteen in all, even partially explained their decision to fight for the Confederacy by referring to national duty. Two, Lacy and G. L. Alspaugh of the 27th Louisiana, were aged twenty or younger. Slightly over half wrote in 1862, not long after their enlistments. None dwelled on the idea of duty in depth, instead mentioning it almost in asides. "I believe it to be my duty to fight for my country," the nationalist B. F. Tamplin wrote his wife bluntly.[68]

Those men who did say more left letters that suggest strongly that duty in their eyes was merely the reverse of the guilt and shame they apparently felt for not enlisting sooner. Such comments place them squarely in what some historians have defined as the southern honor culture. In the antebellum southern mind, according to these scholars, "honor" embodied much of a traditional, masculine, pre-Christian warrior code. It meant status and reputation among white men as conferred by the wider community. The honorable man, whether a small farmer, powerful politician, or soldier, shaped his actions so that he would be acknowledged in the present and remembered in the future as brave and manly, a ferocious defender of hearth and home. To accept charges of cowardice or unmanliness without retaliation immediately marked one as dishonorable, lessened status, and undermined renown. These individual concerns also translated into an exaggerated sense of family and regional honor.[69]

Considerations of honor have become a major component of understanding the Old South. One might argue as well that in 1861 the white South behaved "honorably" by choosing war rather than accepting continued insults and a kind of emasculation. Historians see honor at work in men's decisions to fight, as well. Michael Barton maintained that honor was the chief trait of a good man as expressed by Civil War soldiers North and South, while Gerald Linderman stressed the importance of honor as a motivator and molder of soldier behavior. It not only sent droves of men into uniform, he maintained, but initially governed their expectations and behaviors, requiring that they be courageous, gentlemanly, and magnanimous to the defeated enemy. McPherson likewise insisted that honor was a powerful motivating force, especially for Confederates, who deemed it more central than duty. Personal, family, and unit honor constantly compelled men to enlist, endure, and fight rather than run. Elisabeth Lauterbach Laskin argued that honor motivated men to enlist rather than debase themselves by submitting to the government as draftees.[70]

One thus might expect honor to be a major factor at work in the motivations of later-enlisting Confederates. But once again, only a few soldiers, primarily those fighting in the Western theater, seemed especially worried about honor in their writings. Cpl. William J. Hart of the 47th Virginia in fact was the only member of the sample from the Upper South to touch on honor when he wrote to his father that men who stayed at home were "cowardly fellows."[71] Proud of doing his duty, Lt. W. J. J. Webb of the 51st Georgia condemned the stay-at-homes as well. And Cpl. John T. Beggs of Louisiana's 5th Battery, Washington Artillery, explained to his sister that "you know me too well to think I could stay at home idle while all my young friends have left their families and friends. George Crawford and John Knowles have left their homes long ago for the same cause and I hope it shall never be said that John Beggs was *afraid to go*."[72]

G. W. Giles of the 35th Alabama likewise admitted to his wife that were it not "for the glorious cause that I am in and the scandle and stigmay that would be left on my Reputation I would certainly Runaway and come Home."[73] Yet such concerns did not deter Pvt. Phillips Fitzpatrick for long. "I have made up my mind to do my duty," he wrote his wife from his camp of instruction in March 1862, "& when the battle is over and the victory won I shall have the profound satisfaction of knowing that I have done my share in the defense of the country." Fitzpatrick hired a substitute just two months later and returned home to manage his lands and numerous slaves.[74] Ultimately, one must conclude that later-enlisting Confederates cared even less about honor and duty than they did political ideology. More to the point, as with ideology, they wrote much less about duty and honor than did the enlistees of 1861.

There is a critical, final caveat, however. Several scholars over the years have maintained increasingly that to Confederates, words such as "subjugation," "liberty," and "states' rights" were no more than code words that really meant the preservation of their right to own slaves in a slaveholding republic grounded on white supremacy. Twenty-two of the sixty-one ideologues (36.1 percent) can be identified as slave owners or the sons of slave owners. Thus, to fully gauge the importance of ideology on later-enlisting Confederates, one must also examine how they regarded the South's "peculiar institution."

2

SLAVERY

"THE PRINCIPLE CAUSE OF THE WAR"

Like many prosperous Confederate soldiers, Sgt. Edwin Fay did not go to war alone. When he left home in April 1862 with Louisiana's Minden Rangers, he took with him a slave only identified as Rich to be his personal body servant. Within a week, Fay already was dissatisfied with his choice. He sent for Rich to bring him his horse, only to discover that his slave was missing. Fay proceeded to "hunt all over Gr. Junction for him, gave a boy a quarter to find him but at last he was brought in—gone skylarking to see some woman. I tried to bump his brains out against a hogshead of sugar and since then he has done pretty well."[1]

The incident in Grand Junction only inaugurated a two-year long cycle of complaint and physical abuse, for Rich could do nothing right in Fay's eyes. When he told his master that a letter had arrived from home, Fay "wanted to break his head for not bringing it and sent him to the Capt's tent for it." Rich was a poor cook, Fay complained, he got sick and had to be nursed, and he was "careless and inattentive." While we have no records that reveal Rich's side of the story, one nevertheless can read between the lines Fay wrote home to construct quite a different view of the man. Notably, the "careless" slave also was a hard-working entrepreneur. Discovering within weeks that the soldiers wanted clean clothing without having to do the work themselves, Rich bought a quantity of lye soap and went into the laundry business. Late in May 1862, Fay complained to his wife that "Rich has sent home 2½ [dollars] by Capt. Wimberly $2 another time and 4¼ by Linn Watkins in a letter to her so he says. I told him he was a fool. Why did he not bring it to me and let me send it off for him. I will make him do it in the future so she will be sure to get it." One suspects that Rich knew better than to give his money willingly to Fay.

As the summer passed, Rich added cooking and the care of the men's horses to his resume, while at the same time openly neglecting the unpaid duties Fay wanted performed. In October, the soldier decided to hire Rich out for the rest of the year in exchange for $45, but that became a problem when Fay "forgot" his slave for a time in Vicksburg—that is, Rich ran away again. Although Fay later repeatedly threatened to send Rich home for good, he never did so, even as Rich accumulated enough money to begin sending gifts to loved ones.[2]

The year 1863 brought more grousing. Rich disappeared yet again; Fay feared the Yankees had him. By May, however, he was back in camp, "a better boy than formerly, tho I gave him a good whipping the other day." In July, Rich broke his leg while caring for Fay's horse, and it cost Fay $40 to leave him in a "very nice family's" care. In August, Rich requested crutches. The next month, he hobbled into camp, only to leave again while Fay was on duty. He was back late in October but took off for good the following spring. "If he went to the Yankees," Fay wrote, "I hope they have killed him ere this."[3]

In contrast, about the time Rich ran away from both Edwin Fay and the Confederate army, nineteen-year-old J. Wallace Comer entered the 57th Alabama as first sergeant. The son of a wealthy planter who owned sixty-one slaves and older brother of a future Alabama governor, the young lieutenant also went to war with a family slave. Unlike Fay, Comer praised the man he brought as an exception to other slaves in camp. "If Burrell holds

Lt. J. Wallace Comer of the 57th Alabama and his body servant, a family slave identified only as Burrell. Photograph courtesy Southern Historical Collection, University of North Carolina at Chapel Hill, P-167/1.

out fast full to the end," Comer wrote from Kenesaw Mountain, Georgia, "& stick to me as well as he has done here to fore & I come out safe a mint could not buy him ther are very few Negroes in the army that are not worth enything to their masters in times like this." What especially delighted Comer was Burrell's bravery. "Burrell is not afraid of anything," Comer beamed, "he came to us the other day while we were on Picket . . . he said he wanted to kill One yankee before the war ended."[4] At some point in 1864, the two men even posed together for a photograph. Relatively relaxed, Comer sits in a chair, his hand on his sword and wearing his hat at a jaunty angle. To his right, Burrell stands awkwardly, hat in hand, wearing the Confederate private's uniform routinely given to African Americans with the army. Yet, as Comer consistently maintained in his letter, Burrell was not really a soldier. He was still a "Negro," while Comer remained among the "masters."

SOME RECENT AUTHORS have used photographs like that of Wallace Comer and the man known only as Burrell, evidence such as the latter's alleged willingness to kill a Union soldier, and other, scattered accounts of varying authenticity and interpretation to argue that tens of thousands of African Americans served a color-blind Confederacy as willing soldiers. Such claims cannot be supported by the preponderance of evidence, or by what we know about the complicated, interconnected lives of slaves and slave owners. In truth, whether well regarded like Burwell or roughly treated like Rich, all but a handful of African Americans in the Confederate army remained until the end of the war exactly what Comer said they were, privately owned slave laborers performing tasks for individual slave owners, or else impressed by the army at large. Ultimately, neither Edwin Fay nor Wallace Comer, nor any of the other slave owners identified among later-enlisting Confederates that are included here in the sample, ever suggested that the African Americans with them in camp were comrades, nor did any eager, volunteer "black Confederates" turn up in this study.[5]

The real historical question at hand is how the institution of slavery influenced white Confederate soldiers' initial, sustaining, and combat motivations, later enlisters included. That is to say, did they really fight to preserve slavery? While acknowledging the central role the sectional argument over slavery played in causing the Civil War, Bell Wiley and those who followed his lead downplayed the importance of slavery in individual Johnny Rebs' decisions to serve in the army. To be sure, Wiley did briefly acknowledge that Northern opposition to slavery led many Southerners to hate Yankees, and he agreed that many Southerners fought to forestall African American equality.[6] As with so many other aspects of the ideological explanation, it was Reid Mitchell who forced a reevaluation of the importance of slavery relative to enlistment. Some Confederates openly joined the army to preserve slavery, according to Mitchell, because they were avowed racists and white supremacists who wanted to keep African Americans unequal and subservient. Others feared the havoc uncontrolled former slaves and abolitionist Republicans might wreak. Still other soldiers' reasoning was more complicated. They saw the region as a land of "economic opportunity" and feared that the destruction of slavery would create poverty and chaos for them individually and for whites in general. Events including John Brown's raid on Harpers Ferry heightened fears of Haitian-style bloodletting and race mixing to the level of paranoia. In the end, Confederates' reluctance to officially arm African Americans as soldiers, only overcome in Congress during the war's last weeks and then in the face of significant opposition, demonstrated that many Southerners' commitment to white supremacy trumped even their devotion to independence.[7]

As noted previously, James McPherson and other historians have similarly maintained that liberty and slavery were the "twin goals for which Confederates fought."[8] Indeed, Randall Jimerson stressed slavery even more than McPherson, maintaining that those "twin goals" were in fact one and the same. While men claimed to enlist and fight for many reasons, the "one basic premise" that connected all of them just beneath the surface was that the North wanted to end slavery. If that hostile, atheistic North succeeded, white Southerners worried, every aspect of Southern society would collapse. Property would cease to have value. Uncontrollable former slaves would become legal equals, and, united with Northern Republicans-abolitionists, would forever deprive the permanent Southern white minority of all constitutional liberties. Once-honorable white men essentially would become slaves themselves, men without honor. "The result," according to Jimerson, "would be to jeopardize all that southerners most dearly treasured—honor, family, home, religion, and their entire social order. As the cornerstone of their civilization, slavery must be protected at all costs."[9]

Two newer works mark the strongest recent statements yet about the centrality of slavery to Confederate enlistment. Aaron Sheehan-Dean stresses that Virginia nonslaveholders enlisted to preserve slavery and thus their political rights and economic opportunities. Chandra Manning likewise insists that both Union and Confederate soldiers understood that the war was primarily about slavery. Many slave-owning Confederates enlisted simply to keep their slaves, while many nonslaveholders joined because they wanted slave property in the future. Without slaves or at least the promise of owning them, some white men would fall to the mudsill of society. More fought because they believed that their orderly, God-given, slave-based society, with its prescribed ranks and roles, both offered the best opportunities for their families—what many defined as "liberty"—and protected their loved ones from violent African American retribution. To question the rules of that society was to question the will of the Almighty.

Whether slave owners or not, white men's masculinity was thoroughly entangled with the power to master slaves. Echoing historian Stephanie McCurry, Manning argues that without the power vested in owning slaves, the family itself might disintegrate. Not only might African Americans enter into sexual relationships with willing white women, but other women might attempt to wriggle from their assigned places in society. Ultimately, white men's economic, social, and political power depended on the preservation of slavery. Thus, whatever the expressed reasons given for going to the army, slavery "served as the cement that held Confederates together even under almost impossibly trying circumstances. . . . For the men who filled the Confederate ranks, secession, the Confederacy, and the war were not about state sovereignty or whether the central government could levy a tariff or build a road. Secession, the Confederacy, and the war were about securing a government that would do what government was supposed to do: promote white liberty, advance white families' best interests, and protect slavery."[10]

Although their emphases differ, all of these later scholars maintain in sum that Johnny Rebs enlisted, remained in the ranks, and fought battles to preserve legal slavery. They also admit that such an interpretation requires a degree of historical interpretation and literary deconstruction, for relatively few of the soldiers they studied wrote blatantly about fighting to preserve slavery.

Elisabeth Lauterbach Laskin, for example, found that only 11 percent of the men in her Army of Northern Virginia samples did so.[11] That observation holds true in regard to later-enlisting Confederates as well. Of the 209 men in the sample who also can be located in the census, 92 (44 percent) were slave owners or came from slave-owning families, a figure that suggests that scholars such as Armstead Robinson and David Williams were too quick to condemn slaveholders and their sons for staying at home while others fought. Indeed, this percentage is much higher than that offered by Laskin, who found that only 16 percent and 18 percent of the Army of Northern Virginia men in her two samples were from slaveholding families. Joseph Glatthaar, in contrast, importantly counting nonrelated residents of households as well as slaveholders and their kin, found that 48 percent of 1862 enlistees in the same army lived in slaveholding households.[12] As Table 3 in the Appendix demonstrates, about a third of the slaveholding soldiers sampled for this study were youths of age twenty or below, while the remaining two-thirds were over the age of twenty at the time of enlistment. Counted differently, almost two-thirds (63 percent) came from the Lower South, where slaves comprised a higher percentage of the total population. Given that 111 of the men in the sample do not appear in the census at all, however, a fact that generally if not always suggests poverty and rootlessness, the real percentage of slave owners in the sample is probably closer to 30 percent, roughly the same percentage that existed among Confederate white families as a whole.[13]

Given the assumed centrality of slavery to enlistment as well as the numbers of sampled slave owners, one still might accordingly expect to find at least a fair number of comments from the slave owners and sons of slave owners, if not others as well. Yet only 8 soldiers out of the 320 examined for this study (2.5 percent) openly named slavery as a reason they fought. Three of them, moreover, did so only in angry reactions to the Preliminary Emancipation Proclamation, which proved an ironic sustaining motivator. Pvt. Charles Terrill, the Canadian-born private and a vocal secessionist in the 2nd Georgia, related emancipation to the North's "fever heat" to end the war. "All slaves are to be freed," he proclaimed, "and horrible insurrection rule the hour."[14] Likewise, Virginian John Dooley, the son of a slave owner who rose from the rank of private to lieutenant, noted the encounter between a family of Maryland abolitionists and his body servant, Ned Haines. "The mistress of the house . . . tried to induce him to desert the service and accept his freedom (which Uncle Sam was depriving his white progeny of and lavishly bestowing it on their blacks)," Dooley spat, but the slave refused to abandon his master.[15]

William L. Nugent of the 28th Mississippi Cavalry wrote his wife in the summer of 1863 that "we are now driven to fight to the bitter [end], if conquest itself be the result. The ruling majority are contending to emancipate our slaves, and if the negroes are freed the country . . . is not worth fighting for at all. We will all be compelled to abandon it and seek some more congenial climate."[16] But none reached the crescendo of the ardent Confederate patriot Sgt. Thomas Smith of the 32nd Texas Cavalry, who sometime in 1862 recorded in his diary the lyrics to T. W. Crowson's song entitled "Run Yank or Die." It included a chorus Smith endorsed:

Hurrah for Slavery for Southerners are the boys
For singing & fighting and stopping Yankee noise.
The whole Confederacy is getting up to cry:
Big Yank, Little Yank
Run Yank or Die[17]

Pvt. J. C. Williams of the 63rd Georgia, not a slave owner himself, took a different tack. He approvingly described to his wife a sermon he heard in camp from a minister turned captain who had assured his listeners that "there was another race of people depending on us for their salvation consequently God would not suffer us subjugation."[18] Three final soldiers mentioned slavery as a cause for fighting the war, but only to deny that this motivation applied to them. At the end of 1863, Lt. T. L. Camp of the 40th Georgia assured his wife that he was fighting only to protect his family. "I have no negroes to fite for," he added, "but I am willing to hang on as long as it will do any good." Pvt. Isaac Walters of the 50th North Carolina likewise identified slavery "as the principle cause of the war."[19] Another Tar Heel, Pvt. James Calvin Zimmerman of the 57th North Carolina, bitterly condemned the war as the slaveholders' attempt to hold their property. "If you will show me a man that is trying to compell soldiers to stay in the army," he wrote his wife, "he is a speculator or a slave holder or has an interest in slaves."[20]

Slavery in short had few open proponents among the ranks of later enlisters. The rest were hardly abolitionists, however. Rather, most were men who routinely accepted slavery and racism as parts of Southern life, and thus as part of their army. They did not defend it in letters home because they did not have to do so. They did write about it, however. Twenty-eight of the soldiers in the sample, about 9 percent, described the activities of slaves brought to the army. Roughly half served in the Eastern theater and half in the Western; none served in the Trans-Mississippi. All but four of the soldiers, however, served in Lower South regiments, tentatively suggesting the greater importance of slavery to men from those states.[21]

Thirteen soldiers out of this group referred at times to their own personal body servants. Other Confederate soldiers regularly hired African Americans enslaved by comrades such as Edwin Fay to do their cooking, washing, or foraging. Cavalrymen had them care for their horses, and soldiers sometimes sent slaves home to gather provisions and belongings or deliver mail. Construction proved another important task. Pvt. James Michael Barr of the 5th South Carolina Cavalry related how his slave joined others to cut logs for soldiers' winter quarters, while Sgt. Maj. Harden Cochrane noted that the slaves in his Alabama unit would live in a separate cabin once built. Pvt. Samuel Pickens of the 5th Alabama related how a slave helped him build a chimney for his tent. Pickens also detailed how body servants gathered food for his mess. African American teamsters meanwhile became so common that Pvt. D. C. Snyder of the 11th Virginia Cavalry expressed surprise when a white teamster drowned crossing a river.[22] Only one sampled soldier repeated stories of enslaved Confederates informally taking up arms to fight, however: Pvt. J. A. McMurtrey of the 9th Georgia Artillery wrote that "the other day a negro man took 12 yankees prisoners by him self and brought them up to his master."[23] There is little evidence that nonslaveholders among the late enlisters resented wealthier men who brought slaves with them to camp, as historian Armstead Robinson averred.[24]

Treatment of slaves by soldiers in general varied. Some, like Edwin Fay, allowed their body servants to make money working for others.[25] Pvt. Andrew Crawford, a new recruit in a South Carolina regiment, begged his mother in February 1865 to send a family slave to do his washing, for "the Negroes charge such exorbitant prices for washing '*and other things*' . . . that a person is either obliged to have a boy or a pocket full of money, or go dirty as a dog."[26] Other men complained that, in the words of Pvt. S. W. Farrow of the 19th Texas, "what few negroes there is here has more privileges than the privates do."[27]

Pvt. Abel Crawford of the 61st Alabama wrote a letter for his "colored bodyguard" Jim Crawford when the latter began to worry that his sweetheart had jilted him. While the white man expressed sympathy for the slave, however, he also did not fully trust him. When a local man claimed that the slave had stolen his watch, Abel Crawford believed it without hesitation. "I called Jim up," he related, "and found him in possession of it but previous to this time he had told the Adjutant Green that he had bought the watch. . . . I made him give the watch back and he has some four or five hundred dollars that I shall take from him to prevent his buying any more watches in like manner." The situation clearly left the young soldier uneasy. "I want Pa to send me some advice about how I should attend to such cases," he pleaded.

"It is the first time I ever knew Jim to be guilty of such a trick and I am in hopes that it will be the last."[28]

Other men needed no advice on how to deal with slaves deemed recalcitrant. The ultimate brutality of slavery on the home front extended to the army as well. Pvt. Grant Taylor described how several comrades in the 40th Alabama whipped to death an officer's body servant after the man allegedly "got drunk, stole and wasted a good deal of lard belonging to Bat and then cursed and sauced him."[29] Sgt. Isaac McQueen Auld of the 5th Florida described a lynching that occurred in his camp in July 1862. After a nearby house burned, "suspicion rested upon a negro who had some articles in his possession that were in the house. He was arrested today and the suspicions were confirmed. The citizens hung him about a mile from camp."[30]

Not surprisingly, slaves such as Fay's Rich tried to flee. Young Lt. Thomas J. Moore of Holcomb's South Carolina Legion wrote the family overseer after the Battle of Antietam that "Stephen . . . is greatly dissatisfied and wants to come home. When I was sick he started to run away from the army but someone saw him and persuaded him to come back. If we ever go into Maryland again he will be sure to leave." Several weeks later, Moore sent Stephen home in exchange for another man named Elihu, whom the overseer bought from a family estate.[31] Likewise, Sgt. Maj. Edwin Rice of Waul's Texas Legion described in his diary how "a runaway negro . . . jumped in the river at Greenwood and drowned himself."[32] Samuel Pickens related the escape of two slaves. Pvt. Henry Gibbs Morgan of Fenner's Louisiana Battery complained to his mother that their slave John had disappeared from camp but promised that when the constable finally found him he would return another slave whom the family needed at home. Morgan went on to ask that, if John had escaped for good, the family send another slave who could cook. Whatever their role in motivation, slave labor clearly helped sustain the Confederate army.[33]

WHILE LATER-ENLISTING Confederate soldiers accepted and indeed often wanted African Americans in their camps as laborers, they drew the line at making them soldiers and equals. A handful of white Confederates such as General Richard Ewell had advocated arming slaves from the beginning of the war. Most famously, in 1863 the Irish-born general Patrick Cleburne had circulated at the highest levels a proposal to arm slaves in exchange for freedom. Yet enlisted men knew none of this, and it was only during the waning weeks of the war that it became a public issue when the Confederate

Congress debated the raising of African American soldiers. As Bruce Levine deftly points out, the grudging decision to arm slaves did not grow out of a conviction that either slavery or the nation had to be sacrificed, as usually suggested. Rather, it arose from the reluctant conclusion by slavery's advocates that the institution already had collapsed under Union pressure, that the Confederacy could not survive without additional troops, and thus that the government must move to arm African Americans while ensuring that postwar black freedom within the Confederacy would be as limited as possible. Not surprisingly, the legislation was a hesitant half-measure. Crucially, no slave owner would lose a single slave without his permission.

Soldiers in the army as a whole followed the debate closely and replicated it in the ranks.[34] Few later enlisters, however, seem to have taken part, for only seven men expressing interest in arming blacks at any point in the war could be located in the sample. All more or less grudgingly supported the idea. As early as November 1863, Sgt. Maj. Marion Hill Fitzpatrick had written, "I had much rather gain our independence without it but if necessary I say put them in and make them fight."[35] A few weeks later, in February 1864, Lt. James B. Jones of the 1st North Carolina Sharpshooters likewise reluctantly supported arming blacks, "hoping that they will help stem the torrent."[36]

A more significant account comes from Capt. Thomas Key, the former proslavery Kansan who had moved to Arkansas before the war. The commander of Patrick Cleburne's artillery later in 1863, Key encountered his commanding officer at the end of the year. "I had scarcely seated myself," Key wrote in his diary, "when he introduced a conversation upon the propriety of bringing into the military service, and at once beginning to drill, 300,000 negroes." Asserting that other general officers supported him, Cleburne further advocated freedom for the soldiers' families as well as the fighting men themselves. Only in such a manner could the Confederacy continue to field armies, while such a plan also would turn emancipation to the South's advantage while taking "the wind out of the sails of Northern Abolitionists and cause them to cease the war." If they did not, Cleburne added, the Europeans once again could come to the Confederacy's support."

At first, Key remained unsure. "This is one of the weightiest questions that has been brought forth since the beginning of this revolution," Key wrote. "It will make or ruin the South. It will conclude the war speedily or cause blood to flow more freely than heretofore." Two days after the conversation, however, Key related his discussion with Cleburne to Charles Swett, another artillery captain in Cleburne's command. Key and Swett slowly brought each other around to the idea. Key notably remembered Swett saying that "he wanted his negro women to keep his wife from the wash tub." "Nevertheless, to close the war and give us liberty he was ready to free his negroes, as he now did not value them above a 'dime each.'" Key concluded that "the idea of abolishing the institution at first startles everyone, but when it is viewed as the means of giving us victory or closing the war, every person with whom I have conversed readily concurs that liberty and peace are the paramount questions and is willing to sacrifice everything to obtain them. All, however," he added, "believe the institution a wise one and sanctioned by God."[37]

Key spoke too soon about widespread agreement. In the end, Richmond suppressed Cleburne's proposal. Only in January 1865 did the question fully reach the public mind through congressional debate and Lee's eleventh-hour advocacy. Pvt. Grant Taylor noted serious opposition to African American comrades within Alpheus Baker's Alabama brigade. "We would have to drill and fight side by side with the stinking things," Taylor complained. "They are to be set free if they fight well at the end of the war if we gain our independence. . . . The men, I believe, are generally opposed to it and a great many declare they will go home if they are put in ranks with us. That is my notion." Taylor closed his discussion with a telling comment about his cause: "And to think we have been fighting four years to prevent the slaves from being freed," he wrote, "now to turn round and free them to enable us to carry on the war. The thing is outrageous."[38]

Pvt. Erastus Willis of the 3rd South Carolina, the son of a man who owned one slave, only disagreed somewhat. "I he[a]r some talk of our leading men puting negro troops in the field," he wrote his father, "but I don't think that will do as well there is a great many men that would not fight eny more but I say aney thing be fore subjugation the negroes I think will be maid free be fore this . . . this seems to be the darkes hour that the confederates ever hav had."[39]

WHILE LATER-ENLISTING Confederates overall expressed much less interest in arming black Confederates than did their other comrades in arms, more held strong opinions on the African Americans who joined the ranks of their enemies after the Emancipation Proclamation. By the end of the war, 10 percent of the men who served overall in the Union army were black men recruited in the Confederacy. Pvt. Jesse Sumner Battle of the 11th

Georgia Artillery Battalion hopefully suggested that the arming of African American Federal troops meant that the Lincoln government was collapsing, "the last resort and a weakness below the dignity of any government."[40] Another Georgian, Pvt. G. H. Burns, hoped that the approach of black troops would undermine Southern unionists.[41] And a third Georgian, Pvt. William Ross Stilwell, wrote, "Aha! Poor Yankee who is afraid to face the music themselves, they think they can send the poor nigger down south to get killed. I think they are nearly played out when they want to fight the South with negroes."[42]

Pvt. James Joseph Williamson, one of Mosby's Rangers, meanwhile viewed black Unionists as amusing cowards in a sort of real-life minstrel show. He described with relish a surprise attack on a Union camp in November 1863. "A lot of negroes were sitting around one of the fires enjoying the warmth as only negroes can enjoy it," Williamson wrote in his diary, "when Capt. Chapman drew his revolver & told them he would shoot the first one who made any noise. The negroes opened their eyes and in trembling accents begged him not to shoot." When a gun did go off, however, "some confusion ensued—The negroes and whites ran about in great alarm. . . . Some of the negroes ran about without knowing what to do. Please massa, don't shoot."[43]

But others reacted with tremendous anger. The lure of killing apparent slaves in rebellion actually helped sustain these men. Sgt. John Crittenden, for example, reported that the 34th Alabama was itching to get at United States Colored Troops (USCT) regiments. Four other sampled soldiers in some manner vowed to fly "the black flag," that is, to take no African American prisoners and offer no mercy. "A negro will never get any quarters from me," Pvt. Willie Sivley wrote his sister.[44] Edwin Fay also vowed to take no prisoners at all, asserting that "the Black Flag will be hoisted after Jan'y 1st '63 and the soldiers of the North will pause ere they covet a resting place under its folds."[45] Pvt. William Ross Stilwell himself told his wife, "I intend to make the wool fly if I ever get the chance. . . . I intend to get me enough of negroes to settle me a plantation down in Dixey."[46] None proved angrier, however, than Capt. Thomas Key, the soldier in the sample most motivated by the slavery issue. Key railed against "the disgusting equalization" and potential for interracial sexual relationships that followed in the wake of William Tecumseh Sherman as he marched to the sea in late 1864. "A trustworthy lady" told Key's ambulance driver "that the day before she departed from Atlanta a big black negro man went to one of the most respected young ladies in the city and offered her $10 if she would come to his tent and spend the night with him. The thought of such an occurrence arouses every nerve in my body for vengeance, and I feel like crying: 'raise the black flag and let slip the dogs of war.'"[47]

In time, a few of the soldiers actually encountered African American troops. Their reactions varied. At Petersburg, Pvt. Samuel Pickens noted that picket firing only flared up when USCT troops appeared across the lines. Reporting the capture of up to 400 African American soldiers at Dalton, Georgia, late in 1864, John Crittenden noted that several were fugitive slaves he recognized from home. "When attacked," he claimed, "they made no resistance at all. All seems anxious to get home again."[48] From the Trans-Mississippi theater, Pvt. John T. Knight of the 22nd Texas wrote in October 1863 that "the men are all anxious for a fight" with the African American soldiers stationed nearby.[49] Sgt. Maj. A. D. Craver of the 26th Georgia Battalion meanwhile described the condition of "captured Negroes . . . at work on the RailRoad between Corinth & Cherokee Ala. . . . the Negroes are dying very fast We have buried 9 here in two Weeks."[50]

The incident that stands out in the letters of late-enlisting Confederates, however, is the murder of surrendering black prisoners taken in the Battle of the Crater. On July 30, 1864, Union miners exploded four tons of gunpowder and blew a hole in the Confederate's Petersburg line that was 170 feet long and 30 feet deep. First white and then African American soldiers poured into what they expected to be a gap, but what turned out to be a deep crater. Initially stunned, Confederate defenders surrounded the crater and killed their attackers with minié balls, bayonets, and clubbed muskets. Three late enlisters described what happened next in some detail. "You could not imagine the slaughter of the blacks," wrote Pvt. Charles M. Hurley of the 2nd Company, Washington Artillery, "why they were piled up by our soldiers."[51] Pvt. T. S. McAlister of the 25th North Carolina reported to his parents that "about half the yankees were negroes. Most of the fighting was done with bayonets and butts of muskets. Blood ran in trenches all around. Finally the negroes and white yankees were overcome; a great many were taken prisoners. Most of the negroes were killed; a few were made prisoners. Oh! The horrors of war."[52]

IN A LETTER WRITTEN in July 1862 from Florida, Sgt. Maj. Harden Cochrane related the tale of "two negroes here who were trying to get to the Yankees." He explained, "They do not belong to anybody in the regiment. I believe one ran away from a plantation near Montgomery, the other pretends to have been hired in Milton . . . and was going to his master." When apprehended, both blamed a white man "with red whiskers and white cloth shoes" for convincing them to flee. Confederate soldiers did indeed locate such a character, "a Dutch man . . . strongly suspected of being a spy" and took him prisoner.[53] Other Confederates meanwhile convinced themselves as well that once-loyal slaves only went into Union lines under duress. Both Sgt. Absalom Burum of Thomas's North Carolina Legion and Lt. E. B. Coggin of the 47th Alabama maintained that Union regiments impressed slaves against their will. In a similar vein, Lt. F. A. Bleckley of the 11th Georgia Cavalry noted that many blacks fled Union lines when they had the chance to come home.[54]

Such hopeful sentiments are not surprising. Before the war and still after Fort Sumter, paternalistic white Southerners made much of the allegedly familial relations between slave and slave owners. A few, such as Pvt. J. R. Parker of the 42nd Alabama, regularly sent greetings from the front to their "People," expressing affection and hopes that their slaves would behave well.[55] "Give my love and respects to all of the nigers," Pvt. O. V. Strickland of the 43rd Georgia wrote, "and tell them that I want to see them."[56] Pvt. E. A. Penick of the 38th Virginia frequently wrote home to tell his slaves to be "Respectful and obediant tell them I say so and they must do it for me & they will find me grateful."[57]

Yet as the war went on, few could ignore the obvious and increasing breakdown of slavery on the home front. Southern slaves were well aware of Northern opposition to slavery, and they grew increasingly hopeful of freedom during the last stages of the sectional crisis and into the war. Often under the supervision of women and less-competent men, slaves increasingly resisted their bondage, sometimes violently. They slowed their work in the fields or refused to work at all, demanded negotiations, confronted authority, disobeyed orders, and fled to Union lines in droves whenever possible. In many ways, the pressure brought to bear on Washington and individual Union commanders by so many individual African Americans deciding to seek freedom pushed the Union inexorably toward emancipation.

Many slaveholding later enlisters, or at least their surrogates, gave in to the realities required to produce a crop. Fleming Jordan, a Georgia slave owner and former soldier who returned to the war in 1864 leading a company of militia, wrote home to ask his wife about why she owed money to his slaves. Other owners fled with their slaves as Union forces and emancipation approached.[58] From Arkansas Post, for example, Pvt. John T. Knight of the 22nd Texas reported that "the planters are runing their negroes today every direction. Some of them are going to the cane breaks. Some of them are going to texas. The people are the worst scared people that I ever saw." Almost two years later, Knight lamented that "our country was filling up with negroes."[59] Yet as Union troops marched through the slave South, African Americans continued to seize the opportunity to flee farms and plantations on their own. Texan Capt. William H. Barnes wrote from Louisiana that once the enemy went through the region collecting livestock and slaves, the institution as a whole broke down. "Some few negroes stayed," he explained, "but they work when & as they please breaking up rich men, Some negroes sauntering a bout like Simpletons."[60] Sometimes, it was the soldiers' own slaves who ran, much to their dismay. Pvt. Isaac Walters of the 50th North Carolina received word in November 1862 that "all of our negroes has left except the old man Willis and carried off two horses and that miles has taken the most part of your bacon. . . . If we can but have peace let the negroes go, if we can but be together we can get along. If there had never bin a negroe I expect we would have bin better off."[61]

Masters encountered other problems as they tried to manage their slave property by proxy. "I am sory to hear of the unsatisfactory conditions of things at the plantation," Fleming Jordan told his wife in the summer of 1864. "There is no middle ground with negroes—one must be positive with them."[62] Pvt. James Michael Barr expressed regular annoyance with reports regarding the behavior of the slaves on his South Carolina farm, whom he already deemed "careless." Of special concern were his brother Henry, left in charge of the farm and now accused by Barr of treating the slaves too softly, and an enslaved driver named Bill, whose allegedly poor care of Barr's livestock brought out even deeper anger. But above all was the perceptibly growing fear that without his presence at home, the slaves were growing increasingly disobedient and lazy. "Why don't you write twice a week," Barr demanded of his wife early in 1863. "I think you can write what all the Negroes are doing who are plowing, what the rest are doing, how they behave and whether they mind you. Have you any trouble to keep them about the house, especially at night and on Sundays? If so write me and I will write to Henry. But if they are not obedient, you ought to get Henry to correct them." But Henry Barr was not up to the task. By the summer of 1863, the Barr slaves were openly slacking off work and complaining as well about their meager meat rations. A test of wills ensued. The owner's long-distance response was to order even more cuts in rations, while chiding his slaves that he had no more to eat than they did. In response, they began to steal his chickens. By the time of his death in June 1864, it was obvious that he already had lost control of his slave property.[63]

Barr was not alone in attempting to quell increasingly restive slaves through intermediaries and threats delivered by mail. John Meriwether, a lieutenant in the 38th Alabama and later surgeon of the 40th Alabama, wrote his wife in July 1862: "I want you to tell Bill if he don't quit using so much corn I shall ruin him bodaciously, when I come home. . . . I am satisfied that he is stealing it and trading it off with some scoundrel." By autumn, Meriwether was considering hiring an overseer, hiring out his slaves, or selling out altogether. "They trouble me more than everything else except this horrible war." Those perceived vexations continued to grow. From Vicksburg in February 1863, he wrote, "I am sorry that Poor Leah gets no better. . . . I don't want to loose her if I can help it, for it would seem as if we don't have any of your Stock on hand out of the whole bunch. What did your Pa do with my Henry? I hope that he has sent him clear out of the country where I shall never hear of him again."[64]

Meriwether was not the only master who viewed his slaves as "stock." Sgt. Edwin Fay threatened to punish a female slave if she continued to defy his orders to produce a child. "Tell Cynthia," he wrote his wife, "that if she does not begin to show some signs that way when I come home that I'll whip her most to death or sell her to the meanest man I can find on Red River. . . . I bought her to breed and I know no good reason why she should not do it. . . . I have no objection to her having a husband but she has got to have children."[65]

Threats to sell slaves were not mere talk, as the slave trade continued to flourish almost until the end of the war. Several late-enlisting soldiers took part, convinced that slavery would survive the war in an independent Confederacy. In 1862, Lt. Benjamin W. Lee of the 22nd Texas advised his correspondent that "under the present circumstances I think it would be better to buy a negro at a big price than to keep their Confederate Money laying idle. My reason is that a negro can be put at work and maid accumulate something."[66] Fay meanwhile noted "likely negro men in Granada going for $150 gold," and added that "if this war closes negroes will bear fabulous prices and I want to buy now while they are low."[67] During the following year, four additional soldiers discussed the buying or selling of slaves. Jesse Battle of the 11th Georgia Artillery Battalion encouraged his wife to "sell the Negroes you spoke of for what you can get for them" and then take the proceeds to pay off debts and taxes as well as to provide provisions.[68] Pvt. John W. Cotton of the 10th Confederate Cavalry likewise encouraged his wife to "buy land or negroes if you git enough buy you a waiter girl."[69]

The common practice of slave rental continued as well. Eleven men in the sample discussed the use of hired slaves at home by their parents and wives. Worried about their loved ones' food supplies, Lt. T. L. Camp, Cpl. J. F. Coghill, Pvt. Henry Mowrer, and Pvt. Grant Taylor all encouraged their families to hire male slaves for field labor. Only Taylor was a slave owner. Lt. J. M. Davidson of the 39th North Carolina and Henry Mowrer tried to persuade their wives to rent women for housework, with the latter writing as late as January 1865.[70] Pvt. Amon Updike of the 53rd Virginia, a non-slaveholder, praised the "firstrate hand" his wife hired for farm work.[71]

So did Pvt. John Cotton, who in 1862 hired a slave named Manuel after he failed to raise enough money to buy him. Manuel was "too big for his breeches" in Cotton's wife's opinion: "He went off Saturday dinner and never came home tell Monday about nine oclock and when he came home I said something to him and he got so mad he jawed me." John Cotton responded that she should send for his father "til he gets him straight." Cotton must have been either satisfied with his father's efforts or simply desperate, for after that he consistently encouraged his wife to rehire Manuel, even if it meant selling "everything you have to sell for all you can," for "if you were to miss a crop it would ruin you." In November 1863, he asked his wife to try to buy Manuel for $1,200, although she seems not to have done so. As late as January 1865, he advised her that "there is a captured negro here that I could buy if I could send him home but I don't see no chance."[72]

Others were more dissatisfied. Fay complained about what his wife had paid to rent a woman. Pvt. Benjamin Mason of Hilliard's Alabama Legion worried after his enlistment that his hired slave "will not do his duty when you write let me know how he is geting along."[73] Pvt. Richard Henry Brooks of the 51st Georgia hired at least four slaves for his wife at the beginning of 1862—Mary, Poll, Rode, and a woman known only as "grand mother." Not long after, he began to argue with Poll's owner over which man was responsible for clothing her. In the end, he traded Poll away. "If I had kept her," he wrote home, "I should have clothed her. It is a general thing when a man hires a negro he furnishes the negro with necessary clothing but as he is so contrary about it . . . tell him I wrote to you to furnish one half." In the meantime, he also told his wife several times not to hire grand mother next year, as the cost outweighed any benefits. When his wife did so anyway, he wrote directly to the owner, a man named Lewis, asking him to take grand mother and Rode back. Lewis apparently refused, for grand mother was still with Brooks's wife that summer. Brooks grew even more exasperated when his wife bought another woman for $3,800, using money that he had planned to use to buy a new farm.[74]

INCREASINGLY, HISTORIANS MAINTAIN that Confederate soldiers fought to preserve slavery and all that came with it. It served as both an initial and sustaining motivator, and in some cases as a combat motivation as well. That was also true of later-enlisting Confederates, although measuring the degree of that support finally depends upon how one chooses to count. Only a handful of men directly averred that they fought to defend the institution. On the other hand, sixty-eight soldiers cited in this chapter, 21 percent of the total sample, wrote approvingly of slavery in one manner or another. Only half of them, thirty-four men, were slave owners or the sons of masters, while thirty-four were nonslaveholders, men lacking an immediate reason to defend the institution. No East-West regional pattern emerges among them either, other than the relative paucity of broadly proslavery statements west of the Mississippi and the increased tendency of men from the cotton states to discuss slavery matter of factly. Only two later enlisters criticized the war for being what they saw as a slave owner's conflict.

If one adds all 92 slave owners to the 34 nonslaveholding vocal supporters of the institution, given the reasonable assumption that those who still held slaves in 1860 surely wanted to keep them, the total of sampled men one might presume were fighting in some manner for slavery but not other ideologies increases to at least 126 (39.4 percent of the total). And if one opts to include the 25 nonslaveholders who wrote in other ideological ways without mentioning slavery, as scholars such as Chandra Manning and Randall Jimerson insist should be done, the figures increase even more, to 151 men and 47.2 percent of the sample. While the numbers vary depending on the criteria used in counting, the sample suggests that slavery in some manner motivated anywhere from at least a third to perhaps even half of the late enlisters who fought in the Confederate army, and especially men from the Lower South.

Given the lack of interest in topics such as the enlistment of African

Americans in Confederate ranks, moreover, support for slavery among later enlisters ultimately seems to have been less ideological than practical. While again noting the limitations of the sample, late enlisters already were less concerned with abstractions about rights and liberties overall than 1861 enlistees, but they were just as determined to buy, rent, keep, and work slaves as the men who went before them. The increasing undermining of the institution that resulted both from Washington's policies and internal self-emancipating actions within the slave community, notably federal policies toward emancipation and African American enlistment but also the tremors launched by approaching Union armies, must be considered as spurs to later enlisters' tardy enrollment in the Confederate army. The breakdown of slavery already touched many of their families directly by the time they enlisted, and as the war dragged on, problems of management and control grew worse.

It would be premature at this juncture, however, to ascribe later enlisters' motivations solely to slavery. To the men who became Confederate soldiers after 1861, the defense of slavery and opposition to emancipation were only the central parts of a larger whole centered in their homes and neighborhoods. As they saw it, the South was being invaded by hateful barbarians who not only wanted to end slavery but to destroy every other vestige of white men's lives in the South, leaving a wasteland in their wake. Home and family, financial security, and the women in their lives all were endangered by Yankees and uncontrolled slaves alike. The bitterness and hatred that grew out of that invasion, and especially the wider war on family and property, including slaves, that Union soldiers increasingly fought was another part of the matrix that motivated many men to enlist and fight at last.

PART II

"FIGHTING FOR THE PROPERTY WE GAINED BY HONEST TOIL"

3

WOMEN

"DO THE BEST YOU CAN"

In March of 1862, blacksmith Henry W. Robinson joined the Confederate army as a musician. After a few weeks of basic instruction in camp, his unit, the 42nd Georgia, hurried to East Tennessee to help safeguard the Confederacy's hold on Cumberland Gap. With a threatening Federal force approaching, the reluctant soldier found himself facing both his baptism of fire and his possible death. His surprising immediate response was to write a song for his wife. That lyric, "To the Girl I Love," amateurishly reflected the melodramatic strictures of mid-nineteenth-century verse, but also touchingly told of the author's personal experience, hopes, and fears. "I've wandered many a wary mile," it began,

Since last I saw thy Sunney Smiles
And many a mile I yet must Roam
Far from the lovely Suns of home

Robinson feared that he would die in the coming fight. "The day of battele looms before," he wrote derivatively, "The headlong charge the cannons roar." If he did fall, he asked his wife not to mourn him too long. But at the same time, he worried most that she would not remember him:

Oh! Think of him one to you
In every thought and action true
As one who loved you unto death
And blessed you with the latest breath

And now Sweet lovely girl farewell
I go Sweet freedoms Ranks to Swell
And perhaps to die for my country's Right
So lovely girl adieu good night."[1]

How well Elisabeth Robinson actually slept after receiving he husband's good night "ballad" is lost to history. His other letters surely did not help. With the Federals temporarily repulsed, he shockingly wrote his wife in July, "I have found me aSweat hart heare by the name of Harriet Elisabeth Shelton. She is as pretty as Red Shoes. You aut to be heare & See her." A comrade, he went on, "took her picture & mine with aSong balled on it yesterday. . . . I had our pitures taken with her handen me a bunch of flowers." After teasing his wife, he admitted at length that he finally had told Harriet that he was a married man, and confessed that he only spent time with the Sheltons for the food they provided him. "She took aharty cry about it," Robinson reported, "& Sade . . . has got foold & she sayes that she ant going to try arey nother."[2]

Henry Robinson was hardly alone in thinking of his loved ones while away in the war facing death. Indeed, the Victorian era as a whole was marked by public demands for the extreme romantic and emotional sentimentality, orthodox Christian morality, masculine self-control and self-sacrifice, and growing importance of a loving, nurturing family that Robinson's lyrics embody. Stereotypes and posturing aside, men no less than women longed for romance, love, and affectionate reassurance. Separating loved ones from each other for perhaps the first extended period of time, the war not only created immediate and aching loneliness but deepened

A fellow soldier's drawing of H. W. Robinson of the 42nd Georgia and his wife, Elisabeth, taken from a letter Robinson sent home from east Tennessee in the summer of 1862. A similar drawing, depicting Robinson with a local woman who had fallen in love with him, did not survive. Robinson died of smallpox at Vicksburg in April 1863. Photograph courtesy Manuscripts, Archives, and Rare Book Library, Emory University, Atlanta, Georgia, MSS 392 (microfilm).

emotional needs among many soldiers irrespective of when they enlisted. Young gallants without sweethearts and wives, steeped in the novels of Sir Walter Scott and the wider culture of the Victorian era, ostensibly sought fair ladies for whom to fight. Husbands and fathers meanwhile regretted the loss of the companionship most had taken for granted and envisioned peace as a joyous personal reunion within the home.

Yet like Robinson, some men and women raised in that culture also simultaneously strayed beyond the bounds of accepted behaviors at a time when war strained traditional boundaries. Paradoxically, the war thus ultimately both reinforced and undermined the mores of wider society. At the same time, soldiers had to deal with the practical issues of being away from home, including how to control farms, businesses, and slaves from far away. Increasingly they turned to their wives not just for emotional succor but for economic support as well, altering gender relations in significant ways. Depending upon the results, relationships with loved ones could sustain or demoralize soldiers, including later enlisters, who rallied to the colors well after that process of reordering society was begun.

CIVIL WAR HISTORIANS long have alluded to the role women played in individual soldier's decisions to enlist and fight, as well as their part in shaping morale subsequently.[3] "Woman," Bell Wiley wrote over a half-century ago, "was of tremendous moment in the life of the ordinary soldier." As other scholars have also revealed, Southern white women at the beginning of the war publically spurred men to enlist, leave home, and do their duty in a powerful example of initial motivation. Gerald Linderman went so far as to term women's demands that men enlist "sexual intimidation." Through letters, photographs, public displays, and memories they then sustained soldiers by reminding them of why they fought. Soldiers in turn dwelled on their loved ones in quiet moments, sometimes happily but often to the point of depression and illness. Many formed into battle line and marched into the fight ostensibly to protect their far-away women from marauding Union vandals. Once victory and peace came, it was to those women, they averred, that they would return triumphantly. Meanwhile, soldiers ached to see other women and marveled at their rare appearances in an otherwise male world. Indeed soldiers longed so much for women's presence and the shadow of an idealized family life left behind in their masculine lives that they sometimes went as far as dressing comrades as women for dances.[4]

Recent historians have expanded greatly on the deep significance of gender in the eyes of male soldiers. In a study of Union troops, Reid Mitchell noted how desperately men in the field missed the feminine sphere of their domestic lives. More than simply dressing up drummer boys in bonnets and skirts, they embraced duties and roles usually assigned to women in peacetime. Notably they learned to cook and clean, console the bereaved, and care for the sick. But the power of domesticity even went beyond such matters, Mitchell added. He stressed the centrality of the idea of the family in the minds of Americans, maintaining that notions of home and family life continually shaped Federal soldiers' gendered language, values, and actions. They routinely saw themselves as "boys" becoming men in the ultimate coming-of-age ritual. Sons of the Revolutionary Fathers and

Mothers, they themselves would be revered as fathers of a future nation, once they disciplined their erring, weaker "sister" states and reunited the American family. In the field, meanwhile, the locally raised company also functioned as an ersatz family, with officers filling the parental roles, fellow soldiers becoming brothers, and the folks back home assuming the places of distant relatives who had to be pleased and reassured. To many soldiers, slaves seemed to resemble children. In Washington, meanwhile, "Father Abraham" looked on expectantly.[5]

Mitchell largely wrote about Union soldiers and domesticity, but he did suggest briefly that it played a role in shaping the Confederate experience as well. For white Southerners, according to Mitchell, the war embodied a more-direct attack on the family and home. In many cases, women were left to fill the defender roles of men. This reality turned the South's traditional patriarchy topsy-turvy. In the end, deepening family responsibilities required men to go home, either as deserters or as the defeated.[6] More recently, a few scholars have specifically examined the relationship between white Southern men, their families, and the masculine call to war duty. Chandra Manning agrees that when compared to the men in blue, Confederate soldiers' patriotism was more limited and centered on protection of home. As the war dragged on and conditions on the home front worsened, they felt especially torn between the nation's demands and the traditional duties of family protector.[7]

Stephen Berry meanwhile maintains that antebellum white Southern men craved love and validation. No man would be complete without winning the love of a woman who then would function as both his chief supporter and the object of his worldly striving. When the war came, boys and men alike saw it as a chance to prove or reinforce their manhood, win renown, and crucially impress the ladies. When confronted with death at its ugliest, unfamiliar discipline once seemingly reserved for slaves, and the isolated emptiness of camp life, they yearned all the more for a woman's love and support. According to Berry, "Each man had planted his patriotism in the sturdier soil of his love of woman. . . . Their woman was their country and their cause, the reason they fought and killed." Their sweethearts and wives thus provided a "*reason* to die."[8]

LATER-ENLISTING CONFEDERATES, however, more likely than 1861 enlistees to be married fathers or underage youths, notably eluded classic forms of "sexual intimidation" in 1861. Despite the legendary romantic ostracism and gifts of belles' undergarments that drove some reluctant men into the army in 1861, only one later-enlisting Confederate, W. H. Franklin, seems to have joined the army due to outright feminine pressure. Still a factory worker in February 1862, Franklin admitted, "I have done quit all the girls. . . . they all scorn me so I have quit them."[9] If anything, the evidence suggests that later enlisters encountered a different sort of pressure from women—encouragement from wives and mothers to stay at home, provide, and protect the family.

White women played many other roles for later enlisters as initial and sustaining motivators, just as they almost certainly did for other soldiers, although additional, comparative studies are required for that to be more fully confirmed. One common way they did so was as positive symbols of home and cause. Soldiers largely lived in a masculine world far removed from life at home, which made the relatively rare sight of any woman in camp a noteworthy occurrence. "Occasionally a *woman* passes camp," Sgt. Edwin Fay wrote his wife in January 1863, "and it is a three day wonder."[10] Lt. Draughton Smith Haynes of the 49th Georgia likewise recorded in his diary, "I have seen three young ladies where I went to get milk, it made me think of old Georgia."[11]

Soldiers stationed near towns might also see local women at church or even at dances and balls, and young ladies often turned out for dress parades.[12] Soldiers encountered women on the march as well. Indeed, in the field, women functioned even more as sustaining motivators, some powerfully. Those who supported soldiers more directly invariably raised spirits. Pvt. James Williamson, one of John S. Mosby's men, described with admiration a poor woman, her husband in the army, who cheerfully offered to share with him what little food she and her children possessed.[13] Capt. William H. Barnes of the 1st Texas Partisan Rangers meanwhile praised the women of Thibodeaux, Louisiana, for their treatment of wounded and sick soldiers. "They are Kind, Generous, Patriotic, and very hospital," he wrote, "a soldier can hardly want for any necessaries of life if they have them and know they are needed and will charge you for none."[14]

Women encountered near the battlefield could especially encourage Confederates to fight as well, and even as strangers provided scattered shadow glimpses of "reasons to die." This was particularly true in the East, where the armies fought in more-populated areas. On the eve of the Second Battle of Manassas, for example, as his 1st Virginia approached battle, Pvt. John Dooley remembered women "waving their kerchiefs from the lighted windows, and more than one voice heard at the piano singing 'Dixie,' 'Bonnie blue flags,' etc. This was all very cheering."[15] Crossing the Potomac into Maryland a few days later, Pvt. William Ross Stilwell wrote that "it is enough to make ones blood boil to see the ladies who had gathered on horseback along the road with Confederate flags flying and cheer for the Southern army."[16]

Women continued to exercise such power even as the war went on. A few soldiers wrote with wonder of sympathetic women they met unexpectedly in Maryland and even Pennsylvania during the Gettysburg campaign. Capt. John H. Harris notably encountered a "good Southern Lady" who shouted to his 44th Georgia, " 'Run um. Confound um. Run um for they are meaner than old Nick. I hope you will kill the last one um.' Beside her," he continued, "was a daughter of some seventeen Summers who seemed to be all of a lady. She waved her handkerchief and clapped her hands for joy."[17]

Lt. John Hosford of the 5th Florida described a similar scene of "beautiful girls as they were cheering us by waving their handkerchiefs and giving 'Huzas' for the 'rebels' and telling us to go and kill all the yanks and throw them in the Potomac." As he passed them by, one "in their excitement, she struck me on the shoulder with her 'kerchief saying 'go it my brave fellow, you are the boys for me,' just then I had a feeling and felt as though I could fight 'old Meade' and all his yankee crew." While Hosford never saw "the fair Damsel" again, he continued to pine for her. "I think I must have loved her," he wrote, not incidentally to a young woman back home, "but alas: she is in yankeedom and I cannot see here again I fear."[18] As late as October 1864, such public demonstrations could embolden soldiers. As John Bell Hood's ragged army entered Florence, Alabama, on its march northward to Tennessee, "the ladies received us with rapturous applause," according to Sgt. John Crittenden of the 34th Alabama. "And many were the 'God bless yous' bestowed upon us as we filed through the streets. Young women old women and little girls thronged the streets." Bitterly, Crittenden added, he saw "no men."[19]

In tones anticipatory of the Lost Cause argument of future decades, a handful of later-enlisting soldiers, such as Sgt. Maj. Marion Hill Fitzpatrick, accordingly hailed "the patriotism and industry of the women," without whom "the Southern Confederacy would soon come to nothing. Many a soldier can now realize the value of woman's work that thought but little or nothing about it before the war commenced."[20] Lt. William L. Nugent agreed that women's support helped morale. "God bless the women of the

South, God bless them!" he exclaimed. "They yet uncomplainingly bear the brunt of privation at home, and hover like ministering angels around the couches of those whom war has crushed beneath the iron orbs of his intolerable car."[21]

Negative examples further placed such women in starker relief. If "good Southern ladies" functioned as symbols of home and cause to soldiers, fallen women represented what could happen if the war was lost and Yankee values became entrenched in the South. Sexual missteps drew the greatest condemnation. Pvt. J. A. McMurtrey, for example, wrote from Abingdon, Virginia, that a sergeant in his outfit "is gone to the hospital he has got the worst of complaints ever caught for a woman."[22] The 11th Virginia Cavalry's D. C. Snyder meanwhile reported that "many, many excellent and un-suspecting ones" had been "ruined and deserted by *brass buttons.* . . . I know of many instances of ladies deceived by married men and many more of ruined characters on the part of young men." Yet the women really were to blame, he added, because of their "eagerness . . . to take up with anyone and a *false* idea that they must have *Beaus.*" Private Snyder pointed with particu-lar horror to a women's school near Lexington that allegedly had been "broken up because of some 20 or more young ladies forever disgraced & ruined by a number of Soldier beaus that encamped in the vicinity last winter."[23]

Capt. Thomas Key was particularly obsessed about the dangers of inter-racial relations, but he roundly condemned other sexual behaviors of young women in north Georgia. With disgust he particularly related how his cousin went to wait upon a woman there only to find her "sitting in the lap of a young man. He said the girls smoke and chew tobacco and drink whiskey as if they are fond of the article." Later Key dined with some fellow officers who "had their arms around the girls' waists or necks, and the girls appeared to enjoy the sport as much as the men. I am disgusted at this state of society." Tellingly, Key added that "women should have an elevating influence upon man; for this reason alone I visit their society." One of the central tenets of Victorian domesticity was that women were the reposi-tories of society's virtues, and they bore a duty to both support and better men. In this, Key concluded, women were failing. "Rumor says that almost half of the women in the vicinity of the army, married and unmarried, are lost to all virtue. Oh, what are we coming to! How shall we preserve our character when the women—gentle, kind, and good women—forsake the path of virtue?"[24]

Men stationed elsewhere made similar complaints that untrustworthy women were undermining their efforts. Particularly galling were reports of sexual scandal back home involving women they knew. Pvt. Newt Bosworth of the 31st Virginia reported with loathing to his father that "*Jane Chenoweth is going to marry a Yankee*" and that "Mrs. Arnold from Beverley left with the Yankees."[25] Pvt. E. W. Treadwell meanwhile was shocked to learn that one of the women who had presented his company with their flag "has brought forth an heair or in other words has had a bastard."[26] Worse yet was Mollie Moreland, who according to Sgt. John French White had given birth to a Union soldier's son.[27] But no one was more disgusted than Sgt. Edwin Fay, who wrote home that a young friend of the family had "been delivered of a bastard and a *black one* at that."[28]

Yet in all of these stories, there also are obvious notes of titillation, hints of repressed urges, and fears of rejection. Indeed, both William Stilwell's self-described boiling blood and John Hosford's sudden "feeling," the latter occasioned by the touch of a woman's unexpected and excited hand, suggest additional linkages between danger, martial ardor, and sexuality even when "good" women were involved. It is no surprise that the youths especially among later enlisters particularly fought a remarkably eroticized war. They had grown up in a society that encouraged emotional linkages of ambition, masculinity, and women's love. A simple touch or the sight of a woman's ankle could arouse deep feelings. As several scholars have noted, the war by 1862 meanwhile had loosened drastically traditional rules of courtship. Flirtation and a desperate search for amusement grew common among both young men and women. Parental control weakened, while the accepted time span of courtship compressed. Escorts became the exception rather than the rule. Young men and women accordingly rushed headlong into romances and even marriage while they still could, before death on the battlefield struck.[29]

Not surprisingly, at least twenty-eight later-enlisting Confederates, almost all young and unmarried, and usually from comfortable families as well, spent much of their spare time courting young women of similar pedigrees with the savoir faire of a frontal assault. Lt. John Earnest of the 60th Tennessee, for example, was constantly on the lookout for attractive young women. On a train from Vicksburg to Jackson, Mississippi, in 1863, he took off his cap to a beautiful woman who "to my great surprise and delight . . . returned the salute with a graceful wave of the hand—and I *believe* her kerchief with it, but *that hand* was so delicately turned that I could see nothing else for gazing at it." The next day, after dreaming about "fairy hands," he took a drive with two other women, and dined that evening with two more. "I feel certain," he wrote, "that Miss Cynthia's auburn curls will be dangling about me or the quiet smile of Miss Ann lighten my dreams." He spent time with "Miss Tillie" too before returning to Vicksburg. There, he received cakes from "our little black eyed friend Miss H. Bell Maxwell" and, when sick, recovered in the country while enjoying the company of a variety of women including "a grass widow, quite young and seeming well accomplished," and a Miss Emma. As Grant's noose tightened around the city, Earnest divided his time between Emma and an unnamed woman he met one day after posting his guard when he "concluded to *borrow a book* from her (as that would be the most plausible excuse to get there and introduce myself). No sooner conjured than done."[30]

Other youthful soldiers, especially during the winter months when active campaigning slowed, apparently beat a similar path to the doors of young women in the vicinity whenever they could. They sought feminine companionship and romance at picnics, parties, and church services; enjoyed evenings of conversation and singing; and regularly accepted meals from the women's parents.[31] In the end, there admittedly is no evidence that later enlisters were any different in this regard than other youths who had joined the army in 1861, except that they made their appearances at a time when Southern cultural traditions already were wavering under the pressure of war, and the path toward the relaxation of some social mores had already been broken. For all of them, however, a subtle form of sustaining motivation was at work. Nearly all of the young late enlisters involved in the social whirlwind seem the end of the day to have been more interested in flirtation and companionship than love and marriage. Indeed, only two wartime romances among late-enlisting Confederates found in the sample seem to have led to the altar, confirming Drew Gilpin Faust's and Susan Barber's assessments of declining wartime marriages in Richmond.[32] The other soldiers more or less admitted that romances served as no more than pleasurable sustaining motivators, keeping up youthful spirits and élan in an otherwise, dreary, dangerous, male-centered world.

FLORIDIAN JOHN HOSFORD revealed a darker side still to wartime romance. He courted a young Virginia woman with "all the poets I could think suitable to the occasion from Burns, Biron and Shakespear." The young woman, however, remained suspicious, telling the lieutenant that "you officers from the South are so tricky . . . she had heard of some of them that had married girls here and actually had wives and loving ones at home."[33] Confirming sexual impropriety on the part of married Confederate soldiers is difficult. As Bell Wiley noted decades ago, it is next to impossible to find records adequate enough even to discuss the matter. Victorians generally did not discuss sex openly as it was, and descendants often hastened to destroy any records that may have cast ancestors in a bad light. Yet official records regarding prostitution, frequent newspaper advertisements hawking various cures for venereal diseases, and newspaper coverage attest to the fact that a sizable minority of Johnny Rebs must have strayed often from Victorian strictures.[34]

Among later enlisters specifically, nine married men in the sample ad-mitted at least to a remarkably active social life with other women, given the strict standards of the day. Capt. Robert Emmet Corry of the 11th Alabama Cavalry, for example, blithely wrote his pregnant wife that he had dined with his former sweetheart the previous evening and that she was now having his laundry done. "She begins to look a little old maidish," he admitted, "but is still as cleaver and good as she can be. I shall call on her again as she calls me Cousin Bob so sweetly and invites me so cordially to do so."[35] Like Pvt. Henry Robinson, both Pvt. James Michael Barr and Sgt. Maj. Marion Hill Fitzpatrick admitted that they socialized with young women who assumed that they were unmarried. "There were some good looking girls there," Fitzpatrick wrote of a local church, "and . . . I should have gone home with some of them as long as they did not know I was married."[36] Commissary Fleming Jordan wrote his wife that "many ladies visit us" and later added, "I have had four kisses since I left—ain't you jeal-ous?" Yet in the end, after bragging of his manliness and popularity, Jordan hastened to assure his spouse that any jealousy would be unfounded.[37] So did all the others. "Don't become jealous when you read this," Surgeon John Meriwether similarly wrote after describing parties and dances where he made "quite an impression among the fair Damsels. . . . I don't *intend that any of them shall captivate* me. You well know that I love the society of ladies."[38]

Despite their husbands' pleas, suspicious wives usually responded any-way with jealous anger, and perhaps for good reason. George Rable suggests the possibility of real infidelity behind such pronouncements, something that Henry Robinson confirmed. Noting the "prety Stock" of women in East Tennessee, he wrote his wife that "if we Stay heare much longer in about 9 months from now thare will be more littel Gorgians a Squalling through this contry then you can Shake aStick at." He added, "I doant in tend to be cald pap So fare from home but thare is a grat meny a pitching in."[39] Even in more innocent cases, Rable adds, dalliances in the field damaged relationships, as when Lt. William L. Nugent wrote his estranged wife to deny hurtful rumors that he had been unfaithful to her.[40]

In comparison to the handful of men who stretched the marriage vow, however, were the eighty-five married later-enlisting soldiers, 80 percent of all sampled soldiers identified as married, who wrote faithfully to their wives and children during the war. From the most educated to illiterates that had others write their letters, later enlisters had followed the soldiers of 1861 into a strange world far from home. During their first year in uniform they invariably expressed their homesickness and deep attachment to loved ones left at home. In general, the letters written from camp by relatively new recruits all contained the same basic elements: I miss you, my health is good or bad, I hope you are well. Often addressed "Dear Wife," letters also expressed the authors' love to spouses and, if they had them, children. Soldiers additionally craved any and all news from home, although word of illness invariably was torturous. Variations did develop from those main themes. Some men sent money or gifts and eagerly anticipated promised enlistment furloughs. Marion Fitzpatrick subscribed to a newspaper for his wife, in hopes that it would help her pass the time.[41] A few added special touches that hinted at physical longing. Capt. William H. Barnes, for example, asked his wife to read "the Bible 'Solomon's Song' Chap 1st verses 14 & 15 & 16."[42] Pvt. William P. Cline, meanwhile, promised, "when i come home i will hug you and kiss you. . . . i will git to com home to sleep with you nex winter."[43]

Were later enlisters all that different from other Confederates in this regard? Ted Ownby argued that Confederate soldiers leaving home exhibited two perspectives. "Stoics" stressed duty and patriotism while minimizing the effects of separation from loved ones. To them, homesickness and emotions were weaknesses, and they referred little to their longings. "Romantics" in contrast fully expressed their feelings of love and pain. Ownby suggests that as the war went on, the romantics grew in number at the expense of the stoics who had formed the majority in 1861. If that is the standard, later enlisters were indeed different from earlier recruits, for the opposite is the case. There were plenty of romantics among them from the beginning, for one thing, men who for whatever reason already had not been able to cut their ties to home and do their duty in 1861. An obvious reluctance to be away in the army usually characterized their early letters. Indeed, married men new to camp surprised themselves with the depth of their longing for home and spouse. As James Marten suggests, separation actually produced a new kind of intense intimacy. Many soldiers related how they dreamed of home, while more than a few admitted weeping at the thought of family members. Matthew Thornton of the 34th Alabama wrote his wife, "I waunt to see you and the 2 children the worst in the world. . . . you are all I study a bout in this world. I think of you till I go to sleep and as soon as I wake up in the morning you are all I study about."[44] Pvt. E. A. Penick confessed that he remained homesick and gloomy for his wife, Mary, and their children. Strolling through a Richmond cemetery for a moment of peace, he was startled to find a headstone that read, "here lies sweet Mary. . . . I looked on untill my eyes became dim and turned back for Camp."[45] Holidays proved especially tough for married recruits. For most, Christmas was the central family holiday. While young men celebrated with eggnog, whiskey, and reveling, older men spent the first Christmas away from home gloomily, writing letters to their spouses and imagining what they were missing.[46]

A few soldiers far from home additionally expressed deep regrets about their past actions. "I think it is wise for people to be seperated sometimes," Engineer Phillips Fitzpatrick wrote after his return to the army in 1864, "for we would not know how much we thought of each other unless such an absence showed more plainly to us how necessary we are to each other." Regretting his "bad treatment" of her as well as the unnamed frailties of a "mean" husband, he added that "you are the best wife and best woman that ever lived, and I often think that I would give a great deal to be a better husband to you."[47] Likewise, Pvt. J. A. McMurtrey of the 9th Georgia Artillery guiltily wrote his wife, "you said that you wanted to see me the worse that you ever did in your life what makes you want to see me so bad do you think I am any better than I ust to be."[48]

Yet as the war passed, the affectionate, often lovesick sentiments expressed in later enlisters' letters actually grew less common. Again unlike the Confederate romantics studied by Ownby, or for that matter the broad spectrum of Virginian soldiers studied by Aaron Sheehan-Dean who "placed increasing importance on their emotional ties with family members," the blatant emotional romanticism of most later enlisters peaked early and declined steadily during the war.[49] To be sure, the numbers are somewhat skewed. Disease, battlefield wounds, and capture meant there were fewer soldiers in the sample to write home. Regardless, soldiers whose letters to their wives featured notable components of romantic love and affection declined from fifty in 1862, to twenty-six in 1863, eight in 1864, and only three in the war's abbreviated last year. Indeed, those figures are deceiving, for some of the men writing romantically after 1862 were new recruits or substitution "principals" returning to the army, and thus were experiencing the same anxieties that their comrades had passed through in 1862.

It was not that men quit loving their wives and children, stopped missing home, or became resigned to Christmases in camp. A minority did become more tenderhearted as time passed, while reports of hunger or sickness still could drive any of them to the breaking point.[50] Rather, a combination of realities were to blame for the new practicality. All affected morale. Casualties simply depleted the number of letter writers. The unpredictability of the Confederate postal service, supplemented by the ad hoc system of furloughing soldiers, visitors, and couriers that soldiers employed in its place, convinced many soldiers that they had been forgotten. Letters alternately pleading and scolding followed. Relationships that were already troubled further buckled at both ends under the strain of separation and accusation.[51] Surgeon John Meriwether, for example, apologized for a "*crazy letter of mine*" in which he accused his wife of thinking he did not love her. "I was in one of my nervous fits," he confessed.[52] Pvt. John A. Wilson of the 35th Mississippi in contrast dismissed his wife's depression and lectured her on accepting her fate. Sgt. Edwin Fay constantly berated his young wife and former student for everything from her ardent Confederate patriotism and her father's business dealings to her poor spelling and inability to weave. Above all, he hounded her to go to Shreveport and personally ask General Edmund Kirby Smith for his release from the army, which she patriotically refused to do.[53] Pvt. E. W. Treadwell assured his wife, "you Mattie are my jewel more precious than gold—the anchor of my Soul—you are the star by which my life is governed." It was true, he admitted, that he had acted badly in the past, "but was immediately sorry to my hearts inmost depths. I had flattered myself that you loved me so well that you did not remember those things against me, but alas I fear that you have treasured up all those little wrongs and even magnified them."[54]

Issues of parenthood interfered as well. Early in 1863, J. A. McMurtrey of the 9th Georgia Artillery sent a long letter home to his wife. Worried that she had grown "forgetfull" about her duties, Private McMurtrey lectured her extensively on her "great duty" of rearing their two children and especially their five-year-old son. "I want you to be very careful about how you let Willie act and talk," he wrote, "because if you let him do wrong he will teach Mary to do the same way." Based on the letter, one gathers that Willie McMurtrey had been a troublesome child during his brief life. "Dont let him fight Mary when at play nor no other time," the father wrote knowingly. "Don't let him fight nor speak cross to you nor any other person at any time make him mind you at all times and places if you don't let us see what will be the consequences and what will become of him." Indeed the father clearly foresaw a dismal future for his son unless the mother intervened quickly. "He will tell lies use bad words spend his time in idleness and fighting the baby and every body else," McMurtrey predicted, "and as he gets older he will begin to play cards and to visit the bar room and then what he will end his life . . . with a rope around his neck. cinda I had rather hear of him going to his grave than to hear that you let him do as he please." God would hold them both responsible for Willie's sins, he added. A year later, however, little seemed to have changed. "Tell Willie," the father wrote, "he must be a good boy or the bad man will get him and burn him."[55]

McMurtrey was more than a husband, lover, and soldier. Like many later enlisters he was a father, in this case the parent of a trying son. Parenthood thus added an additional dimension to relations between husbands and wives that began before childbirth. In the mid-nineteenth-century South, giving birth was a dangerous trial that threatened the lives of mother and child alike. The separations of wartime, combined with the expected results of brief furloughs, increased the dread of pregnancy. In August 1862, when Pvt. William Ross Stilwell of the 53rd Georgia learned that his wife Molly was pregnant with their second child, his first reaction was sorrow. "I was afraid of it when I left but did not say anything about it," he wrote, adding that she should not be afraid. As her "time of sickness" drew near, he became increasingly anxious that she would die in childbirth. "If I lose my Molly I lose my all," he wrote her from Fredericksburg on New Year's Day, 1863. "If I was to lose you I would not want to fight any more for what is life or liberty to me without my Molly." Weeks passed without a letter from home, driving Stilwell to the brink of madness. Night after night he wandered a pine forest near his regimental camp, crying out of fear and loneliness. "Oh God," he exclaimed in February, "deliver me from having the pain of mourning for the one that I love with love stronger than death. . . . If it were not for the faith I have in God's goodness, I could not stand it. I cant stand to be absent from you when you are to be sick. Molly, I thought I had a heart like a man but I confess that I am nearly ready to give up. Oh, I would give anything to hear from you tonight." Eventually, good news arrived; Molly had given birth to a daughter. Like most new mothers married to later-enlisting Confederates, she left the name to her husband. He named her Virginia, in honor of where he served. Three months later, he asked Molly to "kiss the children for me. . . . I am your devoted loving and faithful husband taken from your bosom without my consent, left here against my will."[56]

Like Stilwell, eight of the ten other men whose wives delivered children during the war greeted the prospect with worry and even expressed guilt that they were not home for the dreaded event. Pvt. Grant Taylor apologized for coming home on furlough and fathering the child, while Lt. William L. Nugent tried to play a helpful role by constantly advising his wife medically. A follower of homeopathy, he counseled her to bathe her nipples in cold water mixed with a tincture of arnica, so to prevent soreness. He also asked her to avoid worry and stress, which would affect her milk.[57] Only Pvt. Henry T. Morgan of the 31st Louisiana chided his pregnant wife for her fears, asking, "Don't you like babys? They are the pretyest things in the world." He continued, "I think you ought not to grumbel. . . . If it is the will of God then we have no rite to say a word."[58]

Soldier-fathers, even those with sons less apparently problematic than Willie McMurtrey, also attempted to continue directing the rearing of their children. Before Fort Sumter, as James Marten has established, Victorian fathers North and South had taken a major role in parenting. The war with its separations increased the desire on the part of fathers to be a part of children's lives while simultaneously making it more difficult. The result was a halting conversation during which fathers called for good behavior while compressing into letters the advice they otherwise would have delivered face to face over a span of many years.[59] Only five later-enlisting Confederates, however, offered instruction directly to their children, and generally it was of the most basic nature: be good and work hard.[60] "I want you to bee good Boys and mind your mother," Harvey Bailey of the 58th North Carolina wrote, "and Bee good Boys and don't fight . . . I want you all to larn your books . . . and learn how to Right and send me a letter." Bailey went on to give his sons detailed instructions for building a fence, keeping the sheep out of the wheat field, and marking his hogs.[61] Sgt. James A. Wilson, a reluctant secessionist serving in the 1st Battalion, Mississippi State Troops, meanwhile advised his son to avoid bad company, "be honist in all your dealings," and "never vote for a man who was infavor of cession or has anything to do with brenging about this acursd war for it is there fault that I now have to be seperated from you perhaps never to see you again."[62]

Later-enlisting Confederate soldiers were more likely to lecture their wives on what they wanted done with their children, while subtly implying that mothers were not up to the task. Seventeen men in the sample did this. "Always set a good example before our little children," Lt. William D. Cole of the 38th Alabama wrote his wife, "you have them with you and I have confidence to believe that you will try to raise them the best you know how. If I thought you would not I would pray to the Lord to remove them while they are small before they get large enough to say that Ma did this or that."[63]

Fatherly concerns among this small group ran the gamut. More than anything else, the men wanted their children and in particular their sons educated, especially given the possibility of the father's death in the field. Pvt. Grant Taylor was particularly angry when his wife's poor money management forced her to withdraw his children from school.[64] Both Pvt. Richard Henry Brooks and Pvt. John W. Cotton wanted their children inoculated against disease. Sgt. Maj. Marion Hill Fitzpatrick meanwhile worried that his son lacked the proper masculine influence. He wanted his son to have a wagon and, as soon as he was in breeches, a knife as well. "Train up our boy to be a man in the truest sense of the word," he advised. But Fitzpatrick also wrote his wife to "be gentle with him. Do not teaze or fret or deceive him, nor let anybody else do it no matter who it is."[65] Pvt. J. C. Williams also counseled kind supervision, admonishing his wife not to "whip" their daughter. "It grieves me to think how I whipped her," he admitted, "but i done it i thought for the best."[66]

Other fathers worried about their children's morals, and particularly about the influences of their friends and playmates. Lt. William A. Stephens of the 46th Alabama did not want his children playing with others he deemed undisciplined, while hospital ward master J. W. Griffin worried about how his children would get along with the children of his wife's family.[67] Pvt. Grant Taylor meanwhile was outraged that his wife had allowed his children to have a party at their house, as such un-Christian affairs often led to "sinful communications." He was especially furious about the guest list, which included several girls who were "none of the best of characters."[68] Surgeon John Meriwether, in contrast, wanted his wife to keep his daughter away from enslaved children lest she "learn any Negro talk."[69]

No one supplied more nagging advice than Sgt. Edwin Fay. From the time he left home, Fay wrote about everything imaginable involving his sons Will Ed and Thornwell, from the children's toys, to weaning the younger boy, to his fears that his favorite, Will Ed, would fall out of a tree. Fay above all stressed the importance of education. "Hear Will Ed's lessons regularly," he directed, lest he grow up like his wife's father and "not be overly fond of his books." Fay also stressed the importance of governing the boy strictly. "Children," he wrote, "should be taught to obey as it is a necessary lesson of a soldier."[70]

The Fays already had lost a daughter before the war. When Edwin learned in August 1862 that his beloved Will Ed had died, the news made him "crazy." He convinced himself that God was punishing him personally by stealing his eldest son. "Thornwell will go next," he lamented, "then you, my dearest, and I be left an outcast. . . . God is cruel to us. My child is in heaven but I had rather he were where I could see him again." In his agony, Fay blamed God, the Yankees, and especially his wife. "How could you write me those cruel words our little Willie is dead," he asked. Surely she had neglected something, he accused; it had to be her fault. She should have sent for "every doctor in the country. Why did you not send for Dr. Webb?" Already unhappy in the army, Fay cast about desperately for a way to get home and see his son's grave, even if it meant hiring a temporary substitute or deserting.

Fay healed slowly and erratically. A month later he admitted to nightly weeping; "it hangs like an incubus upon me." He also behaved increasingly cruelly toward both his wife and remaining son, claiming that he had "become perfectly hardened. If I have got to lose all my children, let them go. I care for nothing now. My boy is gone. My punishment is greater than I can bear." Months later, he predicted that after the war the family would only be "comparatively happy . . . but never will we be as happy as when our darling Will Ed was alive. No child we may ever have can ever fill his place."[71] When Fay did deign to send advice and orders about Thornwell, it was only in order to make him another Will Ed. "Teach him to mind, not to be cryer," Fay wrote early in 1863, ironically after describing how he still wept for Will Ed, "no baby-talk . . . I want to make him all Will Ed was if possible." Alarmed at learning that Thornwell stuttered, Fay directed his wife to "put a

"PROPERTY WE GAINED BY HONEST TOIL"

small pebble in his mouth when he tries to speak and that will break him I think." Fay also obsessed in letter after letter about having the child's wagon repaired.[72]

Fay's was an extreme case, but he was not alone. Childhood mortality rates in mid-nineteenth-century America were significantly worse than modern figures, and parents had good reason to fear losing children. They grieved nonetheless. Lt. William Nugent's daughter died after two months. Pvt. John W. Cotton mourned the death of his daughter. Although he tried to believe that her death was God's will, Cotton admitted to frequent weeping. He also felt deep guilt about not being home for the girl's illness and death, yet admitted, "I shall dread to come home for I no I shall miss her so much she will not be there to fondle on my knees with the rest of the little fellows."[73] John Cotton was hardly unique in the end; nor were later enlisters apparently all that different in this regard from earlier recruits who also were fathers. The greater proportion of married men among post-1861 recruits, however, at least meant that more later enlisters were likely to worry and suffer as Fay and Cotton had.

WHITE SOUTHERN MEN, according to Stephanie McCurry, were not just sons, husbands, and fathers. They also were masters of their immediate worlds. While one usually associates the word "master" with slaves, all white male heads of households living in a slave society, despite the size and value of their property, were masters who wielded almost unlimited power over their lands and dependents. Within their fences and the walls of their houses, male householders resembled kings in their castles. With support from the church and courthouse, they asserted that power over wives, children young and old, and hired laborers, if not slaves as well. It was the male head of the family who decided if a daughter should go to school, if sons should plant corn or cotton, or if the family should worship as Methodists or Baptists. Likewise men controlled politics and government, reinforcing power based on race and gender. The goal was to produce "liberty" —economic independence rather than dependence. It was that independence that made political and social equality possible for all white men. To be sure, planters, yeomen, and poor white men engaged in an uneasy, ritualistic dance that publically suggested social and political equality among all white men, but that equality never truly existed. The Civil War, fought according to McCurry to preserve those "small worlds" of male independence, thus struck white men at the foundation of their worlds.[74]

In focusing on women's roles in affection and morale building, nearly all historians of Civil War soldiers have missed this added, crucial dimension of Confederate gender relations. Married men away from home suddenly found themselves more than homesick and lovesick. They also had become uncomfortably and absolutely dependent upon wives, parents, other relatives, and even slaves for the continued operation of their theoretically masculine little kingdoms during the worst of times. Later-enlisting Confederates, more reluctant to leave home in the first place when compared to the soldiers of 1861, initially responded by not letting go entirely, trying to maintain their patriarchal power over the household through the mails.[75] During their first year away from home, thirty-six men among those sampled sought information and sent detailed instructions to wives and other surrogates about what they wanted done, fifteen (42 percent) from the Upper South and twenty-one (58 percent) from the Lower South. Husbands routinely inquired about the garden, traditionally the preserve of women. In a society long dependent upon "hogmeat and hoecake," the men also devoted great attention to learning about the condition of their crops and livestock, and whether their families had enough to eat. Men told wives what and when to sow and reap. Pvt. Grant Taylor became almost obsessive on the subject of buying the salt so necessary for preserving meats.[76] Pvt. John S. Battle of the 11th Georgia Artillery meanwhile worried enough about the family's sow that he instructed his wife to "nurse her close, probably you had better stop reading this and feed her."[77]

Others entrusted their wives with financial duties, such as buying and selling crops, livestock, and land. At their husbands' direction women paid and collected debts and accomplished other tasks. Aside from worrying about salt, Grant Taylor mailed his wife specific directions to buy corn and to sell his cotton and steers, but only at a certain minimum price. He also told her to stop renting out his oxen and wagon, to buy a comrade's farm, and to pay the taxes. From the first, however, it was clear that Malinda Taylor had plans of her own. Taylor had only been in the army two months when he learned that his wife had sold two cows. Taylor approved, but also promptly cautioned her not to sell a yearling as well.[78]

Such trust came slowly for other soldiers. Unwilling to leave women solely in charge, they initially turned to male relatives and neighbors, hired hands, and overseers. Many received similar letters filled with instructions. Often such arrangements fell apart as men quit or went to the army. Pvt. E. A. Penick of the 38th Virginia left a son in charge but by summer concluded that he needed to retake the reins. At other times, wives were reluctant to listen to men. Pvt. Isaac Walters, for example, chided his wife for not heeding his father's advice.[79] Pvt. James Michael Barr's initial refusal to trust his wife, Rebecca, twelve years his junior, led only to chaos. When Barr left for the army in January 1863 he placed his farms and slaves in the hands of his brother Henry and an enslaved driver named Bill, as noted in the previous chapter. Henry proved a passive manager, while Bill's decisions often angered Barr. As a result, the soldier began sending home sheaves of letters, not only to his brother, but to his wife as well. Having instructed Henry Barr on when to plant, harvest, gin the cotton, sell cattle, or pay debts, James Barr also asked Rebecca to tell both Bill and Henry what they needed to do. As time passed, conditions at home worsened, and he became more impatient with his brother's poor management. Barr ignored Henry more and more and came to rely on his wife. By summer, Barr was sending orders for Bill and his other slaves directly to Rebecca. She in effect had become his farm manager.[80]

Some women did not want such responsibilities. They responded by asking to give up the farms and move elsewhere, usually back home to their parents or siblings. Faced with the prospect of properties going to ruin, husbands usually opposed abandoning farms, however.[81] "If you could positively make out to liv at home," Ward master J. W. Griffin wrote, "I would of much rather you would stay be cause my place would go to nothing. . . . if you think that you can make out whare you are and think it best I want you to do the best you can for yourself and children as I can't be with you to do for you you must do the best you can."[82] After the Seven Days Battles, meanwhile, Pvt. Jesse C. Knight wrote that he hoped that even if he died in the war his wife would remain on the farm and raise their children there.[83]

As time passed, most of the men slowly realized the futility of running a farm or business long-distance through an absolutely unreliable mail service, even as many wives gained confidence in their decision making. Slowly, out of necessity, soldiers came to put their reliance in their women at home, at least for the duration of the war. In 1863 another twenty-nine men sent farm advice and direction home to wives or surrogates, including as many men save one from the Lower South (68 percent) but six fewer from the often-closer, war-torn Upper South. While a few of them doggedly continued trying to run their farms from the front, most had accepted the reality only a few had embraced the previous year. Increasingly, orders came sparingly, replaced by hopeful inquiries and tentative suggestions. Men additionally praised their wives more and more for their hard work, industry, and wisdom.[84] Above all, soldiers encouraged their wives to temporarily take the initiative and do the best job of running their farms that women could be expected to do. "Do the best you can" became a widespread cliché, its very usage suggesting the commonality of the experience. "You said you want me to give all the advice I could," John W. Cotton wrote home. "I don't know how to advise you unless I new how . . . every thing was going on you can tell what is best to do."[85] "Jane you asked me in your last letter for advice," Sgt. Thomas Hendricks wrote his wife, "but unless I was at home to see how everything goes and how the times are I do not know whether my advice would be best or not. . . . After one has been from home a good while he cannot tell so well how to advise. Do the best you can."[86]

Men did not surrender control completely or across the board. Pvt. J. A. McMurtrey bristled at his wife's perceived foibles, in this case at her visiting habits. "I want you to stay home and eat your own meat and bread," he wrote, "and tell every body to do the same and if they don't do it don't you feed them let every dog wag his own tail for times is too hard for people to visit now I don't want to work at 12 dollars a month and you feed other folks nor other folks feed you."[87] Texan S. W. Farrow likewise discouraged his wife's visiting, convinced that the rumors she was hearing only depressed her already troubled spirits. "If there is any of your neighbors that does not think that you are not as good as they are," he wrote, "or that you are not fitt to keep their company you must let them alone. . . . You know what I told you about visiting some people in the country. I know that you are lonesome, and also your disposition, but . . . you must amuse yourself with the children the best you can."[88]

Other soldiers grew annoyed when they learned of difficulties between their wives and other relatives. Surgeon John Meriwether begged his wife not to grow estranged from his sister, reminding her that "wherever my home is, there hers must be as long as she can live or wishes to live with me."[89] In contrast, he warned his wife away from her brother, who had angered Meriwether while the two men were stationed at Vicksburg. Pvt. G. H. Burns meanwhile urged his wife not to go to live with her parents, for they would insult him in his children's presence. "Damned be he who dare to do it," Burns added, "don't move back up amongst those Devlish people who tried to ruin me so hard."[90]

In 1864, an additional twenty-six men wrote home about family and farm concerns, far more than wrote affectionate love letters. Again, two-thirds came from the Lower South. A minority, including James Michael Barr and Grant Taylor, continued their attempts at micromanagement. Among the others, advice to "do the best you can" sometimes still came with ruminations on growing more corn, caring for animals, paying debts, or seeking counsel from friends and parents. The phrase itself as well as the context suggest that men did not expect a first-rate job from wives; the best they could do might be little indeed. As Drew Gilpin Faust suggests, women themselves still did not want unlimited control. The end result was a muddled compromise. Leaving their wives in charge of their property for nearly all the men involved clearly was a temporary expedient.[91] Worse, disagreements over decisions made continued to strain marriages. Pvt. E. K. Flournoy told his wife that her plans to abandon the family farm and move "has thrown me in more trouble than any thing has since this war commenced. . . . my dear that will never do. in the world if you do that I consider that we are ruined forever my dear you must consider on it and just think for A moment what will become of our stock and everything else I fell like we are almost ruined now and if you brake up and leave home you will find that it is the worst thing that you have ever done." Martha Flournoy's best, in other words, had not been good enough.[92]

HOW ARE WE TO consider the role of women in understanding why later-enlisting Confederates fought? Almost none of the men seem to have joined the army because of women's "sexual intimidation." Indeed, scattered evidence suggests the opposite. They did see women as symbols of their cause once they had joined the ranks. Women encountered while in the army could buoy morale if they proved loyal and true Confederates, but they also could undermine the spirits of men if they acted otherwise. By the same token, women at home left a mixed motivational legacy. More than keeping the proverbial home fires burning, they increasingly kept farms running as well. While there is no evidence that soldiers came to see their wives as equals, they did increasingly acknowledge and praise the contributions of wives. Ultimately, however, women like Martha Flournoy nevertheless often came up short in the eyes of husbands. Problems at home, strained relationships barely succored by the mails, and failing farms undermined the morale of men who clearly cared a great deal about their property. In the end, the effect of women as sustaining motivators for married men especially is at best mixed.

A bigger problem still loomed as well. The women and children at home and the little kingdoms of lands and goods also found themselves in the paths of the enemy, while their ostensible protectors fought far from hearth and home. That aspect of women at home, as targets and potential victims of the Union army and uncontrolled slaves, added a significant dimension to gender relations among later enlisters.

4

HATRED

"VANDAL HORDES"

Eighteen-year-old Robert W. Banks worried about doing his duty. He seemingly had every reason to fight to preserve slavery as well. His father, a wealthy Mississippi attorney and planter, owned seventy-eight bondspeople. The younger Banks, a classmate of Harden Cochrane at the University of Alabama, was also a devoted Confederate nationalist. Yet when he wrote to his father after the Battle of Shiloh about joining the army, he said little about his country or honor, and nothing about his wealth, the family's slaves, or women. Instead, the young student stressed the reality that Union troops had crossed the border into Mississippi and were approaching his Columbus home. Given that invasion and the dark character of those carrying it out, it was time for him to join the army. " 'Our own Sunny South,'" he proclaimed with the oratory of a collegiate debating society, "with all her flourishing institutions of a short time back is now in a perilous condition— about to be overrun by a merciless and implacable foe, and 'tis the duty of every 'freedom loving' son of hers to rally to her rescue, and drive the hireling invador back, or nobly perish in the attempt, as did many a gallant brave on the bloody field of Shiloh."

"Twelve months ago," he hectored his father, "you would have burned with honest indignation if any one would have hinted that Mississippi would be invaded in so short a period and that you would not consent for me to strike a blow in her defense. Yet this very thing has happened. I know that there are many in the C.S. who have completed their education and are now amassing vast fortunes, who could go to war and do not. If such men do not do their duty, is that any reason why I should neglect mine?" In the end, young Banks must have been persuasive, for his father granted his permission at last. Within weeks the youth had joined the newly formed 43rd Mississippi.[1]

BANKS WAS HARDLY the only Confederate soldier to cite Union invasion as both an initial and sustaining motivating factor. It clearly mattered to many of the soldiers of 1861. More to the point, fifty-five of the later-enlisting Confederates in the sample, 17.2 percent, wrote about it as well, almost as many as who wrote about political ideology and far more than those who referred to duty or honor. About a third came from an Upper South whose borders had been violated already, but the bulk of them came, like Banks, from a Lower South that by and large only encountered Federal invasion at the time of their enlistment. A scant few wrote of invasion, moreover, without simultaneously damning the invaders. Later-enlisting Confederates believed by 1862 that Union soldiers were merciless hirelings and blood-thirsty barbarians who would make war on women and children, wreak havoc on their property and the Southern landscape, free the slaves to enact their own vengeance, and leave nothing but desolation. They had to be turned back.[2]

It was not always so. As Reid Mitchell and Jason Phillips both have demonstrated, many Southerners in 1861 expected Northerners to prove weak adversaries and all but laughed at them. Pasty-faced clerks and factory drudges who had never fired a gun, effete, white-gloved New England Puritans, and raucous, buffoonish Irish and German immigrants were stock figures in the Southern mind by the beginning of the war. Such lesser men surely could never be a match for a manly Southern soldier raised in the outdoors and fighting for a righteous cause. Indeed the word "Yankee" itself came loaded in 1861 with now-forgotten meaning, as it initially referred only to the stereotypical New Englander, a money-grubbing, meddling, back-stabbing hypocrite whose cowardice would prevent him from ever becoming an effective soldier. The timid, tight-fisted Yankee undoubtedly would pay the crude, whiskey-soaked immigrant scum of his cities to do his fighting for him. Such hirelings, brutish men motivated by pay rather than conviction, hardly could be feared either. Such expectations led the first waves of Confederate recruits to famously boast of their expectations of whipping ten Yankees each. One also must wonder if that lack of respect for the Northern soldier helped keep thousands of later enlisters at home during the war's first years.

To be sure, other Southerners expected worse from the beginning. They warned in fervent oratorical flourishes against Lincoln's demonic hirelings and fanatics, depicting Northern soldiers as depraved savages who would stop at nothing to rape the South both figuratively and literally, and free the slaves as well. Bell Wiley lists a hatred of the enemy grounded in the North's opposition to slavery and fears of racial equality as a major reason for Confederate enlistment in 1861. Yet only as the war dragged on into 1862 did this latter image gain ascendancy over the more benign one. In part, this was because Union soldiers soon proved their mettle on battlefield after battlefield. The "hirelings" and "pasty-faced clerks," it turned out, could fight.[3]

Still another, critical factor was the manner in which the war evolved. As Mark Grimsley points out, many Union commanders at the beginning of the war, and indeed a majority of Northern civilians, embraced a "conciliatory" policy designed to win back the hearts and minds of the majority of white Southerners they presumed still loyal to the Union. Convinced that a minority of slave owners had led the deluded, ignorant masses into secession, and moreover persuaded that both history and international law called for protecting innocent civilians in the line of fire, commanders such as Winfield Scott, George B. McClellan, and initially Lincoln himself called for a humane war that would demonstrate the Union's army's good intentions. Civilians should be kept safe from danger. Their property, including slaves, was to be protected. Officers would prevent foraging and punish malefactors. Advocates of conciliation predicted that before long, the dormant Unionism of the South would revive, and the rebellion would end.

But efforts at conciliation soon collapsed in failure. Encountering more and more Confederate civilians and soldiers who fully embraced secession, it became harder and harder for Billy Yank to believe in the reality of widespread Unionism. Few wanted to protect civilian property anyway when such duty came with tongue lashings from diehard secessionist women. Guerrilla attacks made Northern soldiers angrier still and led to an exponentially growing desire to exact retribution. Common Federal soldiers themselves, beginning with those in Appalachia and the Western theater, accordingly rejected the conciliation the brass desired. Sometimes they did so on ideological grounds but more often because of empty bellies and cold nights. Foraging for food, fence rails, and other items followed, and the wise officer was the one who did not stand in the way of his men.

In the winter of 1861–62, in ostensibly Unionist enclaves such as Missouri as well as West Virginia, conciliation gave way even in the upper echelons as well to what Grimsley calls "pragmatism" or "war in earnest." Some early proponents of conciliation, notably Benjamin Butler, Ulysses S. Grant, and Henry Halleck, finally lost hope of winning back most Southerners to the old flag. The war was to be won on the battlefield, not in Southern minds. Northern forces would continue to protect real Unionists to be sure, but open secessionists deserved punishment. More importantly, Union soldiers needed to eat. Soldiers now had permission to take necessary food and supplies, destroy public and quasi-public property, and retaliate for guerrilla depredations with fire and sword. Charles Royster maintains that the new recruits who entered the Union army after June 1862 acted from the first as if terror was a standard policy. Faced with a series of defeats, the Northern public soon rejected conciliation as well, as it did stubborn proponents such as McClellan and Don Carlos Buell. So did Congress and the Lincoln administration, which now increasingly allowed soldiers to live off the land and confiscate secessionists' property. The Preliminary Emancipation Proclamation in September 1862 announced the final death knell of conciliation.[4]

White Southern men, crucially including those who had not enlisted in the Confederate army in 1861, thus confronted a war at the beginning of 1862 that not only was spreading into the Lower South but was also evolving rapidly into a conflict increasingly characterized by attacks on property and what they deemed theft and vandalism. As Joseph Glatthaar has explained, such "plundering cut to the very core of their sense of masculinity."[5] The early rhetoric regarding Northern barbarians now rang increasingly true in

Southern ears. As white Confederates angrily reacted to emancipation, as discussed in Chapter 2, they also responded simultaneously to other facets of "war in earnest." Indeed, they were parts of a whole. Foraging, pillaging, and similar depredations committed by Union soldiers against Southern people and property, coupled with emancipation and local invasion, finally spurred some men in the sample to enter the army in 1862.

Most of them were older men with a real stake in the outcome. Virginian John Dooley was one of only a handful of youths who enlisted citing even in part enemy depredations. He condemned the destruction in his native state committed by his "ruthless foes. . . . A wanton cowardly foe whose brutal orders have been too faithfully executed by a depraved and savage soldiery." Later in the year, Dooley compared his enemies to demons.[6] Enlisting in the 60th Tennessee near the end of 1862, twenty-year-old East Tennessean Pvt. John Earnest, a former student at Emory & Henry College and the grandson of a prominent local slave owner, likewise cited the alleged crimes of Yankee invaders. To him they were "vandals. . . . infernal hordes" who aimed to wreak "vengeance upon an unoffending people."[7] Texan Sgt. Thomas C. Smith echoed similar sentiments when he referred to Federal soldiers as "the vile invader" after joining the 32nd Texas Cavalry.[8]

When his brother Willie was captured by "our much detested foe" early in 1862, George H. Chatfield enlisted as a private in the 37th Alabama after failing to raise a company of his own. It was time for other men to do the same, he added, as the "threat of immediate invasion" made it necessary for his neighbors "to defend their wives and children, their homes and friends. . . . Methinks I can almost hear the voice of my brother saying to me: Brother, will you let me stay here in the hands of our enemy and not try to help me by giving them a full sound of the best cartridge from an old Enfield? Then my blood boils and the face will answer no."[9]

Less poetically, fifteen older men in the sample condemned Union soldiers during 1862 with the same angry slurs repeated again and again: "villains," "vandals," "devils." As Jason Phillips points out, history books, Southern religious periodicals, spread-eagle nationalist speeches and editorials, and Confederate popular culture all effectively propagated certain words and concepts that then were endlessly recycled and repeated by individual Johnny Rebs. So it was with the notion of Union soldiers as property vandals.[10] To be sure, men added their own favorite epithets. To Lt. William L. Nugent of the 28th Mississippi Cavalry, the "ruthless" bluecoats were also murderers and thieves, "the poor deluded victims of a false and aggrandizing policy."[11] They were cowards as well. Pvt. E. A. Penick of the 38th Virginia described Federal soldiers on the Peninsula as "skulking behind logs and trees with their long range guns,"[12] while Pvt. William Ross Stilwell depicted enemy soldiers before the Battle of Fredericksburg as "afraid to fight us."[13]

It was Northern soldiers' theft and destruction of property, however, including the "theft" of slaves, that raised the greatest ire. "What a horrid specticle is presented here," ultra-nationalist Sgt. John Thurman wrote from west Tennessee, "how madning & sickning to the heart of a Patriot. Beatiful residences as rent & torn by the shells & balls from the Enemys Gun Boats Beatiful gardens & fields left to go to ruin as the tread of the invader comes." Thurman within days fought in the Battle of Shiloh. He wrote to his wife afterward, thanking God "that it is as it is with one that I am still spaired to give what aid I can in freeing my Country & avenging the wrongs that are inflicted on us by a merciless foe."[14] Later in the year, Sgt. J. B. Sanders of the 37th Mississippi defended his decision to enlist by pointing to "how many poor women are passing through our lines to escape the disgrace of the federals soldiers."[15]

No one in the Western theater exhibited more hatred for Union soldiers than the Harvard-educated Edwin Fay, the son of a Vermonter, who repeatedly condemned them as "abolitionists," "Yankee abolitionists," "double dealing Yankees," "vandals," and "vandal hordes." After speaking with some Michigan prisoners in June 1862, Sergeant Fay concluded that "they would lie as fast as a horse could run." Two months later he condemned Union soldiers for "destroying everything, stealing negroes. . . . ransacking houses . . . leaving the country almost a wilderness. Cursing and insulting the men and sometimes proceeding to even greater lengths with the women." Worse still, he added, they were giving white people's clothing to former slaves. By the end of the year, Fay's rage was reaching fever pitch. When he found a dead Union officer after a cavalry fight, Fay "printed Abolitionist on an Oak Board and stuck it at his head for the Yankees to see."[16]

As the pragmatic policy moved from west to east in the war's second year, so did enlistments and now-familiar Confederate complaints about depredations and destruction. In May 1862, Sgt. John French White of the 32nd Virginia wrote his wife that "an enemy cruel . . . is destroying the peace and happiness of a whole country. O that the day may soon dawn when he shall be compelled to stop his invasion and depredations."[17] Lt. Lafayette Henderson of the 46th Virginia hoped in September 1862 that Lee's army was laying waste to Pennsylvania in revenge for Federal conduct in his home state. "They are a great deal worse than a parcel of run away negroes," he wrote his wife about the enemy, "worse than thieves."[18] Two months later, Lt. John W. Hosford of the 5th Florida contrasted the beauty of the Blue Ridge Mountains with the "desolation . . . lain in this vicinity by the invading enemy. Cornfields are laid waste, houses are tenetless, fences are burnt and even little towns are vacated."[19]

Mark Grimsley maintains that 1863 saw another shift in Union policy toward Southern civilians. Beginning with Grant's Army of the Tennessee at Vicksburg during the early weeks of 1863, the pragmatic policy metamorphosed into what Grimsley calls "hard war." Union commanders starting with Grant now began to order the systematic, large-scale confiscation of food, livestock, and other property. They also called for the complete destruction of railroads, factories, and anything else useful to the Confederate war effort. The goal was less to feed Union soldiers than to deny vital supplies to the uniformed enemy, break Confederate civilians' will to continue the fight, and thus hasten the end of the war. Instead of occupying territory with troops needed elsewhere, Grant as general in chief also called for a series of massive and destructive raids across the Confederacy that would crush the rebellion. William Tecumseh Sherman's Jackson, Mississippi, campaign of July 1863 heralded the new policy, and he later refined it in February 1864 in his Meridian campaign. The March to the Sea, as well as Philip Sheridan's campaign in the Shenandoah Valley, marked the pinnacles of hard war. As Grimsley as well as Charles Royster add, hard war— "destructive war" as the latter calls it—was not "total war" in the twentieth-century sense. There was less destruction of private property than some modern observers assume, and civilian murders and rapes were rare. Hard war in the end less resembled the campaigns of World War II than it did the English forced marches of the Hundred Years War.

Grimsley is quick to add, however, that hard war hardly seemed restrained to Southern civilians and soldiers.[20] He is correct. Indeed, the hatred expressed by Confederates in 1863, including later enlisters, rose proportionally and developed regionally with the destruction occasioned by the rise of hard war, thus becoming a significant sustaining mechanism. Sixteen examples can be found in the sample. From the vicinity of Vicksburg in January 1863, Lt. John Earnest of the 60th Tennessee again condemned the "vandals" in Grant's army. "The infernal hordes call for more blood," he proclaimed, "their fiendish appetites are still insatiate, though the accomplishment of their object is now grown into despair. Yet, with no other object than vengeance upon an unoffending people [they] rush on to desolate more hearthstones and make more lonely hearts."[21]

Writing from western Tennessee two months later, Capt. Samuel Ridley of the 1st Middle Tennessee Battery meanwhile lamented that his family had to live within Union lines and "draw every thing they get to live from the enemy. . . . But what can be done to release them," he added, "nothing I suppose but to whip them yes I feel that I could murder the last one of them and this will be my feeling as long as I live. . . . I have a hatred for them that I can never get over."[22] Across the river in Arkansas, the Shibley brothers worried that the "ruthless invaders and pillagers" might turn on their home-town.[23] A Confederate at Vicksburg, Surgeon John S. Meriwether of the 40th Alabama, denounced Grant's men as "scoundrels" and condemned their "heathen, savage conduct."[24]

Pvt. Grant Taylor, also serving in the 40th Alabama, noted the destruc-tion his enemies had caused. "They burnt up nearly all the houses, corn & steam mills for thirty miles," he wrote his wife, "& carried of lots of negroes. I never saw such destruction of property." What particularly shocked Taylor was that Federal soldiers could not see how depraved they were. Standing guard over two Union prisoners, Taylor heard to his amazement that "the north was determined to conquer the south and restore the Union if there were men enough in the north to do it."[25] Edwin Rice of Waul's Texas Legion actually spoke with several Federals during a truce to bury the dead and likewise expressed surprise that "they don't seem to have any idea of giving up the war and say they will stick to it until we are willing to go back in the Union or forced in."[26]

The already deep hatred of Mississippi native and Greeneville attorney Lt. William L. Nugent for Grant's army increased dramatically in 1863. Where once they had been "vandals" and murderers, the Yankees were now in his estimation "cannibals" as well. They also were "voracious," not to mention "haughty."[27] Sgt. Edwin Fay meanwhile continued his tantrums. Frustrated with both home front Confederates and his government in Rich-mond, he asserted that "there is only one thing keeps me there" in the army, "and that is absolute hatred of the infernal Villains" who had invaded the South "for desire of gain." In his letters, Union soldiers alternately were "dastardly Yankees," "damnable villains," "Vandals," "Vandal hordes," "aboli-tionists," "Abolition scoundrels," "an accursed race," and "devils incarnate." Many were "low bred dutch some of whom cannot understand a word of

English." Others wrote letters home laced with "vulgarity." Overwhelmed with rage, Fay vowed never to give quarter. "I expect to murder every Yankee I ever meet when I can do so with impunity," he swore, "if I live a hundred years. . . . peace will never be made between me and any Yankee if I can kill him without too great risk. The Thugs of India will not bear a comparison to my hatred and destruction of them when opportunity offers. There can be no fellowship between us forever."[28]

By the late spring, such dire sentiments were common back East as well. Pvt. Samuel Pickens lambasted Union soldiers as thieves and foreign hirelings. James Michael Barr verbally skewered "the nasty low lived Yankees" and declared that "there is no honor or justice abot the Yankees. If they cannot take off, they will burn up."[29] Sgt. John French White of the 32nd Virginia lamented to his wife in May 1863 that "we are separated by a wicked and cruel enemy."[30] Reacting to the death of Stonewall Jackson at Chancellorsville during the same month, Lt. John Dooley cursed "the dastardly government against which he drew his unblemished sword." There were no such men in Union field command, he later added, but Robert Milroy, then headquartered in the Shenandoah Valley, was the "Yankee citizens . . . favourite butcher." And even Milroy paled in comparison to Benjamin Butler. "The inhuman barbaraities and insulting ruffianism was not so often the action (perhaps was never so) of the veteran Northern soldier," Dooley wrote in June 1863, "as of the low hirelings who skulked in forts and cities distant from the battle field and who continually fashioned their conduct on such leaders as Ben Butler."[31]

The winter of 1863–64 brought much the same. Sgt. Maj. Marion Hill Fitzpatrick condemned federal prisoners as "devils" and described some prisoners as "the sorriest looking men I ever saw. It makes me mad to even think of submitting to such demons in human form."[32] In October, Sgt. W. Y. Mordecai of the Richmond Howitzers described the destruction in and around Culpeper, Virginia. "We cannot tell what kind of buildings stood between the great number of blackened chimneys on every side through Fauquier and Culpeper [Counties]," he wrote his mother, "but in addition to these there is the framework of many a handsome residence stripped of all that could be useful to these fiends in building hovels & the walls, where they remain, covered with obsenity—How much longer will the just retribution for these things tarry?"[33]

From their winter quarters in Dalton, Georgia, soldiers in the Army of Tennessee prepared for their spring campaign. Pvt. G. H. Burns of the 34th

Georgia described a grand review of troops and praised his fellow soldiers who were "battling for freedoms cause against a merciless foe God help us to drive them back to their place off our soil and may it never be poluted again by their footsteps."[34] Lt. Ben Robertson of the 44th Mississippi meanwhile warned his sister against Yankee raiders who would "destroy every thing you have."[35]

Confederates in Virginia and North Carolina expressed similar thoughts. Harvey Bailey of the 58th North Carolina vowed that he "wood Bee willing to do any thing if we could whip the miserable thieves."[36] Commenting on the recent Kilpatrick-Dahlgren Raid against Richmond, and in particular on the reports that Ulric Dahlgren carried orders to burn Richmond and kill Jefferson Davis, Capt. John H. Harris of the 44th Georgia condemned the "hellion clan. . . . This is certainly one of the most feutile and wicked plots ever conceived by men presuming to be civilized. It would make the cheek of the savage tingle with shame."[37]

The 1864 Atlanta and Overland campaigns, beginning early in May 1864, brought a new round of vicious fighting and also verbal condemnation. Confederate soldiers, including late enlisters, continued to describe their foes as thieves and vandals, criminals against property whose valor came from the whiskey bottle. Lt. Thomas J. Moore of Holcombs's South Carolina Legion mourned the death of a friend at the "foul hands of a despicable foe!"[38] To Lt. William L. Nugent, they were now "outlaws." A group of prisoners taken from Sherman's army, he added, were "wretchedly uniformed, miserable specimens of humanity. They look more like cut-throat mercenaries."[39] Like other soldiers, both Lt. F. B. Ward of the 5th North Carolina Cavalry and Sgt. Absalom Burum of Thomas's North Carolina Legion attributed the courage of Federal soldiers to their being drunk.[40]

Capt. Thomas Key meanwhile continued not only to condemn the enemy at every opportunity but to suspect that their real intentions involved spoiling the purity of Southern white womanhood. Not only were Northern soldiers thieves and vandals, they were "Abolitionists" and race mixers as well, "the base and amorous race of Puritans which has degraded itself and villified and slandered the Southern ladies." The real goal of the "misceginators," he maintained, was to provide black men with white Southern women. Sherman meanwhile was "one of the most heartless men that has ever disgraced a nation. . . . He is as great a brute as Butler, save in a different way." Key saved his most personal venom, however, for one unfortunate Yankee, Sgt. Leroy L. Key of the 16th Illinois, a prisoner at Andersonville.

When he received a letter from the desperate Union soldier, who evidently hoped that the Confederate artillery captain was a lost brother who might help him, the latter wrote back, "you are no brother of mine, and if you were I would disown you."[41]

By this time, a few Confederates hated white Yankees so much that they began openly to relish the idea of killing all of them in much the same way they yearned to raise the Black Flag against African American troops. Surgeon William P. Head of the 16th Texas Cavalry, stationed in Louisiana, looked forward to Sterling Price's Missouri Raid as a way to "visit some of the calamity of an invading army upon those that delight in subjugating and despoiling our southern Homes."[42] Lt. J. D. Padgett of the 24th South Carolina boasted that the men of his regiment planned to take no prisoners. Such sentiments of combat motivation ultimately found expression at places such as the Crater and in the diehard resistance that characterized some Confederates up to Appomattox and beyond.[43] Admitting that his comrades had all but given up, young South Carolinian J. T. Bleckley avowed in March 1865, "I cant belive God will ever allow men to propser that has acted like the yanks hav in Georgia and Carolina. The men say we are whiped and there is no use in fighting any longer. But I say fight them as long as we can get any thing to eat. I get mader and more determined every day."[44]

MEN WHOSE FAMILIES LAY in the path of the enemy exhibited special worry and hatred. There were still only a few in 1862. Learning of the fall of New Orleans, John T. Beggs of the 5th Washington Artillery expressed frustration that he had not been in the city to defend his family. "Ginnie," he told his sister, "I hope your womanly spirit will not fail you in this calamity as we can only trust in God and fight it out."[45] Capt. S. T. Foster of the 24th Texas Cavalry, reading that Corpus Christi had fallen to Union forces, likewise wished he had been at home to fight. "If I have to be killed," he wrote his wife, "I want it to be in defence of my home—and I don't want the enemy to get between me and my family."[46]

In August, Sgt. John French White expressed "surprise to hear that the Yankees encamped in my field. . . . I was sorry to hear of the destroying of the fence and other property and that no corn was ground on the place." What worried him most at the time, however, was the rumor that his wife had been poisoned. Two months later, White learned of a second visit from the enemy, during which they had threatened his wife at gunpoint. This time, he was outraged that his family had been "so shamefully . . . disturbed by the Yankees. No more though than I expected on their retreat," he continued. "I never have desired to take the life of any one but I do think if I had been at Cousin M the night you spoke of it would have afforded me the pleasure to have killed that villain, and also the scamp that pointed the pistol at you." Nonetheless, he counseled her not to flee to Richmond, but rather to stay at home and protect their house and belongings.[47]

In 1863, however, as Union conciliation gave way to pragmatism, the numbers of affected men grew exponentially, especially in the West. Rumors of troop movements in familiar neighborhoods elicited the greatest anxieties for loved ones. Like White, some men urged their wives to stay put and ride out the storm. Edwin Fay encouraged his wife to buy a gun and defy the enemy until he arrived home.[48] Others wanted their families to flee to safety in the West. After the fall of Vicksburg, William L. Nugent encouraged his wife to move to Texas and live with a relative. His demands increased when he learned that the Union army planned to establish "a negro camp" near his home. "I hope you will not delay a moment in getting out of the way," he wrote. "Either go across the River into the interior of Texas or come over here: anything but being kept in close proximity to a camp of demoralized negroes."[49]

Texas did not offer such an obvious refuge to its citizens, however. "I hardly know how to advise you," Surgeon William P. Head wrote his wife after hearing rumors of an invasion of his home state. "I do not want you to remain in the Yankies lines and if our army should have to fall back from red river I wish you to keep in their advance. I have seen so much distress with those that remained home with a view of saving their property that I cannot advise any one to remain within the federal lines."[50]

Along with the "hard war" policies of 1864 and the steady advance of Union arms came new concerns, again almost completely from Westerners. Reports of families left without supplies agonized soldiers. Frightened men wrote to their wives encouraging them to seek refuge with relatives in safe areas.[51] But such places increasingly seemed few and far between. Pvt. Abel Crawford of the 61st Alabama wrote a young woman that "it seems you had the courage to hold on" despite a Federal incursion, "but I guess you wouldn't have anywhere to run if you were to start, for it seems the Yankees are everywhere."[52]

HATRED, TO BE SURE, was not an all-powerful emotion. As postwar reconciliationist accounts indicate, fraternization between soldiers did occur as well, and hands really did reach across the proverbial bloody chasm. Yankees in the flesh could seem less diabolical than in theory. Battlefield courage could be acknowledged. After battles, sympathetic soldiers sometimes gave wounded foes food and water and provided medical aid. Others joined together to bury the dead. During informal truces they swapped tobacco for coffee, exchanged newspapers, and "jawed" with the men across the lines. Complaints about officers, anger at the politicians, shared religious sentiments, and expressed wishes to give up killing and go home all could create a temporary degree of solidarity. James I. Robertson maintains that fraternization increased steadily during the war, peaking in 1864, while Gerald Linderman goes beyond him in asserting that mutual suffering created bonds that outweighed antipathy. Linderman aside, however, historians from Bell Wiley and Robertson to Jason Phillips have warned against inflating the true degree of fraternization between Johnny Reb and Billy Yank. As Randall Jimerson suggests, the simple fact that such incidents were so unusual helps explain the many accounts that survive. Wiley himself implied that Southern soldiers' hatreds were deep and less easily jettisoned than those of Northern men.[53] "Hatred and fighting," Wiley concluded, "far outweighed friendliness and intermingling," as far as Confederates were concerned.[54]

Such wariness seems justified, for later enlisters at least were not especially interested in making friends across the lines. Only fifteen of the sampled later-enlisting Confederates (5 percent) described moments of fraternization, generally involving trading among pickets. Most of the descriptions, ten, were written in 1863, suggesting that for them the practice peaked earlier than for the set of men Robertson studied and did not survive the brutal campaigns of 1864. Pvt. Richard Henry Brooks of the 51st Georgia, for example, described how Confederate and Union soldiers at Fredericksburg made "little sail boats an put tobacco in them and Let them sail across the river to them and they will put in Coffee an Soda an Pocket knives an many other Little things and send it back to us. They say they are tired of the war an so are we."[55] Lt. E. B. Coggin of the 47th Alabama described a Christmas truce during which Federals actually crossed the river to "Swap or Boys Coffee and Shugar for tobacco that seam to Bee as friendly to us a that ar to one another."[56] From Petersburg, South Carolinian Lt. Thomas J. Moore described speaking with "Billy" on picket as well as arranging local nighttime truces.[57]

Even when it occurred, however, fraternization had its limits—often literally. Almost half of the accounts include mention of an intervening river or entrenchment. There were less visible barriers as well. Officers consistently frowned on the practice. Pvt. James Michael Barr was willing to acquire goods he wanted across the lines but continued to hate Yankees just the same. Pvt. John W. Cotton meanwhile worried that by trading with the enemy, he was helping to augment their presumably scarce provisions. His fellow Alabamian, Sgt. Maj. Harden Cochrane, suspected that erstwhile friendly pickets were in fact spies, and accordingly lied about the location of his camp as well as the whereabouts of other units.[58]

The threat of violence also remained in the air during every encounter. Cpl. J. F. Coghill of the 23rd North Carolina wrote from Virginia about trading newspapers with the enemy but added that "if they were to come at cross they would certainly find a warm reception."[59] Lt. E. B. Coggin was wary of crossing the river himself "for ther is Dainger of them taking us prisners ef ther head officers was to hapen tu Be there."[60] Such fears were not unfounded. Cpl. Thomas J. Newberry of the 29th Mississippi wrote from Tennessee that Union pickets across Lookout Creek were "very anctious fer a conversation and want to trade coffee for tobacco. We have orders not to speake to them some of the boys talks to them and trades them tobercco for coffee. . . . Sometimes the boys gets them to come over to trade and then they take them priseners."[61]

Four additional soldiers described contacts they had with Union soldiers after combat. Pvt. Hiram Smith Williams dug a grave and carved a headstone for a soldier who died in the hospital. Pvt. E. A. Penick of the 38th Virginia, however, drew an imaginary line when he encountered several wounded Federals after the Battle of Second Manassas. Some "seemed truly pentinant for being engaged in such an unricheous war, while others would rave & curse the rebels as they call us." The one who most affected him, however, was a New Yorker who "beged me to stay by him untill he died, which I did. He had a little money which he gave me and beged me to let his wife know when and how he died. . . . I wrote to his wife and enclosed the note $10 in the letter. . . . I feel proud that I did even that much for a dying Christian which he bore every testimony."[62] Lt. I. M. Auld of the 5th Florida similarly drew a line between good Yankees—Christian men who claimed to oppose the war—and bad ones. At Chancellorsville, Auld encountered a wounded Federal who called out, " 'Boys, for God's sake don't retreat, just whip us but today and the war will close.' I gave him a canteen of water and promised him that we would not retreat, and passed on."[63]

By far the largest number of later enlisters who wrote of encounters with individual Union soldiers, nineteen men, referred to Union prisoners of war. Most were unimpressed. Pvt. John Shibley and his brother William, both serving in the 22nd Arkansas, dismissed the first Federal prisoners they saw as "very poor specimens of Humanity."[64] Lt. Draughton Smith Haynes of the 49th Georgia referred to the prisoners he saw as "decidedly the cheapest looking set I ever beheld."[65] While Pvt. Samuel Pickens of the 5th Alabama described a "filthy, miserable, wretched set."[66] Such impressions could lead to abuse. Pvt. Henry T. Morgan of the 31st Louisiana wrote his wife that Union prisoners in Alexandria were "treated bad."[67] J. C. Brightman of the 18th Texas, a surgeon's assistant at Camp Ford in Tyler, Texas, described what that bad treatment could look like. "When the Yankees make their escape from the stockade," he wrote, "we hunt them down with negro dogs. They have none make their escape yet. . . . The Yanks think it is very hard to be hunted down with dogs, like so many run-away negroes."[68]

Capt. Robert Dickinson of the 21st South Carolina offered a somewhat more positive appraisal. He described the men captured on James Island in the summer of 1862 as "a good looking set of men all young and well built and rosy faces . . . and as fair and clean as though they had just come out of a band box. . . . We didn't take any of the Massachusetts men for they all run at the sight of our boys the prisoners were Pensylvanians and farmers at home and native born Dutch & Irish . . . there is not one genuine Yankee among them." Yet even Dickinson later described prisoners taken from the 79th New York in the Battle of Secessionville as "a brag Regiment. . . . all stimulated with Whiskey."[69] Pvt. Creed Thomas Davis of the Richmond Howitzers meanwhile expressed wonder that captured Union prisoners were "New Englanders and not foreigners."[70]

Other factors usually had to be present to create much sympathy. Sgt. Maj. Draughton Haynes described two fellow Masons he befriended, one of whom "intends coming south" to "purchase slaves & settle."[71] Another Mason, Sgt. Absalom Burum, dismissed most Union prisoners as drunks but got along well enough with a Mason from Ohio that they exchanged addresses and promised to write.[72] As in other cases, however, later-enlisting Confederates expressed the most sympathy for Union soldiers willing to repent of their perceived evils. Eleven men reported some manner of defeatism and repentance in Northern soldiers as far as invasion and the war were concerned. Both Cpl. John T. Knight of the 22nd Texas and Lt. T. J. Rounsaville of the 13th Texas Cavalry wrote that the Emancipation Proclamation had disillusioned Union soldiers to the point that they were deserting in droves. J. C. Brightman estimated that half of the prisoners in Camp Ford would take an oath of allegiance to the Confederacy if it would gain them release.[73]

Human sympathy, a sense of shared suffering and neglect, and the desire for scarce coffee, in short, could occasionally bring combatants together, but those factors only went so far in mitigating later enlisters' fervent hatred of the Yankee. In most cases, Johnny Rebs, including later enlisters, only sympathized with Billy Yank when the man in blue was wounded or else expressed Christian faith or, better still, doubts about his own cause. Balanced against the seventeen soldiers who more or less spoke sympathetically of Union soldiers once encountering them, in short, are the close to sixty who by and large did not change their minds at all about their loathing of the "vandal hordes."

Comparatively speaking, hatred of the invading enemy in sum motivated about as many later enlisters in the sample as did political ideology and involved all of the facets of soldier motivation from enlistment to battle. When one remembers that so much of that hatred involved the same Union army tactics and strategies that also brought about the collapse of slavery, it is difficult not to conclude that states' rights ideology, the even more broadly held determination to preserve slavery and protect home, and the hatred that developed toward those who seemingly went to war to bring down both were inexorably linked in a tangled web of initial and sustaining motivations. The lawless vandals of Confederate rhetoric, after all, were not just fanatics and hirelings who threatened the home folks, but were also allegedly abolitionists and miscegenationists as well.

Yet, in the end, for some later-enlisting Confederates, even all those factors combined still were not enough to motivate enlistment. Facing economic ruin in a war that especially hurt poor men and their families, some additionally demanded something else—cash on the barrelhead.

5

PAY

"FIGHTING FOR MONEY INSTEAD OF THEIR COUNTRY"

In the spring of 1862, Pvt. J. H. Lee enlisted in the newly formed 43rd Alabama. He did not do it for states' rights, or to preserve slavery, or even out of any apparent hatred for the invading Yankees. Nor did he say anything about high-flown notions of honor or duty. What he most cared about was that his family needed money. "We have not drawed one red cent yet," he then complained to his wife from camp the following May, "and from what I hear among the boys they havent more than one third of them ever drawed half of there bounty yet." A week later, he told his father the same thing. Indeed, a disillusioned Lee now angrily alleged that the Confederacy had broken its contract with him, and he wanted to sue for his release. "Pa," he asked, "there is one thing I want you to do for me, that is, to . . . ask judge

Oliver hear the case will be where they don't pay a soldier his bounty. I have been told by severel men that if they do not pay a soldier his money as soon as he is mustered in to service he is at liberty to come home if he sees cause to do so." That was exactly what Lee wanted. "I do not wish to stay here if I can get out of it," he wrote his father. "Many men grumbling, want to go home. We are treated like dogs."[1]

The bounty to which Lee referred was the product of the Confederacy's continuing need for men. A month before Fort Sumter, the Confederate Provisional Congress in Montgomery had authorized President Jefferson Davis to raise up to 100,000 recruits for a term of twelve months. After the war began, new legislation called upon Davis to accept additional units for a period of time he deemed sufficient. An opponent of short enlistment terms, Davis seized the opportunity to enlist men for the duration of the war. Enthusiasm and expectations of a short conflict both ran high, and the recruiters ended up turning away men. The Battle of First Manassas, however, coupled with Lincoln's decision in its wake to build a massive army, spurred the Confederate Congress to again act. New legislation authorized the recruitment of 400,000 additional men, but only for terms no longer than three years.[2]

The number of volunteers coming forward as a consequence disappointed Congress's hopes. By the end of the year, with the conclusion of the war nowhere in sight and a massive Union host massing, the Richmond government faced a frightening manpower crisis. Within weeks the twelve-month enlistments would run out, and expectations were rife that many disillusioned men would head home for good. Congress was desperate to prevent that. Thus, on December 11, 1861, it passed yet another new law. Men willing to reenlist would receive a bounty of $50, a sixty-day furlough, and transportation home. The army also would allow them to reorganize themselves into new units and elect all of their officers. Importantly for this study, the legislation further promised the bounty to new recruits who were willing to enlist for three years or the duration of the war. A week later, additional legislation authorized the War Department to begin raising companies of new men. Subsequent acts over the next few weeks extended to new recruits the right to elect their officers and to serve with units based in their states. Indeed the final act of the Provisional Congress authorized bounties to soldiers old and new as soon as the surgeons pronounced them fit for service.[3]

Fifty dollars in Confederate money in early 1862 was still a sizable sum, carrying as much purchasing power as $700 today.[4] Yet while the bounty and local supplements as well brought in new recruits, they still did not produce enough during the first three months of 1862. Accordingly, the Confederate Congress in April took another, more far-reaching step: conscription. Urged on by Davis, a Confederate government created on the avowed pillars of individual liberty and a limited central government declared that every man between the ages of eighteen and thirty-five was subject to three years of military service unless exempted. The upper age limit went up to forty-five the following September and to fifty in 1864, while seventeen-year-olds eventually became eligible as well. Civil servants as well as a wide range of industrial and white-collar workers would receive exemptions, and the later law of September 1862 allowed one exemption for every twenty slaves on a plantation. Men already in the army, whatever their original terms of enlistment, would have to serve three years or the duration of the war. But the new law also continued the provisions of the December legislation in authorizing bounties, furloughs, and the election of field officers. The hope was that men still not in the army would choose to enlist immediately in a company and regiment of their choosing rather than be drafted into organizations chosen for them. It also maintained the older practice of allowing men to send substitutes, providing that those men were not otherwise subject to the draft.[5]

It was in the shadow of the December and April legislation that the men considered for this study enlisted. Some historians have assumed as a result that it must have been the threat of the draft especially that led to their military service. Historians as otherwise interpretively diverse as James McPherson and Mark Weitz contend that, forced into the service and separated from their wives and children, later enlisters would prove unwilling combatants more likely to shirk duty or desert than earlier enlistees. J. H. Lee's desperate pleas to get out of the army initially seem to embody that description. Indeed, faced with the reality of remaining in the service, Lee hastily turned to hiring a substitute once he realized that military service was not just another job he could quit. His father found a willing man, but too late, for with the September legislation the proposed substitute became eligible for the draft as well. In the end, Lee remained in the army. Hospitalized in the summer of 1862, he later served as a nurse and detailed carpenter—in what McPherson disparagingly called "bombproof" assignments—before assignment to the 1st Confederate Engineer Troops. There his relative safety came to an end. It was as a sapper with that unit that he was captured during the Battle of the Crater on July 30, 1864. He died in captivity weeks later, still a Confederate soldier and a combat veteran.[6]

"I FOUND I COULDANT git in to work," Pvt. Theophilis Frank wrote his wife from camp in October 1863, so he joined the army, enlisting in the 48th North Carolina. "I thought I might as well go for I couldnent well help it yet i went without being taken."[7] To Frank, just as to J. H. Lee, soldiering boiled down to just another job, except that it was one that came with heightened danger and a powerful threat to demand the work willingly or unwillingly. Most Civil War historians, of course, are emphatic: Civil War soldiers seldom fought for money.[8] Russell Johnson, however, offered a rare demurral. Maintaining that scholars have "routinely divorced ideology from the context of their civilian lives," Johnson argued that many men from the unskilled and artisan classes of Dubuque, Iowa, joined the Union Army precisely for the steady work and wages it provided at a time when the war, the initial economic depression of 1861, and industrialization in general were marginalizing them otherwise. Combined with bounties and the coercion of conscription, regular wages made the military a reasonable choice for unemployed and underemployed urban men. To be sure, most later-enlisting Confederates were not urban wage earners like the men from Dubuque, increasingly squeezed out of their trades; yet no one would deny the increasing economic straits on the Southern home front as inflation, shortages, speculation, and government policies designed to feed and clothe troops in the field made life increasingly difficult. Many later enlisters did increasingly need money.[9]

Yet their numbers are not great. Thirty-five of the men considered for this study, 11 percent, enlisted at least in part for the Confederate bounty and what two men tellingly called their "wages."[10] The letters of an additional three men suggest inconclusively that they probably signed up in part for pay as well. Over half fought in the Eastern theater of the war, while seven out of ten came from the Deep South. The great majority of those who can be confirmed as bounty men, twenty-five, enlisted in 1862. An additional nine enlisted in 1863, and one man, seventeen-year-old South Carolina farm laborer L. R. Dalton, joined Hampton's South Carolina Legion as a private in 1864. By then, the bounty had doubled to $100.

As a group, what is most notable about bounty soldiers is their economic status. Contrary to expectations, not all were poor. At one end of the scale were six slaveholders; while five men owned over $5,000 of personal property. Of the seventeen soldiers who appear in the census, the mean average value of land holding was $683, the median average was $500, and the modal average was zero. In regard to personal property, the mean was $3,104, the median $800, and the modal $5,000. But here the census is deceiving. Fifteen of the bounty men cannot be located in the census at all, which suggests that most of them were all but propertyless. Adding them to the totals would produce an overall picture of poverty indeed. At worst, assuming that none were property owners, the averages fall to a realty mean of $382, and the median and modal averages become zero. Despite the presence of a few wealthy men such as merchant James Montgomery Lanning, in other words, most men who enlisted for the bounty money really did need it. What they wanted to do with it, in most cases, was send it home to their families. While a few kept some to meet needs in camp, eight of the men specifically sent home part or all of their bounties as well as pay as soon as receiving it, or else promised to do so when the money came in.[11] It was, Pvt. Richard Henry Brooks maintained on Christmas Day, 1862, "the dearest money I ever had in my life."[12]

Like other workers in mid-nineteenth-century America, men who enlisted for the bounty, like J. H. Lee, were not shy about demanding their money, the promised furloughs, or their rights in general.[13] Pvt. Harden Cochrane described the situation in the newly formed 2nd Alabama Cavalry as of June 1862. When company captain Joseph Pegues went from their camp in Florida to Montgomery in order to pick up the men's bounty and pay, a Confederate bureaucrat refused to comply, citing technical errors in the pay roll. "This created some dissatisfaction with some of the company," Cochrane reported. "There are some men who do look like they are fighting for money instead of their country." He went on to identify one man as "the greatest growler. His whole mess seems dissatisfied."[14]

A few days later, Cochrane's lieutenant received a letter from Pegues, indicating that the bounties would be paid at last. "This must be good news to some of our men," Cochrane complained, "who have had their 'bounty' for their theme ever since I have been here. They have talked so much about it that I am really tired of hearing it. There does seem like something has been wrong about the men not getting their bounty sooner, for I believe some men really needed it for their families, but I don't think they should talk of it like they came to the war for it."[15] Cochrane's comments in the end seem to confirm that many Confederates enlisted for bounty money. Yet among the men in the sample compiled for this study, there are still fewer bounty-oriented recruits than men who cited political ideology or invasion; and there are far fewer still than those apparently motivated in some manner by slavery. Perhaps cash incentives alone, especially those often delayed or devalued by inflation, were just as ineffective as the Confederate government concluded.

THE BOUNTY, OF COURSE, was not an isolated policy and cannot be viewed as such. If it was the carrot designed to spur enlistment, the draft was the accompanying stick. "Our company have reorganized and made a war company," thirty-eight-year-old Alabama militiaman W. V. Fleming wrote from Mobile in May 1862, "there is a few of us that is not subject to the conscrip that has not joined the company for the war and do not expect to." Fleming indeed went home, not to return until 1864, but the men of draft age remained.[16] An estimated 120,000 other Confederate soldiers served unwillingly in the army as conscripts, while another 80,000, according to Larry Logue, enlisted as a result of its implementation. A representative sample of 320 later Confederates thus should have turned up eighty to one hundred conscripts. Yet in the entire course of this study, only eight confirmed draftees could be identified.[17] Such a paucity of written records, when compared to the high number of total conscripts, suggests at the least a high level of illiteracy and poverty among drafted men, making their war in many ways truly "a poor man's fight." Elisabeth Lauterbach Laskin, who found only 9 drafted men among the 647 in her comparable sample and 58 conscripts among the 1,825 men in ten sampled companies, additionally wondered if literate conscripts were too embarrassed to write about their status.

Ultimately, such small sample sizes preclude reliable conclusions or real analysis. What can be said about the few conscripts studied here is that economically they ran across the spectrum. Two Clover brothers of North Carolina, both of whom entered the 6th North Carolina in June 1864, do not appear in the census at all, nor does Pvt. Neill McLaurin of the 4th North Carolina Cavalry. Pvt. W. A. Crouch of the 1st Arkansas Cavalry did. A thirty-year-old self-described artist and jeweler from Arkansas, he entered the army in the fall of 1862. A husband and father, he owned no real property and only $250 of personal property. North Carolina school teacher Thomas Elliott was not much better off. When he entered the army in 1862, he owned $150 of real property and $300 of personal property. In contrast were two men from slave-owning families. Eighteen-year-old Pvt. Samuel Baker's family owned $5,000 worth of realty and eighteen slaves. Pvt. Homer Adams of the 13th Alabama, the only sampled conscript from the Lower South, also came from a wealthy family that claimed $10,000 of land and $19,000 of personal property, including seventeen slaves.[18]

What tentatively seems to have united such disparate men, based on their limited writings, were their roots in the more reluctant to secede Upper South (Adams excepted), their apparent unwillingness to serve for any of the other reasons previously discussed, a marked unhappiness in the army once enrolled, and a slow, final adjustment to the reality of service. All evinced strikingly close family ties as well. John Clover wrote of missing his "native land," a phrase that suggests the extreme localism historian Mark Weitz describes. Both of the Clover boys complained of "hard times here" and called life in camp the "hororablest life that ever I lived," but added that they and their fellow draftees "all get a long well together."[19] Adams meanwhile hoped that his teacher's position would win him a release. It did not, and he went on to be captured at Gettysburg. Crouch would see action as well.[20] Elliott ached to get home and admitted that being in the army "don't suit me at all," but went on to write that if he had to stay in the rank, he hoped to get in the cavalry. "I had rather go on a horse back than to take it on foot," he wrote his wife.[21]

In addition to the eight conscripts are seven additional men, all but two again from the Upper South, who openly admitted that they volunteered only to escape the draft and find more congenial surroundings. Pvt. James Calvin Zimmerman wrote that he "never voluntiered until I saw there was no chance to keep out of going then I was forced to go."[22] Three others easily fit McPherson's description of shirkers. Pvt. H. C. Harris of the 40th Alabama railed against "the Congressmen that made the conscript act."[23] Pvt. A. D. McBride's father persuaded his son to enlist and find a safe place to serve, writing him that "I do not think you will be safe to come home without a furlough certifying that you have volunteered into the service and if you ever have to go in it may be the sooner the better as all the companies may soon be filled up on the coast and you will be sent to Virginia." McBride did as he was instructed, but he let his wife know that he was unhappy about being the army. He ended up in Virginia anyway.[24] "I was to smart to go before the board to be examined," Pvt. W. P. Farnsworth likewise wrote his brother. "I volunteered and got my detail when I was mustered into service." He soon found himself out of harm's way in Atlanta, toiling in a quartermaster's company commanded by an in-law. "It is better than standing Sentinel these rainy nights," he boasted.[25]

Draftee Joseph Joyner's career turned out differently. Like young William Lacy, Joyner was the son of a powerful politician and Confederate official, and something of a nationalist as well. He also clearly remained the pet of the family in 1862. In February of that year, he finally decided to enlist so that he could fight in the 7th North Carolina, where two of his brothers already served. His father fumed, insistent that any son of his should serve only as an officer. "I would not object to a lieutenancy in any company," he wrote his father, ". . . but considering the opportunities that now present themselves it would seem very idle speculation for me to expect an office of any importance at the present time." Joseph insisted that he had made the right decision, as he had been only one step ahead of the conscript officials. "The draft," he explained, "was reported to be very near at hand. . . . R. C. Williams arrived here on last (Sunday) evening *by way of Weldon*, he says *they were drafting there on that day*." Yet Joyner ultimately proved to be no "sneak." He went on to rise to the rank of sergeant, and he emerged as a tough soldier and diehard Confederate by war's end.[26]

Historians generally maintain that men who joined the army earlier, especially those from the middle and upper classes, looked down on conscripts as cowards and shirkers.[27] Only a few late enlisters in the sample evidenced such opinions, however, suggesting less of a distance in perception than existed among the recruits of 1861. Sgt. W. Y. Mordecai judged conscripts unintelligent, to be sure, while Pvt. E. W. Treadwell of the 19th Alabama pronounced them poor soldiers. Sgt. Edwin Fay expressed support for the "tyrannical" law that none the less would fill the ranks and end the war, as long as he could get out of the army himself.[28] But overall only a mere handful of later enlistees, seven, agreed. Two notably supported the law only because it would force particular men into the army. Pvt. Richard Henry Brooks expressed joy that the draft forced "old John Bird" into the ranks, and wished "it would get a few more that is there that I could name."[29] Pvt. William Pinckney Cline asked his wife for a list of all the local men taken up by the draft, but especially wanted to know if his hated rival, Mark Hewitt, was among them. In a similar manner, Sgt. A. G. Jones of the 5th North Carolina Cavalry wanted to see all the local Unionists forced into the ranks.[30] Lt. William L. Nugent gleefully hoped to see "the nice young gentlemen quake in their shoes, and . . . 'come to the centre.'"[31]

William Pinkney Cline of the 26th North Carolina. A blacksmith before the war, he enlisted reluctantly in 1862 and deserted in August 1863. Imprisoned at Castle Thunder in Richmond, he returned to his regiment in 1864 only to die in the Wilderness. Photograph courtesy Southern Historical Collection, University of North Carolina at Chapel Hill, P-5019/1.

But just as many, eight others, expressed their reservations about conscription. Capt. Joseph R. Manson felt sorry for the men taken. "They looked so dejected," the captain wrote his mother. "You can tell one as far as you can see him. They are so troubled that they become fit subjects for disease and so many of the poor fellows will die in camp."[32] The others less sentimentally worried about the effect of the draft on the home folks left behind. Pvt. E. W. Treadwell thought that the drafted men would "do much more good at home making corn and taking care of their familys."[33] Pvt. William A. Collins of the 48th North Carolina agreed that the draft would leave "many a home desolate and besides that I am affraid there will be a many poor wife and children will have to suffer for bread."[34] Pvt. C. W. Bunker, an 1863 enlistee and the son of the celebrated "Siamese twin" Eng Bunker, worried that the drafting of the man he had engaged to cut wood for his wife would leave her to freeze in the winter. Pvt. William Ross Stilwell supported conscription in theory but opposed his brother being drafted. So did Lt. William L. Nugent, who approved of the draft for cowardly stay-at-homes but thought that a relative was too sickly to stand the strain of life in the military. Sgt. Maj. Harden Cochrane also worried about an uncle and encouraged him to join his company rather than wait for the draft.[35]

Overall, we are left with a conundrum. The Confederacy drafted over a 100,000 men, but few are represented in the sample. Surely many more joined because of the threat of conscription. Moreover, few later-enlisting Confederates wrote about the draft as it affected them or others, or about draftees as a group. It is reasonable to assume that many of them enlisted under the threat of conscription, and thus felt a degree of solidarity with conscripts, but few left positive confirmation to undergird that assumption. Perhaps as with slavery, the draft was such an obvious factor that they did not have to draw attention to it.

KEEPING WITH ESTABLISHED practice going back to the American Revolution, the Confederate Congress as early as October 1861 allowed a volunteer to provide a substitute to take his place, providing that no more than one man per company per month did so. The new conscription law also allowed drafted men to employ substitutes. As long as the substitute was healthy and not already eligible to be drafted, he could take the place of the "principal." Enlisted men already in the army could also obtain substitutes at the one per month rate as long as company captains approved. Despite the expected public shame associated with hiring a substitute, the market for such proxies in the Confederacy exploded overnight as men swallowed both the vaunted Southern honor historians wax eloquently about and their reputations. Advertisements filled Southern newspapers, with offered payments rising from $500 in 1862 to $10,000 by the end of 1863, not to mention the principal's bounty. Other men simply offered their land. Professional brokers appeared, offering for a fee to match wealthy principals with boys under the age of eighteen, old men, and others whose health or mental abilities otherwise precluded service. Sgt. Edwin Fay even described a "negro boy" who brokered a deal between one of Fay's comrades and a substitute.[36] "There is a great fever for putting in substitutes now," Joseph R. Manson of the 12th Virginia wrote his mother, "and unfortunately every day poor fellows are found who will sell their lives for money."

Not surprisingly, substitutes soon developed a poor reputation among 1861 enlistees and even the more willing recruits of 1862. Manson, for example, called them "the meanest soldiers in the army."[37] Many officers simply refused to accept them, and the secretary of war soon called for a complete overhaul of the system. Congress, however, did nothing directly at first, although raising the age limit for the draft to forty-five not only cut into the supply of potential replacements but deprived many principals of substitutes already employed, since the government considered hired substitutes in that age range draft eligible. Many principals sued the government as a result. Few won their cases, and the War Department concluded that men who had lost the services of their substitutes were again eligible for service, no matter the sums they had paid others to fight for them.[38]

By mid-1863, substitution in the Confederacy had reached scandalous proportions. Men already in the army, including 1862 later enlisters, lambasted the so-called cowards still at home hiding behind the practice. Many viewed conscription and substitution as creating a "rich man's war and poor man's fight." Morale suffered accordingly. Substitution proved militarily questionable as well. Substitutes frequently never appeared in camp or else deserted later, sometimes repeatedly. The Bureau of Conscription flatly maintained that no more than 10 percent of hired substitutes ever reported for duty. Criminals made money selling forged papers. A group of officers in the Army of Tennessee led by commanding general Braxton Bragg finally demanded that Davis and the War Department overhaul the entire system but especially prohibit substitution. Late in December 1863, the Confederate Congress did so, and declared that all of the men who had hired substitutes were now eligible again for service. By January 9, 1864, they were to enlist or be conscripted. Many turned to the courts for protection, but outside of North Carolina they found little succor. Yet substitution in a way continued. While men could no longer leave the army by providing a substitute soldier, they could at least gain a furlough in some armies by recruiting an additional soldier.

Ultimately, 70,000 Southern men hired substitutes to take their place in line of battle.[39] As with conscripts, however, substitutes' correspondence is difficult to locate, suggesting that the Confederate government was correct in asserting that relatively few paid substitutes ever bothered to actually serve. Only six men in the sample can be identified firmly as substitutes, and three of them enlisted as recruits in 1864, only providing furloughs for the responsible men. One, Pvt. George Marion Coiner of the 59th Virginia Cavalry Battalion, came from a wealthy family that owned $11,550 worth of realty as well as eight slaves. A veteran of the 52nd Virginia, Coiner fought at Antietam, left the army, and reentered as a substitute for unknown reasons in 1864. Two others, J. C. Brightman of the 18th Texas and I. B. Cadenhead of the 34th Alabama, do not appear in the census, and were probably poor. Cadenhead, like Coiner, was a veteran who had fought previously in the 45th Alabama.[40]

Indeed the substitutes of 1862, with the apparent exception of Pvt. Charles Terrill, were desperately poor men. Joseph Lambeth was a forty-four-year-old Virginian with no land, no property, no given occupation, and four children. Pvt. George Ashby was the son of a widowed seamstress who owned $190 worth of real property and no personal property of worth in 1860. His case suggests the complexities of the practice. In March 1862, Ashby's mother agreed to supply her son as a substitute for a man named James Bartlett in the 6th Virginia Cavalry. In exchange she would receive the latter's bounty as well as $30 a month, a laborer furnished one day every month, two-and-a-half barrels of corn, and cloth. She soon wrote her son's commanding officer, however, demanding that he be released from the army because she was not receiving "the state pay" as well. She also demanded that her son "bring both of his Blankets back with him as i am scears of bed clothes."[41]

It is somewhat easier to find men like Bartlett who wanted to employee substitutes. Thirty-six soldiers in the sample, 11.25 percent of the total, with three-quarters hailing from the cotton states, contemplated hiring a substitute at some point. Fifteen of them did so in 1862, near the beginning of their experience in uniform, which suggests certainly a reluctant parting from civilian life.[42] Phillips Fitzpatrick was a notable case. In March 1862, the Alabamian and owner of sixty slaves had joined the army out of an ardently expressed love for his new country. He rose quickly to the rank of sergeant. By May, however, he was stationed outside of Mobile, bored, and ready to go home to his plantation. "I don't think there is going to be any fighting down here," he wrote his wife glumly, "and I am getting somewhat tired of Dog River and camp life generally." Moreover, there was talk that his overseer might soon enter the army himself as another man's substitute, jeopardizing his control of his slave property. Accordingly he contacted a local man to consult with his father-in-law about finding a replacement. He was unwilling to pay $1,000 a year as some men were, he added, but would be happy to pay less.[43]

As May dragged into June, Fitzpatrick grew both impatient and annoyed with his broker, who had yet to deliver an adequate replacement, and with the Confederate bureaucracy as a whole. A fellow soldier had secured the monthly substitute, he wrote, and while his officers rejected that man on the basis of health, Fitzpatrick suspected that his time was running out. He thus implored his wife to more involve her father, and at the same time to open negotiations with a local blacksmith named McAfee who might be willing to enlist. Suspecting that the blacksmith was under the age of thirty-five and thus ineligible to take his place, Fitzpatrick openly encouraged his hired agent to convince the man to lie about his age. "I think if you talk to him," he wrote, "you could convince him of the great advantage of being over 35. At least get him to swear that to the best of his knowledge and belief he is over that."[44]

McAfee agreed to the deal only to back out at the eleventh hour. Fitzpatrick blamed the go-between. "This is twice he has fooled me," the soldier complained, "and if he fools me again it will be by really getting a man." At his wit's end, Fitzpatrick went into the city himself to find McAfee, only to conclude that he had left town to work on gunboat construction. Fitzpatrick left an outstanding offer of $1,000 and waited impatiently for a reply. At last, McAfee wavered. Fitzpatrick, hesitant to lose him again, sent his wife detailed instructions on what to do next. "Let me know as soon as he consents," he wrote. "As soon as he assents to come tell Albert to take him before a Justice of Peace and make the affidavit that, to the best of his knowledge and belief, he is over thirty five years old, and tell him to send it down to me as soon as he does it, by this presenting this affidavit to Capt Semple it will have the effect of putting me first and prevent and body else from putting in a man until McAfee has been examined and pronounced unfit for service or mustered in."

Fitzpatrick finally made it out of the army, but not for good. By May of 1864, he was once more in uniform and back at Mobile, attached to the Engineering Department and assigned to the hospital at Dauphin Island, Alabama.[45] Others were less lucky. Pvt. William Ross Stilwell considered hiring a substitute after a friend did so, and his regimental sutler offered him fifty dollars a month to clerk for him, but Stilwell never followed through. Lt. William D. Cole sought a substitute but simultaneously feared that he had waited too long, for he was about to be elected lieutenant in the 38th Alabama. Capt. Lafayette Henderson's wife asked him to get a substitute in November but he lamented that it was too late.[46]

Cole and Henderson, like Phillips Fitzpatrick, Fleming Jordan, and Daniel C. Snyder, were prosperous men and slave owners. But less-wealthy men sought substitutes as well. Pvt. H. E. Neal of the 53rd Virginia secured a substitute in September and went home to rejoin his bride only to be called back later. One presumes that subsequent legislation made the substitute eligible for service in his own right. As late as March 1865, Neal, a man who owned no property in the 1860 census, would offer the king's ransom of $1,000 to a man who would trade a detailed position in the rear for his. Weary of his rainy camp and leaky tent, Pvt. H. C. Harris told his sister in language reminiscent of slavery that "if I only had enough money to buy myself free & that money was all that I ever expected to have I would give it freely, willingly, to shake off the youke that galls and binds me here. Give me freedom above all. . . . let all go out that can get out by paying for a substitute."[47] Some poorer men turned to family members to find willing men at home. Pvt. C. D. Epps asked his wife to offer first $50 and then $75 to potential replacements, while Pvt. Elijah M. Odom of the 35th Mississippi wrote his wife to go as far as $150 after experiencing his first shelling and a slight wound at Vicksburg. Neither appear in the census, which suggest that they were offering what for them were considerable sums.[48] Sgt. James Wilson, a comrade of Odom and seemingly equally poor, lamented that his agent had failed to find a substitute and told his wife, "I would give all that I am worth for a man."[49] None in the end escaped the army. Indeed, Cole, Epps, and Wilson died of battlefield wounds, while Henderson and Odom became prisoners of war.

Others sought substitutes as well. Starting in the summer of 1862, Pvt. Grant Taylor repeatedly asked his wife to negotiate with an older man in their neighborhood. At first he offered "old Riley" $50 a year for the duration of the war, although he admitted privately, "I am willing to give the land, houses, and all if he would go." When the man initially refused to join the army for any price, including the better offers with which Malinda Taylor competed, she countered with a promise of $800 in cash, 160 acres of land including the corn planted on it, seven cattle, three pigs, four bee gums, and a pair of shoes. Grant responded that he would prefer that Riley "take all of the land and less of the stock but make the best trade with him that you can." In the end, Riley delayed too long. In August, his captain refused to accept any more substitutes. "We will have to endure it," Grant concluded.[50]

Despite his deeply expressed disgust for Yankees, Sgt. Edwin Fay began attempting to get out of the army as early as May 1862, citing the defection of other men as well as his self-perceived delicate health and alleged concern for his family. He was willing to fight for a year, he explained, but not for the three now required. From the first he pinned his hopes on the draft exemption granted to teachers like himself, but was willing to go the substitute route instead if necessary, proposing to offer "my horse, bridle and saddle, and $400 per year as long as the war lasts." Told by "a little squirt of a Captain" that he had relinquished his draft exemption when he enlisted voluntarily, Fay pretended to ask his wife for permission to pursue the matter honorably. "I don't think I could bear the reproaches that would be heaped on me," he shammed, "but if you desire it my dearest one I will come home at any cost." He added that if he stayed in the army, she surely would become a widow. Later in the letter, he let it slip that he had already decided to appeal his denied exemption to Gen. Sterling Price. In the meantime, Fay also provided her detailed instructions on how to secure and send to his camp a substitute, and better a young boy than an old man. Since only one man a month could provide a substitute, "I want him before anyone else can come in."[51]

Fay pursued the matter doggedly into the summer. The experience of combat whetted his desire to get home; he told his wife that he had proven his courage under fire and could now leave the unit honorably to come home to her and either resume teaching or else become a guerrilla; the latter became a constant fantasy. He upped his proposal to $2,100 for three years, plus his horse and equipment. "If this is not good wages," he suggested, "I don't know it for a man can't begin to make it at home." When his captain told him that he would accept no more substitutes, Fay reacted by angrily demanding the same rights granted to other men who had left the company in that manner. Undeterred, he offered an immediate $1,000 to anyone who would take his place after learning of the death of his son. Only in August did Fay admit the failure of his attempt to find a substitute. He accordingly turned back to the chimera of securing his teacher's exemption, which would see him placing increasing pressure on his wife and his school's board of trustees, and also began campaigning for the rank of lieutenant, which he noted would give him the right to resign.[52]

The year 1863 saw no let up in the desire for substitutes. Sixteen men in the sample discussed finding one that year. Pvt. Samuel Baker's mother implored her son to accept a substitute three months after he joined the 4th Virginia Cavalry, as "we have already lost one in this *horrid* war." Baker tried, but his preferred man could not receive permission from his father. Baker's mother blamed her husband for not trying hard enough to save their remaining son.[53] Another youth, Lt. Thomas J. Moore of the 18th South Carolina, the son of a slave owner and a former student at South Carolina College, was willing to pay "1,000 dollars more for a substitute" in November 1862, specifying "any one over 50 years of age stout and well. . . . A substitute in Richmond is worth $1,500." Still in the army the following spring, Moore wondered "What is the matter? Have you tried or are none to be had." He went on to recommend a man supposedly "anxious to substitute" and authorized his correspondent to up the offer to $2,500.[54]

Older men tried to find substitutes as well. Although officers could resign, and thus needed no substitute, Capt. John Blair of McClung's Tennessee Battery hired one at a bargain for $25. Merchant James Montgomery Lanning joined the 18th Alabama in January 1863 only to secure a replacement two months later. "My days of Soldiering have ended at least for a while," he wrote in his diary, prophetically as it turned out, since he was back in the ranks within a year.[55] When Gen. James H. Lane rejected Pvt. A. E. Shore's proposed substitute, he turned to his lieutenant, who promised to find him another man in exchange for "2.60 galons of Brandy & Whisky I want you to hold on to the Brandy & Whisky for it may be a Friend to me yet." The lieutenant failed; Shore was captured at Gettysburg.[56] Pvt. J. A. Patton of the 47th North Carolina asked his wife about hiring one, although he personally leaned against it, preferring to tough out his enlistment. Already reduced from sergeant to the rank of private, James Wilson's last letter before his death at Vicksburg detailed his hopes for finding a substitute.[57]

Cpl. Thomas J. Newberry of the 29th Mississippi meanwhile suggested substitutes for his father and underaged brother, who had been called into active service with the militia. He implored his father especially to secure a discharge or else find a substitute, "for you are not able to stand it for you can do more at home." Indeed, within a month, Newberry was trying to convince the brother to fill in for his father if no one else would.[58] Pvt. M. R. Norman of the 63rd Virginia likewise wondered if a relative should seek a substitute, while considering it himself. "If he gets eny boddy with him," Norman wrote his wife, "I want to no their name you must write their names to me if there is eny boddy that wants to fight so bad that is there if they will come out here they can get as much as they can."[59]

As the year passed and legislation tightened, men began to give up hope of securing permanent substitutes. One loophole remained, however. Men in the Army of Tennessee and in the Trans-Mississippi who could bring in a new recruit would at least receive a furlough. "Ould general brag has isued an order," Pvt. John W. Cotton wrote his wife in October 1863, "and says that he will give any man a 40 day furlow if he will recruit to his company." Cotton aimed his sights on "ould man kelly," writing his wife to tell Kelly that he would "do all I can for him if he does come . . . tell him he will never find a better regiment nor one that has more privilege." Kelly wanted more, however, namely $700 for a few months in the ranks.[60]

Although efforts to find substitutes were usually unsuccessful—Pvt. Abel Crawford of the 55th Alabama noted in December 1863 that "recruits you know are kind of scarce"—eleven of the men in the sample tried anyway, appealing to neighborhood boys and old men as well as relatives.[61] When Pvt. A. M. Sewell learned that a new recruit was on the way to the 39th Georgia, he asked his wife to catch the man and persuade him to "represent me as we live near each other & I can get a furlow on him."[62] Pvt. S. W. Farrow even tried to entice his brothers into the 19th Texas so that he could get a furlough. "I would not advise any one to go into the army if they can help it," he wrote his wife, "but if either of them would come a sixty days Furlough would be very acceptable." John T. Knight made a similar appeal to a relative.[63] As in other substitution transactions, money changed hands. Pvt. A. J. Edge was willing to pay a local man $50 to enlist; Pvt. Grant Taylor made an offer of $200; and Pvt. W. H. Tamplin promised $300. Drummer Tamplin added that other men in the 11th Texas were offering $500.[64]

PVT. JAMES MICHAEL BARR was yet another soldier who tried to find a temporary replacement in order to gain a furlough. Indeed, he admitted that he would like to find a permanent substitute were his unit sent to the active front in Tennessee from South Carolina. But at the same time, Barr realized that the practice was crippling the Confederate war effort, and he hoped that Congress would pass a law to force all the men who had hired substitutes to enter the army. "Oh, pity to the Seventy-five or Eighty Thousand who have substitutes," he wrote. "Why they would make us a pretty large Army, could guard some place I think pretty well and perhaps turn the invading Yankees. May the time come soon when they will all have to come out."[65] In the end, Barr, like most of the men discussed in this chapter, remained in the ranks. Even those who managed to get home sooner or later found themselves back in line, thanks to tougher Confederate legislation.

When all is said and done, Barr was right about the corrosive effects of substitution. As his comments demonstrate, substitution undermined confidence in the government and reinforced the notion of "rich man's war, poor man's fight." Of the men in the sample who sought substitutes, eight do not appear in the 1860 census. Of those who do, the majority, sixteen, were prosperous slaveholders, with a mean average of fifteen slaves and a median of eleven. The successful seekers of substitutes were all slave owners, men with the money required to hire a man to fight in their stead. The substitutes themselves, at least the ones who did eventually take up their muskets and fight, seem to have been wretchedly poor.

The evidence also tentatively confirms the government's conclusion that most substitutes never served in the army at all. While thirty-three men sought substitutes with varying degrees of diligence once in camp, only four were successful, and only six substitutes can be found in the survey results. For those who sought replacements, the hope of a substitute in the end seems to have been more of a safety valve and a morale booster than anything else, and perhaps as well a way to mollify worried loved ones at home.[66] Many of the successful clearly ended up back in uniform whatever their cash outlay for a substitute. For a few others—the brokers and newspapers that sold advertising space—it meant profit. For the Confederacy, it meant tens of thousands of men leaving the army without a real replacement. Barr was right; 70,000 additional men would have comprised a full field army the Confederacy desperately needed.

Other aspects of conscription were equally inadequate. Only twenty-eight men in the sample enlisted even in part for bounty money, suggesting that the lure of gain generally did not outweigh other causes. The vast majority of later-enlisting Confederates sampled for this study volunteered for other reasons, with ideology and hatred of the enemy providing more motivation and slavery proving more central still. Only seven of the Confederates surveyed were drafted; while an additional four clearly enlisted to escape the draft. Given the real numbers of draftees in Confederates service, their absence in the written record is striking. One is confronted by the looming shadow of a segment of Southern society, poor and illiterate, forced into the army without recourse and then lost to scholars who rely on traditional written records. To be sure, those incomplete records obscure the motivations of other men, dampening numbers, and we cannot know how many men enlisted with the draft in mind but never stated that to be the case.

Finally, even when bounties, substitution payments, or the draft did play a role, they should not be considered out of context. When soldiers accepted money to fight, it usually was out of need rather than greed. That is to say, soldiering for wages and bonuses, as well as avoiding or leaving military service, were simply other ways for certain men to provide for and defend their families. That role of family leader and defender was central to white Southern society. Conscription as well as voluntary enlistment thus were shaped by the needs of wives and children, dependents who needed monetary as well as physical protection during wartime. Unwillingly, even these men were fighting for their families and property.

PART III

"WE ARE A BAND OF BROTHERS AND NATIVE TO THE SOIL"

6

RELIGION

"LET US MEET IN HEAVEN"

Before the war, Capt. Joseph R. Manson of the 12th Virginia was a comfortable farmer and the owner of five slaves. A graduate of Randolph-Macon College, he also served on Sundays as a lay leader in his local Methodist church. Manson the soldier wrote little about religion, however, until after the Battle of Chancellorsville in May 1863, a struggle in which his regiment played a conspicuous and bloody role. Following the fight, the thirty-two-year-old officer emerged a changed man. He now fervently urged his wife to "pray to God to bless & preserve each other and prepare us for a better inheritance." The Almighty, he advised her, "can bring us safe through all the furnaces of affliction and will no doubt take us home at last." He also asked her to pray for an "end to this bloody war. . . . Surely we will be a better people after our heavy chastisement for our iniquities."[1]

In the aftermath of the Gettysburg campaign that followed, Manson wrote his mother a letter that ran along similar lines. He thanked God for allowing him to survive the battle, but wondered at His mercy. "I have frequently asked the question when I have seen men fall near me," he admitted, "why that ball, or that shell did not strike me. I feel God preserves me for some wise purpose perhaps," he went on, "and I hope for some good which I may be instrumental in accomplishing and I thank Him for it. Or it may be in answer to your prayers," he added. What now truly baffled him, he confessed, was how "wicked, profane and depraved" men without faith could go into battle and face death. It was only his hope of Heaven that allowed him to do so, he told his mother.[2]

By November 1863, such questions consumed him. He wrote his sister a long letter that month that briefly noted his new camp, his expectations of battle, the lack of potatoes, and his sadness that his "bad" son Ashby, age six, had knocked out a few teeth. But what Manson really wanted to discuss was their faith. His "continued prayer" was for peace, he wrote, but he knew that it would only come when the Southern population was sufficiently punished for its sins. For his part, it was the nearness of death in battle and a recent bout of dysentery that had forced him to adopt "a clearer and more heart piercing view of the grim monster." Nothing aided spirituality more than constant thoughts of death, he advised. The optimistic notion that death might be decades away was "a dangerous delusion of the Devil. . . . In this life I lead it is not surprising that I should think of a *sudden* death." He did not want to die, he admitted, "such are the claims of family & such the desires to complete my own unfinished plans in life," but that was in God's hands. He was a poor Christian, he added, "too cold and calloused," but despite his sins God had given him the grace to strive toward righteousness and now listened to his prayers. "I would like to feel that my example has done good to those who love me and would be influenced by my conduct," he added pointedly. Someday, if his loved ones followed suit and strove as hard as he labored for righteousness, all of them would meet in heaven. That would require more than mere church attendance, however, he warned, for even "good services" limited "proper zeal." Serious study of the Bible and other devotional writings was required, as were prayer and good works. In closing, he urged his sister to join him on the "heavenly road."[3]

Throughout the rest of the war, Manson remained obsessed with an almost mystical expression of Christianity. For sixteen months, from November 1863 until February 1865, he kept a "spiritual diary" that recorded his journey down the narrow path with God. Although he commanded troops at Petersburg the entire span, he rarely mentioned them or the war in his journal. To him all that was "a life of pain" best blocked out. Only once did he mention battle and the loss of two friends, although several alarms clearly reawakened his fears of death. Instead, the diary is full of constant praise of God, frequent self-loathing over what Manson perceived as his weak faith, and his longing for peace and home. Almost daily, except when resented duties interrupted, Manson retreated for hours into "secret prayer" and "secret communion" with God, praying for his family, an end to the conflict, and a heavenly afterlife where he would live eternally with his loved ones. Aside from a few references to Christian friends, in other words, Manson seems to have withdrawn entirely from his comrades. Indeed, only three times did he mention attending formal church services in camp, and he dismissed President Jefferson Davis's proclaimed day of fasting and humiliation on November 16 as a necessary exercise that nonetheless left him cold and typically worried about his piety.[4]

In his single-minded zeal and passionate pursuit of personal communion with God, Joseph Manson is an extreme example of how Confederates embraced Christianity during the war as a sustaining motivator. Yet at least in his practices and concerns, the Virginian provides a useful introduction to later-enlisting Confederates and their faith. Like Manson, many brought familiar practices of faith with them to camp but only experienced fervent spiritual rebirth after surviving battle. Moreover, like the pious captain, most remained emotionally connected to home, attempting to direct the spiritual paths of their loved ones in order to achieve a never-ending reunion in the afterlife. They prayed constantly for family members while simultaneously asking for more prayers in return. That inability to cut their emotional ties to family meant that most did not fully embrace the legendary camp revivals that characterized the Confederate army beginning in the winter of 1862–63, and instead practiced an almost solitary faith. Later-enlisting Confederate Christians on the whole were more likely soldiers who alone or in their messes studied their Bibles, said their prayers, and dreamed constantly of rejoining their loved ones, either in this world or the next. Indeed, their experiences vary so dramatically from the familiar revival trope that one must call the entire canon into question.[5]

"FAITH IN GOD," according to James I. Robertson, "became the single greatest institution in the maintenance of morale in the armies."[6] It would have been surprising had it not. Victorian America was steeped in Protestant Christianity. While perhaps fewer than 30 percent of Americans were formal church members in 1860, double that number regularly worshiped. As Drew Gilpin Faust points out, that meant that four times as many Americans worshiped on an average Sunday as voted in the 1860 presidential election. Even the most worldly Civil War soldiers grew up in a culture molded and supervised by a devout and powerful Protestant minority of believers that set the definitions of morality and respectability for the society as a whole. North and South increasingly diverged, however, as the war approached. Southerners' faith remained oriented toward personal salvation. It was evangelical, premillennial, conservative, and orthodox, expressed more often than not in Baptist and Methodist congregations, with the Presbyterians running a distant third. Most Northern churches fit the same description to be sure, but increasingly others aimed to redeem society as a whole through social action that would make the United States a more Christian nation. The South also had little of the utopianism and heterogeneous panorama of other 'isms'—notably abolitionism—that characterized vocal religious minorities up North. In regard to slavery, the Southern clergy simply considered the institution divinely ordained and the matter settled. Some did call for a more humane brand of slavery that protected families and allowed literacy, but most preachers proclaimed that politics were none of the church's business. Growing sectional schisms among church people over Christianity and slavery formally broke up the Baptist and Methodist churches into Northern and Southern bodies a decade and a half before the political nation followed suit.[7]

When secession did come, Civil War armies became, in James McPherson's words, "arguably, the most religious in American history."[8] Yet while most Billy Yanks were religious men, most scholars have maintained that Johnny Rebs trumped them in piety. Confederate nationalism, as discussed earlier, was built on openly Christian rhetoric. Patriotic ministers assured congregations that the Southern way of life, slavery included, was not only in accordance with the scriptures but indeed helped fulfill them. Freely borrowing from American exceptionalism and millennialism, Southern religious and political leaders increasingly maintained after Fort Sumter that the Confederacy in fact was the new Israel and its citizens the new chosen people.

Confederate soldiers did not comprise an army of Christian crusaders according to historians, however, not at first anyway. Doubters, backsliders, and vocal skeptics always comprised a significant portion of the Southern nation's military. Moreover, piety ebbed and flowed in the Confederate army along with campaigning, victory, and defeat. The first eighteen months of the war produced army camps that strayed far from resembling Christian communities. Freed from parental and societal expectations, soldiers anxious to assert their masculinity instead cut loose from their moral moorings. Drunkenness, gambling, profanity, and licentiousness became rampant in both armies, while pious soldiers sometimes found themselves a shunned minority, condemned as weaklings. Elisabeth Lauterbach Laskin suggests that even many of the devout embraced faith only as a way to combat homesickness by repeating comforting rituals connected to home. Chaplains who might have stemmed the moral breakdown of the Confederate army were in short supply, and the Southern religious establishment generally did not involve itself in military missions in fear of blurring the separation of church and state.[9]

Much of this had changed by the winter of 1862–63, however. Steven Woodworth powerfully asserts that the experience of combat and the nearness of death in the summer of 1862 drove scores of men back to their knees. Many went into the fight with their cards and liquor thrown aside, prayers on their lips, and a hopeful conviction that their lives were in the hands of Providence. Strict Calvinists could try to accept death in the field as part of God's infinitely wise plan, while Arminians hoped to sway Him with prayers and moral living—but both wanted assurance of a heavenly afterlife. And while Confederate victory may have been God's plan, most agreed that serving in His army did not erase the need for personal conversion and salvation. Thus, following the massive blood-letting and ultimate failures of the Maryland and Kentucky campaigns, and moreover fueled by an outpouring of Christian publications dispatched by worried Southern denominations, a massive revival broke out in winter encampments. Beginning in Stonewall Jackson's II Corps of Lee's Army of Northern Virginia and then spreading westward across the Mississippi, Sunday services, prayer meetings, hymn singing, and baptisms grew increasingly common as men enthusiastically dedicated themselves to Christ. Soldiers east of the Mississippi River formed nondenominational Christian associations that provided not only fellowship and support, but also attempted to clean up camp life and shame sinners. Trans-Mississippi soldiers established their own nondenominational sect. Meanwhile, the Confederate cause basked in the aura of a holy crusade, complete with national fast days and celebrations of thanksgiving.

The summer campaign season of 1863 interrupted the military awakening, but during the following winter, revival flared back up to new heights. Most Confederate generals and officers openly supported the revival, and a few commanders actually were baptized themselves. Prominent divines descended upon camps. The vicious, constant fighting of 1864 that culminated in the trenches of Petersburg and the debacles at Franklin and Nashville halted the revival, and the last months of the war according to most historians witnessed considerable backsliding. Nonetheless, throughout the rest of the war and especially at critical moments following significant defeats, piety and a more generalized Christian morality sustained the average Confederate soldier.[10] "It may not be an exaggeration," McPherson concludes, "to say that the revivals of 1863–64 enabled Confederate armies to prolong the war into 1865."[11] Until the bitter end, many Confederates remained convinced that God surely favored them and would bring them a triumph once the Confederate nation had repented of its collective individual sins, notably greed and impiety. Christian theology easily explained their suffering and defeats as the chastening discipline necessary before victory. Presidential days of fasting and repentance meanwhile reinforced the soldiers' tendency to continue to equate the Confederacy with the divine order and their military service as service to God. Accordingly, at least the "diehard rebels" Jason Phillips describes expected God to deliver a miraculous, Old Testament victory as long as even a single dim ray of hope remained. Nothing sustained soldiers more than faith.[12]

THE SPIRITUAL ARC most Confederate soldiers allegedly took during the war is familiar, but how did later-enlisting Confederates fit into the path? Not comfortably, in fact. Many of them to be sure were at least some of the time, if not throughout the war, religious men. Of men in the sample, 122 (38 percent) discussed religion in their writings at least one time, most of them considerably more than once. Their reluctance to enlist in 1861 also meant that arriving in camp at last inserted them into a military pilgrim's journey already in progress. Only a handful of religious men who came to the army in 1862 thus found and condemned the much-discussed dissipation and sin of the early war period. Pvt. E. A. Penick was one. He complained of "disipation and digridation."[13] Pvt. William A. Collins of the 48th North Carolina likewise wrote his minister from nearby Petersburg that

"Old Satan" was active in his camp, "trying his wily arts and power to entangle men by his deceitful and cunning tricks and sorry am I to say that he has at this time many poor souls . . . laboring in his service."[14] Farther west, Pvt. W. J. Peel of the 1st Arkansas Mounted Rifles described his comrades as drunkards, gamblers, and overall "a set of 'not men' but Devils. with red noses and blackened eyes, raged and out of money . . . this class of men is not fit for the army or any place else."[15]

Sgt. Thomas C. Smith of the 32nd Texas Cavalry also condemned the vices of his company's camp as vehemently as any man could. Gambling was rampant, he lamented. "Some 3 or 4 propose a game at cards *just for amusement*," he recorded in his diary in September 1862. "The game commences and soon they wish to play for something, say 25 cents to make it interesting. . . . Spectators soon get interested and they propose a game, so soon the whole camp is taken up. . . . Thus we see the Young man who has been brought up in a different way is led off step by step and he is almost a confirmed Gambler." Worse yet were the "horrid oaths calling upon God to send their Soul to hell, etc, etc. while others use all sorts of Vulgarity Blackguard talk, which *sickens me at once*. Oh! How can I withstand all?" he wondered.[16] Cpl. Friedrich Niebuhr, a young German-speaking Texan, expressed similar disgust once his unit, Waul's Texas Legion, took to the field. "Here you hear nothing but cursing and swearing," he lamented to his parents. "All Christendom seems to have disappeared even with those where you would believe it the least. Since we left Grenada, you don't hear any sermons any more. You don't know when it's Sunday. It is a sorrowful time."[17]

What is most important about these jeremiads is how rare they are. Among the fifty-three later-enlisting soldiers in the sample who discussed religion at any point in 1862, complaints about sinful fellow soldiers were the exception rather than the rule. Much of the discussed wickedness and wildness, if it existed at all, apparently had already subsided by the time many of the new recruits started arriving in camp. Pious later-enlisting Confederates were more likely instead to complain about the absence of religion caused by the war instead of about outright sin. Military routines and active campaigning simply meant that soldiers like Niebuhr or the men of the 3rd Tennessee Cavalry "never know when sunday comes."[18] Yet even then, the worst already had passed. As Woodworth demonstrates, most soldiers by 1862 had access to Bibles, although, as Pvt. Jesse Battle complained, "I think it is very little used in camp as a general thing." Religious tracts circulated as well. More to the point, preaching generally was available in town or camp. That not all took part was due in part to lack of interest, but also to military necessity. Battle, a faithful man and regular reader of scripture, admitted, "I have not heard but two sermons since I have been in camp. I believe there is preaching in Camp Lee every Sunday evening," he added, "but in consequence of my being in the city on guard for three Sundays past, I have not been able to attend."[19]

Other men did enjoy services in the first half of the year. On the eve of the Seven Days Battles, Joseph Kauffman, a private in the 10th Virginia of Jackson's corps, described a June weekend of preaching in camp that featured the general's chief of staff, theologian Robert Dabney. The men reassembled on Sunday evening for holy communion, which Jackson received along with the rest.[20] Pvt. William A. Collins wrote from Petersburg a few days later that his unit had preaching every Sunday, reporting on "as touching a sermon as I ever heard it was indeed affecting to see the tears rolled down brawny cheeks of the soldiers as they sat around the ground." He attributed his survival after a Federal bombardment to the Almighty. "God certainly was with us to preserve us," he wrote his minister.[21]

Western soldiers reported the same. From Mobile, Pvt. Grant Taylor discussed prayer meetings, critiqued the Methodist minister who preached to his unit, and described a revival that began in mid-July. Hospitalized in Dalton, Georgia, Pvt. J. H. Lee related how a nearby Methodist quarterly meeting attracted soldiers and brought ministers to his facility. The 35th Mississippi's James Wilson wrote in May that he "went to church & herd an excellent sermon."[22] The Shibley brothers, serving in the 22nd Arkansas, described a service led by a minister from a nearby town. "His text was the first chapter of John and 29th verse, 'behold the Lamb of God, which taketh away the sin of the world.' He did tolerably well," the brothers added, "some parts however were rendered rather curious."[23] The Shibleys' confusion may have been due to listening to a clergyman from a different denomination, which was nonetheless a common occurrence before and during the war. Others did the same. "I went to meeting las Sunday," the Primitive Baptist John W. Cotton wrote approvingly, "and I herd the roman catholieks and presbyterians both preach and we had meeting at our camp that night."[24] When services were not available at all, many men clamored for them. "Tell John to come down and preach for us," Pvt. G. H. Burns wrote his wife. "I never saw people so keen to hear preaching."[25]

Later-enlisting Confederates, in short, encountered a camp experience that already was in the process of evolving away from the notorious bacchanalia of 1861. What they now added to the mix was a pronounced family orientation that kept them mentally and spiritually connected to home while simultaneously undermining to an extent the cohesion between pious soldiers in camp.[26]

Some new recruits, anxious about their families, essentially had left God in charge to protect them.[27] "God will protect us all," Pvt. J. M. Davidson of the 39th North Carolina wrote his wife, "if we only put our trust in him I may be slain in Battlle. . . . but I trust in God."[28] Likewise, the former seminarian William S. Lacy wrote his mother that he thanked God for his family and that "he has shielded me thus far & he can if he will carry me thro."[29] The 38th Virginia's Pvt. E. A. Penick agreed, reminding his wife not to "forget that you and the dear children are in the Hands of a kind father Protection who will support purity though all the trials of life."[30]

Penick's admonition to his spouse to remain pure is significant if relatively commonplace. Husbands and fathers of the era, and not just later enlisters, were not only the household's political actors and economic decision makers, as discussed in a previous chapter. They functioned as well as spiritual leaders. Family worship, centered on daily prayers and Bible readings, were an integral part of the pious antebellum household. Married soldiers gave up that leadership with difficulty. Thus they not only attempted to run their farms from a distance through wives and middlemen, as discussed in Chapter 3, but also tried to continue directing their families' private spiritual lives.[31] "You must write me word," Pvt. Elijah Odom of the 35th Alabama asked his wife, "if you have obeyed the Gospel of Our Lord & Savior Jesus Christ, I often wish I was with my family to lead in family worship."[32] Learning of his son's baptism, Sgt. Edwin Fay mandated "a careful observance of the Sabbath. Do try and interest Will Ed on Sunday by reading or telling him religious stories. Try and teach him that it is wrong to play on the Sabbath."[33] Pvt. Miles Lewis of the 22nd Georgia also tried to provide his child with religious instruction of the most basic kind. "Tell Mary the good man take care of her Pa," he wrote "& if he lets him live he will come home some day." Unlike Fay, Lewis praised his wife for her efforts, writing, "I was very glad to hear you pray with the children often . . . and that you enjoy religion so well it does me more good than anything else."[34]

Soldiers likewise encouraged their wives to worship publically at church. To be sure, Pvt. Jesse C. Knight of the 50th Georgia emphasized the pleasurable social aspects of churchgoing, "to go a bout and see the people and be in company."[35] But thanking God for protecting him since he left home, a pious Jesse Battle wrote his wife that "your meeting will commence next Friday, How I would like to be there. I feel like there will be a good meeting at Old Bethesda this year. I hope there will at least be you, and the children must go and enjoy it, that's a privilege I can't enjoy here."[36] Ward master J. W. Griffin meanwhile expressed happiness that his wife's meeting had proven successful.[37]

Pvt. Henry T. Morgan of the 31st Louisiana, however, expressed outrage at his wife's independent decision to leave his Methodist church and become a Baptist. "Ellen," he bitterly wrote, "i was perfectly thunder struck when I heered that you had joined the baptist and i havent got over it yet. . . . You said that you wished that i was at home to join the church. Have you forgotten that I belong to the Methodis? Or do you call that a church? You have woonded my fealings very much in the way you have acted. . . . I wouldnt give one Methodid church fore every Baptist church in the universe." For Morgan, however, the bottom line involved his children's worship. "Don't make baptist of the children untill i come home, if you please," he begged. "Let me have one Methodis now in that little flock." A month later, his wife's apparent betrayal, coupled with a lack of additional letters from home, still stung. "The ware and the Baptist and the sickness is a nuff to make a man go crazy that don't have fare to go no how," he worried, "as i am one of that class. Don't be astonished if i go that road." The letter that finally came did little to reverse his perceived course toward madness. "You gave my church a great rekmendation in your last letter," he complained. "You said that you dident belive ther was but one church. Then you don't believe that the Methodid has any church at all. You are a hard case i am fraid, but," he added finally forgivingly, "who woodnat praise their own church."[38]

Such a personal rebellion as Ellen Morgan's was rare, however. The most common admonition to relatives simply was to pray. Pious soldiers prayed themselves, of course, for their families, and for their own survival. Serving near Savannah, the 63rd Georgia's Pvt. J. C. Williams credited prayer with the Federal navy's decision to shell another part of the coast.[39] "I pray for you when I pray for my self," Pvt. G. H. Burns wrote his wife. "I go in my tent and pray to the Lord to hold me in his arms and do with me then I pray for you that the lord would give you grace to bear your troubles & be a husband to you till I get back."[40] Pvt. E. B. Coggin prayed "that the lord may Stand By you and my children in sickness and in helth and that he may bee with you all thrugh the journy of life."[41] Pvt. Grant Taylor prayed both to survive the war and to accept God's will if he did not. He admitted that he found it difficult to pray in camp. "I try to pray," he reported, "but one has a poor chance to hold communion with his Maker here when he can scarcely get to be alone a minute and on every side hear oaths of the most horrid kind mixed up in every conversation."[42]

Georgia gunner Jesse Battle meanwhile sent his wife the words to "Another Day of Soldier Life," which he found in "a little him book" distributed to soldiers entitled *Hymns for the Camp*. Two stanzas referred specifically to prayer:

> Thy grace, O God, hath kept us whole;
> To thee we lift our praise;
> Accept the homage of each soul,
> And keep us all our days.
>
> Keep us in safety through the night,
> And with us those we love:
> Save us, we pray thee, by thy might,
> In battle and above.[43]

When soldiers wrote about prayer, however, it usually was in the role of leader of family worship. From that traditional household pulpit, they encouraged their loved ones to pray properly. Some wanted prayers of victory and peace. To Sgt. John French White, prayer was a way for his wife to fight for the Confederacy, "as you can wield no other weapon for the Sunny South."[44] Sgt. Edwin Fay wrote that Christians at home had to pray "that this horrid war may be speedily closed."[45] John F. Davenport of the Alabama Legion similarly asked his wife to "put your trust in god and ask him to be with our armes and then *rest satisfide* that he will do for the best."[46] Capt. Robert Dickinson of the 21st South Carolina placed the outcome of the war squarely on the shoulders of civilians in prayer, but doubted that they would respond appropriately. "Morality is fast losing its influence upon society especially the city," he complained. "Religion is not spoken of at all by any in a sincere manner, and yet it is said that this war rests upon the god of battles if our country christians don't pray very hard I don't know what will become of the soldiers and the destinies of this once glorious land." The only hope, "in a providential point of view, is the Northern people being more wicked than we are."[47]

Cpl. Friedrich Niebuhr similarly placed the onus of victory or defeat on the actions of civilians. "May God help us and soon bring this war to an end," he wrote in October from Mississippi, "so that all may return home again. Pray for that, and when enough people will do that, and are God-inspired, then peace will come again." A few weeks later, he expanded on his theme. "If only the hearts of men would turn to God," he wrote, "and become converted to God, then I believe peace would come soon—Pray hard for it."[48]

Just as many soldiers, however, asked loved ones to pray for them person-ally. "Never cease to pray to Almighty God that he may keep us from all harm," Pvt. William A. Collins wrote his father.[49] "Hole out faithful," Pvt. Miles Lewis wrote, "live for God, pray for me."[50] Pvt. E. B. Coggin asked his wife "to pray to the lord that he may guide you when you Do rong."[51] Sgt. Edwin Fay asked that his wife and son not "forget his father in his prayers, for I don't believe a bullet can go through a prayer and it is a much better shield than the steel armor with which Oliver says many Yankees were clad."[52] Grant Taylor enlisted his entire hometown church. He asked his wife to "continue to pray for me. Tell the brethren to pray for me at their prayer meetings. I have great faith in the efficacy of your prayers. If you see Brother Smith tell him howdy and tell him to remember me in his prayers."[53]

Requests for prayers and admonitions to wives and children to lead good Christian lives both pointed to an ultimate object that soldiers grasped hold of from the moment of their enlistment. Sickness in camp and battlefield casualties constantly reminded men that death could be imminent. No matter the number or fervency of prayers, most admitted that they still might die if that death was consistent with God's providential plan. Faced with the real possibility of never getting home, of never seeing loved ones again, pious soldiers increasingly fixated on the world to come as a new and better home, a place for a family reunion that could not be blocked except through a refusal to follow Christ.

Resurrection and the heavenly afterlife, of course, always had been a central tenet of Christianity. The Apostle's Creed, which dates to the early centuries of Christianity, ends with expressions of belief in "the resurrection of the body and life everlasting." Beginning in the mid-eighteenth century, however, Americans increasingly began to imagine heaven not as a myste-rious unworldly place but rather a better version of the life they already knew, a realm just above the clouds where loved ones lived together as families and active souls housed in corporal bodies reached perfection in the absence of work, pain, and death. Dozens of books appeared after 1830 that made this view of heaven common if not universal. As a result, mid-century American Christians expected to live in heaven not in ethereal angel bands but in their Victorian, racially segregated, nuclear family units, just as they did on earth.[54]

This was the domestic vision that shaped Confederate soldiers' notions of the afterlife, a perfected vision of homes they knew and from which they could never again be "parted" by war. What the reality of life and death in uniform added was a new immediacy. Pvt. G. H. Burns, for example, wrote often of his faith, his prayers, and his trust in God. It was only after his brother died in camp of measles, however, that he began to think of "the morning of the great day when I will see him not as I saw him last pale and cold but dressed in a white robe, praising god forever & ever." They would not be alone. "I hope the day will come," he wrote his wife, "when we will all meet if not on earth high up in heaven where my dear brother is gone."[55]

"Let us meet in heaven" became the dominant cliché, and it grew pronounced in the late summer of 1862 as soldiers confronted the possibility of never returning to their earthly homes. "We must trust in providence and tri to meet in heven if we meet on earth no more," Pvt. A. J. Edge wrote his wife.[56] "I want to meet you all in haven whear wares and fightings will be ore," John F. Davenport wrote from Cumberland Gap, "whear wives and husbands part no more, whear parance and children each other greete, wheare all is joy and plesure sweat."[57] On the way to the Virginia front, Pvt. William P. Cline told his wife, "if we don't never meeat in did world i hope to mean you in a beter world but i wod like to see you all wontz more if i don't i wont you to remember mez on till deth."[58]

A heavenly reunion, however, required faithfulness on the part of all concerned. If one partner rejected salvation, eternity together would prove impossible. Thus men encouraged wives to be faithful, to pray, to attend church, to raise up the children as Christians, all toward the end of being together forever in the next world. When his unit was sent to Virginia in mid-July, Pvt. Richard Henry Brooks wrote his wife that "the Chance for us to meet again in this life is very Slim yet time may bring us together once more. Should we never meet on earth again let us try to meet in a better world than this. . . . I will try to Live the best I can." An immediate effect was that the soldier gave up alcohol. In the meantime, his wife needed to make sure the children attended church regularly.[59] Capt. Robert Dickinson meanwhile reminded his wife that the final decision to allow a reunion was God's. While he expected to be with her in paradise, "I may be mistaken, we will leave it for him to decide."[60]

THE CONCLUSIONS OF THE campaigns of 1862 coincided with the real beginnings of religious revival in Confederate camps. Rev. Francis Milton Kennedy, the young regimental chaplain of the 28th North Carolina starting in January 1863, left a busy record of sermons and prayer meetings, not to mention the distribution of tracts, visits to the sick and wounded, and gatherings of fellow divines. The revival, especially in the West, included some late enlisters among the fold. "We have had some good preaching here in our camps of late," the 34th Alabama's Pvt. Thomas Warrick wrote from Tennessee. "One was baptised yesterday morning by a missionary from Montgomery Ala and 3 were baptised last night by a Campbellite preacher."[61] From Kentucky four days after the Battle of Perryville, Lt. J. M. Davidson "heard an excellent sermon" and "felt the force of the prayer and responded Amen!" A few weeks later, writing from Tennessee in anticipation of combat, Davidson added that he read his Bible "a good deal" and prayed "for wisdom & understanding to better prepare myself for an exit into eternity at any time. I know I am not what I would wish to be," he added, "a good Christian but I Pray to God to enlight my mind and make me what I should be."[62]

Yet, in retrospect, surprisingly few later enlisters in the sample seem to have taken part in the legendary revival. Most of them in fact did not report participating in the prayer meetings and services that characterized the camp revival, a finding that in itself opens real questions about that event's full extent and depth, as well as scholars' tendency to see it as the only form of soldier piety. Those who did generally participate, moreover, did so only in the spring of 1863, right on the eve of the campaign season. Through the winter that preceded it, even the most religious men among later enlisters instead preferred to continue along as they had before, maintaining their closest emotional and religious links to the folks at home, sharing their religious thoughts and hopes in letters with wives and parents, and praying for an ultimate family reunion that involved, in J. M. Davidson's words, "the same undivided little Family that God has given me on earth."[63] Sgt. John French White of the 32nd Virginia likewise lodged his faith at home. After the Maryland Campaign and the deaths of two of his brothers, he promised that when he came home he would "call around our little family alter our little family in prayer & praise as an acknowledgment of our thankfulness and gratitude." He added in passing that a regimental chaplain finally had come, and that prayer meetings as well as preaching had followed, yet he remained lonely. Notably, he did not offer his prayer of thanksgiving in camp, but rather kept it as something for home.[64]

On guard duty at the end of November, Pvt. Grant Taylor meanwhile listened to soldiers "profaning the sacred name of God as though they never had to appear at the judgment seat of Christ. . . . I turned from this babel of confusion and thought of home my dear earthly home and the dear ones I left behind perhaps never more to behold them again in Eternity." Taylor drew hope from contemplating the night sky, "where my Blessed Savior reigns. . . . that sweet home where I hope to safely arrive one day, and where I hope to meet you my dearest earthy friend." Later that winter, after a bout of typhoid fever, he admitted that only the existence of his wife and children caused him to want to remain living.[65]

Such men continued to try and direct their families' spiritual lives from the field. Pvt. William Ross Stilwell told his wife that it was time to begin teaching their son to pray, and that she should join the church and have the boy baptized. John W. Cotton not only encouraged his wife to attend church but also forbade a funeral for his daughter until he came home.[66] Just as in farming and financial matters, however, at least a few had to acknowledge their wives' rough equality. Pvt. Henry Morgan's wife, Ellen, for example, stepped up her unsuccessful efforts to win her Methodist husband to the Baptist faith; while Lt. J. M. Davidson notably entered into an informal contract his wife drew up "in us both setting out a fresh for Zion."[67]

For older, married men such as these, army prayer meetings and camp preaching proved at best a poor substitute for worship at home with loved ones, or even in a real church in town. In January 1863, Pvt. Elijah Odom sent home a letter decorated with drawings of the Bible, the Ten Commandments, and the Lamb of God, as well as a scroll bearing the names of his eight children. He wrote that he had been to preaching several times in Jackson, Mississippi, but then turned quickly to his wish to worship instead with his family at home and his hopes that his wife would join a church.[68]

Other men shunned the revival meetings. A lonely Cpl. Friedrich Niebuhr wrote his family that he prayed alone every evening, imagining that his loved ones were doing the same. "Here one often might despair but what help would that be?" he wondered. "If I did not know that so many pray for me and continue to do so, oh, then I would be overcome."[69] Sgt. Edwin Fay

Elijah Odom's letter of "Lords day," January 11, 1863, was written from a hospital in Jackson, Mississippi. The hand-drawn illustration depicts Christian images linked to the names of his wife and children. Odom enlisted in the 35th Alabama largely for the bounty, spent much of the war seeking a way out of the army, and found solace in his faith. He was captured at Vicksburg. Photograph courtesy Mississippi Department of Archives and History, Jackson, B1/R75/B1/56.

also preferred to worship alone and claimed that the revival of faith he experienced after the doubting and anger following his son's death grew out of his own private Bible readings and conversations about predestination with a single comrade. The two Shibley brothers, concerned for their parents after a Federal raid, turned to each other and adopted a paraphrased version Psalm 46 as their bulwark.[70] Private devotions were especially important to men such as the 18th Alabama's James Lanning who believed themselves surrounded by ungodly men. "Boys playing cards while I read the Bible," he recorded in his diary, "these are evil days—may God help us."[71] Pvt. E. K. Flournoy credited not the revival but the wickedness in camp for convincing him to give up smoking and cursing. "I never cared anything about preaching," he admitted, "but there is so much wickedness here that I have become disgusted and turned for the better. I intend to belong to the church when I come home."[72]

A few other soldiers shied away from the revival because of those leading it. A lack of chaplains contributed in some cases. Cpl. A. G. Jones of the 5th North Carolina Cavalry wrote that his regiment had no chaplain and heard its sermons from their major, a Presbyterian layman. When the chaplain of the 34th Georgia went home in February 1863, Pvt. G. H. Burns suggested that a friend might come to replace him. But others could not lay aside their denominationalism. Near Mobile, for example, Lt. John Meriwether wanted little to do with a "Parson . . . preaching his Methodism at a shouting voice to the soldiers under a large arbor made expressly for the purpose."[73] Catholics such as Lt. John Dooley felt left out as well. While he admired the sincerity and power of the revival in the Army of Northern Virginia, he nonetheless dismissed the entire affair with mild condescension, viewing it as something chaplains cooked up to sway rough, untutored farmers. His fellow soldiers in the 1st Virginia, he added, were in contrast far too urbane to give up their secular amusements to please a Methodist chaplain who soon would abandon them anyhow for the safety of home.[74]

Then there were those who simply felt unworthy to participate due to unspoken sins. Sgt. Maj. Marion Hill Fitzpatrick, for example, had asked his wife for prayers since entering the army, but only after the Second Battle of Manassas began to worry that he had strayed from the true path to salvation. God had spared his life, the soldier wrote, but he feared that "I am not as thankful as I ought to be. . . . I have wandered far from the path of duty as a Christian, and am often troubled about it." Months later, he continued to struggle. After the Battle of Fredericksburg, he reported that three comrades had joined the church, but "as to my part I have gone entirely wild and if I ever get back I shall have my name taken of the church book for it is a shame and disgrace to the cause of Christ for it to be there. But the Lord has spared my life so far for some purpose I know not what."[75]

As spring passed and summer arrived, and with it marching and fighting, some later enlisters did throw themselves at last into the now-waning camp revival. Fitzpatrick was one. "We have preaching every night and Sunday," he wrote. "Several have joined the church."[76] As late as the march to Gettysburg, the 53rd North Carolina's Lt. James E. Green wrote: "12 or 13 men belonging to Ramseur's Brigade was Baptized. it is the first Soldiers I have seen Baptized since I've been in service." Later, at the end of August, he enjoyed his first communion service while in the army."[77] Similar activities occurred in the West. From Tennessee, Lt. J. M. Davidson described "a great feeling pervading our camp with the soldiers crying, 'Oh Lord what must I do to be saved?' We have regular prayer meetings," he added, and preaching as well. "I can give you this assurance of my hope of heaven," he told his wife, "that I love Christ and his disciples and that I hate sin. I love to go to church and be with Christians which is evidence that I am not altogether lost."[78] Farther west, the Shibley brothers reported preaching and "a slight revival of religion in progress in our brigade," which they hoped would counteract "the wickedness" of an army "greatly contaminated by our stay at Little Rock."[79]

But others still continued to merely observe from the sidelines. From Fredericksburg at the end of May, Lt. John Hosford of the 5th Florida wrote home while his comrades attended preaching. "It is sublime to visit one of our humble Churches," he wrote. "We have no music save of vocal and that consists of our men's voices who has been exposed to all the dews of heaven and cold till it is somewhat hoarse and harsh." Yet Hosford skipped the service himself.[80] Lt. William Ross Stilwell meanwhile described "considerable religious feeling in the army. Last Sunday we had preaching in our regiment; and there were about thirty or forty members. . . . We have a chaplain by the name of Toy, but he can't preach much." A few days later, the former Episcopal clergyman and now general William Nelson Pendleton preached, Stilwell reported, and "there were eleven baptized."[81]

In general, later-enlisting Confederates maintained their lack of interest in camp services—when they occurred at all—through the summer of 1863. They remained oriented toward home and focused on a personal relationship with God. Men who prayed did so on their own, just as they read their Bibles. They attended local churches when possible but above all continued to impress upon their families the necessity of faithful living if they were ever to meet again.[82] After the fall of Vicksburg, for example, a despondent Pvt. A. J. Edge of the 52nd Georgia wrote his wife that he had "nothing else to studey about but you and abute dying that is all. . . . I hope god will give Me faith to baire all ove it and I hope that all ove us will Meat one this urth on time More."[83] Pvt. S. W. Farrow admitted that he washed his clothing during part of "the first preaching I have heard in twelve months" because he had acquired soap, and he asked his wife to forgive him.[84]

In the end, spiritually minded later-enlisting Confederates offered a variety of excuses and complaints to explain why they did not participate generally in the army revival of 1862–63, but most of them involved home. Newer to the field than more veteran comrades and often not serving in the most active theaters, later enlisters still hesitated to let go of the spiritual center their homes had recently provided. They also found the spiritual atmosphere of the camp wanting when compared to the idealized Sabbaths and deeply missed family gatherings they had left behind. Sinful comrades, allegedly half-hearted chaplains who lacked the commitment or courage to tough out army life, and a general malaise about service stood as obvious roadblocks to embracing the awakening launched by the veterans. What most required was what the veterans already had experienced: more desperate trials on the battlefield.

IN AUGUST, PVT. ISAAC BARINEAU of the 8th Florida wrote from Virginia with the sad news of a friend's death. His "one consolation" was that "his soul is in Heaven." He begged his wife to live so that they might meet there as well one day. "All of my mess is doing this as near as they know how," he added, "to reach that happy place where there will be no more war, I do hope and pray that if we are not permitted to meet you all on earth again we will be permitted to meet in heaven where we will part no more."[85] While the sentiments were familiar, there was a significant change. Barineau expected to meet not only his kin in heaven, but his army comrades as well. They had in a sense, become family too. While few later enlisters went as far as the Floridian did, many were changed nonetheless. In the aftermath of the fighting at Gettysburg and Vicksburg, losses that even shook men serving elsewhere, more and more later enlisters like Barineau began to describe their participation in a new, more fervent round of camp-based prayer meetings and services. The great army revival of 1863–64 had begun, and this time many more later enlisters were among the throng.

Lt. J. M. Davidson described the revival in his camp, explaining that "a great many men are seeking religion, the mourners bench is crowded."[86] Pvt. J. F. Coghill received a letter from his wife describing revivals at home and responded that "a revival is going on here amongst our soldiers. A good meny have been converted the meeting are still going on."[87] Pvt. William Ross Stilwell similarly described meetings taking place "most every day." He added, "I attend preaching most every day and prayer meeting every night." Within weeks, he was speaking at meetings, testifying to his "unshaken" faith.[88]

The revival to an extent now superseded denominational rivalries. The young minister William S. Lacy, newly appointed chaplain to the 47th North Carolina, complained that the regiment contained not one fellow Presbyterian. Adding that a Methodist preacher was conducting a protracted meeting nearby, Lacy admitted, "I never attended one before and it is hard for me to know what to do. I cant fully approve of his Methodist machinery," Lacy added, "but there is so much interest in the different Regiments and in mine that I have to throw myself with the current. I hope much good may be done even with the means."[89]

Soldiers appreciated the ecumenical sentiment. The 43rd North Carolina's Capt. Ruffin Barnes admitted that he had been "concerned about the Salvation of my Soul pretty much since I left home," but only acted when "our Preacher . . . saw my condition & I told him how I had been disturbed about the welfare of my soul. He said he knew there was a great change in me after talking with me awhile. He told me I ought to connect myself with some Christian Church. I told him I preferred Joining the Methodist Church & I joined the Church the 3d day of August & was baptized last Sunday." He was not alone. "The soldiers all seem to be taking a great deal more interest in going to hear Preaching than they have done," he wrote. "Our Chaplain has been Preaching to our regt. every night for two weeks. A great many have become very Serious on the Subject of Religion since he has been Preaching so much."[90]

Some soldiers attributed the revival to traditional causes, namely the moving of the Holy Spirit and the stirrings in their own souls. A few others referred to the more earthly actions of loved ones. T. T. Hoskins of the 9th Virginia Cavalry, for example, noted the revival going on in his regiment but acknowledged his mother as the one who had encouraged him to read his Bible daily.[91] More, however, consciously or subconsciously pointed to battle and its wake. Seriously wounded at Gettysburg, Sgt. John William Watson turned to God after concluding that he would not survive the war. "There is a revival going on richmond," he told his wife. "I have been to church 4 times sence it comence and I want to go tonight if nothing prevents." By late October he was attending church "3 or 4 times every week and twice Sunday." In the midst of frenzied worship, however, he repeated a familiar refrain. Adamant that his loved ones join him in the Promised Land, he asked his wife to "strive to enter in at the strait gate so that if should never meet in earth that we may meet in heaven."[92]

Men in Virginia had already experienced the great part of their fighting for the year, but elsewhere the killing and dying continued. From the battlefield at Chickamauga, Pvt. A. M. Sewell asked for prayers and expressed hope that he would meet his wife in heaven.[93] Stationed nearby, Pvt. G. H. Burns wrote of the "preaching every day and night I can set hear and hear two and three preachers preaching at once."[94] Captured at Vicksburg, Pvt. Grant Taylor was exchanged and returned to the Army of Tennessee in October to find "a great revival going on here and has been for several weeks. There is preaching every night and from 50 to 100 mourners. They say that 190 have joined the different denominations." Taylor yearned to take part, and he went to hear preaching nightly. Yet he admitted, "I feel very cold and distant most of the time. I sometimes feel almost crazy." In November, his 40th Alabama was stationed on Lookout Mountain, "a dangerous position." His response was to ask for prayers.[95] Nearby on Missionary Ridge, James Lanning had worried for weeks that marching on the Sabbath would bring disaster to the Confederacy. Now he concluded after studying the books of Daniel and Revelations that the end of the world was exactly eight years away.[96] Fighting continued on the South Carolina coast as well, and there too revival flared up in November, involving the by now usual occurrences of preaching and baptisms.[97]

Yet for later enlisters at least, the revival did not roll on through the winter like a mighty stream. Indeed, for all Confederates, it seems to have been a more sporadic affair than some texts suggest. December brought an official day of fasting and prayer, yet Lt. James Green recorded in his diary that by then "some keeps it, but a grate many pays no attention to it."[98] In fact, a harsh winter and the coming of another Christmas season away from home all seemingly placed a sudden damper on the revival as a whole. In

Virginia, Chaplain Francis Milton Kennedy of the 28th North Carolina recorded in his diary that he had led or at least participated in nine services in September and five in October, but over the next three months he noted only six more. Once more, the thoughts of men squeezed together in tiny shanties drifted toward loved ones. Instead of large meetings, soldiers instead reported small Bible studies and nostalgic thoughts of holidays past. On Christmas Day itself, Capt. Thomas Key worried that his children had no presents from Santa Claus,[99] while a homesick and depressed J. W. Griffin, the ward master now himself a patient in a Richmond hospital, described his life as a "burden" and expressed hope to meet his family in heaven.[100]

January passed similarly, and large-scale services only resumed the following month as winter finally began to wane. In Virginia, Lt. James Green's 53rd North Carolina constructed a "chapel" for their services.[101] Revival flared up again in the Army of Tennessee as well as in James Longstreet's detached force, spending a miserable winter in East Tennessee. Pvt. G. H. Burns described "plenty of preaching" in Dalton, Georgia; while Sgt. John Crittenden reported "a good deal of interest is now taken in religious matters."[102] Pvt. Hiram Smith Williams, also writing from Dalton, bitterly condemned his commanders for requiring duties that violated the Sabbath. Sunday, he complained, "is now passed by our military rulers here in inspecting the soldiers, at least the better part of it." Williams contrasted the usual Sunday routine with a presidential day of fasting and prayer that had occurred on April 8. "Strict orders were issued for all soldiers to observe it faithfully," Williams observed. "No work, no duties to be performed and all were requested to 'Fast' during the day or until four o' clock P.M." The actual fasting, he continued, was "the subject of much ridicule by the boys who *fast* every day," yet the observance "was religiously observed throughout the army." Yet Williams drew a subversive moral. "Now who has been the most power and who is more readily obeyed," he asked rhetorically, "the Creator of the world or the President of the Confederacy? What consistency. What faithful obedience to the powers that be."[103]

Although he prayed fervently for victory and peace, Capt. Thomas Key agreed with Williams that hungry "soldiers did not fast much, if any, more than usual, for rations are so scarce that they contend it is a fast all the time."[104] Pvt. William Ross Stilwell, serving under Longstreet, found it more difficult to take part: "I don't feel the same solemn obligations as in days gone by. I suppose the reason is that fast days come so often with me of late that I can't feel right." Yet in the end, Stilwell fasted as well.[105] He was not alone. Elsewhere in the West, the revival gathered steam and reached a climax at the end of April, when battle once again beckoned. In the Army of Tennessee, soldiers reported nightly sermons that reminded Thomas Key of the camp meetings of his youth. Sgt. John Crittenden described hundreds in attendance. Many soldiers, both Key and Crittenden happily reported, had at last given up profanity and other sins. Pvt. A. J. Edge told his wife that eighty men had joined the church the previous week. Baptisms were a daily occurrence, he added, for men had realized that they needed to prepare for death.[106] "A great revival is still in progress in our Brigade," Pvt. G. W. Burns wrote from Dalton on May 2. "Last Sunday our Brigade took the sacrament I never saw such a crowd of preaching there were 17 sprinkled and 12 baptized in the creek."[107]

In Virginia, the scene was much the same. Lt. James Green, like his fellow Confederates west of the mountains, regarded the fast day as something of a flop, yet he otherwise continued to attend sermons and was baptized himself at the end of April.[108] Pvt. William Stilwell reported "a very good meeting" once his brigade rejoined Lee's army: "Many have joined the church and many more I think will join yet." He aided the cause by distributing tracts to grateful readers.[109]

Yet through the winter and spring, other later enlisters still remained turned inward, focused on their families and their God instead of the camp revival. Private reflection became more pronounced as well as fighting loomed, especially among men facing battle for the first time. Pvt. James Michael Barr's 5th South Carolina Cavalry left the coast of his home state in March and went to Virginia. Facing battle for the first time, Barr skipped church to write his wife, fearful that they would never meet again except in heaven. Another South Carolinian, J. W. Tindall of the 20th South Carolina, regarded his unit's transfer to Virginia as all but a death sentence. He sent his wife final instructions on child rearing and told her he hoped that "we may meete in heaven when we will regain each others company" if he did not survive "this miserable war."[110] On his way back to Virginia, John F. Davenport tried to pray for his ill wife, "but it seamed to me like my prair never got higher than my head."[111] In the West, other men asked for prayers from their loved ones while reminding them to act so as to ensure their reunion in the next world. Pvt. J. A. Frierson went them one better, asking his entire church at home to pray for him.[112]

In the Trans-Mississippi, the revival continued unabated for months. Sgt.

James T. Wallace, a Missouri cavalryman, wrote at the end of May that "we organized our Christian association. We have a great revival of religion among us many were converted and Christians comeforted & Backsliders reclaimed. this was truly the greatest revival I ever saw." Throughout the summer, he noted preaching, baptisms, and "considerable sensation amoung the people," culminating in the creation of the Church of the trans-Mississippi.[113] In the Eastern and Western theaters, however, the situation changed dramatically. With May came the opening rounds of the Atlanta and Overland campaigns. The relentless, day-after-day fighting, among other things, prevented many men from writing letters. When they did pause to write about religion, the sentiments were basic: pray for me, be good Christians, let us meet in Heaven.[114] J. W. Tindall, shifted from garrison duty to the Richmond front with the 20th South Carolina, was the most expressive. "The lord will take care of me through all my troubles and through all the troubles of life," he wrote. "Live in the discharge of your Christian duties and the lord will bless you and your family and save us at last in heaven."[115]

With the end of June and the beginnings of the sieges of Atlanta and Petersburg, however, revivalism again resurfaced. Nightly preaching took place in camp again throughout the summer, and new converts appeared at last at the altar. A few men, of course, expressed cynicism. Sgt. John Crittenden complained that "the Chaplains of our Brigade seem to have forsaken us altogether. They are back with the wagons lying around the cook places and Quartermasters."[116] Capt. Thomas Key asserted that many men went to church only to get out of the rain, while he himself went in part to see pretty women. Yet most soldiers who wrote about faith were sincere in their worship. Their basic hopes generally were familiar.[117] Pvt. J. H. Lee wrote his wife from Petersburg that he had resolved "to try to live a pious christian life. . . . to live a different life to what I have been living all my life. I am resolved to reform & flee the wrath to come." He hoped to survive the war, he added, but if not, he hoped to "meet you in an upper & better world where parting will be known no more."[118] J. W. Tindall expressed similar hopes. "The soldiers all seem interested in the welfare of their souls best interest," he wrote only days before his own death. Pray for me, he asked, let us meet in heaven.[119] After Harvey Bailey died of his wounds outside of Atlanta, Maj. E. H. Hampton of the 29th North Carolina wrote the widow that "Harvey said that he was prepared to die . . . he is going to a better land." For Hampton, the message was clear. "You now have a tie in Heaven that you never had before," he advised, "and a tie that will serve as a silver chord to draw you and your children to the Lord."[120]

A few soldiers of course added prayers of victory. Pvt. William Ross Stilwell boldly asserted that he was fighting for God and Christianity as well as for the Confederacy and his family, while Capt. Thomas Key described a September 15 fast day service in the Army of Tennessee that featured prayers for an independent Confederacy. Most religious later enlisters, however, at least those who had survived the onslaught, continued to think primarily of their souls, their families, and heavenly reunion as the rest of the year passed and another, the last of the war, began. Adding to the personal thrust were the pressures of continual warfare as well as an apparently growing lack of reliable chaplains to preach. Men at the front complained increasingly of poor sermons or the lack of any services at all. The result, as the 11th Virginia Cavalry's Pvt. D. C. Snyder reported, was an upsurge in sin, specifi-cally drinking, among the officers of his regiment. Some soldiers, such as the men of the 45th Georgia, took matters into their own hands, building a church in winter quarters and holding prayer meetings and Bible study while their chaplain comfortably furloughed the winter at home.[121]

As the war ground to a close, a few men continued to hold out hope. Their Christian faith convinced them to fight on, providing a powerful sustaining motivator. The demands of fighting, however, meant that most of the few documents written by later enlisters who still survived emanated either from west of the Mississippi, where worship remained most regular, or from prisons. Among the former, Pvt. Henry T. Morgan damned the withering faith of civilians in both God and country and told his wife that "if thare ever was a time that peopal needed religion it was now. Ellen we have a prayer meeting in our tent every night."[122] What is most notable in these admittedly few letters and diary entries is the almost complete absence of theodicy, the explanations of why good Confederate Christians continued to suffer and die in what increasingly looked like a losing cause. As other historians have noticed, many Confederates sought to explain their losses as a chastening experience that purged and prepared them for a miraculous victory and nationhood. Such arguments sustained their will to fight. Few later-enlisting Confederates, however, seemed to share this belief.[123] Thus, when defeat came, it shook the few pious later-enlisting Confederates who commented on it. "Truly the Lord has forsaken his people," now-captain

Edwin Fay lamented. "I fear the subjugation of the South will make an infidel of me. I cannot see how a just God can allow people who have battled so heroically for their rights to be overthrown."[124]

"I HAVE ONLY TWO objects in life," Lt. Ben Robertson of the 44th Mississippi wrote his sister from near Atlanta in May 1864, "one is to whip the Yankees & the other is to go to heaven both of which I expect to accomplish."[125] Although he ultimately failed in at least one of those goals, Robertson's words aptly sum up the role of Christian faith to later-enlisting Confederates. Given the times, it is not surprising that many of them were religious men. At some point during the war, 122 discussed religion: 46 in 1862, 59 in 1863, 50 in 1864, and 4 in the first chaotic months of 1865, figures clearly skewed by casualties in the war's later years. Privates figured notably among the religious; while officers seemed to have remained more aloof. Stated differently, expressions regarding God appear twice as often as expressions of loyalty to country. Yet a majority of the sampled later enlisters never wrote about religion, and relatively few of those who did saw themselves as Christian knights in a holy crusade.

As we have seen, later enlisters were less nationalistic and less eager to enlist than other Confederates. When they did go to the army more or less reluctantly, they had trouble letting go of home, and not only of their farms and families but of their religious lives as well. While many did go on to participate in the revivals, notably that of 1863–64, most nonetheless maintained distances from their more veteran comrades' much-discussed religious enthusiasm. As the next chapter suggests, that distance was not on religious matters alone. But as for religion, later enlisters' faith instead repeatedly reverted to the individual and family-oriented forms that it took before the war. It centered around shared prayers with loved ones and the mutual obligations of family worship, all toward the end of a family reunion in a heavenly home to come if not the home they knew. The realities of battle and camp and the stench of ever-present death only reinforced those tendencies. Thus, unlike the soldiers examined by Reid Mitchell, who felt increasingly isolated and alienated from home as the war progressed, later enlisters' faith actively worked to help maintain soldiers' ties to home while to a degree lessening feelings of alienation and separateness. In the end, one wonders if later enlisters really were that different from their more veteran comrades after all, a question that only more comparative studies of religion can answer. At any rate, it does not undermine the sincerity or indeed the reality of their Christian faith to recognize that later-enlisting Confederates turned to God in order to seek shelter from the storm of war in the Rock of Ages, and that they ultimately took seriously and indeed surprisingly literally the words of John Newton's venerable and beloved hymn: "Thro' many dangers, toils and snares, I have already come / 'Tis grace has brought me safe thus far, And grace will lead me home."[126]

7

COMRADES

"ALL MY NEIGHBOR BOYS"

Born in Ireland, Pvt. L. H. Mathews may have possessed his countrymen's fabled way with words, but words also could land him in trouble. As a reporter for the *Pensacola Observer* at the beginning of the war, Mathews made the mistake of describing too accurately Braxton Bragg's plans to seize Fort Pickens. A furious Bragg promptly had the correspondent arrested for treason. Acquitted, Mathews continued his press career until March 1862, when he joined the 1st Florida Infantry. From November 1862 until February 1863, he served as a hospital steward but then rejoined his company in the field.[1] A month later, writing from the regiment's winter encampment in Tullahoma, Tennessee, he composed a poem entitled "Our Mess." With a practiced wit and obvious affection for his comrades if not lyrical genius, the soldier described in 110 rhymed lines the four men with whom he ate his meals, smoked, and slept.

"Our 'mess' is composed of as jovial a set," he boasted, "As ever a camp-fire or cottage has met." Capt. Augustus O. MacDonnell, "wiry and witty," had just returned from furlough. "The captain's a gentleman of the old school," Mathews explained, "Not made by the tailor part fop and part fool." As for the others, "John T." longed to go home and marry. Regimental adjutant James H. Nicholson was "as loving a spouse, As ever drank Champagne, but 'Jeems' don't carouse." Completing the mess was Lt. William Miller, who was, in the poet's estimation, "as truly serene, As our friend Dick in our warfare is green." Mathews depicted a warm if cramped cabin, filled with smoke, good humor, and a running dinner debate over the evils of alcohol, and then went on to describe the men's after-dinner pursuits. "One's reading the 'Rebel' another the "Friend," he wrote. "The 'Floridian & Journal' just came to John T. / Whose looking for items from our homes near the sea . . . And Dick is again reading that letter o'er / Which he must have read fully ten times before."[2]

Despite its subject matter—men at war—"Our Mess" actually fits snugly into the conventions of nineteenth-century women's domestic verse, celebrating the commonplace joys of a happy home, complete with an admired "spouse" and domestic virtues.[3] Nor was Mathews alone in envisioning his mess in such a familiar manner. A diary entry of the New Jersey–born Alabama infantryman Pvt. Hiram Smith Williams written in March 1864 depicted his mess in even more strikingly gendered terms. "The head of the mess is a tall 6 foot 4 speciman of a piny woods genius from South Ala.," Williams wrote approvingly. "As he is the oldest man we all call him 'dad' while he designates us as his 'gals.' He has three single ones, *Jane*, *Sal*, and *Amanda*, the last cognomen being the one he gave me. The two married ones is Mrs. Green and Mrs. Hedgepet. We have rare old times now and then," he added with apparent understatement. "Amanda's" affections, however, notably did not extend beyond the mess to the rest of the company. Sharing a cracker with one of his messmates, Williams cynically added that "No. 1 is the rule here in the army. I doubt if any of the company would divide with me if I was out and they had anything. 'Take care of No. 1.' That is it."[4]

SCHOLARLY RESEARCH ON soldiers going back to World War II stresses the role that camaraderie plays as a sustaining motivator. The modern military bases much of its doctrine on the central place occupied by the fierce loyalty of soldiers toward their closest friends, men willing to fight and die for each other when other motivators fail. Yet historians of Civil War soldiers came late to the notion that close ties among small groups of comrades also increased morale and fighting efficiency in that era. Although he described in great detail the peer pressure that encouraged enlistment, living arrangements in field and camp, diversions, and the friendships and kin relationships that undergirded messes, Bell Wiley never went beyond the descriptive to ask how interrelationships psychologically sustained Civil War armies. Nor did most other historians. It was Gerald Linderman who first addressed, albeit briefly, the importance of comradeship to Civil War soldiers. He interpreted it as a coping mechanism that soldiers developed in reaction to growing feelings of isolation from home and to dark thoughts that the war had made them murderers unfit for civilian society. In their messes especially, soldiers sharing the miseries of war emotionally bonded in small groups that imperfectly replicated the family life they feared they had lost. In a similar tone, Reid Mitchell agreed that soldiers feared what the war was making them. Both Mitchell and Larry Logue maintain that, given the limited range of models, soldiers fell back on the family as a familiar form of a nurturing relationship.[5]

In contrast to those scholars, James McPherson maintained forcefully that the "primary group cohesion" developed in messes and companies was one of the most powerful sustaining motivators of the war. In his appropriately named *For Cause and Comrades*, he drew upon John Lynn's description of the roughly similar French *ordinaire* to assert that the battlefield and camp created "a true band of brothers whose mutual dependence and mutual support" kept armies functioning. Men who might otherwise have fled camp and field did not, sometimes because they feared the censure of their comrades but more often because of the intense emotional bonds they felt toward their closest comrades. Sharing and surviving the experience of combat strengthened those bonds, as did the not-uncommon presence of real brothers, other relatives, and hometown friends in locally raised companies. Blood ties aside, men spoke of all their fellow soldiers within the primary group as family, resisted separation, and mourned their loss. The downside of such relationships, unfortunately, was that attrition could shatter a morale built solely on such emotional ties. That it did not, McPherson maintained, was due to the ideology and patriotism that also sustained soldiers. Civil War soldiers truly fought for cause *and* comrades.[6]

A few scholars counter that the importance of male bonding within the army has been overstated. Stephen Berry notably doubted whether the Southern ethos of masculinity actually permitted close ties between men. According to Aaron Sheehan-Dean's somewhat similar argument, men did model camp life when they could on the familiar routines of family life, often took pride in the meals cooked in their messes, and came together as they shared the sacrifices and suffering of war. Yet he argued that relationships between soldiers never superseded the bonds that tied men to their real families, who after all were sacrificing and suffering as well. Sheehan-Dean's Confederates thus fought for cause and family, not comrades.[7]

In previous chapters, this study asserts that patriotism and ideology were less important to later-enlisting Confederates than to Confederate soldiers as a whole, while ties to home remained strong, if strained by distance. But what of camaraderie? For many, it was indeed a significant factor, providing that the comrades in question were also relatives and friends from back home.

OF THE SOLDIERS INCLUDED in the sample, eighty-two (25.6 percent) discussed the men in their messes as well as other comrades. Ten did so negatively. The unpleasant Edwin Fay notably made few friends and often disparaged even them. When one messmate deserted, Fay was left for a time with only his regimental captain. At another point, he complained that no one would tend to him while he was sick because his fellow soldiers had concluded that he was malingering. Yet while Fay was infamously hard to get along with, he was not alone in encountering difficulties in the mess. William S. Lacy, for example, became the chaplain of the 47th North Carolina in the late summer of 1863. He complained after arriving in camp that the regiment's ranking officers and members of his mess clearly did not welcome a man of the cloth in their midst. While Lacy eventually made friends, others were not so lucky. Young Andrew Crawford left his captain's mess and determined to strike out on his own, asking his mother to send him a frying pan and sauce pan. W. H. Robertson of the 44th Mississippi described how one of his messmates quit the group after an argument. Lt. Thomas J. Moore complained that some of the men in his mess were doing so little to support the others that he would no longer share food from home with them.[8] Pvt. G. H. Burns likewise fumed that four of messmates were "such hogs I wont give them any thing they wont cook and we have to divide our meat when we draw it to keep them from eating it all up."[9]

Alabama sergeant John Crittenden similarly fussed that a messmate was "the laziest, meanest good for nothing boy that ever lived. Sometimes we cook our meals and put it away. he will then go and eat it himself. He cares nothing for anybody but himself, And few cares for him." (What finally broke up Crittenden's mess, however, was not conflict with the "good for nothing boy" but the men's crafty calculation that they would receive more food if they divided into pairs.)[10] Meanwhile, the 51st Georgia's Lt. W. J. J. Webb wrote his father to tell him, "I am now messing to myself." He explained, "Burnett & myself do not get along as smooth as we once did. he acted the dog with me. . . . he is now messing with Col. Anthony who has not drawn a sober breath in several days."[11] And Pvt. Jesse C. Knight of the 50th Georgia complained that while on the march he had "taken sick and [been] left in the woods" by his comrades "to live or dy as best as I could."[12]

These men nonetheless were exceptions. Most of the sampled men in the subset, seventy-two soldiers (24 percent), wrote positively of their messes and closest companions. Twelve did so in a general manner, to be sure, listing the names of their comrades, reporting briefly on their health, and relating anecdotes involving cooking and curious sleeping arrangements.[13] But twenty-three late enlisters expressed deeper sentiments that square with McPherson's observations regarding close emotional bonds and primary group cohesion. Soldiers expressed pride in their army friends, as when Pvt. William J. Hart wrote his father that a "cowardly fellow" still at home "wont stand it like me and Joe Robinson."[14] Others referred to their closest friends as family. "We all live like so many Brothers," Pvt. E. A. Penick of the 38th Virginia wrote of the five other men in his mess. Men like Penick tended their friends when sick and pined for them when away.[15] "I have been very lonely since all the officers of the company have left except myself," Joseph R. Manson similarly confessed. "George Bernard was indeed a very pleasant companion but he has gone off sick."[16] When he was detailed, Pvt. Charles Croom wrote his wife, "I hope they will not keep us long on the detail. I miss my friends, and I miss the good meetings we were having when I was there."[17] "O! to be without friends is horrible," the 27th Louisiana's Pvt. J. A. Frierson exclaimed. "Ike Best left camp this morning; to nurse his brother; so he leaves me without a friend."[18]

The men also deeply mourned their lost comrades. Writing of the death of his friend, for example, Pvt. J. L. J Lear of the 1st Tennessee Artillery recorded in his diary that "we as soldiers and friends have much to lament. As a soldier there was none that could surpass him and as a man he was a true upright man."[19] At Gettysburg, Pvt. Samuel Pickens mourned the death of messmate George "Tean" Nutting. So did Nutting's brother-in-law, John S. Tucker. After the battle, Cpl. J. F. Coghill similarly mourned his friend Rial Stewart. "I loved Rial as a Brother," he wrote his family, "and I would do enything I could for him he was a brave and knoble young man but alas he has fallen in the cause of his beloved country."[20] The young chaplain Willie Lacy wrote from Petersburg that a recent fight had cost him "my most especial friends—and ever since the engagement have felt lonely. . . . I have been messing and sleeping alone until today."[21]

What one cannot say with certainty about these twenty-three soldiers is how many of the friendships described predated the war. Extant records only provide clues. Given the local composition of initial wartime units as well as the opportunity for later enlisters to choose their outfit, it is obvious that many relationships did emanate in peacetime. Additional correspondence, moreover, makes it evident that kinship and neighborhood ties within units were common, and that they often strengthened military bonds just as they had in the *ordinaire*. Twenty-two men in the sample specifically wrote of serving with various cousins, uncles, and nephews. "I feel greatly rejoiced to be with so many of my near relations," Pvt. J. M. Davidson of the 39th North Carolina wrote. Later, he expressed delight that his regiment was to serve in "Cousin Bob Vance's's" brigade.[22] Lt. W. J. Barron of the 4th Alabama Cavalry, a prisoner at Johnson's Island, wrote with undisguised regret when his cousin's husband was exchanged, leaving him "lonely—sad and discontented as you could imagine."[23]

Nine other men described serving with brothers-in-law. Alabamian Pvt. John W. Cotton soldiered with two. When John Meriwether left the 38th Alabama to serve as the surgeon of the 40th regiment, he tried to take his brother-in-law with him, afraid that he would have to eat and sleep by himself. Pvt. John Fowler of the 16th South Carolina secured a furlough and attempted to raise $400 in order to retrieve his brother-in-law's body from a hospital cemetery.[24] After Pvt. Grant Taylor's brother-in-law, Ide Teer, was captured along with most of his company at Noonday Creek, north of Atlanta, Taylor was beside himself. "I feel very lonely to-day," he wrote, "for they never make any better men than Ide. And a brother he has been to me and I feel that I have lost a true friend." Four months later, Taylor remained inconsolable. "Since poor Ide was taken away," he wrote his wife, "I have no bosom friend to go to. I am lost. I am like some poor bird that has lost its mate."[25]

The relative most commonly served with was a brother, as discussed in correspondence by eighteen soldiers.[26] As with friends and other relations, such blood ties could strengthen a regiment, but they could also undermine morale when kin were lost. J. M. Davidson admitted that he felt "entirely lost" when his brother left the 39th North Carolina.[27] Lt. Thomas J. Moore of the 18th South Carolina described to his sister in great detail the death of their brother, his search for the body, and how he himself dug the grave.[28] When Pvt. G. H. Burns's brother died, Burns lamented that he was "left hear alone far from home and no one to sooth my sorrows or wipe away the . . . tear from my eyes." Although he later joined a new mess, Burns never reconciled himself to the loss.[29] Pvt. S. W. Farrow noted "the boys from our settlement" still serving with him in the 19th Texas, but added that none could replace his brother. "I am lost since daniel is dead," he admitted, "though I suppose that I have friends with me I miss him a great deal . . . if I were to get sick no one would take as good care of me as he did."[30]

Besides Farrow, an additional twenty-six later enlisters wrote of serving in the same units with confirmed friends from home, usually with brief messages regarding their health and compatibility, and sometimes with mourning for their loss.[31] Equally indicative of the strength of neighborhood ties are the twelve men whose comradeship extended beyond the regiment to local men in other units. Those soldiers regularly noted reunions with neighborhood men encountered in camp or on the march. Pvt. G. H. Burns briefly shook himself from his grief when in Vicksburg he ran across some neighbors serving in the 39th Georgia. Pvt. John W. Cotton of Alabama's Hilliard's Legion wrote his wife about happily encountering some men from his Georgia hometown who had moved on to Texas and had news of his uncle.[32] Pvt. Grant Taylor rejoiced when he learned that his 40th Alabama would be brigaded with units that contained "all my neighbor boys in the different Reg.," but his mood soured a few months later when his brother-in-law's regiment marched out of Vicksburg.[33]

Pvt. William Ross Stilwell also frequently described visiting family members and friends in other regiments. He wrote most often, however, of his closest friend and brother-in-law, William Darnell, who served in the 27th Georgia. Despite serving in another regiment, Stilwell visited him as often as possible. In autumn of 1862, Darnell tried unsuccessfully to transfer into Stilwell's 53rd Georgia. That winter, Stilwell fretted until learning that his friend had survived the Battle of Fredericksburg, only to worry anew when Darnell became ill. When the 27th Georgia moved south to the Carolinas the following year, Stilwell expressed sadness that "we will never get together any more I don't suppose." Of Darnell himself, who had gone home with another illness, Stilwell demanded, "why don't you write me?" He continued, "I fear we will never get together any more unless you get a transfer to our regiment."[34]

It is clear that for many later-enlisting Confederate soldiers, men like Stilwell and Taylor, camaraderie was a significant sustaining motivator. Yet one must be careful not to push its importance too far. Of the seventy-two men who wrote positively of their relationships with comrades, just over half referred specifically to family members and friends from home. It is reasonable to assume that at least some of the others did so as well, only in allusions and references incomprehensible to the modern eye. Thus for later-enlisting Confederates, the primary group cohesion of messes and companies—true bands of brothers and other kin—must be seen as an extension of antebellum Southern localism transferred to army camps rather than as a function of the camps themselves. The deep loneliness men expressed when old friends and kinfolk were lost, combined with the apparent difficulty in forging new "families" out of the survivors, reinforces the notion that for a majority of later-enlisting Confederates, camaraderie was simply yet another representation of their deep, unyielding ties to kin and neighborhood.

GIVEN THE HIERARCHICAL nature of Civil War commands, William Ross Stilwell simultaneously belonged to several units, and he was proud of all of them. As much as he missed William Darnell, he tellingly never attempted to join his friend's regiment, but instead tried to get Darnell to join his. During the Seven Days Battles, Stilwell's 53rd Georgia, brand-new and undrilled, had wavered in the fight and become an object of derision. After the Battle of Antietam, where his comrades took heavy casualties and fought well, Stilwell rejoiced that "it will be said no more that the 53rd Georgia regiment won't fight." Eight months later, he described how his comrades had captured two stands of enemy colors at Chancellorsville. "I hear of no prisoners taken from our regiment," he added, "they don't surrender." Stilwell's pride extended beyond his regiment. "Our brigade covered itself with glory," he boasted, "they whipped a whole corps of Yankees." He also praised the entire Army of Northern Virginia, writing, "we in our army keep our armor bright and our powder dry, and when they come we let fly and sure to be a Yankee die. We don't do like the army in Mississippi," he added, "get run off with a few bombs."[35]

Unit pride such as Stilwell's can be seen as a manifestation of primary group camaraderie writ large. As with the mess, scholars have long recognized the importance of esprit de corps, the deep affection some men held for their companies, regiments, and brigades. Bell Wiley described volunteer companies as extensions of proud antebellum communities and related how the breaking up of brigades and the consolidation of battle-worn regiments later in the war undermined morale. Both James I. Robertson and Reid Mitchell compared companies to families, with officers filling the necessary parental roles. James McPherson strongly related unit pride to sustaining motivation. Primary groups cemented together with the glues of kinship and camaraderie, while significant in themselves, were also the building blocks of locally raised companies and state-organized regiments. Pride in the regiment, growing out of primary group cohesion and constantly reinforced with the shared experiences of camp and battle, turned the unit at best into one great mess of fraternal comrades. Men expressed fierce pride in their regiment, looked down upon others as inferior, and cringed if their beloved outfit sullied its reputation. Regimental and national colors became the tangible symbols of that loyalty, and were defended to the death. Unit pride thus functioned as another major sustaining motivator.[36]

For later-enlisting Confederates, however, unit pride proved much less important than primary group solidarity. While seventy-two soldiers wrote positively of their messes, about half, thirty-eight soldiers in all (11.9 percent), expressed any pride at all in any of their larger units. Only one served in the Trans-Mississippi, moreover, with the others divided almost evenly between East and West. About half of them, eighteen soldiers, wrote positively of their regiments, focusing like Stilwell almost exclusively on the units' fighting prowess and reputation to the exclusion of other qualities.[37] Pvt. H. W. Robinson, for example, admitted that his 42nd Georgia lacked discipline, much to his brigade commander's annoyance. "Ginrel Stevenson ses the 42 Ga is a Scandel to this Brigade," he reported, "becas we will Shoot at a fuss with out Seeing any person he wants us to wate tel we See them when it is So dark that we Cant See our hands before us." Even worse, the men of the regiment "runaway over to the other side have the gard hous allways Crowded, our Soldiers fro Steeling & Running out in the Contry & giting drunk." As far as Robinson was concerned, however, none of that mattered, for in battle the regiment had held its ground while the Tennesseans of the brigade ran.[38]

Fewer men still, ten soldiers, praised their companies. While soldierly skills and bravery remained important to them, the men writing of their companies were more likely to point to less-warlike attributes. Lt. William L. Nugent celebrated both his company's gentlemanly demeanor and its skill on the drill field. Thomas J. Newberry of the 29th Mississippi likewise boasted of his company's expert drill as well as its marksmanship.[39] Capt. Samuel Ridley of the 1st Tennessee Light Artillery meanwhile was proud of his men's willingness to obey his orders. Pvt. J. A. Patton of the 47th North Carolina boasted, "our company is considered the best in redyness I never saw a more peaseiable pasel of men in my life we hoald pray meetings twise a week."[40]

In his superb analysis of Union Civil War regiments, Gerald Prokopowicz maintains that a soldier's strongest loyalties involved his company and especially his regiment. The company was his "family" and the regiment his "hometown." In contrast, the larger military organizations—brigades, divisions, corps, and armies—never attracted much attention or affection. Not only were they too big to permit familiarity among soldiers, regional and state rivalries undermined their esprit de corps. Moreover, generals constantly reorganized the larger units and, in so doing, further prevented the development of strong loyalties. As a result, soldiers routinely thought of themselves as members of companies and regiments, but not members of their corps or army. According to Prokopowicz, the result was a double-edged sword. On the one hand, strong bonds within the regiment helped prevent the disintegration of armies. But on the other hand, he maintains, the dramatic emphasis on the regiment made larger organizations overly decentralized and less effective.[41]

As one might expect, only eight sampled soldiers expressed pride in their brigades, almost as many as the number of sampled later-enlisting soldiers who wrote approvingly of their companies. Most focused on battlefield exploits, as men also did with their regiments. Typical was Sgt. J. D. Joyner of the 7th North Carolina and the celebrated Branch-Lane brigade of Tar Heels. "Our Brigade uses scarcely any thing but yankee equipments," Joyner boasted to his mother. "It has fought the yankees 11 times . . . and whipped them everytime."[42] In contrast, Cpl. John T. Beggs of the 5th Battery, Washington Artillery, believed that the best thing about Daniel Adams's Louisiana brigade was the "splendid band . . . that plays morning and evening."[43] Lt. J. M. Davidson of the 36th North Carolina meanwhile expressed delight when his regiment went to Vicksburg to join Evander McNair's Arkansas brigade. The Georgians with whom they had served previously, Davidson charged, "seemed to think themselves better than other soldiers that had been in the field all this time made fun of our men's clothing and the way they drilled which created a hard feeling that the N Carolinians will never git over."[44] Davidson went on to praise his army, as did three others.[45] Yet in retrospect, he was an exception. Most late enlisters never suggested that they felt much pride in their units at all, and those few that did largely did so only once or twice. Unit pride simply does not seem to have been a major sustaining motivator for them.

BOTH THE SECRET OF Confederate military success and the greatest weakness of the Rebel army, Bell Wiley asserted, was its officer corps. "Given brave, efficient, and respect-inspiring leaders from lieutenant to brigadiers," he wrote, ". . . Southern soldiers were insurpassable." On the other hand, poor commanders weakened the army beyond repair. Johnny Reb was hardly unique in the annals of military history when he carped about his officers or chafed under their discipline, but the particular complaints he lodged offer considerable insight. Well into the war, Confederate officers at the company level were often a kind of comrade: hometown leaders, familiar faces equally untrained as soldiers, and often elected by peers in hotly contested elections. They were not truly economic and social equals, of course; as explained earlier, officers tended to be a few years older, notably wealthier, and more likely to pursue nonfarming professions. Yet within a South that boasted that every white man was as good as another, all had at least talked a rough political and social equality. Now, with the war, men who once considered themselves peers before enlistment found themselves shoehorned into a system of hierarchical military discipline that brought out both the best and the worst. According to Wiley, bad officers included the pompous peacocks who strutted about as if they were superior to enlisted men, the layabouts who avoided the worst of camp and field, and the cruel martinets. Drunken carousers and incompetent drill masters earned their share of derision as well, but the worst reproaches awaited men who proved cowards under fire. Men serving under unpopular officers might ridicule them, shame them, or even occasionally try to kill them, but whatever the response the situation eroded morale. On the other hand, soldiers admired and followed those officers who kindly and willingly shared their men's burdens, administered fair and flexible discipline, treated them as republican equals, led from the front, and did not waste their men's lives.

In general, subsequent scholars have not deviated greatly from Wiley's path, although Reid Mitchell additionally stressed the role of officer as surrogate parent. Ultimately, all agree with the modern military that good leadership was and is both a sustaining and a combat motivator.[46]

Only twenty-six later-enlisting Confederates (8.1 percent) lauded their immediate superiors, however. Those who explained their positive feelings —six did not do so—pointed to various attributes. The pious Pvt. E. A. Penick, for example, respected his captain's Christianity. Lt. I. M. Auld of the 5th Florida meanwhile lauded his captain's skills as a disciplinarian, while adding that this admiration put him in a decided minority.[47] Nine soldiers pointed to officers' courage under fire, such as Pvt. Charles Terrill of the 2nd Georgia, who lamented the loss of his colonel. "A braver man never fell," Terrill wrote. "He was insensible to fear, bombs and bullets were to him a pastime. I verily believe that it was a matter of perfect indifference to him whether he was killed or not."[48]

Courage, however, seemingly did not matter as much to later enlisters as did fairness. Nearly twice as many men as those who lauded bravery described the good officer as the one who treated his subordinates with kindness and egalitarian respect. A few noted the importance of special favors. Pvt. John W. Cotton's newly elected lieutenant, for example, promised to try to get him a long-desired furlough.[49] The 19th Texas's Pvt. S. W. Farrow gleefully reported that his captain "excuses me from duty to go fishing whenever I want to go."[50] Cpl. John T. Beggs of the 5th Company, Washington Artillery, wrote that his lieutenant had given the men a gift,[51] while Michael Nihill of the 10th Texas praised his captain for walking along with his men during a retreat rather than riding a horse. "Because his men had to walk, he wanted to walk with them," Nihill told his mother. "He wished to share their toil with them."[52]

More soldiers, thirty-six (10.9 percent), criticized particular immediate officers for various sins. Texan Capt. William H. Barnes, for example, complained when his colonel prevented regimental elections and appointed two favorites to office. The case went all the way to Richmond and the secretary of war intervened. Surgeon John Meriwether of the 40th Alabama meanwhile described his colonel as "a perfect *Humbug*,"[53] while to Grant Taylor, all of the officers were "big headed."[54] William D. Clover of the 62nd North Carolina minced no words in describing his anger when his popular captain was convicted in a court-martial and replaced by "shit briches Kelley . . . I think they will brake up the company he should be my captain I will go home and be conscripted first."[55]

Most strikingly, and in contrast to the conclusions of the current literature, only four complained of an officer's cowardice.[56] Instead, later enlisters focused on three other problems. Eight of them complained of immoral behavior and especially drunkenness. The 51st Georgia's Lt. W. J. J. Webb, for example, wrote his father than Lt. Col. Oliver Preston Anthony "has not drawn a sober breath in several days. Col. Anthony got very mad with me a few days ago while on the march," Webb continued, ". . . asked me if I would take a drink. I refused and wished that every drop of whiskey in Va was mixed with the waters of the Potomac."[57] Likewise, Pvt. D. C. Snyder of the 11th Virginia Cavalry launched into a tirade when his wife wrote him about women who had attended a ball with Confederate officers. He savaged them as the beneficiaries of "wire-working deception. . . . Our army (and I say it to its disgrace) is filled with officers who were drunken, immoral, worthless characters before the war in a majority of cases."[58]

Another fourteen men cited incompetence. Pvt. Samuel Pickens criticized a regimental captain for turning them out of their winter cabins at bedtime. Pvt. John Shibley of the 22nd Arkansas complained of favoritism in granting officer's rank to well-connected men who seemed only to argue constantly with each other. Lt. William L. Nugent similarly scorned his colonel for appointing his incompetent son to his staff in order to protect him from the draft.[59] "Our Commander does not know himself ten minutes a head what he will do next," Capt. William H. Barnes complained. "I learn of the Col Sometimes what he expects to do; and sometimes he does that, and sometimes he does something else."[60] Lt. Thomas J. Moore of the 18th South Carolina wrote his sister that it would be "hard to find a bigger fool" than his captain. "He cannot write a pass without mis spelling wrong half a dozen words," the former student complained. "He will be your best friend to your face behind your back your worst enemy. He is partial in his company, his associates are the lowest characters and they all believe that when they die they will go *to him*."[61]

Incompetence went hand in hand with what twelve later enlisters perceived to be tyrannical harshness and cruel treatment.[62] Several cited exhausting drill. "It does seem at times," Pvt. Hiram Smith Williams wrote, "as though the Captain tried to see how much he could get for us to do, and he seems to have an idea that no one of us can ever get caught."[63] Pvt. A. E.

Shore similarly complained about a dress parade during which his colonel ordered his men to "doubel quick" ten minutes while he "slipt out of it" and retired to his tent.[64] Pvt. John W. Cotton meanwhile complained that his allegedly drunken colonel also was "getting titer every day he has got 30 or 40 in jail some for one thing and some for another he had two taken this morning for deserting there post last nite the hole regiment I think would be glad if he was dead." In retrospect, some of Col. Charles T. Goode's actions may have been justified. After the colonel released a suspected bushwhacker, Cotton reported that "some of us men went with him and when they had got him about half a mild a cross the river they tride to hang him and they could not get him by enough off of the ground to choke him to death and they shot him twice and left him hanging there and the colonel found it and had six of them arrested and put in jail."[65]

Overall, the attitudes toward officers expressed by later-enlisting Confederates differed from those of 1861 enlistees. Most wrote little about their superiors. Those who did discuss them, moreover, evinced surprisingly little concern with combat prowess or its corollary, cowardice. What mattered instead were the same qualities men expected from supervisors in peacetime: competence, fairness, and a rough egalitarianism. In other words, they simply wanted their leaders to be what they had been ideally at home, good bosses and generous patrons.

WHILE CONFEDERATE SOLDIERS interacted daily with company-grade and regimental officers, they glimpsed their generals only infrequently. Such occasions usually were striking enough to merit comment. During the retreat from Pennsylvania, for example, South Carolina lieutenant Alex McNeill noticed Robert E. Lee sitting on the southern bank of the Potomac. The sight cheered the weary soldier. "Still the same expression warmed up his features," McNeill wrote his wife, "as when success had attended all his efforts."[66]

Bell Wiley suggested that Confederates such as McNeill admired in their commanding generals the same practical qualities they wanted in other officers: courage, competence, fairness, kindness, hard work, sobriety, and an unwillingness to risk their men's lives without cause. Other scholars have followed suit.[67] But as Reid Mitchell first maintained, generals increasingly filled another sustaining role as well. As loyalty evolved in the minds of white Southerners, generals such Lee, Stonewall Jackson, and J. E. B. Stuart became powerful new symbols of the Confederacy. Gary Gallagher has gone so far as to assert that by 1863, Lee and his army had become synonymous with the Confederacy in the minds of Southern civilians, just as George Washington had been identified with American independence. As long as the noble, pious, and lion-hearted Lee and his lieutenants remained in the field, vanquishing one hapless Yankee general after another, hope in eventual victory and nationhood survived. More than Jefferson Davis, generals such as Lee and Jackson thus personified the Confederacy and kept it afloat during years of war. Other scholars, notably Elisabeth Lauterbach Laskin and Jason Phillips, have built upon Gallagher's interpretation to maintain that general officers also produced such responses within the army. Faith in their commanders' tactical skills, according to Phillips, reinforced by inspiring grand reviews and the repeated sights of enemies cut down in droves, sustained morale and kept Confederates in the field.[68]

Later-enlisting Confederates match this description to a point. Sixty-six sampled soldiers (21 percent) commented on their own generals, most in brief comments and asides that reflected little real contact. Fifty of them specifically praised an array of brass, running from Patton Anderson and Patrick Cleburne to Robert Toombs and Alfred Vaughan. Twenty-six generals only merited one mention each. In contrast, twelve soldiers praised Stonewall Jackson while nine expressed their admiration for Joseph Johnston, and another ten lauded Robert E. Lee. As a group, those who explained their reasons deemed generals praiseworthy for their manly appearance, egalitarian kindness, and especially their military prowess. There were variations. Jackson's admirers almost universally praised his skills on the battlefield, while Lee's adherents were just as likely to stand in awe of his persona.[69] Sgt. Maj. Marion Hill Fitzpatrick, for example, described Lee as "the best rider I ever saw. . . . I cannot look at him with his gray hair and beard only with feelings of awe and almost devotion." But the general also was a fighter who was "too smart" for U. S. Grant.[70]

In contrast, twenty-eight men wrote negatively of eighteen general officers, ten receiving only one mention each. Even Lee found the occasional critic, but few men other than Joe Johnston appeared on both lists. On the whole, Braxton Bragg, John Forney, and Johnston attracted the most opprobrium from men serving under them. Severe discipline undermined several of the generals' reputations.[71] Writing to his wife, for example, Pvt. J. H. Lee of the 43rd Alabama noted that a sick man had died after Forney denied him a furlough. The general, Lee went on, "says all the way for a man to get out of this war is to die out. Our orderly sargeant called his name three times this morning before he marked it out, it looked like they hated to discharge him after he had been dead 6 hours." Lee added that several of his comrades hoped to shoot Forney while in action.[72]

The 11th Alabama Cavalry's Capt. Robert Corry, meanwhile, regretted that his outfit had come under Nathan Bedford Forrest's command, for Forrest was "a rash man and fond of going into danger."[73] The opposite kind of leadership, however, accounted for fully half of the critics' attacks. Cpl. R. M. Head was typical when he wrote a friend, "I don't think that ole Brag evry aught to have con toral of any thing withought it was sum ole woman chickens."[74] On this point, both positive and negative commentators agreed. While later enlisters wanted company-grade and regimental officers who primarily were fair and competent men, they still expected their generals to look the part and know how to fight.

Some few expected military prowess from other soldiers' generals as well. As Jason Phillips has noted most cogently, constant rumors of distant victories, Northern political collapse, and foreign intervention became major sustaining motivators for many "diehard" Confederates. Rumors of improbable battlefield successes, even in relative backwaters, especially countered local defeats.[75] Relatively few sampled later-enlisting Confederates, however, only seventeen in all, paid much attention to the successes of generals beyond their immediate front. Theaters of service divided them almost evenly, with seven in the East, five in the West, and another five in the Trans-Mississippi. There was one notable variation among them, however. Supporting Gary Gallagher's findings, the men in the Trans-Mississippi and West paid an inordinate amount of attention to rumors of Lee's victories in Virginia.[76] The Shibley brothers of the 22nd Arkansas, for example, wrote from Louisiana in August 1863 that Lee's Pennsylvania invasion had been "imminently successful. He has defeated the enemy in every engagement and taken 15 or 18 thousand prisoners. This will in some degree counterbalance our losses at Vicksburg and Port Hudson. Gen. Lee's army is still on Federal soil and in excellent spirits and fine condition being stronger now than ever before. It seems to be that if the Confederate government is able to invade the North it certainly is entitled to a place among the nations."[77] In contrast, men in the Eastern theater put much less hope on the less successful Western armies. They were just as likely to point to successes elsewhere in the East, as did Pvt. Isaac Walters, who took heart from Jackson's 1862

Valley Campaign, or Thomas J. Moore, who wrote exuberantly of the Confederate capture of Baltimore that never was.[78]

IN MANY WAYS, later enlisters were much like their fellow Confederates. They valued comradeship and good leadership. A deeper examination, however, highlights many apparent differences as well. Camaraderie for them ultimately was a more extreme extension of common home-based relationships of kin and neighbor. Separated from their "neighbor boys" by death or distance, many experienced difficulties creating new bonds among fellow soldiers from other counties and towns, a phenomenon that in the literature seems less frequent among veterans. Later enlisters' relationships with company and regimental officers also were grounded in antebellum hierarchies. They were less likely to expect courage of their officers and focused instead on qualities such as competence and fairness that also described peacetime work supervision and leadership. Relatively few expressed unit pride, or worried a great deal about their generals or the distant campaigns of other Confederate armies. Far from home, in short, later-enlisting Confederates generally retained a local focus that made their messes and companies mere extensions of the places they left behind. Indeed, in stark contrast to the soldiers historians have described as increasingly alienated, for later enlisters, military service seems to an extent to have helped maintain local ties and undermine that alienation. Indeed, continuing kin and neighborhood relationships, as well as reciprocal bonds between men of different status, strengthened communities with new, overlapping webs of masculine relationships and egalitarian demands that stretched beyond the community proper to camp and field. Yet at the same time the survival of community ties within and beyond the army also produced insularity, demands for conformity, and suspicion of outsiders. In the end, such relationships simply were not elastic enough to respond effectively to dwindling messes or to prevent war weariness and even defeatism among soldiers, although even then they shaped those responses. As the next chapter will demonstrate, even deserters usually went home in small familiar groups of relatives and neighbors.[79]

8

WEARINESS

"WE HAVE SUFFERED ENOUGH"

Pvt. Hiram Smith Williams was cold, wet, and depressed. A reluctant soldier to begin with, the New Jersey–born Alabama resident, former carriage maker, journalist, and amateur actor had delayed enlisting until May 1862, and then managed to get himself detached to duty in the Mobile shipyards. Called into active service only in February 1864, his first reaction was to seek a transfer into the Confederate Navy, which he considered safer. His effort failed, and he soon found himself at the front in Dalton, Georgia, assigned to Alexander P. Stewart's Pioneer Corps. Although he still enjoyed playing the role of "Amanda" in his unusual, gender-bending mess, Smith could see little else ahead of him that was cheering. One chilly, stormy night in April, on guard as the rest of his comrades slept, Williams broke regulations, sat down beside the fire, and penned an untitled, forty-eight-line poem that expressed his gloomy mood about "the Present so dark [and] so dreary." He was, he confessed, "weary":

Weary indeed of a poor soldier's life
Weary of all this mad turmoil and strife
Weary of roll-call, weary of drilling
Weary of marching and weary of killing
Weary of labor in sunshine and rain
On breastworks and baricades oft done in vain

He was "weary" of other things as well: long nights, guard duty, shelling, seeing wounded men "writhing in torture [and] pain." He was "weary of battle, though glory be there / Of winning green laurels for others to wear." But mostly, he was weary of the war and the leaders who would not end it:

Oh, where are our statesmen [and] have we got one?
To end what our demagogues madly begun
Not one in our land to start into life
With brain and with nerve to stop this sad strife
Alas for our country! Alas for our day!
If we wait for battle to stop this mad fray

Too much blood has already flowed like a river
Too many fond hearts have been parted forever
Too many farewells with tears have been spoken
Too many fond circles already been broken
Footsore and weary over paths steep and rough
We have fought, we have bled, we have suffered enough

"I honestly believe," he added in a cynical postscript, "that the above lines contain the real and true sentiments of ninety-nine hundreths of the soldiers composing our armies and at least four-fifths of those out of the army. Yet what newspaper would dare publish them at the present time? What a sad commentary on *Liberty*, on *freedom*." In retrospect, the former thespian's words admittedly sound hyperbolic, if not melodramatic. He had, after all, never been in combat—although that soon would change—and he had suffered on the whole much less than his peers in the Army of Tennessee. Yet Williams's poem still raises a significant question about the war weariness of later-enlisting Confederates. How many of them were weary, believed that they had seen and suffered enough, and simply wanted the war to end?[1]

BELL WILEY WOULD HAVE suggested that Williams was not alone. Poor rations, threadbare clothing, and infrequent pay were daily reminders to many men of the Confederate nation's inability to provide for its soldiers. Family hardships made worse by privation, the apparent actions of greedy speculators, and the inability to get home on furlough to help out further depressed spirits. Declining civilian support and patriotism forced many soldiers to question their reasons for serving. Lengthening enlistment demands placed additional burdens upon soldiers already in the field, even as other men sought to avoid military service entirely. Hatred of the stay-at-homes grew. Simultaneously, and without any hint of irony, the monotony of camp and the rigors of the march, as well as the terrors of battle, led soldiers to earnestly advise friends and family members to stay out of the army if they could do so. While most merely grumbled and complained as soldiers often do, some actively sought to escape the army. Men pleaded sickness, avoided duty, and, increasingly, deserted. In February 1865, the Bureau of Conscription reported over 100,000 deserters abroad in the country, a figure Wiley judged overly conservative.

Wiley further stressed that morale ebbed and flowed with events over the course of the war. Homesickness undermined morale from the first, but conscription, resentment, privation, and battle created a serious crisis of war weariness and depression in the winter of 1862–63. Military and government authorities recognized the problem and responded with a range of correctives from furloughs to sham battles and grand reviews that kept morale relatively high during the following winter. The religious revivals noted in Chapter 6 played an additional role in buoying morale. None of these measures, however, could fully withstand the blows of military defeat and the subsequent loss of territory toward the end of 1864, notably involving the fall of Atlanta and John B. Hood's brutal defeats at Franklin and Nashville. Many soldiers became despondent and gave up on the war during this second, deep morale crisis, whether or not they fled from the ranks.[2]

Gerald Linderman also argued that the realities of war, so unlike the naive expectations young men brought to service, undermined morale and led to widespread disillusionment. The ugliness of battlefield death, disease, harsh discipline, the ill treatment of enemy civilians, the boredom of camp, and the drinking and gambling that followed all rudely shocked recruits who expected war to be grand and glorious. Once hoping to prove their courage on the battlefield, soldiers increasingly sought merely to survive the war, according to Linderman, and return to an allegedly ungrateful civilian world that they believed had exploited and dismissed them.[3]

Linderman's work, however, remains an exception. Despite the publication of several specific studies of desertion,[4] the general tendency among most recent historians of Civil War soldiers has been to counter Wiley and Linderman, acknowledging but minimizing despondency and defeatism while focusing upon those whose morale remained reasonably high. Reid Mitchell agreed to an extent that Confederate soldiers in particular grew disillusioned as the war dragged to an end, particularly poor Johnny Rebs who blamed the rich for everything from conscription and impressment of the families' stores to speculative extortion and corruption. Seemingly betrayed, unable to provide for loved ones even as others profited from the conflict, their loyalty to the Confederate experiment remained lukewarm at best. Many deserted. But most, Mitchell added, did not. Thanks to the racial solidarity, hatred of the enemy, religious faith, and bonds of camaraderie discussed in previous chapters, most Confederates remained loyal to the bitter end. In general, later scholars have echoed and amplified Mitchell's essential points. Jason Phillips, for example, importantly added to the list of explanatory factors the abundance of morale-building rumors involving miraculous victories, Northern defeatism, and Yankee atrocities. Chandra Manning meanwhile argued that only the Confederate government's eleventh-hour decision to arm black troops finally led to a widespread conclusion among soldiers that the war was lost, and even then they continued to fight until April 1865. Aaron Sheehan-Dean concluded that desertion among Virginia troops actually peaked in 1862 and declined thereafter due to a combination of their proximity to home, peer pressure, and punitive measures.[5]

James McPherson took on the Linderman thesis most directly. Citing both Linderman's reliance on limited and published postwar sources and his interpretation of them, McPherson countered that duty, honor, belief in republican liberty, and, for Confederates, the determination to keep African Americans in bondage sustained all but the worst deadbeat soldiers throughout the war. Desertion and defeatism did increase, McPherson admits, but he implies that within the army it was largely a problem of married men anxious over their dependents and especially "conscripts, substitutes, and bounty men" who lacked "a sense of duty and honor"—that is, men like Hiram Smith Williams who had strenuously avoided the battlefield. Overall, most soldiers remained true to their cause.[6]

Given such assumptions about the linkage between cause and morale, and adding to them what this study has suggested about the lesser importance of ideology, camaraderie, and corporate worship within the army among later-enlisting Confederates, one would expect them and especially older men with families to exhibit a somewhat higher degree of war weariness, disillusion, and even desertion than the enlistees of 1861. And indeed, over a quarter of the sampled soldiers, eighty-four (26.25 percent), described some sort of war weariness at least once during the war. A closer study of their comments, however, reveals that bad morale even among later enlisters was not so widespread as one might expect; and when it occurred at all was usually just as sporadic and event driven as it was for their more-veteran comrades.

WHILE SOME NEW RECRUITS among later enlisters discovered that they enjoyed camp life in the first months of 1862, and even boasted of better health and weight gain, a few openly longed for home. Young Pvt. William A. Collins wanted out of the army even before the regimental doctors had examined him, and expressed regret that he was healthy enough to be approved. Seventeen-year-old Pvt. G. L. Alspaugh of the 27th Louisiana meanwhile claimed to "like soldiering" but still wanted to go home as soon as possible. "Ma," he wrote, "I did not know how good I loved you till I got to be a soldier."[7]

Older men were more likely to express initial dissatisfaction, however. North Carolina schoolmaster Thomas J. Elliot, lacking a draft exemption, railed against wealthy stay-at-homes who avoided military service while he had to go to the front lines. "I don't think money ought to get them out of it," he huffed to his wife, "they are no better to be out than myself, my life is as sweet to me as theirs is to them."[8] Some did more than complain. Pvt. Harden Cochrane reported that a man in his company drowned himself soon after arriving in camp. "He left a child 11 days old at home," Cochrane added, "and his mess was broken up when he got here. He was troubled generally."[9] Others deserted, many only to be caught and returned. Sgt. Edwin Fay described the April execution of a bounty jumper, while Pvt. H. W. Robinson related how six captured deserters at Cumberland Gap received thirty-nine lashes each, a brutal punishment that at least served the purpose of frightening him into line.[10]

Fay went on to point out a second reason for poor morale, a growing disillusionment with the gritty reality of army life, as opposed to the romanticized ideal men brought with them. From the outset, he complained about poor food and treatment, describing his rations as "pickled Beef that even our negroes will not eat." Worse yet, his officers were of poor quality, and the nation's management of its troops was scandalous.[11] While Fay was typically shrill in both his complaints and his constant desire to go home, he was not alone in expressing shock at the army's shortcomings and especially its discipline, which reminded more than one man of slavery. Pvt. G. H. Burns, for example, described himself as a slave who "must go to a Master when we want to go . . . even to the post office."[12] Lt. William L. Nugent meanwhile complained of incompetent officers and "the suicidal policy of our Government" that he feared would result in the loss of Vicksburg and Corinth.[13] Pvt. John Thurman of the 3rd Tennessee Cavalry, a fervent secessionist, wrote after the Battle of Shiloh that "the Confederate army here is in the most imaginable disorder and if it is to be taken as a sample of our ability to win our independence, it is exceedingly doubtful I assure you. I could tell you things I saw on the battle field," he added, "that I consider a burning shame to southern honour and shivelry."

Similar complaints about army life continued unabated, but as the summer of 1862 passed a third theme developed.[14] Sheer homesickness set in as the war dragged on without resolution. A few new soldiers could think of little else. "I wount to see you and the children very Bad," Lt. E. B. Coggin wrote from Petersburg, "But I am two fur off to Come to See you though I had Not for got tou Nor I never Shal my heart is fild with greef and my eyes with tears to think that we ar so far apart that I cannot See you and my Sweet little Children."[15] Another, Pvt. S. W. Farrow of the 19th Texas, explained similar sentiments. "I can tell you that I have not learned to love to stay away from you yet," he wrote his wife. "I spend many a lonely hour in camps. . . . I shall never be satisfied in the Army I am anxious to see you and my sweet children."[16] Pvt. William Ross Stilwell told his wife that he thought of her constantly. "I think if it were not for my family that I would make a good soldier," he wrote, "but when I think of you and Tommy and that is all the time most, it makes me feel bad."[17]

Active campaigning released men from the tedium of camp and drill while keeping them too busy and exhausted to ache for home, but it brought its own discontents. Pvt. G. H. Burns complained from the line of march that "we have been draged and pulled about until we want to run into the rascals and stave them up & be done with them but we are draged from post to pillow for no purpose that I can see."[18] Hoping to obtain a cadetship or any other position that would get him out of the ranks, Pvt. Robert Banks of the 43rd Mississippi similarly wrote his sister, "I am not dissatisfied except I dislike these forced marches and suffering for food and water and accomplishing no good by it."[19] Having met the Federal "rascals" in battle, meanwhile, Pvt. William Ross Stilwell concluded that he had seen enough. From Antietam, he opined that "it looks like they are going to kill all the men on both sides before they stop." A few weeks later from Fredericksburg, he confessed that he "wouldn't care much if the Confederacy was broken up into a thousand fragments anyhow for they treat the army like so many dogs. . . . Nothing but war would do the people and they have just it in all its bitterest crimes." As for ideology, he added, "they may talk of liberty and they may talk of me dying in war but I want to live with my family and live in peace. . . . If this is independence don't want it. I had rather take bondage."[20]

Victory proved a tonic for many complainers, but soldiers who experienced defeat or at least inertia often sank further into despair. Lt. William L. Nugent, for example, continued to fret about conditions in his home state and the potential loss of Vicksburg. Rather than be sent elsewhere, Nugent wanted his regiment to serve near home where it could defend the city, and he railed at his generals for not letting them protect it.[21] Other men were anxious to return home because they were convinced that the Confederacy already was all but defeated. "I would Give this Southern Confederacy," Pvt. John H. Hundley of the 21st North Carolina wrote from a hospital, "if it ware in my power to be at home with you and the children once more."[22] Lt. John Meriwether of the 38th Alabama agreed. "I am entirely worn out with the life of a Soldier," he explained. "My Dear I am going to quit if I can, sure. For I believe I had soon let the infernal yankees have all I have than be killed off by degrees with cold & filth."[23]

Anger at the government crystallized into class-laden rumors, such as the allegation that impressment officials were actively targeting poor men with foodstuffs and other supplies, or that Confederate authorities planned to prevent wives from writing to husbands in the army.[24] Resentment of both the rich and the powerful at home festered as well. Sgt. Thomas Wayman Hendricks of the 12th Alabama Cavalry, homesick and angry, blamed a few ambitious wealthy men for his suffering. Pvt. A. M. Sewell of the 39th

Georgia agreed. "The war is composed of privates & I suppose over too thirds of them were poor men that is neaded at home," he explained, "& i am in faver of them having there rites I am in faver of all the privates going home & then who would carry on the war then the officers wouldn't you know." Like other soldiers, Sewell fantasized about the privates of both armies jointly agreeing to quit the war and go home, and the wealthy be damned.[25] The wife of Pvt. C. D. Sides, a soldier who had joined the 5th North Carolina solely for the bounty, cherished the same notion, that both sides "should lay down our armies and go home," but her spouse found it unrealistic. "As long as the men puts up with everything the Big men puts on us," he countered, "Just so long the war will last and there is so many fools that think that everything that is done by the great men is Just right and that makes me mad." A week later, Sides again attacked his "good Secession neighbors" who were "steping about with their wives and Snotty negroes" while spreading "Confederate lies" about peace.[26]

Discontent worsened during the winter of 1862–63. As Table 4 demonstrates, reported incidents of desertion, already a growing problem through the autumn, increased dramatically in December, and levels remained high across the Confederacy until spring. Men described some deserters leaving individually but more often told of small kin and neighborhood groups of five to fifteen men, soldiers who displayed in their flight an often-ignored facet of wartime camaraderie. While writers identified a handful of them as Unionists or bounty jumpers, most were depicted as simply hungry, weary, and angry at their treatment.[27]

At a few western camps, frustrations and the desire to go home reached dangerous levels. Stationed at Cumberland Gap, William D. Clover of the 62nd North Carolina became convinced that he and his comrades would die of disease while wealthy men avoided service. He surrendered his musket, refused to don his newly issued uniform, and began to discuss mutiny with some of his fellows.[28] Lt. T. J. Rounsaville of the 13th Texas Cavalry meanwhile reported from Pine Bluff, Arkansas, that his comrades were furious that with the one-year anniversary of their enlistment approaching, they were to be kept in the army and even denied promised furloughs. What finally touched off a collective response, however, was a particularly rancid issue of beef. The Texans "lit up some torches & formed the company & gathered the drums and mes pans and martch over the branch and buried it and fired several paltoons over it & then stack up head and foot boards, then march up to Col. Burnett's head quarters for a speech." The colonel took the impromptu mock funeral seriously and moved quickly to diffuse the situation. "The Col. taken the stump," Rounsaville continued, "& told us that he did not think hard of us for burning brand but he did not want us to stack arms and attempt to go home, thos he said he was unaware that pork could not have been procured for us, for the damed old Arkansas never did have any thing in it from the start. We have a great deal of dissatisfaction through out our regiment," Rounsaville added, "simply because our time is about to expire & no prospect of going home very soon, just raving and pitching about it & swore they will not stand it. They say they will go home or die, it is nearly a unanimous thing through out our Regiment."[29]

Writing from the same seething encampment, the 22nd Texas's John T. Knight related that his hungry comrades were "not going to drill any longer than today. Some of ours are under guard for refusing to do duty." Four days later, he mysteriously reported that several "Catholicks" had been "shot all to pieces" in retaliation.[30] The Shibley brothers meanwhile described to their parents a confrontation in the 3rd Arkansas that occurred there in September. "There are but few guns in that regt.," they explained, "and they are old rifles. These the insurgents collected and provided themselves with ammunition. About 8 o'clock they formed into a mob and marched past two regiments calling out to the men 'Fall in, all that want to go home.' Rumors were rife that 3 or 4 hundred had deserted. But when morning came it was determined that only 28 were gone. About 40 men have deserted that regiment. The insurrection is I think effectively quelled." But a month later, they admitted that "there is great dissatisfaction and in camps two or three Companys stacked their guns yesterday and demanded their pay. They finally took them up again by the Col. Prather promising that the money should be paid as soon as it comes on."[31]

From Vicksburg, Pvt. John Wilson related a similar crisis in the 35th Mississippi. "There is more dissatisfaction in the army than I had any idea of," he wrote. "The men swear that they will not fight any more. There was 30 left hear last Thursday night & has not been heard from. There is others making preparations to leave. I am fearful that there will be a split between ourselves before Christmas. We cant hear nothing talked of hear but Home Sweet Home! All have got the home fever & nothing will do them but home. It is nothing to hear men say they will not fight & that they will throw down there arms & go home."[32]

Military authorities responded to defiance and desertion with a host of punishments, ranging from confinement and hard labor to the ball and chain to the lash. Other deserters received a death sentence. Frequently but not always, men sentenced to be shot had not only fled the army but had gone over to the enemy and been recaptured. In general, later enlisters sympathized with the prisoners but admitted that the sight of executions kept them in the ranks.[33] From the troubled Pine Bluff encampment, Lt. T. J. Rounsaville maintained in late March 1863 that desertion had lessened inversely with an increase of executions, but he still lamented their necessity and cruelty. "They both resided in the City of Houston" he wrote of two men who were shot, "& one of them with a wife and three little children to moan his loss, also one was executed yesterday for the same offence, a young man some 20 years age, he had been sick for three weeks I hear not out of bed, but was taken out to be shot, he looked very thin & meager, was an object of pitty." At least fifteen more awaited the same fate, he added, for "there is little chance for a deserter to escape death."[34] Executions ultimately discouraged desertion, but they elicited little love for the country or the army. Pvt. S. W. Farrow described the executions of two men as "Cold blood murder,"[35] while Pvt. C. D. Sides of the 5th North Carolina enthusiastically approved of the method but groused that already "men die fast enough in this confederacy, but big men rule."[36]

In general, such pronounced discontent reached its nadir among new regiments in the West that winter. The Pine Bluff and Vicksburg garrisons were particularly troubled. But even there, the new year and coming of spring seemed to bring hope to some men. J. A. Wilson, who recently had worried about mutiny, noted in February that rumors of peace had put his comrades in a fine mood. For other men, all it took was winter clothing and decent food to stop the grumbling. Lee's victory at Fredericksburg helped some men stationed from Virginia to Texas cope with the brutal winter. As the roads thawed, Army of Northern Virginia soldiers in particular looked forward to more battlefield victories and a successful conclusion to the war. Others pinned their hopes on foreign intervention or the Democrats in Washington. Sgt. Edwin Fay believed every promising rumor he heard about Northern upheaval and the collapse of the Lincoln administration, while even Pvt. A. M. Sewell expressed hope that rumors of Union officers' resignations and midwestern Democratic rebellion meant a quick end to the war.[37]

Overall, low morale in 1862 ran at relatively steady levels, with a slight increase beginning with cold weather in October 1862 that reached its acme in February 1863. Desertion followed, spiking in December and peaking in

March before a flurry of executions and other punishments partially beat back the tide, although reports of desertions and shootings remained at relatively high levels until active campaigning began. Indeed as late as June 1863, Capt. Ruffin Barnes of the 43rd North Carolina, serving in Lee's Army, reported desertion levels so high in his regiment that no soldier could leave his camp without a commissioned officer, while Pvt. M. R. Norman of the 63rd Virginia described his encampment in Southwest Virginia as surrounded by guards. It also was around this time that Pvt. C. D. Epps of the 6th Georgia Cavalry, one of only two admitted deserters in the sample, went into the guardhouse for briefly taking off for home.[38]

Men whose families lay in the path of the enemy expressed special discontent. Pvt. John W. Cotton described the distress of some of the Alabamians in his outfit. "A heap of them talks of going home," he related, "but very few of them goes. . . . A heap of them says there famileys is out of provisions."[39] Men who feared Federal occupation of their home territories fared even worse. "From all accounts you are now completely hemmed in by the enemy," Lt. William L. Nugent wrote his wife, "and will soon learn by heart, as a child, the oft told tale, the recital of their outrages and the invocation of divine punishment upon them. I have given up all hope of ever saving anything from the crash that will inevitable follow close upon the heels of the termination of the present conflict." But still, he soldiered on.

So did most others. Indeed, never did more than nine sampled men in a month admit to their own bad morale, and even those levels declined slightly beginning in March and then precipitously in June.[40] Morale in fact remained surprisingly good among most late enlisters when viewed month by month, and it was improving as the spring of 1863 passed. Even the death of Stonewall Jackson after the Battle of Chancellorsville, which made such an impact on the civilian population's spirits, elicited only two comments. Victory on that field, indeed, proved a powerful sustaining motivator. Two battlefield defeats, however, soon reversed the trend. Eight sampled men, not all serving under Lee, judged the results of his Pennsylvania campaign distressing. Pvt. William Ross Stilwell had seen enough of the North during the Maryland campaign the previous autumn, and had no desire to return.[41] Joseph Manson of the 12th Virginia agreed. "I was sorry when it was begun," he wrote his mother, "I am glad it is over. I never expected we would have the ability to wage invasive warfare and I had enough of Maryland last year to satisfy me that we could never fight successfully upon that soil." What bothered him particularly was that Confederates "acted very disgracefully in Pennsylvania towards the civilians. . . . I felt when I saw how our men were going on that nothing but disaster would follow and in truth I was associated with an armed mob under the broadest license and not with a disciplined army such as General Lee has had under his command." Unless foreign intervention developed or Southerners abandoned their wickedness, he concluded, the Confederacy could not win the war.

Some refused to wait on the British and promptly deserted for home. William F. Wagner, a private in the 57th North Carolina, wrote frequently of post-Gettysburg desertions in his regiment and admitted that he was tempted himself. His wife's disapproval as well as concerns for his honor eventually dissuaded him.[42] Other men were not so concerned with appearances. Notably, Pvt. William P. Cline of the 46th North Carolina is, along with Epps, the only other admitted deserter in the sample. Blacksmith Cline enlisted early in 1862, expecting the war to be over within months. He went on to fight at Antietam and Fredericksburg, but he never grew comfortable away from his wife and smithy. Cline's discontent worsened when he learned that former soldier Mark Hewitt was harassing his wife as well as spreading rumors that Cline had consorted with prostitutes. As early as May 1862, Cline had threatened to return home to kill Hewitt. Only after Gettysburg, however, and despite being shaken by the sight of a deserter's execution, did he begin to seriously plan his flight. He was both discouraged about the war and angry that Hewitt remained out of uniform. Cline wrote that "the men is all out of heart the most of them thinks that we are whipt." A few days later, he added, "i don't think that it is worth our while to be fiten hire eny longer for we cant never whip the yankes i have a noshen to quit and come home." And so he did. Yet a month later, Cline returned to his unit voluntarily, for reasons unknown. He spent forty days in Richmond's Castle Thunder wearing a ball and chain and remained under arrest until February 1864. Released, Cline rejoined his outfit in time to fight and die in the Wilderness.[43]

Distress over Gettysburg paled in comparison, moreover, to the depression and defeatism that followed the fall of Vicksburg. News of the city's loss initially sank civilian and soldier morale and led to numerous desertions among all Johnny Rebs. Sixteen men among those sampled expressed their shock and dismay over the fall of the city. The most affected, of course, were the unlucky men captured within the city. One of them, Sgt. J. B. Sanders of the 37th Mississippi, admitted that he saw "no prospect now of the South ever Sustaining it . . . we have lost the Mississippi and our nation is sundered and they is not a nuf left to fight for. I don't look for any thing else but total an a highlation of the entire population of the South if she continued to carry on this war."[44]

Other stunned soldiers, such as Capt. J. B. Rounsaville, served west of the river. "Deep gloom among our officers and arms on this side," he wrote his family. "Cut off from all communication, for the Feds can soon take Port Hudson, then Richmond, and we are gone up I fear. Very near that now."[45] After Port Hudson fell as well, J. C. Brightman of the 18th Texas concluded that "one thing is certain: It is going to have the most demoralizing effect of anything that has occurred during the war. You can hear the expression every day by our men that we have 'gone up the spout,' They have lost confidence in our officers on the other side of the Mississippi," he added, Lee included.[46] Pvt. S. W. Farrow of the 19th Texas wrote a flurry of letters after the fall of Vicksburg that described his defeatism and that of his fellow soldiers. Farrow hoped that somehow the Federal Congress still might relent, but all he really wanted was a furlough.[47] Others refused to wait; Pvt. John Knight described men "leaving all the time" with " 'Spanish furlous.' " Indeed Knight ultimately profited from desertion by collecting abandoned weapons and selling them to men who remained in the ranks. Ominously, he decided that when the time came, he would sell his too before he fled.[48]

All of the other men expressing Vicksburg-spun low morale served in the Western theater. Echoing others, Lt. William Duncan Cole of the 38th Alabama reported that morale in the Army of Tennessee had plummeted to new lows because of the loss of the city, coupled with the results of the Pennsylvania campaign and conditions within Bragg's army. Soldiers stationed in Mississippi were more despondent still. Lt. William L. Nugent, long a Cassandra when it came to Vicksburg, expected the war to be over before the new year.[49] "We air whipt now if we nod hit," Pvt. A. J. Edge of the 52nd Georgia lamented, "and we air beginning to no hit we have not got a nuff men here in the west to hold old Grant a bit he can whip us here ever fit and he has don hit eve fit we hav had with him."[50]

As Jason Phillips points out, some soldiers rebounded quickly, thanks in part to hopeful rumors but also because it remained unfathomable to many that the Confederacy could lose the war. The simple fact that the Confederacy survived through August, for example, helped J. C. Brightman regain his hope, as did rumors of French intervention. Yet a general malaise dragged on into the autumn and beyond for many sampled soldiers, who now added the summer's defeats to an ever-lengthening list of woes. Some actively discouraged relatives from coming to the army. Pvt. A. E. Shore ached for the war to end and blamed its continuance on state governments and newspaper editors. Others took off for home; desertion in August as reported by sampled men far surpassed the previous highs of March. Loyal men dismissed many deserters as soft or as shiftless criminals before the war but had more trouble ignoring fleeing family men who had served well. While the Army of Tennessee was rent with the worst morale and desertion problem, the situation in the Army of Northern Virginia remained far from rosy. Pvt. Samuel Pickens reported the flight of twenty-one deserters from the 12th Alabama. Chaplain Francis Milton Kennedy of the 28th North Carolina spent so much time visiting condemned men in Gen. James Henry Lane's Brigade that the general angrily reprimanded him for leaving camp. Between September 1863 and the end of the year, the Methodist Kennedy counseled fifteen condemned men, baptizing some and even dispensing communion to two Lutherans of the 18th North Carolina.[51]

Still and all, almost all of the later enlisters in the sample, even those most tempted to desert, ultimately refused to run. For them, desertion was an observed phenomenon both attractive and repulsive that left them emotionally tied in knots. "This is indeed a dark day for the Confederacy," Pvt. William Ross Stilwell wrote, "hundreds of our men are deserting and those that remain are discouraged and disheartened and people at home whipped and want us to give up. To give up is subjugation," he went on, "to fight on is but dissolution, to submit is aful, to fight on is death. Oh, what shall we do?" Stilwell himself was not yet ready to quit, but he had little faith in his comrades' resolve.[52] Like Stilwell, Lt. William Duncan Cole refused to resign, citing his loyalty to the men of his company. Still, he confessed that it was hard to keep fighting. He feared that "all enjoyment for us as a Southern People has forsaken us forever." The Army of Tennessee, he reported, was "low spirited" and "at the end of our row." Battle loomed, he added, and he expected defeat. "I had rather be in Africa at this time than in the Confederacy," he lamented, "we are in the last place now that is." While he partially censured Tennessee troops within the army for threats of refusing to leave the state, he saved his worst jibes for politicians and ideologues. "It is quite an easy thing for some to say that they had rather die than submit to subjugation," he wrote, "but when they have to act they generally do as little as any one else."[53]

Three Army of Tennessee soldiers singled out one notable politician for derision. Jefferson Davis had arrived in the West to review and rally the troops. Pvt. Grant Taylor sarcastically compared his president to a "smoked dried herring."[54] "Some of the boys speak of going to see him as though he was a monkey show," Pvt. Abel H. Crawford of the 55th Alabama noted a few days later. "I am anxious to see him myself provide he can tell me when the war is going to close, but if he cant I don't care anything about Seeing him."[55] Once the president had come and left, Lt. Ben Robertson of the 44th Mississippi bitterly criticized him. "Our soldiers are in worse spirits than I ever saw them," he wrote his sister. "Many are down upon Jeff Davis for stamping them as cowards. It was no the fault of the soldiers that caused our defeit at missionary Ridge. The blame belongs to the Officers combined with the fact that the enemy had four to one against us."[56]

As winter approached and passed, more men did finally give up. Capt. Robert Corry of the 11th Alabama Cavalry described how "all of Captain Sheets company deserted night before last—The Captain at the head."[57] Lt. James Wallace of the 9th Missouri Sharpshooters reported that his brigade's battery had refused to participate in a grand review because they would not accept the officers chosen for them. At Dalton, Pvt. A. J. Edge expressed little faith in his comrades, reporting that "old Grant is goying to come against us with about one hondred & fifty thousand strong when he dos hit we will have to run or fit one but hit will be running i do espect for we hav bin in the [habit] of running all the time."[58]

Edge for the moment only worried about possibilities, but other men suffered real defeats. For them, morale wavered critically. The 3rd Mississippi's Pvt. Willie Sivley wrote his sister after Sherman's forces launched the Meridian campaign and drove Leonidas Polk's force back into Alabama. "Our good old State has gone up," he lamented. With his comrades outnumbered, he went on, it was "useless to fight." Thousands had deserted during the retreat but, Sivley added defiantly, "we art whipped by a long shot."[59] Pvt. S. W. Farrow, in contrast, was not so sure. His morale had never been high before his unit went into action, and now it plummeted. As his division retreated across Louisiana from Nathaniel Banks's army, Farrow complained of hunger and "dissatisfaction in camp. the men are literally starving here a great many are talking of leaving the field and they will do it if they are not better fed. every reasonable, sensible man can see that we had better quit before times gets any worse. . . . the soldiers all believe that we will go back to the Union . . . we are overpowered by an overwhelming force and Texas will be invaded before two months unless something is done to prevent it."[60]

There were fewer discordant voices in the Eastern theater that winter, however, and all save one strikingly were from troubled North Carolina. Pvt. A. H. Massey of the 31st North Carolina was especially ready to go back into the Union. Writing his sister from Petersburg in April 1864, Massey doubted that the long war he opposed would ever end. At best, he hoped that William W. Holden, the outspoken Raleigh newspaper editor and leader of his state's vibrant peace movement, would win the upcoming election as governor and somehow take North Carolina back into the union. "I never want A nother vote given," he wrote, "unlese it is a unon vote the time has Bin when A unon man Did not have librity to talk but the time will Bey when thay will say what thay think And I pray to See that Day Cum."[61] Pvt. William F. Wagner of the 57th North Carolina agreed, convinced that the war was lost. When the "Big men drawed up a resilution" against Holden's peace movement, Wagner reported, "most of the solegers voted for peece and now they got it published that we had voted to keepe on the war we never voted that a way we voted to have peece on some terms." He added that "the solegeres is nearley all willing to go back in the uniion a gain and that is what I think they aut to doo. . . . we aut to staid in the union in the first plase."[62]

Yet Massey and Wagner were in the end only exceptions that proved the rule, and indeed even they remained in the ranks and later fought again when required. Pvt. Grant Taylor's response was far more typical. Captured at Vicksburg in July, Taylor lamented in October that he felt as if he had "sacrifized everything for a phantom." Two months later, hospitalized in Georgia, he described all of his fellow patients as "generally low spirited and [they] think our cause is gone." And at the beginning of the new year, he confessed in words reminiscent of Private Massey's, "I am glad the Yanks ran us off Lookout Mountain for it does seem to me that we would have been bound to have frozen if we had staid up there without shelter as we were." Yet Taylor reenlisted for the war, explaining that at least it gave him a better chance of a furlough and seeing his loved ones again.[63]

Overall, neither expressions of poor morale nor reports of desertion that winter ever reached the levels of July and August 1863, although month-by-month totals do reveal a somewhat worse situation than during the previous winter, peaking during the first four months of 1864.[64] Most of it, moreover, was confined to the West and especially to the recently defeated Army of Tennessee; Lee's men remained in relatively good spirits. Later enlisters west of the mountains especially had little faith in their political leaders, complained of officers' special privileges, and damned stay-at-homes and speculators for undermining the war effort. They were cold, poorly clothed, and hungry to boot. After the Chattanooga battles, they watched as comrades slipped away for home. Yet even for most of them, defeat still remained unthinkable. The religious revivals of the winter played a significant role in providing men with hope, as did new rumors of faraway victories and peace talks. Executions played a part as well in stifling some desertion; Lt. William A. Stephens described seeing nineteen men shot in one day at Dalton, Georgia. Thus expectations of both life and death kept the army together.[65]

IN MAY 1864, the Union army unleashed the massive, coordinated assaults in Virginia and Georgia that Grant had planned over the winter. Unlike previous campaign seasons, the early summer of 1864 would be marked by constant, grinding, daily clashes. Later-enlisting Confederates involved in those near-constant struggles barely had to time to eat and sleep, much less discuss their morale in letters home, although frequent complainer A. E. Shore managed to write his brother that he envied his arm amputation, as it had gotten him out of the army. Meanwhile, reluctant soldier James Pickens of the 5th Alabama cursed his decision to enlist, prayed for peace, and threw away his weapon on the way to the hospital at Spotsylvania. After that, he spent much of his time seeking a way out of the service. Only in September, with the beginning of trench warfare at Petersburg and the demoralizing fall of Atlanta, did more than a handful of men again take up their pens and pencils to write home. Many clearly were worn out and apprehensive.[66] "Our army is considerably demoralized," a bitter Lt. Ben Robertson reported from Lovejoy Station after Atlanta's loss. "None of them have any confidence in the generals. Hood & [Stephen D.] Lee has not nor ever had the confidence of a single soldier in the army. . . . Hood is no more a general than is your negro girl & all this disaster is caused by his blindness."[67] James Montgomery Lanning of the 25th Alabama agreed, and added that when Jefferson Davis again came to visit the army, "his brigade refused to cheer him, "not from any animosity towards him but for the Simple reason they did not feel like it."[68]

Yet while soldiers reported low spirits and scattered incidents of desertion, morale actually rebounded once again among later enlisters; their October correspondence was notable for an almost complete lack of negative expressions. The reason was politics. Observant Confederates had fol-

lowed the Union's presidential race for months, and now impending elections and the possibility of a Democratic victory followed by some sort of
negotiated settlement briefly renewed hope and sustained them in their
struggles, even though candidate George B. McClellan's avowed intention
to continue the war somewhat tried enthusiasm. Lincoln's reelection in
November blasted those expectations. Pvt. Charles M. Hurley of the 2nd
Company, Washington Artillery, hoped that the Democrats would stage a
revolution as a result.[69]

For other late enlisters, another dark winter now beckoned, as did tight
rations, homesickness, and escalating concerns for loved ones in harm's way.
Capt. William V. Davis of the 30th Mississippi reported that some of his
comrades were reduced to eating cats and dogs. More fighting awaited
many of them as well, from Petersburg to middle Tennessee.[70] Hood's
subsequent defeats at Franklin and Nashville shook men such as John W.
Cotton, who admitted that it looked "like the yankeys has got the upper-
hand on us I would like to here of some terms of peace before they runn
clear over us." Charleston would soon fall, he added, for "our soldiers are
very much disheartened and the most say we are whiped."[71] Sherman's
march through the Carolinas sank the hopes of others. Men grasped at
straws; both Pvt. John Putnam and Pvt. Grant Taylor hoped that the ru-
mored death of Jefferson Davis would bring an end to the war, while
Alabama cavalryman Sgt. Thomas Wayman Hendricks put his faith in the
peace movements of Georgia and North Carolina. A few soldiers likewise
hoped that Alexander Stephens's meeting at Hampton Roads with Lincoln
would result in a peace settlement, and that its failure somehow would
renew patriotism. Pvt. Henry T. Morgan of the 31st Louisiana reported that
men in his command had turned to God, adding that "we see them nelt
down all bout in the woods praying for peace."[72] Sgt. John Crittenden
reported with some desperation that both he and a comrade had dreamed
of peace, which he hoped was a favorable omen. Others simply sought
furloughs, transfers, and passes to go home. Mississippian Pvt. Willie Sivley
begged his family to flee to Texas, while Capt. Edwin Fay fantasized about
escaping to Brazil. Some deserted, although if the letters of soldiers can be
believed, fewer than had fled the previous winter.[73]

But despite the despair around them, most of the later enlisters still alive
and in the ranks did not give up hope. During the last months of the war,
many indeed fit Jason Phillips's description of veteran "diehards." Referring
to the conditions Lincoln enunciated at Hampton Roads, Pvt. Willie Sivley

proclaimed that he would "rather fight him twenty years than to submit to any such properstitions our cause looks very gloomy at the present. But I am in hops that there is a brighter day now at hand."[74] In March 1865, Capt. Thomas Key smiled on the Confederacy's last day of fasting and prayer and affirmed that he believed "that the Supreme Ruler will soon reward the Sons of Liberty for their prayers with a great victory."[75] Former state legislator F. A. Bleckley of the 11th Georgia Cavalry meanwhile lectured his correspondent on her defeatism. "You seem to think we are whiped and many other things," he wrote angrily, "that is disheartening you are mistaken. For if we do not gain our independence this war will continue during Lincoln's present administration and God only knows how much longer—we must prepare for the worst." Defeat would be so dishonorable, he added, that the Confederacy would never give in.[76]

Other men agreed. Both Pvt. L. R. Dalton of Hampton's Legion and the 53rd North Carolina's Lt. James E. Green were home at the beginning of April but actually left to return to their regiments. More amazing was Cpl. Martin V. Kees of the 33rd Mississippi, who had enlisted three years earlier for the bounty. Furloughed on April 21, Kees stayed at home nearly a month but then, on May 16, started back to his company. Arriving in Jackson the next day, he found out that the war was over and received his parole from occupying Federals. Pvt. William D. Alexander surrendered only at Appomattox. W. H. Robertson was still with Richard Taylor's army when it surrendered in Alabama a month later.[77] Lt. Thomas Grisham of the 28th Louisiana Cavalry would have held on even after that if he could have. "Better that the fight had continued four, yea, eight more years," he wrote, "than our Country should have been humiliated, and our noble flag *trailed in the dust*."[78]

In Galveston, Texas, Lt. Lee Faulkner too remained defiant and spoiling for at least one fight despite his conviction that the Confederacy finally was defeated. "I thank my God I have not been at home for the last twenty months," he wrote his wife, "that I have deprived myself of the greatest and almost only pleasure I have on earth . . . to assist in rescuing Our Country from the grasp of the greatest tirants on earth. My efforts have I fear been in vain," he went on, "though I shall return home feeling a consciousness that I have done my whole duty though I have never been in action. Tis the general opinion that general Magruder will make an effort to hold this place. . . . I am determined I will never be surrendered am Satisfied when we are attacked we will be defeated. . . . So long as we have an army I expect to be with it and if our people then resort to the brush I am with theme there so long as there is the least ray of hope."[79]

BELL WILEY DESCRIBED two distinct periods of low Confederate morale and desertion, the winter of 1862–63 and that of 1864–65. Jason Phillips added a third, the period just after the defeat at Gettysburg and the loss of Vicksburg. Taken together, the two historians present an accurate view of ebbing and flowing morale within Confederate arms that this study of later-enlisting Confederates bears out. For late enlisters and especially those stationed in the West, the period after Vicksburg was particularly dark. Yet for all their anger, complaints, and depression, most who left written accounts remained with the colors once joining them, until illness, wounds, death, or the end of the war forced them away. Thousands upon thousands deserted to be sure, and letters from them no doubt would alter the conclusions given here. Unfortunately and frustratingly, however, we have only two accounts in the sample from those soldiers, privates William P. Cline and C. D. Epps. The latter's reasons for deserting remain unclear, but Cline ran from a combination of worrying home concerns and a deepening conviction that the war already was lost. Notably, both also returned to their units voluntarily, fought another day, and died as a result—Epps from his wounds at Chickamauga, and Cline in the Wilderness. Even their disillusionment and demoralization, in other words, did not prevent these most-obvious "skulkers" from actively fighting and dying for the Confederacy on the battlefield, the final test of later enlisters' motivations.

9

BATTLE

"THE ELEPHANT"

Pvt. John Dooley's baptism of fire took place at Second Manassas, on August 29, 1862. Marching with the 1st Virginia in James Kemper's brigade, Dooley and his comrades realized that they were approaching the scene of battle when they suddenly walked past several dead Union soldiers. Gunfire immediately broke out ahead of them. "We are told about midday to load our guns," he wrote later, "and this was my first loading with intent to *kill*." Obeying the order, the youth admittedly "trembled with excitement and, I may add, with fear, for I was never *very* brave." Dooley's captain took him aside, advised him on "loading and keeping cool," and in so doing steadied the young soldier. The regiment then deployed into line and marched across the flank of an enemy brigade. Federal artillery opened fire, the shells "ploughing up the open field over which we are going." As they approached John Pope's exposed flank, "our Brigade was ordered again *to load*. Oh, how scared I felt!" Dooley confessed. "If I could only stay out of the fight with honor how gladly would I have done so!" Under fire the regiment double-quicked to the front and took cover behind a rail fence. "I was very much frightened," Dooley went on, "and I am sure I wasn't the only one."[1]

The 1st Virginia ended the day in reserve, but its work was hardly done. Late the following afternoon, James Longstreet unleashed his crushing flank attack on Pope's bluecoats. Part of that involved the 1st Virginia charging an enemy battery. "Again we form into line," Dooley remembered, "and now dashing thro' a cornfield; the bullets whistle thro' the leaves and ears and send many a brave comrade to his last account. But we have no time to think; such is the excitement, such the feeling with which I am inspired that I rush on with the rest, completely bewildered and scarcely heeding what takes place around." Chaos loomed ahead; a wave of Confederates fell back in disarray, "some shouting for us to *go back*—others to advance—some to *lie down*. Still on we went double quick all the time right over the flying broken Brigade and up the hill." At the summit they opened fire. Dooley found himself "among dismounted cannon, broken caissons, bleeding horses, the dead and dying." Bleeding as well, his colonel approached him, asking him to "'bear me witness that I was the first man on that battery.'"[2]

By this time, the 1st Virginia had come apart. Joining a few dozen comrades, Dooley chased away another group of enemy soldiers and took possession of a knoll overlooking the center of the battlefield. Below them the battle spread out in a tableau of smoke, color, movement, and finally victory. While the view was awe inspiring, the immediate scene was less romantic. "Oh, the horrid scenes around us!" Dooley exclaimed. "Brains, fractured skulls, broken arms and legs, and the human form mangled in every conceivable and inconceivable manner."[3]

In the aftermath of the Confederate victory at Second Manassas, Lee again moved north, taking his army into Maryland. At South Mountain, Kemper's Brigade moved belatedly and unsuccessfully to check a Federal advance into Lee's rear. Dooley most remembered encountering a frightful Federal barrage that drove him to the breaking point. He was about to run to the rear when one of his captains unexpectedly slapped him on the back, "saying 'Hurrah for you! You are one of the 1st Va. I know you'll stand by us to the last!' What could I do under such circumstances? Was I to run and prove myself a coward? No Sir!"[4]

South Mountain in the end proved only a preliminary bout to the Battle of Antietam. Kemper's brigade, down to about 200 effectives, began the day in the Confederate center, but after noon was shifted to the right, to blunt Ambrose Burnside's assault. "There may have been other troops to our left and right but I did not see any," Dooley complained. When the approaching Union line rose and charged, the regiment unleashed a volley and "fled back through the cornfield. Oh, how I ran! Or tried to run through the high corn." Afraid of being shot in the back and dishonored, however, he "frequently turned half around in running, so as to avoid if possible so disgraceful a wound." The brigade as a whole, largely comprised of 1861 enlistees, ran to the position held by Robert Toombs's Georgians and formed up in their rear. There John Dooley ended the day, a veteran in the Army of Northern Virginia.[5]

WHILE THIS STUDY thus far has examined the initial and sustaining motivations of later-enlisting Confederates, a third factor must be explored as well. *Combat motivation* was the final leg of the tripartite model developed by John Lynn and extended to American Civil War scholarship by James McPherson, who defined it as "what nerved them to face extreme danger in battle."[6] In many ways, scholarly debates over combat motivation resemble those concerning initial and sustaining motivation. Historians who downplay the importance of ideology in the decisions of men to enlist and remain with the army likewise see little relation between ideas and the willingness to pick up a rifle, fall into line, and risk death in battle. Both Bell Wiley and James Robertson largely concentrated on describing rather than interpreting the battlefield experience of men like John Dooley. Anxious to come to grips with their enemies—to "see the elephant" in contemporary slang—Johnny Rebs going into their first battle felt all sorts of emotions, from extreme fear to anger to apparent indifference. Most were nervous, afraid of death and divine retribution, but also worried that they would play the coward. Some did run, but most held their ground. While remaining outwardly calm, they nonetheless revealed their inner tensions when they threw away possessions, overshot the mark, or screamed the rebel yell. The experience of combat itself proved chaotic, and thick smoke, explosions, and shaking earth beneath their feet made it even more frightening. After the battle, men fell into exhaustion and depression, not only because of their own exertions, but also because they had to face the horrible carnage of mangled dead and dying men, many of the latter screaming for water or their mothers. The horrible sights occasioned by nineteenth-century weapons led them to hope earnestly never to fight again. Yet fight most of them would, and as veterans they would be calmer and steadier on the field, and more indifferent to the suffering that followed.[7]

Gerald Linderman took many of these threads and wove them into an early analysis of motivation for battle. He insisted that proving one's courage was the chief combat motivator of raw Civil War soldiers. Unbloodied soldiers approached battle with mixtures of anticipation and concern, he maintained, because culturally and psychologically they had built it up into so many final examinations of their manhood. They hoped not to feel fear, and if they did, they at least hoped that their comrades would not notice. Soldiers thus strove to control themselves and remain, in the lexicon of the times, "cool." Such courage might well help them survive, or at least offer them the meaningful "good death" Victorian Americans craved. The realities of battle, however, undermined their assumptions. Death, often hideous, displayed no discrimination or apparent respect for the brave. Increasingly cynical veterans accordingly jettisoned their scorn for the comrades who dodged shells or preferred to dig in for protection, as well as many of the other moral and religious values they brought with them to the war.[8]

Reid Mitchell offered a variation on the theme. Agreeing with both Wiley and Linderman that raw recruits entered battle aching to both establish their manhood and crush the foe, Mitchell focused on how soldiers overcame the dismaying disillusionment that inevitably followed. Battle was ugly and terrifying madness. To survive it and keep fighting, soldiers required some sort of motivation beyond proving their courage. Those combat motivations not surprisingly dovetailed with the factors that brought men to the army in the first place and then sustained them in camp and field. For some, a sense of duty, patriotism, or the belief in a just cause carried them through battle. Others relied on God's grace, or else nurtured their hatred for the Yankees. Some simply embraced killing, while more worried about what the folks back home would think of them if they ran. After their first battle, the psychological transformation from civilian to soldier already in process quickened, as did the "hardening" process, enabling soldiers to better prepare for the next encounter with the enemy.[9]

More recent works, including those written by Joseph Glatthaar, Earl Hess, and James McPherson, essentially follow Mitchell's path while adding variations. McPherson pointed to the physiological effects of adrenaline. Stimulating the "fight or flight" response, that stress-induced hormone temporarily made combat soldiers both stronger and more furious, inducing "battle rage" or "combat narcosis." The body's reaction to an adrenaline surge also later induced the exhaustion and fear that characterized men after a fight. Hess, in the fullest exploration of Civil War combat to date, maintained that veterans and especially younger ones increasingly became inured to the "dirty job" of killing the enemy. For all of these scholars, however, the signal question remained, what enabled men to choose fight instead of flight, not once but many times? To answer that, historians referred to the panoply of ideals that first sent soldiers to war—patriotism, political ideology, love of home—and the comradeship that sustained them while in uniform. While Glatthaar does admit some growing cynicism and depression in the war's latter stages, both Hess and McPherson summarily dismiss Linderman's conclusions and instead argue forcefully that most soldiers held on to their idealism and their causes. It was those beliefs that enabled them to face battle again and again.[10]

Later enlisters, this study argues, were both less ideological than 1861 enlistees and less imbued with camaraderie and especially unit pride. How then did they approach and experience combat, both initially and later on as veterans? And were they more likely to shirk, straggle, and run? During the course of the war, ninety-one soldiers among the sample, 28.7 percent, described at least one battle experience. With a few exceptions, and despite the spur of ideology, those men largely proved to be willing soldiers, driven to defend their kin, homes, and property in an acceptably manly fashion not so unlike their comrades of the class of 1861. What made them notably different was not their character, but rather their health and age.

THE SAMPLED LATER enlisters who first went into battle during the spring and summer of 1862 almost exclusively fought in Virginia. Rushed to the defense of the capitol as George B. McClellan's massive army moved up the Peninsula, they publically resolved to do their duty to the Confederacy, defeat the enemy, and honor their families with their courage, even if that meant death on the battlefield. Political ideology, coupled with love of family and the masculine imperative to be a hero, drove only two of them, however, and then only in part. Under fire for the first time at Yorktown, the

38th Virginia's Pvt. E. A. Penick leaned back against a tree and wrote his wife, "proberly for the last time," that he did not fear death as long as he died courageously, "like a man." He claimed to be eager for action and confident of success in the looming battle, one that hopefully would "be the last to ensure our independence." Penick's first active skirmish in the Yorktown fortifications reinforced the importance of those intertwined combat motivators. He insisted that "every gun I fired the other night I thought of you my Mary and the freedom of those dear children."[11]

Farther west, ardent secessionist ideologue Sgt. John Thurman was similarly proud that he had fought at Shiloh for "our rights as free men," and he expressed gratitude to God that he had been "spaired to give what aid I can in freeing my country & avenging the wrongs that are inflicted on us by a merciless foe." He also assured his wife that his children would never need to blush for anything he did on the field, for in the ultimate test of manhood he had "stood it better than I thought I could." Indeed, he continued, he had been at the head of the column when his 3rd Tennessee Cavalry had charged the foe, and he had "shot a Yank dead in his tracks."[12]

No other sampled later-enlisting Confederates writing in 1862, however, connected independence or Southern rights directly to the combat experience. Most soldiers simply described the experience as best they could without any editorializing at all. Of those who did expand their narratives, proving their courage and masculinity to themselves and their loved ones mattered most. As Linderman suggested, fighting with "cool blood," as the 48th North Carolina's Pvt. William A. Collins put it, truly mattered.[13] A few clearly had wondered beforehand how they would measure up. Louisiana gunner Cpl. John T. Beggs, for example, expressed both pride and surprise that he had fought as well at Shiloh as he had. Initially, he admitted, his first sight of a wounded comrade shocked him. "His eyes looked like they were burned out," he related, "his face like a map of charcoal and blood, and one hand entirely blown off." Yet Beggs nonetheless left his silenced artillery piece, asked to join an engaged gun crew, and "had the satisfaction of sending a few loads of shot and cannister into their midst which made them howl." That zeal continued the following day, when he volunteered to drive his gun after the regular drivers "played sick. . . . One ball came in about six feet of me," he went on, "but I did not leave my post, although I have been in better places." All in all, he concluded, the mysterious experience of battle had made a better man out of him. "Ginnie," he concluded, "you recollect how I used to get sick at the sight of blood and could not eat fat meat! Well, it is not so now. I confess the first dead man . . . made me feel a little squeamish, but when a man gets once into the fight the killed and wounded seem to excite neither fear or hardly pity. . . . As to fat meat, I can eat it raw with as much relish almost as I used to eat butter."[14]

Like Beggs, Sgt. Maj. Marion Hill Fitzpatrick also found himself drawn to combat. Released from the hospital in the wake of the Seven Days, he strode so steadily to reach his regiment that he blistered his feet on the way to Manassas. Despite the pain, he still placed himself in the thick of the fighting until he was wounded at Frayser's Farm. At Antietam, Fitzpatrick volunteered to fight as a skirmisher, "being just hotheaded enough to love the excitement." He was later wounded again at Fredericksburg.[15]

Other men reacted differently, however. Sgt. Edwin Fay notably ended up far from Fitzpatrick on the spectrum of battle experience. Although he had skirmished at Corinth, Fay's first true combat experience was at the Battle of LaGrange in September. He claimed that he had been so anxious to get at an enemy battery than he taken the lead in his attacking cavalry column. Reaching a rail fence, however, he "jumped down . . . and tore down the fence, and before I could get to my horse again the Command charge was given. Jack [his horse] rushed by me at the head of the Column and I charged forward on foot after him to within 20 or 30 yards of the battery, but my horse being obscured in a cloud of dust and no chance to catch him with a hundred of being trampled to dust by our own men, I rushed back to the fence." Fay remained there in the rear while his regiment made two additional attacks on the enemy guns. "I found my horse at the fourth charge," he went on, "but I did not get into the fight at all on account of losing him." After the fight, some of his fellow soldiers ignored his strained excuse and charged him with cowardice. "My conscience is clear on the subject, however," he huffed to his wife, "and whatever may be said will not affect either you or me."[16]

Soldiers who missed battle were more likely to claim illness. Pvt. William Ross Stilwell wrote that he sickened during a forced march to Richmond, straggled thereafter, and finally broke and ran when friendly fire hit his outfit at Savage's Station. Later, at Antietam, he happily missed the battle entirely when detailed to guard Gen. Paul Semmes' baggage.[17] After composing a lengthy account of the fighting at Malvern Hill and the rout of his unit, Cpl. B. Wylie Scott of the 57th Virginia admitted that he had been in the rear the entire time: "broke down with sore feet I was excused by out 1st sergeon from keeping in line."[18] The 5th Florida's Sgt. I. M. Auld fell out sick the night before the battle with "about half the regiment" and spent the next day "in the fight nearly all day trying to find" his regiment. He admitted that he only caught up with his regiment the next morning, but added that his brother only wandered into camp a day later.[19]

While one is tempted to suggest that perhaps more than their physical ailments kept such men out of battle, as many historians have done, allegations of cowardice fly in the face of the overall spirit of recent solider studies that demands that one takes soldiers at their word in regard to other matters, such as political ideology. In fact, if one approaches the subject of "skulkers" consistently and accepts their explanations on that subject in the same manner, quite a different conclusion emerges. From the first, later enlisters were a sickly lot. It is rare to find extended accounts of later-enlisting Confederates who do not describe in some detail the illnesses of their comrades and themselves. As with other "fresh fish," diseases such as mumps, measles, various fevers, and even smallpox took their toll. While 1862 proved the worst year, recurrent epidemics occurred throughout the war. Poor diet and sanitation meanwhile made typhoid, malaria, and especially diarrhea a common experience. Moreover, the physical exertions required by the military experience affected the sort of older men who came to the army after 1861. Many not only complained of aches and pains but increasingly described chronic rheumatism. Men were hospitalized, some repeatedly. Not surprisingly, later enlisters often weakened on long marches, fell out, and finally became unable to keep up with the army. Illness, battle, and in inability to cope with stress further winnowed their numbers as time passed, and complaints of exhaustion and physical injuries continued until the end of the war. If one accepts later enlisters' accounts of illness and injury as well as their comments on nationalism and camaraderie, in short, one must conclude that a sizable percentage of them were not "sneaks" at all. Instead, they simply were less able to bear the exertions of camp and field than their predecessors, and thus were more likely to straggle, sicken, and miss battle when the time came.[20]

As they first experienced battle, whether from the front or by a fence in the rear, soldiers who did get into the fight also expressed surprise at the reality as compared to what they had imagined, as well as the physical and psychological transformation it wrought. Like volunteers who had gone before them, they discovered that battle was noisier, more confusing, and literally more earth shattering than any of them expected. Some marveled that instead of being afraid in combat, they felt exhilaration, or exhaustion, or that they simply and methodically continued to load and shoot despite enemy fire. Battle and adrenaline sharpened some soldiers' senses; despite the chaos and carnage of the battle of Gaines Mill, Sgt. Maj. Marion Hill Fitzpatrick remembered that he fired exactly seven rounds.[21] During the Confederate evacuation of Cumberland Gap, another soldier, Pvt. H. W. Robinson of the 42nd Georgia, "saw the Elephant with his tail up we Run on the left wing of the enemy before we new it & tha opend fier on us & the balls came like hail but we never waited for eny command we just cut loos on them."[22]

Yet the experience of combat clearly unnerved others. Reflecting back on his first skirmish at Yorktown, during which he notably had killed a Federal officer at long range, Pvt. E. A. Penick remembered himself as "more than I really were. When I had cooled off, I thought I really was not me." As a result, the pious Penick had trouble accepting praise for his sharpshooting, and indeed felt only guilt. "O the Horrors of taking a fellow man's life," he exclaimed.[23] Pvt. Joseph Kauffman of the 10th Virginia admitted that he "scarcely had any idea how it went in a battle," but after the Battle of McDowell in the Shenandoah Valley, he confessed that he never wanted to be in another one.[24] Pvt. James P. Garrison of the 8th Alabama wrote from Richmond a month later, "I have went thru with it so fare but I don't know how long I will but I am in hops i will go thru with it and git home to yo again safe if i doant git in to an nother batel . . . I am in hoping that it wont com on at tall."[25] Lt. John H. Harris of the 44th Georgia remembered how anxiously he yearned to get to Richmond and fight, but after his regiment lost over 300 men at Mechanicsville, the lieutenant admitted that having "seen the 'He Elephant,'" he wished he had been still back in camp.[26] The legendary elephant was an even more frightening sight to others. When the 20th Georgia deployed as skirmishers at Malvern Hill, Lt. H. J. Hightower took out his sister's letters, wept, and prayed that he might survive to see her again.[27]

When the smoke cleared, newly baptized soldiers almost universally expressed shock at the carnage of the battlefield, bathed in blood and littered with wounded soldiers and human remains. "I have seen some of the most awful sights since I have been here that ever any man was permitted to look at," Stilwell wrote from Richmond, "men lying in great piles, dead and dying, some with no legs, no arms, nose or eyes shot off our out. . . . God deliver me from ever seeing another battlefield."[28] After Antietam, stretcher bearer Charles Terrill of the 2nd Georgia expressed a similar wish. "I never again wish to witness another battle—blood and carnage have no charms for me," he confessed. It was not fear that made him feel so, he added quickly, but rather "disgust. My very gorge rises at the mangled mass of humanity, to be witnessed on all sides."[29]

As they contemplated the mangled corpses of others, soldiers wondered how they had survived. The pious ones made sure to thank God for their deliverance. As members of two connected communities, the company and the hometown, soldiers also undertook the related duties of reporting casualties and outlining the performances of comrades and unit.[30] "I have a sad tale to tell," Pvt. John French White of the 32nd Virginia wrote after Antietam, "that is painful beyond description to me. . . . we have engaged in a hard fought battle if not the hardest of the war and Bro. A & S. H. was killed & that is not all our regt was eat up terrible . . . not less than fifty killed & wounded. Bro A & S. H. were both shot in the head & killed instantly. . . . Poor cousin Mary and Sister I am afraid there hearts will break."[31]

Even as they reported feeling sick at their first sight of the carnage, later-enlisting soldiers noticed the almost immediate beginnings of an emotional hardening to the sight of dead men that already had changed veterans. After Second Manassas, Hightower, who had wept in terror before his first battle, described how he calmly stripped a dead Yankee of his shoes.[32] "I have changed much in my feelings," Marion Hill Fitzpatrick likewise announced. "The bombs and balls excite me but little and a battlefield strewn with dead and wounded is an every day consequence."[33] Like those who had experienced "hardening" before them, they were becoming veterans.

FOR LATER ENLISTERS who had already become veterans in Virginia or Tennessee, the battles of Fredericksburg and Murfreesboro only marked another bloody milestone on a now-familiar path. Men like Sergeant Major Fitzpatrick continued to fight hard and make sure that their families realized it. Pvt. William Ross Stilwell meanwhile expressed the joy that came once again with guarding Semmes's headquarters while his regiment fought at the front.[34] For a host of other later enlisters, however, the winter of 1862–63 introduced the proverbial elephant to numbers of men stationed west of the mountains. For a few, that happened along Stones River. "I have seen the Monkey Show at last," Pvt. Thomas Warrick wrote his wife, "and I don't Waunt to see it no more I am satisfide with ware." Like so many soldiers, Warrick described the grisly aftermath more than the fight itself, except to note that his 34th Alabama "fought like tigeurs."[35]

Most new veterans, however, wrote that winter from along the Mississippi River. Large numbers of 1862 recruits, many comprising new regiments from the Old Southwest, had moved steadily into garrisons along the river and especially to Vicksburg, where increasing Federal pressure and skirmishing convinced them of an imminent attack. The Vicksburg theater thus became an area full of later enlisters. The expected Federal assault came at the end of December when William Tecumseh Sherman's force attacked at Chickasaw Bluffs.[36] Pvt. Henry T. Morgan missed the battle due to illness and was disappointed. Pvt. Grant Taylor fought. "I did not dread it in the least," he wrote. "I feel that God was my protector and I had a chance to defend you and the little ones."[37] Pvt. H. W. Robinson too was in the thick of the fighting. Describing in detail the Federal assault, Robinson explained how "the yankeys come like tigers . . . the Balls come as thick as hail we pord it in to them some too every man stood like a lion I stood in a open place with Sevrel Round me & while I would be loading my gun I would look Round & See Some one gaping for breth & Some shot too dead to gape but we Raised the yell & pord it in So thick that tha could not Stand tha took to these heels for Safty." When the firing ceased, Robinson was shocked to find "but one living man left & he had his leg broke. . . . I never got tutch but the next time may be mine you doant no what kind of afeeling it put on me to See men Shot down like hoges & See aman tore all to peases with a Shell after he is dead."[38]

Federal gunboats shelled Vicksburg sporadically through the winter and into the spring. In mid-April, David Dixon Porter's fleet ran past the city's batteries and soon began ferrying Grant's men across the river into Mississippi. Grant marched to Jackson, turned westward back to Vicksburg, and drove John Pemberton's troops back into the city. In anticipation of another assault, Confederate authorities poured into Vicksburg's defenses every man available from quieter nearby commands, including large numbers of unbloodied later enlisters.[39] One of them, Sgt. Maj. Edwin Rice, moved into the entrenchments on May 17 with the infantry elements of Waul's Texas Legion and experienced his first skirmishing the next day. Grant's first massive attempt to pierce the Confederate position, Rice's first fight, failed on the following morning. "During the rest of the evening we hugged the west side of the hill to escape the minnie bullets from the Yankee sharpshooters," Rice admitted, "one of the bullets grazed the top of my hat."

Grant tried again three days later. Rice and his fellow Texans responded with bravery but also inexperience and confusion. "We were immediately ordered to the rear of the works to assist in case it became necessary," he recorded in his diary, "but after being there 15 or 20 minutes, the boys rushed into the pits, some without orders and some obeying a wrong order, and commenced firing." The line held, while a piece of shrapnel hit Rice in the arm. "This was properly the first time the Legion has ever been in a fight," he concluded, "and they acted nobly."[40] Grant settled down for a siege that lasted until John Pemberton's surrender on the Fourth of July. Many later enlisters became at that point prisoners awaiting parole. As Bell Wiley noted, the defenders of Vicksburg endured heavier fire, more intolerable conditions, and more danger than any other troops of the war, and a sizable percentage of them had been later enlisters.

Meanwhile, the Virginia front heated up as Joseph Hooker struck Lee at Chancellorsville. All of the sampled Army of Northern Virginia later enlisters who described that battle in any detail had been in action the previous year. Yet aside from relating events, notably their successful attacks against the enemy, all reacted differently. Capt. John Harris's detailed account included an aside about drinking fresh water and sugared coffee, while Pvt. I. M. Auld related how he had stripped a dead Yankee of his sword and provisions.[41] In contrast, Lt. James E. Green of the 53rd North Carolina only described the horrible futility of attacking Federal works as "the worst piece of Gnl. ship I have ever seen" and "the awfulest time I have ever seen."[42] Lt. W. J. J. Webb meanwhile affirmed that he had fought "in the service of my country" and expressed curiosity about why he had "felt secure from harm and very much unconcerned about my own person." He concluded that he probably had been "saved by prayer not my own but those of others."[43] Still guarding baggage, Pvt. William Ross Stilwell tried to explain how he could write a letter in the midst of the Federal dead. "You may think it strange," he wrote, "but anybody that has seen as much as I have does not pay attention to it. Dead men are so common that I get used to it, though I always try to pay due respect to them."[44]

For T. T. Hoskins, a schoolboy who had just joined the 9th Virginia Cavalry, the baptism of fire came a few weeks later at Brandy Station. Deployed as a sharpshooter, he professed to be cool, writing his father that the battle reminded him "more of 'bird hunting than any business I was ever engaged in, both parties hiding behind tree stumps & cover . . . firing on each other whenever a head was left uncovered. I am almost certain I killed one," he continued, 'and probably more. . . . When a yank would show himself someone would draw a bead on him and he would fall dead as a wedge."[45] After Brandy Station, Lee's army headed north again, eventually meeting the enemy at Gettysburg. Later enlisters, like other soldiers, differed strongly on Lee's leadership there. "I don't think Lee has gained enything by this fight," Lt. James Green complained after fighting on Culp's Hill, "though we did not get whiped by a long shot, but Lee fought them in there own country & on there own choice of Position, not having the means of carring back our Wounded & for severel other causes, I think he had better let it a loan."[46] Pvt. William Ross Stilwell admitted he did not know which army had won, but "a few more battles and our regiment will be all gone. It isn't much larger now than our company when it came out."[47] Sgt. W. Y. Mordecai of the Richmond Howitzers agreed, but only to a point. "The position of the enemy in the centre could not have been taken by mortal man," he admitted, yet he added that "gen Lee has accomplished every thing he desired except fighting the Yankes in a strong position & exchanging many of his valuable lives, for many more such as they. . . . Our army is still in fine condition & needs one more chance to finish . . . Meade."[48] A month later, Joseph Joyner of the 7th North Carolina decided that the enemy's "inactivity has proven to me that their successes have not been quite so complete as they first anticipated." True, his army had lost a battle, but their forefathers lost battles in the Revolution only to win the war. "I am just as sanguine of success as I ever was," he went on, "and am willing to continue the struggle to the bitter end and achieve our independence."[49]

Joyner would have to wait until 1864 for that continuance, however, for aside from skirmishing and jockeying for position, Virginia remained relatively quiet for the remainder of the year. The one notable exception was A. P. Hill's ill-judged attack at Bristoe Station in October. The shocking carnage of that battlefield amazed Lt. John W. Horsford of the 5th Florida after Union forces retreated. "Of a few we could only find some pieces of the body," he wrote, describing the burial of the slain, "such as a hand or two or three fingers. Sometimes a foot, or part of a foot, sometimes a whole arm, or half of the head, and bodies mangled in every conceivable condition." God would judge all of them for such acts, he feared. "My heart has ached when I have seen them carelessly buried or cramed in a grave to small to receive the body, with no coffin or shroud and the clod thrown over them as roughly as the Irishman throws his clay in digging a ditch."[50]

But the war went on elsewhere, on less-renowned fields from South

Carolina to Louisiana and Arkansas. On July 4, the same day that Vicksburg fell and Lee began his long retreat from Gettysburg, Confederates under the command of Theophilius Holmes attacked but failed to defeat the Federal garrison at Helena, Arkansas. "I must ever denounce the course of a great many of our leading Officers," Lt. William Shibley announced afterward, "for unmitigated lieing and misrepresentation. We were told that the Federals were entirely ignorant as to our approach; that the city would be very easily taken and every thing in like manner. . . . when we came to the battle-field and saw the true state of affairs, men saw that they affair had been grossly misrepresented, their courage failed and no small part of our Regt and I expect of others also failed to go in to the battle to any extent." Neither Shibley nor his brother, a veteran of the battle of Prairie Grove, wavered, he added.[51]

In northwestern Georgia, Bragg's Army of Tennessee took on William S. Rosecrans's force at Chickamauga. Pvt. John W. Cotton had been in a small contest during the previous June at Monticello, Kentucky, but expecting worse at Chickamauga, even his own death, he found himself longing for some of his wife's homemade brandy, as "it would help my feelings and maby I wouldnt study so much about home."[52] The Confederates drove Rosecrans back into Chattanooga, but in November a reinforced Federal force commanded by Grant fought its way out of the city. Pvt. Grant Taylor noted that he badly sprained his ankle retreating from Lookout Mountain to Dalton, Georgia, but added that he had never been afraid. "I felt that I had trusted my all in the hands of my blessed savior," he wrote. "I felt like I would not be killed and if I did that it would be merely a release from trouble and an entrance into the joys of my blessed savior."[53]

DURING THE WINTER OF 1863–64, desperate Confederate authorities once again stripped garrisons in quiet backwaters of available fighting men and dispatched them to the main armies of Lee and Joseph E. Johnston, in expectation of a renewed Federal onslaught in the spring. Many paroled Vicksburg prisoners rejoined the war as well. For men who thus far had escaped combat in backwater sectors, the expectation of battle could be particularly unnerving. Pulled out of the Mobile shipyards, Pvt. Hiram Smith Williams admitted in February that he found reports of a Federal approach "somewhat uncomfortable. As long as I could not see the enemy, I felt a certain sense of security, but now that there was a prospect of meeting them face to face; just the thought caused a tremor to run over me."[54] Young

Pvt. Jo Francis of the 51st Alabama Mounted Infantry, equally untried, took heart from the confidence expressed by his veteran comrades.[55]

Veterans among later enlisters reacted differently to the coming storm. Like Francis's fellow soldiers, many actually looked forward to the coming battles, at least in hopes that they would bring an end to the war. For at least a few of them, calls to duty, honor, and country, as well as masculinity, still mattered. Pvt. J. C. Stone of the 6th Virginia Cavalry believed that if the stay-at-homes would join him in the ranks, the army could force the enemy to "seek shelter in his own land."[56] "It may be my lot to fall in the contest," Sgt. C. B. Watson of the 45th North Carolina explained, "but if I do I fall in a good cause."[57] "When the order comes to fall in," Sgt. Maj. Marion Hill Fitzpatrick likewise avowed, "I will buckle on my armour, seize my enfield, and put forth with energy and devotion to my bleeding country." He added that having missed much of the fighting in 1863 due to illness, "I shall regret it much if I miss this," for he worried that his comrades might think him afraid. "Some body is always ready to say he is playing off or that he is a coward if a man fails to be in the fight," he explained. "I do not fear being accused of this, but I do not want anybody to even think it of me."[58]

When the fighting began, a new host of unbloodied troops saw the dreaded elephant for the first time, and in a ghostly new form. Largely, they held up just as those who had gone before them. Conscript N. J. Clover of the 6th North Carolina described the fighting and his wound at the Battle at Plymouth, North Carolina. All of nineteen, Sgt. Wallace Comer of the 57th Alabama complained only about the body lice and the generals who held his unit in reserve rather than allowing them into the front lines. Shifted unwillingly from the South Carolina coast to Virginia, Pvt. James Michael Barr first saw action at Drewry's Bluff. "I never want to be in a hotter place than I was," he confessed. Yet, he added, he had been "very cool, took it much better than I feared I would. I would be willing to do it again under the same circumstances." A few days later, after more fighting, he admitted, "I am satisfied to never get in another fight. Hope I may not, but if duty calls me I shall be in our Service." Duty called again at Trevilian Station in June; Barr lost a leg and died of his wounds weeks later.[59]

Pvt. Creed Thomas Davis of the Richmond Howitzers, only in uniform a month, first experienced battle at Spotsylvania Court House on May 10. Two days later, a Federal assault temporarily pierced Lee's line at the famed "Mule Shoe." "It was the most terrible and awful day of my life," Davis wrote the next day, ". . . I am completely exhausted; sick as well as demoralized.

Have eaten nothing scarcely, and am bad off with the dysentery. I am scarcely able to stand up unassisted, being so weakened." He briefly went to the hospital but, afraid of being judged a "skulker" by his comrades, returned to his company. "It looks bad to be in the hospital when a battle is expected momentarily," he explained. Yet after another day's fighting he returned, too ill to remain in the ranks.[60]

In the end, even Pvt. Hiram Smith Williams bore up under fire. During the Battle of New Hope Church, the pioneer's task was to dig breastworks. "We were in a more exposed place in fact than behind those breastworks," he explained. "Nearly all the boys got down behind trees. . . . I do not claim to be blessed with any extra amount of bravery, but at all events, I can safely say I did not exhibit quite as much cowardice as some in the company."[61]

As the summer passed, all soldiers, those who had enlisted in 1861 as well as those who followed, experienced a new kind of war. It was unrelenting, marked by constant fighting, daily advances and retreats, the constant physical labor involved in the construction and repair of earthworks, and unremitting bloodletting. The sheer volume of killing, the numbers of lives lost, shocked even the hardest veteran and drove many men to psychological collapse. Yet if their letters can be believed, most surviving later-enlisting Confederates still remained motivated to fight, convinced that victory would end the war. In Georgia, to be sure, soldiers admitted frustration that Sherman would not offer open battle, yet even most of them remained confident that at some point, Johnston would defeat his foe.[62]

A few men actively sought out danger. Along the Chattahoochee River, "for the first time since I have been in service," nurse Robert Williams of the 34th Alabama "got a chance to take a Rifle and go with my 2 Brothers John and Fred in to Battle and although it was Death to many it was Sport to me. I have not enjoyed any thing half so well since I have been in the service," he continued, "it done me good to poke lead at those who had so cruelly treated the fair sex of Ga. and you need not doubt but I did all I could to avenge them for their conduct."[63]

In June, operations in the major theaters took another unfamiliar turn as siege warfare opened in Atlanta and Petersburg. The defenders of Atlanta now included Georgia militiamen—"Joe Brown's Pets"—as well as regulars. One of their captains, Fleming Jordan, had served briefly in the 44th Georgia before resigning due to illness. Jordan described the men of the 6th Georgia Militia as "long faced and despondent." The militia as a whole, he went on, "as a general thing feel themselves badly whipped. I do not think they may be relied upon in an open field." Many had deserted, he added, yet those who had remained had fought well so far, better indeed than he had expected.[64]

The siege of Atlanta ended in September, but at Petersburg, operations dragged on until early spring. As noted in a previous chapter, several later enlisters were involved with the fighting at the Crater in June. Others experienced life elsewhere in the "ditches." "We hav been in our Earthworks for 45 days," Lt. William R. Hughes of the 41st Alabama wrote from Petersburg a month later, "from 50 to 500 yards of the yanks. . . . we throw hand grenades, or hand bums at one another occasionally."[65] As the weather turned cold, Sgt. Maj. Marion Hill Fitzpatrick remained defiant. Criticizing civilians for their poor morale, he maintained that he and his comrades remained true to the cause, "resolved to die rather than submit to Yankee Rule and never; never give it up. . . . We will rise again and again and fight them till they will gladly leave us alone." As late as March 1865, he remained both defiant and hopeful.[66]

In the West, the situation was different. After Atlanta fell, John Bell Hood marched the army north to Tennessee. Among the increasingly gaunt host was thirty-four-year old Pvt. H. R. Rodgers of the 46th Alabama. Rodgers had enlisted in March 1862 but sickened quickly and eventually hired a substitute. Only in October 1864 did he return to the army. He fought for the first time at Franklin on November 29. Rodgers is exactly the kind of soldier one might expect to skulk, yet he did not. At Franklin he charged with his unit, and two weeks later he was captured at Nashville. Interned in Camp Douglas, he died late in January. Like a majority of later enlisters, in other words, even as reluctant a soldier as Private Rodgers fought at last. His particular combat motivations for taking part in the charge at Franklin remain murky, but if he was like most later-enlisting Confederates, political ideology and the fear of "Yankee rule" probably were not major factors. Neither was the defense of slavery nor an especial hatred for the men in blue. More likely, Rodgers fixed his bayonet and hesitantly charged out of emotions associated with the necessities of courage, comradeship, and manhood. Later enlisters who had not seen combat, steeped as they were in the Southern masculine ethos, quietly wondered if they were cowards. In battle, some fell to the rear, and after fighting, some sought safe assignments. There is absolutely no evidence, however, that more later enlisters did so than those soldiers who enlisted soon after Fort Sumter, although the percentage of men leaving combat accounts at least suggests that a smaller cohort

"Petersburg, Va. Dead Confederate soldier with gun," photographed on April 3, 1865.
Given his youth, he almost certainly was a later enlister. Photograph courtesy Library of
Congress, Washington, D.C., LC B811-3175.

actually saw action to begin with. Most of those who did fight, moreover,
proved their heroism—to themselves, their comrades, and their loved ones
back home. As the war continued, the war hardened them just as it did
others. Always oriented toward home, many clearly stepped into line with
the hope that just one more battle would end the war and allow them to
return to their loved ones and familiar environs. If they died in that battle,
they hoped that God would take them to their eternal home, to await
a blessed reunion. Like their initial and sustaining motivations, in other
words, the combat motivation of most later-enlisting Confederates was
wrapped up in kin and neighborhood.[67]

AT APPOMATTOX, LEE famously stated in his farewell message that "the Army of Northern Virginia has been compelled to yield to overwhelming numbers and resources."[68] That statement touched off a long controversy among students of the war over the reasons for Confederate defeat, a controversy that shows no sign of abating despite its increasing redundancy. Some generally agree with Lee and maintain that when all was said and done, the Confederacy lost the war on the battlefield, at least in part due to the Union's stronger battalions. Others pointed to the many internal divisions and weaknesses within the Confederacy that undermined it from within.

The experience of later-enlisting Confederates, however, does not fit neatly into either "externalist" or "internalist" scholarly interpretations. On the one hand, later enlisters often did reflect a Confederacy divided against itself. For many reasons, most personal, eligible older men chose not to go to war in 1861 to fight for their new nation. When they did rally to the colors later on, it often was reluctantly, because of the pressure of conscription, the need for the money provided by bounties, and a host of other local concerns wrapped up in protecting their families, property, and neighborhoods. As a group, older later enlisters in the army remained more Janus-faced, always keeping a steady eye on home. They supported slavery as much as the next white Southerner, but they were less likely to use the ideological arguments favored by so many of the recruits who went before them. Stirring words such as "subjugation" and "liberty" roused them comparatively little, as did "duty" and "honor." They hated the war above all, hoped for peace, and wanted to go home, preferably the one on earth but, barring that, at least the reconstituted one above.

Yet in the end, they still marched, fought, killed, and died for the Confederacy on dozens of battlefields. If late enlisters betrayed an obvious weakness in uniform, it was not a notable, comparable lack of combat motivation or a pronounced tendency for shirking and seeking bombproof jobs. As a group, they were not cowards. Called upon to engage in combat, most seemingly fought to the best of their abilities and despite a weaker sense of unit pride and a small-group cohesion that embodied both the strengths and weaknesses that grew out of its localist orientation. Instead, one must look to the soldiers' sheer physical limitations, the results of age and hard toil. While youths came of age and grew up in uniform during the Civil War, older men simply aged. Concerns about family and farm induced constant worry and stress. Camp life and marches wore them down physically, while injuries and ailments constantly landed them in hospitals and convalescent camps. Many did not survive; the historian studying later-enlisting Confederates regularly notes the men whose letters stop in mid-war, as well as the accounts of men writing their last, sad missives from hospitals.

Thus in the end, in one sense anyway, Lee was right. The Confederacy really did run out of soldiers and yielded to "overwhelming numbers." But as the general knew himself, it was a process that began long before Appomattox. It was not just that the North, allied with Southern-born African Americans, could supply more soldiers than the white South. Part of the Confederacy's ultimate problem was that the thin gray line of white men the South called up in the war's second year and beyond always were too few in number, too old, too divided in heart and soul, and physically not always up to the task before them. Later enlisters could and would fill the ranks and kill in combat, but many of them could not always march and fight as well as their new nation needed them to do. As the gospels surely reminded some of them during their trials, "the spirit indeed is willing, but the flesh is weak."[69] Lacking sufficient manpower both in terms of quality and quantity, the thin gray line of later enlisters proved insufficient, and the Confederacy yielded at last.

The modern historian often meets enthusiasts who openly exclaim that they wished they had lived during the Civil War era. Such sentiments surely would baffle later-enlisting Confederates, most of whom simply longed for the "cruel war" to end in their favor so that they could return to their families and farms. To most of them, and especially the older men, the war was not a noble adventure, but rather something akin to a natural disaster, a tsunami of four years' duration that brought suffering, stole lives, divided families, destroyed property "gained by honest toil," wrecked communities, and left nothing as it was before. Their perspective, of course, was not the only one of that generation; the popular modern habit of equating "the South" with the prosecession white South breeds more confusion than clarity. For the enslaved, the war brought a joyous "new birth of freedom" in Lincoln's memorable words, one that sadly proved too limited in the years that followed. For others, both Southern Unionists and the mass of Northerners, the result was national unity and the beginning of a march toward modernity, industrialization, and power. It is impossible to imagine that the world would be a better place today without a united America standing against the goose-stepping "vandal hordes" of a later century. It was the "Blue and Gray" Division, after all, led by the heirs of the Stonewall Brigade, who stormed Omaha Beach at Normandy. But for the reluctant Rebels at least, the Civil War in the end was never a glorious pageant to be endlessly reenacted, celebrated, and used for political gain. We would do well to remember that for them, it was instead a devastating horror ripe with pain, fear, loss, and loneliness, soaked in mud and the blood of kin and neighbors. "Alas for our country!" as Hiram Smith Williams wrote for so many of them, "Alas for our day!"

APPENDIX

TABLE 1. Combined Database of Sampled Soldiers
(N = 320)

Note: The names of men under the age of twenty in 1862 are *italicized*. The names of men who were slaveholders or from slaveholding families in 1860 are in **bold**.

Name	Reg't[1]	Age[2]	Head[3]	Mar.[4]	Occ.[5]	Real[6]	Personal[7]
Adams, Homer	AL	24	N	N	7Cl	10,000	19,000
Adams, Spencer	AL/MS	12	N	N	9	10,000	19,000
Albright, James W.	VA	25	Y	Y	7E	1,500	3,300
Alexander, James S.	SC	33	Y	Y	1	7,500	850
Alexander, William D.	NC					Unable to locate in census[8]	
Allison, Jonathan	AL					Unable to locate in census	
Alspaugh, Granville L.	LA	15	N			Not in census	
Armstrong, Charles J.	AL	25	N	N	1	300	400
Arthur, R. Admire	VA	36	Y	N	6	0	400
Ashby, George	VA	16	N	N	6	190	0
Auld, Isaac	FL	42	Y	Y	7P	0	5,000
Aylett, William R.	VA					Not in census	
Bailey, Harvey	NC	34	Y	Y	1	1,200	638
Baker, Samuel M.	VA	16	N	N	1	5,000	13,560
Banks, Robert W.	MS	17	N	N	4	3,000	200,000
Barineau, Isaac	FL					Not in census	
Barnes, Ruffin	NC	32	Y	Y	1	2,500	2,000
Barnes, William H.	TX	30	Y	Y	7G	600	200
Barr, James M.	SC	30	Y	Y	1	1,200	14,920
Barron, W. J.	AL	25	N	N	7Cl	0	0
Barrow, James H.	VA					Not in census	
Bates, Robert	VA					Not in census	
Battle, Jesse S.	GA	32	Y	Y	1	1,000	8,000
Beggs, John	LA					Not in census	
Bell, John W.	AL	32	Y		1	3,000	8,000
Bell, William R.	AL	33	N	N	3	0	3,000
Berryhill, William H.	MS	32	Y	Y	8C	730	1,800
Black, William J.	VA	15	N	N	9	15,000	250
Blair, John	TN					Unable to locate in census	
Blakley, W. L.						Unable to locate in census	

Name	Reg't[1]	Age[2]	Head[3]	Mar.[4]	Occ.[5]	Real[6]	Personal[7]
Bleckley, F. A.	GA					Not in census	
Bleckley, J. T.	SC					Not in census	
Bosworth, S. Newton	VA	17	N	N	7C	0	750
Bradford, H.	FL					Not in census	
Brightman, John C.	TX					Not in census	
Brooks, Richard H.	GA	25	Y	Y	3	0	200
Browning, John K.	AL	27	N	N	3	0	10,400
Bunker, Christopher W.	VA?					Not in census	
Burns, George H.	GA					Not in census	
Burum, Absalom J.	NC	32				Not in census	
Cadenhead, I. B.	AL					Not in census	
Cadwallander, James M.	VA					Not in census	
Cameron, Bluford A.	TX	27	Y	Y	7T	2,250	400
Camp, Thomas L.	GA	27	Y	Y	3	0	1,470
Capehart, William R.	NC	22	?[9]	?	1	16,600	35,400
Carneal, Lafayette J.	VA	15	N	N	1	9,000	16,000
Chatfield, G. H.						Not in census	
Chenault, David W.	KY	34	Y	Y	1	91,240	9,600
Chesternut, D. A.	GA					Not in census	
Childers, David R.	MS	34	Y	Y	7T	1,000	3,000
Clement, Abram W.	SC	17	N	N	4	0	0[10]
Cline, William P.	NC	26	Y	Y	1	50	300
Clover, John A.	NC					Not in census	
Clover, N. J.	NC					Not in census	
Clover, William D.	NC					Not in census	
Cochrane, Harden P.	AL	17	N	?	4	Not in census	
Coggin, Ebenezer	AL	27				Not in census	
Coghill, John F.	NC					Not in census	
Coiner, George M.	VA	17	N	Y	1	11,550	2,445
Cole, William D.	AL	31	Y	Y	1	1,500	6,000
Collins, William A.	NC	18	N	N	1	300	158
Comer, J. Wallace	AL	15	N	N	9	23,000	65,000
Copland, William	SC	25	Y	Y	3	0	264
Corbin, Henry	VA	37	N	N	6	0	0
Corry, Robert E.	AL	32	?	Y	7En	Not in census	
Cotton, John W.	AL	29	Y	Y	1	1,200	800

Name	Reg't[1]	Age[2]	Head[3]	Mar.[4]	Occ.[5]	Real[6]	Personal[7]
Craver, A. D.	GA	26	N	N	9	0	0
Crawford, Abel H.	AL	17	N	N	1	16,000	33,000
Crawford, Andrew	SC	13	N	N	7Me	10,000	8,000
Crittenden, John	AL	26	N	Y	7T	0	1,150
Croom, Charles	NC	15				Not in census	
Crouch, W. A.	AR	28	Y	Y	7Ar	0	250
Culp, James P.	NC					Not in census	
Dalton, L. R.	SC	15	N	N	6	1,500	600
D'Antignac, Auvergne	GA	16	N		9	150,000	181,000
Davenport, John F.	AL				Unable to locate in census		
Davidson, John M.	NC	30	Y	Y	7Me	500	7,700
Davis, Creed T.	VA	18	N	N	7Cl	0	0
Davis, William V.	MS	31	Y	Y	1	2,400	925
Denney, David M.	AL	31	?	Y		Not in census	
DeWitt, Marcus B.	TN	25				Not in census	
Dickinson, Robert	SC	31	Y	Y	8G	2,500	1,600
Dooley, John	VA	17	N	N	7Me	13,000	80,000
Dull, John P.	VA	27	Y	Y	3	0	738
Earnest, John G.	TN	17	N	N	4	25,000	20,000
Edge, Andrew J.	GA	17	N	N	1	5,000	19,190
Elliot, Thomas J.	NC	22	N	N	7T	150	300
Ellis, Jasper	NC	23	N	N	1	140	400
English, John J.	NC	19	N	N	3	0	600
Epps, Commodore D.	GA					Not in census	
Evans, George K.	VA	40	N	N	1	1,200	2,500
Farnsworth, W. P.	TN					Not in census	
Farrow, Sam W.	TX	38	Y	Y	8M	0	2,500
Faulkner, Lee	TX					Not in census	
Fay, Edwin H.	LA	28	Y	Y	7T	0	10,000
Figgatt, Charles M.	VA	24	Y	Y	7Bt	0	2,000
Fitzpatrick, Marion H.	GA	25	N	N	6	2,340	4,120
Fitzpatrick, Phillips	AL	30	Y	Y	3	0	65,000
Fleming, William V.	AL	38	Y	Y	1	200	700
Flournoy, Elijah K.	AL	22	N	N	1	2,750	4,332
Foster, Samuel T.	TX	31	Y	Y	7A	300	200
Fowler, John G.	SC	21	Y	N	3	0	300

Name	Reg't[1]	Age[2]	Head[3]	Mar.[4]	Occ.[5]	Real[6]	Personal[7]
Francis, Joseph H.	AL	15	N	N	7P	6,600	22,000
Frank, Theophilus	NC					Not in census	
Franklin, James C.	NC?					Unable to identify in census	
Frierson, Jacob A.	LA					Not in census	
Galloway, Armistead	AL	22	Y	Y	1	600	192
Garrison, James P.	AL	25	Y	Y	3	0	0
Giles, G. W.	AL	29	Y	Y	8P	0	150
Gillis, Daniel	GA	33	N	N	1	600	2,242
Gillis, Malcolm	GA	14	N	N	1	900	3,010
Gillis, Neil	GA	19	N	N	1	600	2,242
Gillis, W. S.	GA	19	N	N	1	900	3,010
Golden, Thomas M.	GA					Not in census	
Goodwin, F. M.	GA					Not in census	
Green, James E.	NC	21	Y	Y	1	550	653
Gregory, William H.	VA	19	N	N	6	10,000	32,311
Griffin, James W.	NC?					Not in census	
Grisham, Thomas	LA	40	Y	N	3	0	600
Gyles, William A.	SC	15	N	N	8P	400	5,000
Harris, H. C.	AL	45	Y	Y	8T	800	1,000
Harris, John H.	GA	33	Y	Y	7Cl	900	2,500
Hart, M. C.	LA?					Unable to identify in census	
Hart, Robert	VA					Unable to identify in census	
Hart, William	VA					Unable to identify in census	
Haynes, Draughton S.	GA	23			7T	Not in census	
Head, R. M.	AL	25	Y	N	8O	0	0
Head, William P.	TX	26	Y	Y	7P	3,200	3,650
Hedrick, Jefferson	NC	17	N	N	1	1,550	500
Henderson, Lafayette	AL	27	Y	Y	7Me	0	16,475
Hendricks, Thomas W.	AL	25	Y	N	1	1,000	2,000
Herron, George S.	MD					Unable to identify in census	
Hightower, H. J.	GA					Not in census	
Holmes, Henry M.	FL	26	Y	Y	7P	75	1,500
Hosford, John W.	FL	27	N	N	7T	0	0
Hoskins, Thomas T.	VA	15	N	N	1	27,544	30,000
Hughes, William R.	AL	26	Y	Y	1	440	695
Hundley, John H.	NC	27	Y	Y	2	0	100

Name	Reg't[1]	Age[2]	Head[3]	Mar.[4]	Occ.[5]	Real[6]	Personal[7]
Hunter, Miles H.	NC	24	Y	Y	3	0	0
Hurley, Charles M.	LA	18	N	N	7Cl	0	600
Inzer, John W.	AL	26			7A	Not in census	
Jarrett, John E.	NC	34	Y	Y	3	0	0
Jeffares, Bennett R.	GA	23	N	N	3	0	220
Jett, Richard B.	GA	31	N	N	1	600	250
Jones, Abraham	NC					Not in census	
Jones, James	NC				Unable to identify in census		
Jordan, Fleming	GA	22	N	N	7Me	6,500	18,975
Jordan, Stephen A.	TN	36	Y	Y	1	12,075	20,000
Joyner, Joseph	NC	17	N	N	7Cl	4,000	7,450
Joyner, Julius S.	NC	20?	N	N	7Cl	4,000	7,450
Joyner, Richard	NC	16	N	N	7Cl	4,000	7,450
Kauffman, Joseph F.	VA	21	N	N	1	1,000	156
Kees, Martin V.	MS	19				Not in census	
Kennedy, Francis M.	NC	26	?		7C	Not in census	
Key, Thomas J.	AR	27	Y	Y	7E	0	15,000
Kilpatrick, Madison	GA	39	Y	Y	1	9,000	17,180
Kirby, Edmund	NC					Not in census	
Kirkland, Moses	GA	27	Y	Y	1	600	450
Kirkland, Richard	GA	17	N	N	3	0	600
Kirkland, Zean W.	GA	20	Y	Y	3	0	420
Knight, Jesse	GA	29	Y	Y	1	500	1,178
Knight, John T.	TX	20	N	N[11]	1	500	7,000
Knight, John W.	SC	24	N	N	8	0	250
Knight, Matthew	GA	31	Y	Y	3	0	115
Lacy, Drury	NC	57	Y	Y	7C	0	12,500
Lacy, Singleton W.	NC	15	N	N	7C	0	12,500
Lacy, William	NC/VA	17	N	N	4	0	12,500
Lambeth, Joseph H.	VA	42	Y	Y	9	0	0
Langhorne, Jacob K.	VA	15	N	N	1	34,800	31,500
Lanier, John M. P.	GA					Not in census	
Lanning, James M.	AL	32	Y	Y	7Me	1,200	16,000
Lawson, Madison	VA	32	Y	Y	1	2,500	2,000
Lear, J. L. J.	TN	15	N	N	7D	2,000	4,977
Lee, Benjamin W.	TX	21	N	N	7Cl	1,500	2,200

Name	Reg't[1]	Age[2]	Head[3]	Mar.[4]	Occ.[5]	Real[6]	Personal[7]
Lee, James H.					Unable to identify in census		
Lee, R. H.	AL	28	Y	Y	7P	15,000	4,795
Lee, Thomas E.	GA	24	N	N	8H	0	300
Lee, William H. H.	SC	19	Y	N	1	3,000	1,600
Leet, Edwin	LA	42	Y	Y	7JP	600	200
Lewis, Miles W.	GA	26	Y	Y	6	0	75
Lewis, Philip P.	VA	25	Y	Y	7T	0	200
Lippard, Jesse	NC	24	N	N	9	0	0
Long, Andrew D.	VA	16	N	N	6	11,600	2,520
Long, James F.	VA	20	N	N	6	11,600	2,520
Luttrell, Harvey W.	AL	36	Y	Y	7Me	600	3,500
Manson, Joseph R.	VA	29	Y	Y	1	3,000	10,000
Mason, Benjamin	AL	36	Y	Y	1	800	265
Massey, A. H.	NC	18[12]	N	N	6	0	450
Massey, Thrush H.	NC	24	N	N	3	0	450
Mathews, L. H.	FL				Not in census		
Mathis, Stephen M.	TN	32	Y	Y	7Me	4,000	1,500
McAlister, Timothy S.	NC				Not in census		
McBride, A. D.	NC				Not in census		
McCulloch, James	GA				Unable to identify in census		
McElhenny, Robert W.	LA				Not in census		
McGhea, J. S. G.	VA	39	Y	Y	1	500	200
McLaurin, Hugh	NC	35	Y	N	8B	5,000	16,364
McLaurin, John D.	NC	24	N	N	6	8,700	2,000
McLaurin, Neill	NC				Not in census		
McLeod, Neil	NC	37	Y	Y	3	0	0
McMurtrey, J. A.	GA	22	Y	N	6	0	0
McNeill, Alex	SC				Not in census		
Mendenhall, John J.	NC	60			Not in census		
Meriwether, John S.	AL	30	N	Y	7P	10,000	10,360
Miller, A. T.	TN				Not in census		
Mobley, Radford E.	AL	29	Y	Y	8C	0	5,000
Mobley, W. R.	NC				Unable to identify in census		
Moore, Thomas J.	SC	17			Unable to identify in census		
Mordecai, William Y.	VA	24	N	N	3	20,000	5,000
Morgan, Henry Gibbs	LA	16	N	N	9	0	9,000[13]

Name	Reg't[1]	Age[2]	Head[3]	Mar.[4]	Occ.[5]	Real[6]	Personal[7]
Morgan, Henry T.	LA	24	Y	Y	1	200	300
Mowrer, Henry	NC					Not in census	
Neal, Henry Edward	VA	22	N	N	6	0	0
Newberry, Thomas J.	MS	17	N	N	1	8,000	11,000
Newell, Andrew J.	GA	27	Y	Y	3	0	0
Niebuhr, Friedrich	TX	23				Not in census	
Nihill, Michael	TX	18				Not in census	
Nobles, J. T.	SC					Not in census	
Nobles, W. J.	SC	24	N	N	8Co	400	100
Norman, Melvin R.	VA					Not in census	
Nugent, William L.	MS	28				Not in census	
Odom, Elijah	AL	35				Not in census	
Padgett, James D.	SC					Not in census	
Palmer, James	MS	26	Y	Y	3	0	0
Parker, Jacob R.	AL	31	Y	Y	1	800	5,399
Patton, James A.	NC	22				Not in census	
Peel, R. M.	AR	16	N	N	1	2,000	1,500
Peel, W. J.	AR	19	N	N	1	2,000	1,500
Penick, Edward A.	VA	40	Y	Y	1	2,450	2,500
Phillips, Albert R.	NC	15	N	N	1	1,200	1,000
Pickens, James	AL	18	N	N	4	209,600	250,000
Pickens, Samuel	AL	19	N	N	4	209,600	250,000
Pugh, Richard L.	LA	22	N	N	1[14]	?	?
Putnam, John	SC	34	Y	Y	3	0	210
Rabb, Kiah	AL					Not in census	
Raines, Thomas T.	GA	21	N	N	1	1,200	11,250
Ramsey, James	SC					Unable to identify in census	
Reid, James H.	VA					Not in census	
Retif, P. E.	LA	36	Y	Y	6	500	0
Rice, Edwin E.	TX					Unable to identify in census	
Ridley, Samuel J.	MS	39	Y	Y	1	20,500	52,440
Robertson, Benjamin	MS					Unable to identify in census	
Robertson, William	MS					Unable to identify in census	
Robinson, Henry W	GA	30	Y	Y	8B	0	25
Rodgers, Hugh R.	AL	30	Y	Y	1	3,500	11,300
Rounsaville, James B.	TX					Unable to identify in census	

Name	Reg't[1]	Age[2]	Head[3]	Mar.[4]	Occ.[5]	Real[6]	Personal[7]
Rounsaville, Thomas J.	TX				Unable to identify in census		
Rucker, W. H.	NC	63	Y	Y	9[15]	3,750	12,000
Sanders, J. B.	MS	30	Y	Y	8B	230	175
Sayger, Allmon	VA				Not in census		
Scott, B. Wylie	VA	23	N	N	9	0	1,200
Sewell, Aaron M.	GA	22	N	N	1	300	590
Shadrick, Allen	NC	30	Y	Y	3	0	0
Shearer, Pharis	MS				Not in census		
Shibley, John S.	AR				Not in census		
Shibley, W. H. H.	AR	20			Not in census		
Shore, Augustin	NC	29	Y	Y	1	700	450
Shore, Edward H.	NC	26	Y	N	1	400	100
Sides, Charles D.	NC				Unable to identify in census		
Sims, William H.	VA	40	Y	Y	1	57,000	128,270
Sivley, William R.	MS/TN	17	N	N	1	22,500	131,400
Smith, J. G.	VA				Unable to identify in census		
Smith, John M.	MS	35	Y	Y	3	0	1,800
Smith, Thomas C.	TX	16	N	N	3	0	1,200
Smith, William A.	TN	15	N	N	7T	132,000	74,500
Smithson, William B.	VA				Unable to identify in census		
Smithwick, Edgar	NC				Not in census		
Snider, William E.	VA	16	N	N	1	4,000	875
Snyder, Daniel C.	VA	30	Y	Y	3	0	1,850
Stapp, Joseph D.	AL	17	N	N	4	1,000	15,000[16]
Stephens, William A.	AL	28	N	N	3	0	5,000
Stilwell, William R.	GA	21			8H	Not in census	
Stone, James C.	VA	28	N	Y	3	0	6,800
Stoutmire, Jacob	VA				Not in census		
Strickland, Oliver V.	GA	17	N	N	1	2,500	20,000
Tamplin, Benjamin F.	TX	23	N	N	1	300	10,000
Tamplin, William F.	TX	19	N	N	1	300	10,000
Taylor, Grant	AL	31	Y	Y	1	500	875
Terrill, Charles F.	GA				Not in census		
Terry, Joseph G.	AL	28	Y	Y	1	1,600	3,368
Thompson, Wilbur	GA				Not in census		
Thornton, Matthew	AL	30	Y	Y	6	0	300

Name	Reg't[1]	Age[2]	Head[3]	Mar.[4]	Occ.[5]	Real[6]	Personal[7]
Thurman, John	MS	29				Not in census	
Tindall, J. W.	SC	37	Y	Y	1	5,000	3,300
Treadwell, E. W.	AL	23	Y	Y	7P	0	750
Tucker, John S.	AL				7Cl	Not in census	
Tuttle, Edwin D.	VA	31	N	N	7T	0	650
Updike, Amon	VA	31	Y	Y	1	1,100	300
Vige, Edmond	LA					Not in census	
Vinson, Benjamin W.	NC	14				Not in census	
Vinson, Daniel J.	NC	16				Not in census	
Vinson, Uriah T.	NC	18				Not in census	
Wade, Horace M.	VA					Not in census	
Wagner, William F.	NC	29	Y	Y	8B	800	800
Wallace, James T.	MO	17	N	N	1	5,000	2,200
Walters, Isaac T.	NC					Not in census	
Ward, Frank B.	NC	27	Y	Y	1	175	1,000
Warrick, Thomas	AL	28	Y	Y	3	0	300
Watson, Cyrus B.	NC	16	N	N	1	2,000	1,500
Watson, John W.	VA	27	Y	Y	1	750	200
Webb, W. J. J.	GA	21	N	N	7A	0	350
Wells, L. R.	NC				Unable to identify in census		
Whitby, Thomas P.	AL	15				Not in census	
White, James	AL	37	Y	Y	1	1,000	2,020
White, John F.	VA	26				Not in census	
White, Obadiah	AL	15	N	N	1	1,000	2,020
Williams, C. W.	VA				Unable to identify in census		
Williams, Hiram S.	AL	27				Not in census	
Williams, John C.	GA	31	Y	Y	Unable to identify in census		
Williams, Robert A.	AL	28	Y	Y	7Ma	350	3,000
Williamson, James J.	VA	25	Y	Y	8P	0	200
Willis, Erastus R.	SC	16	N	N	1	3,000	2,500
Willis, James I.	SC	23	Y	Y	1	1,000	250
Wilson, James A.	MS				Unable to identify in census		
Wilson, John A.	MS	31	Y	Y	5	0	4,000
Wilson, Samuel	NC	33	Y	Y	3	0	3,768
Wood, Dallas	FL	16	N	N	4	0	0
Wood, Robert	GA	40	Y	Y	3	0	8,000

Name	Reg't[1]	Age[2]	Head[3]	Mar.[4]	Occ.[5]	Real[6]	Personal[7]
Woolwine, C. R.	VA	16	N	N	3	3,000	1,600
Yager, Richard F.	MO	21	N	N	8F	11,200	8,000
Zimmerman, James C.	NC	27	Y	Y	1	1,300	550

1 State of regiment's origin.

2 Age in 1860.

3 Whether head of household in 1860 census, excluding obvious nonrelated employers.

4 Likely married in 1860. The 1860 Census does not explicitly reveal marriage, so this column is based on the assumption that a woman of similar age and with the same surname as the soldier-householder is a spouse rather than sister.

5 Occupation. When none is given, that of the head of household is indicated. Key: 1 = "Farmer" or "Planter," Landowner; 2 = "Tenant" or "Renter"; 3 = "Farmer" or "Farm Manager," No Real Property Listed in Schedule I, Probable Tenant; 4 = Student, 5 = Overseer or "Negro Manager"; 6 = Farm Hand, Farm Laborer, or Laborer; 7 = Professional or Businessman; 8 = Craftsman or Skilled Worker; 9 = No Occupation. Categories 7 and 8 are further broken down as follows: 7A = attorney; 7Ar = artist; 7Bt = bank teller; 7C = clergyman; 7Cl= clerk; 7D = dental surgeon; 7E = editor/printer; 7En = engineer; 7G = government worker; 7JP = justice of the peace; 7Ma = manufacturer; 7Me = merchant; 7Pa = painter; 7P = physician; 7T = schoolmaster/teacher; 8B = blacksmith; 8C = carpenter; 8Co = cooper; 8F = freighter; 8G = ginwright; 8H = harness maker; 8M = mechanic; 8O = overseer; 8P = painter; 8S = boot maker/shoemaker; 8T = trader; 8W = wheelwright. This key is a modified version of that used in Frederick A. Bode and Donald E. Ginter, *Farm Tenancy and the Census in Antebellum Georgia* (Athens: University of Georgia Press, 1986).

6 Value of realty owned by head of household in 1860 census, excluding obvious nonrelated employers.

7 Value of personal property owned by head of household in 1860 census, excluding obvious nonrelated employers.

8 This phrase means that there were too many men in the census with similar names to make a positive determination.

9 Information refers to his father, George Washington Capehart. The son cannot be found in the census.

10 Property refers to Clement himself, who was a student at The Citadel.

11 Knight was married by 1862.

12 Here I choose the oldest of the three Massey sons with names beginning with "A."

13 Property belongs to guardian.

14 In what seems to be an oversight, the census is blank for the father, including property, although the slave schedule shows him to be the owner of 291 slaves. Barnes Lathrop identifies William Thomas Pugh as a wealthy sugar planter. See Lathrop, "Confederate Artilleryman," 373.

15 The titular head of household was listed as "insane." Property is listed as belonging to Rucker's mother.

16 Real property is mother's; personal property is his.

TABLE 2. Sampled Soldiers by State
(N = 320)

State	Men[1]	Percentage of Sample	Estimated Percentage of All Confederate Soldiers[2]	Difference
Alabama	56.5	17.7	9	+8.7
Arkansas	6	1.9	3	−1.1
Florida	7	2.2	2	+0.2
Georgia	46	14.4	11	+3.4
Kentucky	1	0.3	5	−4.7
Louisiana	14	4.4	6	−1.6
Maryland	1	0.3	2	−1.7
Mississippi	18	5.6	7	−1.4
Missouri	2	0.6	3	−1.4
North Carolina	65.5	20.5	15	+5.5
South Carolina	22	6.9	6	+0.9
Tennessee	9.5	3	12	−9
Texas	17	5.3	6	−0.7
Virginia	55.5	17.3	14	+3.3

1 Men who served in two regiments from two states are counted as one-half for each state total.

2 McPherson, *For Cause and Comrades*, 179.

TABLE 3. Sampled Slave Owners or Men from Slave-Owning Families
(N = 92)

Name	State	Age	Head	Number of Slaves
Adams, Homer	AL	24	N	17
Adams, Spencer	AL	12	N	17
Auld, Isaac	FL	42	Y	7
Baker, Samuel M.	VA	16	N	18
Banks, Robert W.	MS	17	N	78
Barnes, Ruffin	NC	32	Y	4
Barr, James M.	SC	30	Y	12
Battle, Jesse S.	GA	32	Y	14
Bell, John W.	AL	32	Y	6
Brooks, Richard H.	GA	25	Y	?
Browning, John K.	AL	27	N	10
Burum, Absalom J.	NC	32		Not in census
Capehart, William R.	NC	22	?[1]	40
Carneal, Lafayette J.	VA	15	N	6
Chatfield, G. H.				Not in census
Chenault, David W.	KY	34	Y	9
Childers, David R.	MS	34	Y	2
Cochrane, Harden P.	AL	17	N	?
Coiner, George M.	VA	17	N	8
Cole, William D.	AL	31	Y	4
Comer, J. Wallace	AL	15	N	61
Crawford, Abel H.	AL	17	N	23
Crawford, Andrew	SC	13	N	8
D'Antignac, Auvergne	GA	16	N	15
Davidson, John M.	GA	30	Y	1
Dickinson, Robert	SC	31	Y	1
Earnest, John G.	TN	17	N	1
Edge, Andrew J.	GA	17	N	33
Farrow, Sam W.	TX	38	Y	4
Fay, Edwin H.	LA	28	Y	?
Figgatt, Charles M.	VA	24	Y	1
Fitzpatrick, Marion H.	GA	25	N	4
Fitzpatrick, Phillips	AL	30	Y	60

Name	State	Age	Head	Number of Slaves
Flournoy, Elijah K.	AL	22	N	3
Francis, Joseph H.	AL	15	N	13
Gillis, Malcolm	GA	14	N	5
Gillis, Neil	GA	19	N	2
Gillis, W. S.	GA	19	N	5
Gregory, William H.	VA	19	N	21
Harris, John H.	GA	33	Y	9
Henderson, Lafayette	AL	27	Y	2
Hendricks, Thomas W.	AL	25	Y	2
Hoskins, Thomas T.	VA	15	N	34
Jordan, Fleming	GA	22	N	26
Jordan, Stephen A.	TN	36	Y	19
Joyner, Joseph	NC	17	N	7
Joyner, Julius S.	NC	20?	N	7
Joyner, Richard	NC	16	N	7
Kilpatrick, Madison	GA	39	Y	25
Knight, John T.	TX	20	N	10
Lacy, Drury	NC	57	Y	6
Lacy, Singleton W.	NC	15	N	6
Lacy, William	NC	17	N	6
Langhorne, Jacob K.	VA	15	N	29
Lanning, James M.	AL	32	Y	4
Lawson, Madison	VA	32	Y	1
Lear, J. L. J.	TN	15	N	3
Lee, Benjamin W.	TX	21	N	1
Lee, R. H.	AL	28	Y	3
Manson, Joseph R.	VA	29	Y	5
McLaurin, John D.	NC	24	N	19
Meriwether, John S.	AL	30	N	38
Mobley, Radford E.	AL	29	Y	13
Moore, Thomas J.	SC	17		
Mordecai, William Y.	VA	24	N	6
Morgan, Henry Gibbs	LA	16	N	7
Newberry, Thomas J.	MS	17	N	11
Parker, Jacob R.	AL	31	Y	5
Penick, Edward A.	VA	40	Y	3

Name	State	Age	Head	Number of Slaves
Pickens, James	AL	18	N	201
Pickens, Samuel	AL	19	N	201
Pugh, Richard L.	LA	22	N	291
Raines, Thomas T.	GA	21	N	13
Ridley, Samuel J.	MS	39	Y	65
Rodgers, Hugh R.	AL	30	Y	3
Sims, William H.	VA	40	Y	116
Sivley, William R.	MS	17	N	69
Smith, William A.	TN	15	N	28
Snyder, Daniel C.	VA	30	Y	3
Stapp, Joseph D.	AL	17	N	3
Stephens, William A.	AL	28	N	3
Stone, James C.	VA	28	N	8
Strickland, Oliver V.	GA	17	N	13
Tamplin, Benjamin F.	TX	23	N	13
Tamplin, William F.	TX	19	N	13
Taylor, Grant	AL	31	Y	?
Tindall, J. W.	SC	37	Y	13
Walters, Isaac	NC			Not in census
Williams, Robert A.	AL	28	Y	4
Willis, Erastus R.	SC	16	N	1
Willis, James I.	SC	23	Y	1
Wilson, Samuel	NC	33	Y	14
Wood, Robert	GA	40	Y	7

1 Information refers to his father, George Washington Capehart. The son cannot be found in the census.

TABLE 4. Soldiers Reporting War Weariness and Desertion, by Month

	Weariness	Desertion
1862		
January	0	0
February	0	0
March	1	0
April	3	1
May	3	1
June	4	1
July	7	1
August	5	3
September	6	3
October	7	2
November	7	1
December	8	6
1863		
January	7	4
February	9	6
March	6	8
April	6	4
May	6	5
June	2	3
July	26	3
August	13	13
September	5	5
October	6	7
November	8	7
December	5	3
1864		
January	9	6
February	9	3
March	10	5
April	9	3
May	5	2

	Weariness	Desertion
June	6	0
July	5	1
August	1	2
September	8	1
October	2	1
November	7	4
December	8	1
1865		
January	6	2
February	6	2
March	3	4
April	2	0
May	1	0

NOTES

ABBREVIATIONS

ADAH   Alabama Department of Archives and History, Montgomery
AU   Special Collections, Auburn University, Auburn, AL
CAH-UT   Center for American History, University of Texas at Austin
CCCWC   Confederate Collection, Civil War Collection 1861–1865 (microfilm),
                Tennessee State Library and Archives, Nashville
CMM, LSU   Joseph T. Glatthaar, ed., *Confederate Military Manuscripts, Series B,*
                Holdings of Louisiana State University (Lanham, MD: University
                Publications of America, 1996).
CNMP   Chickamauga National Military Park, Fort Oglethorpe, GA
CWMC,   Civil War Miscellaneous Collection, U.S. Army Military History
    USAMHI   Institute, Carlisle, PA

Duke	Special Collections, Duke University, Durham, NC
EU	Manuscripts, Archives, and Rare Book Library, Emory University, Atlanta, GA
Leigh, USAMHI	Lewis Leigh Collection, U.S. Army Military History Institute, Carlisle, PA
LSU	Special Collections, Louisiana State University Libraries, Baton Rouge
MDAH	Mississippi Department of Archives and History, Jackson
SHC-UNC	Southern Historical Collection, University of North Carolina at Chapel Hill
TSLA	Tennessee State Library and Archives, Nashville
UAL	W. S. Hoole Special Collections Library, University of Alabama, Tuscaloosa
UAR	Special Collections, University of Arkansas, Fayetteville
UGA	Hargrett Rare Book and Manuscript Library, University of Georgia, Athens
USAMHI	U.S. Army Military History Institute, Carlisle, PA
USC	Caroliniana Library, University of South Carolina, Columbia
VHS	Virginia Historical Society, Richmond
VS	The Valley of the Shadow, http://valley.vcdh.virginia.edu/.

INTRODUCTION

1 These are the original lyrics. Only later versions, shorn of any reference to slavery or other kinds of property, begin, "We are a band of brothers and native to the soil/Fighting for our Liberty, With treasure, blood and toil." See Wiley, *Life of Johnny Reb*, 155.

2 McPherson, *Ordeal by Fire*, 142–45, 149–51, 164–68; Robinson, *Bitter Fruits of Bondage*, 33; Wiley, *Life of Billy Yank*, 17–37; Wiley, *Life of Johnny Reb*, 15, 19, 25.

3 Russell, *My Diary North and South*, 77.

4 Ibid., 79, 82, 86.

5 In comparison, the Union army eventually contained 46,000 conscripts and 118,000 substitutes. See McPherson, *Ordeal by Fire*, 168, 181–82, 357. On "cowards," see Gordon, *"I Never Was a Coward."* On desertion, see Weitz, *A Higher Duty* and *More Damning than Slaughter*. On soldiers' religion, see Rolfs, "Religious Compromises," 121–44; Woodworth, *While God Is Marching On*; Phillips, "A Brothers' War?" 67–90.

6 Wiley, *Life of Johnny Reb*, 11–12, 15–27; Wiley, *Life of Billy Yank*, 15, 40–44, 358–60; McPherson, *For Cause and Comrades*, 91, 94. Brief versions of this discussion are found in Noe, "Alabama," 165–71; and " 'Battle Against the Traitors,'" 124–25.

7 Barton, *Goodmen*, see especially 5, 24, 31–33, 40–43 (quotations 24, 41); Robertson, *Soldiers Blue and Gray*.

8 Linderman, *Embattled Courage*; Anderson, *Blood Image*; Berry, *All That Makes a Man*; Glatthaar, "Afterword," 250–51; Logue, *To Appomattox and Beyond*; Sheehan-Dean, "Blue and Gray," 9–16.

9   Berry, *All That Makes a Man*, 171.

10 Reid Mitchell, *Civil War Soldiers*, esp. 1–35. See also Reid Mitchell, *Vacant Chair*.

11 Glatthaar, *General Lee's Army*, 29–41; Hess, *Liberty, Virtue, and Progress*; Hess, *Union Soldier in Battle*; Jimerson, *Private Civil War*, 10–24; Manning, "This Cruel War," 2, 28–31; Manning, *This Cruel War*; 4–32; McPherson, *For Cause and Comrades*, 5, 16–27; Williams, *A People's History*, see esp. 73–81, 191–96. McPherson first introduced his interpretation in *What They Fought For*. The phrase "slave society" is taken from Berlin, *Many Thousands Gone* and refers to a type of society with values and economics than rise directly from slave labor.

12 Jimerson, *Private Civil War*, 10; Williams, *People's History*, 191–96.

13 Manning, *This Cruel War*, 4–6, 12, 21–38 (quotations 29, 32).

14 McPherson, *For Cause and Comrades*, 6; McPherson, *Ordeal by Fire*, 165, 168, 181–82, 357.

15 Later-enlisting Confederates generally are studied only in biographies and unit histories. Two splendid examples are Glatthaar, *General Lee's Army*, 200–207, 358–60; and Richard Lowe, *Walker's Texas Division*.

16 Manning makes a distinction in her dissertation, "This Cruel War," but not in the book that followed, Manning, *This Cruel War*. Another example is Elisabeth Lauterbach Laskin, "Good Old Rebels."

17 Wiley, *Life of Johnny Reb*, 322–47; Linderman, *Embattled Courage*, 2.

18 McPherson, *For Cause and Comrades*, ix, 6–8, 102–3.

19 Osborn, "Letters of Robert Webb Banks," 142.

20 Crow, *Diary of a Confederate Soldier*, 14.

21 B. Wylie Scott, Fort Siler, NC, to Ella Merryman, May 4, 1862, Merryman Papers, VHS. Throughout the notes, I standardize place indicators when possible by providing only the closest town given and the state. Thus, the theoretical "Camp Smith, 4 miles from Jones, Virginia" would be listed as "Jones, VA."

22 W. H. Franklin, Chatham, VA, to Brother, Feb. 12, 1862, Franklin Correspondence, Duke. Franklin, a devout Christian, later served in a Confederate hospital.

23 M. C. Hart, Port Hudson, LA, to Nehemiah Williams, Nov. 10, 1862, Hart Letter, Mss 4553, Reel 6, CMM, LSU.

24 Glatthaar, *General Lee's Army*, 202; J. M. Davidson, Clinton, TN, to J. M. C. Dunn, May 13, 1862, Davidson Papers, EU; Holland, *Keep All My Letters*, 49.

25 Cash and Howorth, *My Dear Nellie*, 41, 46.

26 Lynn, *Bayonets of the Republic*, 19–35 (quotation 24–25).

27 Lynn, *Bayonets of the Republic*, 35–36; McPherson, *For Cause and Comrades*, x, 12; Reid Mitchell, *Civil War Soldiers*, 56–75.

28 Glatthaar, "Roundtable Discussion."

29 Lynn, *Bayonets of the Republic*, 43.

30 Civil War Soldiers and Sailors System. I am grateful to both Gary Gallagher and Carol Reardon for reminding me of the importance of identifying rank.

31 McPherson, *Ordeal by Fire*, 357–58.

32 Wiley, *Life of Johnny Reb*, 347.

33 Ibid., 330; McPherson, *Ordeal by Fire*, 358–59.

34 McPherson, *Ordeal by Fire*, 358–59.

35 Figures are computed from Tables 1 and 2. Here I also follow the method outlined in Bode and Ginter, *Farm Tenancy and the Census*.

CHAPTER 1

1 Ryan, "Harden Perkins Cochrane, part 1," 281; Twenty-Eight Alabama Infantry Regiment.

2 "Harden Perkins Cochrane," 282.

3 Ryan, "Harden Perkins Cochrane, part 2," 68; Noe, "Alabama," 163–65.

4 Durkin, *John Dooley*, xiii, xviii, xix, 70 (quotation 70). Dooley kept a diary from August 1862 until July 1863. Captured and imprisoned on Johnson's Island, he rewrote much of it, elaborating at several points. After the war, he added still more text, but I have used only entries from the original diary.

5 Gallagher, *Confederate War*, 73.

6 Escott, *After Secession*, quotation ix; Escott, "Failure of Confederate Nationalism," 15–28; Powell and Wayne, "Decline of Confederate Nationalism," 29–45; Weitz, *More Damning than Slaughter*, 16–33; Robinson, *Bitter Fruits of Bondage*; Williams, *A People's History*; Williams, *Rich Man's War*; Williams, Williams, and Carlson, *Plain Folk*.

7 Beringer et al., *Why the South Lost*, see esp. 64–81, 336–67, 426–27, 440–42 (quotations 64, 442). The authors' thesis reflects in turn an early essay by Stampp, "Southern Road to Appomattox," in his *Imperiled Union*, 246–69.

8 Potter, "Historian's Use of Nationalism," 34–83 (quotation 63–64). An earlier, abridged version appeared in the *American Historical Review* 67 (1962): 924–50.

9 Gallagher, *Confederate War*, 70; McCardell, *Idea of a Southern Nation*; Channing, "Slavery and Confederate Nationalism," 219–226; Thomas, "Reckoning with Rebels," 3–14; Thomas, *Confederacy as a Revolutionary Experience*; Thomas *Confederate Nation*, see esp. 145–48, 221–44, 277, 284–306.

10 Faust, *Creation of Confederate Nationalism*, quotations 6, 7.

11 Rable, *Confederate Republic*; Rubin, *Shattered Nation*.

12 Barton, *Goodmen*, 33; Berry, *All That Makes a Man*, 171; Reid Mitchell, *Civil War Soldiers*, 1–2, 20–22, 56–57, 191; Reid Mitchell, *Vacant Chair*, 37.

13 McPherson, *For Cause and Comrades*, 21, 27, 90–116, 212n15 (quotation 94).

14 Gallagher, *Confederate War*, 63–111; Carmichael, *Last Generation*; Sheehan-Dean, *Why Confederates Fought*.

15 W. R. Sivley, Vicksburg, MS, to Sister, May 27, 1862, Sivley Papers, SHC-UNC.

16 Smith, *Here's Yer Mule*, 16, 39. See also William A. Collins, Camp Mangum, NC, to Father, Mar. 27, 1862, Collins Papers, SHC-UNC

17 J. F. Coghill, Williamsport, MD, to Pappy, Ma and Mit, July 9, 1863; and Coghill, New Market, VA, to Mit, Oct. 27, 1864, Coghill Letters, SHC-UNC.

18 A. G. Jones, Stevensburg, VA, to Parents, Aug. 21, 1863; and Jones, Camp Racoon Ford, VA, to Father, Sept. 11, 1863, Jones Family Papers, SHC-UNC. See also Hubbs, *Voices*, 238.

19 John Thurman, Memphis, TN, to Wife, Mar. 17, 1862; and Thurman, Barnsville, to Wife, Mar. 26, 1862, Thurman Papers, SHC-UNC.

20 John Thurman, Corinth, MS, to Wife, May 5, 1862; and Thurman, Tupelo, MS, to Wife, May 17, 1864, Thurman Papers, SHC-UNC.

21 Moseley, *Stilwell Letters*, xiv, 5, 11, 66, 127 (quotations 5, 11).

22 Ibid., 51, 133, 196, 275. See also "53d Ga. Vols."

23 Lowe and Hodges, *Letters to Amanda*, ix, 26, 27, 67, 95.

24 John Crittenden, Tupleo, MS, to Bettie, June 3, 1862; and Crittenden, Marietta, GA, to Brother, June 24, 1864, Crittenden Papers, AU.

25 Mays, *Let Us Meet in Heaven*, 21n28, 58, 131, 156.

26 Wiley, "*This Infernal War*," 4–6, 92, 96, 126, 291, 305. Reid Mitchell refers to Fay as a "perpetual grumbler" and "a particularly paranoid man," while Gerald Linderman calls him "delicate and timid." See Linderman, *Embattled Courage*, 92, 305; and Reid Mitchell, *Civil War Soldiers*, 58, 177. For a similar sentiment, see H. C. Harris, Mobile, AL, to Sister, Nov. 2, 1862, Harris Letter, UAL.

27 Wiley, "*This Infernal War*," 153, 326, 329, 350.

28 For "the country," see Phillips Fitzpatrick, Cantonment Walter, to Mary, Mar. 26, 1862, Fitzpatrick Papers, ADAH. For "my country," see G. H. Burns, [?] Station, TN, to Wife, Nov. 13, 1862, Burns Letters, CNMP; Griffith, *Yours Till Death*, 14; Benjamin Franklin Lafayette Henderson, n.p., to Jane, Nov. 28, 1862; Henderson Letters, ADAH; Jesse C. Knight, Chatham County, GA, to Wife, June 24, 1862, Knight Family Papers, UGA; H. W. Robinson, "To the Girl I Love," Robinson Letters, EU; B. F. Tamplin, Houston, TX, to Retincia, Mar. 24, 1862, Tamplin Letters, CMM, LSU; W. J. J. Webb, Fredericksburg, VA, to Mother, May 23, 1863, Webb Papers, Leigh, USAMHI. For "our country," see D. R. Childers, Chattanooga, TN, to J. W. Palmer, July 22, 1863, Wood Papers, UGA; R. E. Corry, Okolona, MS, to Lizzie, Nov. 25, 1863, Corry Confederate Collection, AU; S. W. Farrow, Camp Wright, LA, to Josephine, Apr. 8 and 16, 1863, Farrow Papers, CAH-UT; Lee Faulkner, Galveston, TX, to Wife, May 7, 1865, Faulkner and Wilson Papers, CAH-UT; F. M. Goodwin, Campbellton, GA, to Susan, July 13, 1864, Goodwin Confederate Letter, UGA; Tom Grisham, New [?], GA, to Friend, May 8, 1865, Grisham Letter, Leigh, USAMHI; William P. Head, Pineville, LA, to Children, June 4, 1864, Head Papers, CAH-UT; John French White, Richmond, VA, to Mattie, May 3, 1863, White Papers, VHS. For "God and country," see A. L. Galloway, Tupelo, MS, to Wife, June 15, 1862, Galloway Letters Collection, AU. For "our bleeding country," see J. R. Manson, Fredericksburg, VA, to Charlotte, May 17, 1863, Manson Diary and Letters, CWMC, USAMHI; and F. Niebuhr, Grenada, MS, to Parents and Brothers and Sisters, Dec. 25, 1862, Niebuhr Papers, CAH-UT. For "the whole country," see John French White, Richmond, VA, to Wife, May 19, 1862, White Papers, VHS. For "our infant confederacy," see William P. Head, Pineville, LA, to Children, June 4, 1864, Head Papers, CAH-UT. For "our little confederacy," see John William Watson, Orange County, VA, to Wife, Mar. 14, 1864, Watson Family Papers, VHS. For "nation," see J. R. Manson, Falling Creek Camp, VA, to Mother, Aug. 9, 1862, Manson Diary and Letters, CWMC, USAMHI. For

"glorious nation," see Cawthon, "Letters of a Private," 541. For "the South," see Haynes, *Field Diary*, 28.

29 Cash and Howorth, *My Dear Nellie*, 109; Terrill and Dixon, *History of Stewart County*, 183, 275, 286, 602–3 (quotation 286); McPherson, *For Cause and Comrades*, 95. Terrill's letter contains additional high-flown rhetoric about "true patriotism," "stoical philosophy," and "the balm of time [that] shall have cicatriced the wounds now bleeding" for the memories of fallen loved ones who "offered their very life blood, a willing sacrifice." I am grateful to Keith Bohannon for his thoughts on Terrill's career.

30 Wiley, *Life of Billy Yank*, 44, 358; Wiley, *Life of Johnny Reb*. Robertson, *Soldiers Blue and Gray*, 5, 30, suggest that the greatest legacies of the Revolution for the Civil War generation were the positive legacies of volunteer soldiers and African Americans combatants. Linderman, *Embattled Courage*, 287, refers to the war solely as a basis for later reunion.

31 Reid Mitchell, *Civil War Soldiers*, 1–2, 4–10, 12, 20–22 (quotations 1).

32 Jimerson, *Private Civil War*, 10–17, 27–33.

33 McPherson, *For Cause and Comrades*, 20–21, 27, 104–16 (quotations 104, 206, 21).

34 Elisabeth Lauterbach Laskin, "Good Old Rebels," 32–50; Manning, *This Cruel War*, 19–22, 28–39; Robinson, *Bitter Fruits of Bondage*, 34–36; Rubin, *Shattered Nation*, 14–25, 58, 147; Gallagher, *Confederate War*, 59, 144, 146.

35 Smith, *Here's Yer Mule*, 16, 39.

36 Moseley, *Stilwell Letters*, 118–19; Hubbs, *Voices*, 147. Manning, *This Cruel War*, 29, notes that few soldiers discussed states rights or the realities of building a new government.

37 John Thurman, Barnsville, MS, to Wife, Apr. 3, 1862; and John Thurman, Monterey, MS, to Wife, Apr. 9, 1862, Thurman Papers, SHC-UNC.

38 Mays, *Let Us Meet in Heaven*, 8–21, 131 (quotation 131).

39 Cate, *Two Soldiers*, vii–10, 18, 22–23 (quotations 22, 23); Hubbs, *Voices*, 78.

40 Burns, Clinton, TN, to Wife, Aug. 9, 1862, Burns Letters, CNMP.

41 Kennedy Diary, Nov. 27, 1863, SHC-UNC.

42 Pharis Shearer, Tullahoma, TN, to Jennie Silvey, Mar. 3, 1863, Sivley Papers, SHC-UNC.

43 Joseph Joyner, Orange Court House, VA, to Mother, Aug. 12, 1862, Joyner Family Papers, SHC-UNC.

44 Hubbs, *Voices*, 233, 238, 252, 261, 353, 371; Moseley, *Stilwell Letters*, 48, 68, 174.

45 Mays, *Let Us Meet in Heaven*, 131, 229; Isaac Barineau, Orange County, VA, to Kate Barineau, Aug. 6, 1863, Barineau Collection, CWMC, USAMHI; T. L. Camp, Dalton, GA, to Mary, Dec. 25, 1863, Camp Family Papers, EU; J. M. Davidson, Harrodsburg, KY, to J. M. C. Dunn, Oct. 12, 1862, and Davidson, Lenoir, TN, to Dunn, [Nov–Dec. 1862], Davidson Papers, EU; S. W. Farrow, Monroe, LA, to Josephine, May 13, 1863, Farrow Papers, CAH-UT; Hartley and Zimmerman, *Fighting 57th*, 128, 143; William P. Head, Pineville, LA, to Children, June 4, 1864, Head Papers, CAH-UT; J. R. Manson, Falling Creek Camp, VA, to Mother, July 27, 1862, Manson Diary and Letters, CWMC, USAMHI; Alex McNeil, Chambersburg, PA,

to Wife, June 28, 1863, McNeil Papers, USC; John S. Meriwether, Vicksburg, MS, to Alice, Jan. 2, 1863, Meriwether Papers, EU; J. T. and W. J. Nobles, James Island, SC, to Father, June 30, 1862, Nobles Papers, USC; H. W. Robinson, Beans Station, TN, to Wife and Family, Apr. 4, 1862, Robinson Papers, EU; John Thurman, Tupelo, MS, to Wife, May 17, 1864, Thurman Papers, SHC-UNC; John William Watson, Orange County, VA, to Wife, Mar. 14, 1864, Watson Family Papers, VHS; John French White, Chaffin's Farm, VA, to Mattie, Nov. 14, 1863, White Papers, VHS; Blomquist and Taylor, *This Cruel War*, 322; Cash and Howorth, *My Dear Nellie*, 131; Cate, *Two Soldiers*, 198; Crow, *Diary of a Confederate Soldier*, 73; Lowe and Hodges, *Letters to Amanda*, 95, 182; Ryan, "Harden Perkins Cochrane, part I," 282; Terrill and Dixon, *History of Stewart County*, 286; Wiley, *"This Infernal War,"* 75.

46 Durkin, *John Dooley*, 93.

47 A. G. Jones, Kinston, NC, to Friend, Jan. 6, 1863, Jones Family Papers, SHC-UNC.

48 Cash and Howorth, *My Dear Nellie*, 110; Wiley, *"This Infernal War,"* 170; E. W. Treadwell, Shelbyville, YN, to n.p., Apr. 7, 1863, Treadwell Letters, ADAH.

49 Lee Faulkner, Galveston, TX, to Wife, May 7, 1865, Faulkner and Wilson Papers, CAH-UT.

50 Griffith, *Yours Till Death*, 13.

51 Cate, *Two Soldiers*, 9, 13, 28, 74, 113, 119, 123; John Crittenden, Marietta, GA, to Mother, June 22, 1864, Crittenden Papers, AU; Fay, *"This Infernal War,"* 102, 242.

52 G. H. Burns, Clinton, TN, to Wife, Aug. 9, 1862, Burns Papers, CNMP.

53 DeWitt Diary, May 26, 1863, CCCWC, TSLA.

54 J. F. Coghill, Orange Court House, VA, to Pappy, Ma, and Mit, Aug. 10, 1863, Coghill Letters, SHC-UNC.

55 Cash and Howorth, *My Dear Nellie*, 134.

56 Pharis Shearer, Tullahoma, TN, to Jennie Silvey, Mar. 3, 1863, Sivley Papers, SHC-UNC.

57 Blomquist and Taylor, *This Cruel War*, 303.

58 R. H. Lee, Mobile, AL, to Wife, Feb, 15, 1862, Lee Papers, Duke; Moseley, *Stilwell Letters*, 201; John Thurman, Barnsville, to Wife, Apr. 3, 1862; and John Thurman, Monterey, MS, to Wife, Apr. 9, 1862, and Thurman, Corinth, MS, to Wife and Children, Apr. 15, 1862, Thurman Papers, SHC-UNC; E. A. Penick, Richmond, VA, to Mary, Mar. 14, 1862, Penick Papers, VHS; B. Wylie Scott, Camp, to Ella Merryman, June 5, 1862, Merryman Papers, VHS; J. C. Williams, Thunderbolt, GA, to Honey, Jan. 12, 1863, Williams Papers, AU. For a negative commentary on those who decried "subjugation" see William Duncan Cole, Burchard TN, to Wife, Aug. 28, 1863, Cole Letters, CWMC, USAMHI.

59 J. F. Coghill, Orange Court House, VA, to Pappy, Ma, and Mit, Aug. 10, 1863, Coghill Letters, SHC-UNC.

60 Cash and Howorth, *My Dear Nellie*, 132; Cate, *Two Soldiers*, 34; James E. Green Diary, 10, SHC-UNC; Leas, "Diary of Absalom Joshua Burum," 34, CCCWC, TSLA; Lowe and Hodges, *Letters to Amanda*, 100.

61 W. R. Sivley, Vicksburg, MS, to Sister, Feb. 25, 1864, Sivley Papers, SHC-UNC.

62 Cash and Howorth, *My Dear Nellie*, 196; William P. Head, Pineville, LA, to Children, June 4, 1864, Head Papers, CAH-UT.

63 E. R. Willis, Richmond, VA, to Father, Jan. 2, 1865, Willis Family Papers, USC. See also Hubbs, *Voices*, 355.

64 Elisabeth Lauterbach Laskin, "Good Old Rebels," 54–55. Laskin notes that discussions of rights essentially disappeared after 1862. For those men referred to in the narrative above, see J. F. Coghill, Orange Court House, VA, to Pappy, Ma, and Mit, Aug. 10, 1863, Coghill Letters, SHC-UNC; John F. Davenport, Tazewell, TN, to Wife, Aug. 20, 1862, Davenport Letters, ADAH; A. J. Edge, Camp McDonnell, GA, to Companion, Mar. 28, 1862, Edge Papers, EU; Cate, *Two Soldiers*, 18, 19, 176; Lowe and Hodges, *Letters to Amanda*, 95; Mays, *Let Us Meet In Heaven*, 131; Hartley and Zimmerman, *Fighting 57th*, 139; William P. Head, Pineville, LA, to Children, June 4, 1864, Head Papers, CAH-UT; Abraham Jones, Stevensburg, VA, to Parents, Aug. 21, 1863, Jones Family Papers, SHC-UNC; Alex McNeil, Chambersburg, PA, to Wife, June 28, 1863, McNeil Papers, USC; John S. Meriwether, Mobile, to Alice, Sept. 24, 1862, Meriwether Papers, EU.

65 "Drury Lacy," Davidson Encyclopedia, http://library.davidson.edu/archives/ency/lacyd.asp.

66 William S. Lacy, Gordonsville, VA, to Ma, Mar. 19, 1862, Lacy Papers, SHC-UNC.

67 Linderman, *Embattled Courage*, 10–11; McPherson, *For Cause and Comrades*, 5–6, 8, 13, 22–24, 35, 36, 168–69; Reid Mitchell, *Civil War Soldiers*, 81–82; Reid Mitchell, *Vacant Chair*, 154, 162–66.

68 B. F. Tamplin, Houston TX, to Retincia, Mar. 24, 1862, Tamplin Letters, CMM, LSU. See also R. E. Corry, Okolona, MS, to Lizzie, Nov. 25, 1863, Corry Confederate Collection, AU; John Crittenden, Tupelo, MS, to Bettie, June 3, 1862, Crittenden Papers RG 765, AU; A. L. Galloway, Tupelo, MS, to Wife, June 15, 1862, Galloway Letters, AU; R. H. Lee, Mobile, to Wife, Feb. 15, 1862, Lee Papers, Duke.

69 Wyatt-Brown, *Southern Honor*, 19–24, 34–48, 350–61; Dickson D. Bruce, *Violence and Culture*, 28; Greenberg, *Honor and Slavery*, xii, 3–23, xii, 8, 32–33, 41–42, 54–62; Christopher J. Olsen, *Political Culture and Secession*. Stephen Berry, in contrast, avers that scholars have overplayed the centrality of honor, as I also suggest here. See his *All That Makes a Man*, 20–21.

70 Barton, *Goodmen*, 13, 14, 36–37; Linderman, *Embattled Courage*, 11–15, 32; McPherson, *For Cause and Comrades*, 5–6, 8, 13, 23–25, 31, 77–84, 134–40, 168–70; Elisabeth Lauterbach Laskin, "Good Old Rebels," 110–15.

71 William J. Hart, n.p., to Father, Sept. 8, 1862, Hart Brothers Letters, CWMC, USAMHI. See also John Crittenden, Shelbyville, TN, to Bettie, Jan. 26, 1863, and Crittenden, Dalton, GA, to Bettie, Mar. 24, 1864, Crittenden Papers, AU.

72 W. J. J. Webb, Fredericksburg, VA, to Mother, May 23, 1863, Webb Letters, Leigh, USAMHI; John T. Beggs, n.p., to Ginnie, [Apr–June 1862], Beggs and Janssen Family Papers, SHC-UNC.

73 G. W. Giles, Meridian MS, to Wife, May 13, 1862, Giles Letters, CMM, LSU.

74 Phillips Fitzpatrick, Cantonment Walter, to Mary, Mar. 26, 1862, Fitzpatrick Papers, ADAH.

CHAPTER 2

1 Wiley, "*This Infernal War*," 31–32.

2 Ibid., 36, 37, 43, 49, 62, 65, 73, 80, 91, 163, 168, 173, 177, 208 (quotations 36, 37, 65, 177).

3 Ibid., 220, 224, 263, 304, 306, 307, 320, 340, 351, 397 (quotations 263, 307, 397).

4 Wallace Comer, Kenesaw Mountain, GA, to Mother and Relatives, June 14, 1864, Comer Family Papers, SHC-UNC. See also Comer's letter of Nov. 16, 1864.

5 Standard, scholarly works on African Americans as slave laborers in the Confederate army include Brewer, *Confederate Negro*; Jordan, *Black Confederates and Afro-Yankees in Civil War Virginia*; and Levine, *Confederate Emancipation*. For some of the most prominent printed examples that promote the idea of thousands of willing "Black Confederates," see Austerman, "The Black Confederates," 37–49; Harper, "Black Loyalty Under the Confederacy," 7–28; and Rollins, "Black Southerners in Gray." In regard to "scattered accounts of varying authenticity," I point to a "quotation" repeatedly posted on the internet, attributed to a book I wrote in 2001, that was in fact both lifted out of context and substantially rewritten. If this is a good example of the "proof" offered by proponents, that "proof" is flimsy indeed.

6 Wiley, *Life of Johnny Reb*, 15, 211, 309; Robertson, *Soldiers Blue and Gray*, 6, 9–10.

7 Reid Mitchell, *Civil War Soldiers*, 4–9, 10, 27–28, 181–83.

8 McPherson, *For Cause and Comrades*, 19–xx (quotation 20).

9 Elisabeth Lauterbach Laskin, "Good Old Rebels," 50–105; Jimerson, *Private Civil War*, 10–21 (quotations 10).

10 Sheehan-Dean, *Why Confederates Fought*, 13–20, 31–37; Manning, *This Cruel War*, 4, 6, 12, 23–39 (quotations 6, 29); McCurry, *Masters of Small Worlds*, esp. 85–91, 214–25, 230, 236–37, 260–61,

11 Jimerson, *Private Civil War*, 11; Elisabeth Lauterbach Laskin, "Good Old Rebels," 53; Manning, *This Cruel War*, 18, 28–30; McPherson, *For Cause and Comrades*, 19; Sheehan-Dean, *Confederates at War*, 34–35

12 Elisabeth Lauterbach Laskin, "Good Old Rebels," 52–53; Robinson, *Bitter Fruits of Bondage*, 49–51; Glatthaar, *General Lee's Army*, 203–4.

13 Otto H. Olsen, "Extent of Slave Ownership," 412–13.

14 Terrill and Dixon, *History of Stewart County*, 285.

15 Durkin, *John Dooley*, 31.

16 Cash and Howorth, *My Dear Nellie*, 117.

17 Smith, *Here's Yer Mule*, 34; Allan, *Allan's Lone Star Ballads*, 35.

18 J. C. Williams, Thunderbolt, GA, to Honey, Jan. 12, 1863, Williams Papers, AU. Williams identified the speaker as Capt. C. W. Howard.

19 T. L. Camp, Dalton, GA, to Mary, Dec. 25, 1863, Camp Family Papers, EU; Isaac Walters, Drewry's Bluff, VA, to Wife, Nov. 16, 1862, Costen Papers, SHC-UNC. See also a letter to Thomas Warrick of the 34th Alabama from his wife, written on October, 9, 1863, in which she reminded her husband that "you hant got no nigero to fite for." Thomas Warrick Papers, ADAH.

20 Harley and Zimmerman, *Fighting 57th*, 151.

21 For a similar argument, see McPherson, *For Cause and Comrades*, 19–21, 106–10.

22 I. McQueen Auld, Palatka, FL, to Mother, July 1, 1862, Auld Letters, CWMC, USAMHI; John T. Beggs, Tullahoma, TN, to Sister, Apr. 5, 1863, Beggs and Jonssen Family Papers, SHC-UNC; John Crittenden, Tupelo, MS, to Bettie, July 5, 1862, Crittenden Papers, AU; Andrew Crawford, Adam's Run, SC, to Mother, Feb. 5, 1865, Crawford Family Papers, USC; Phillips Fitzpatrick, Cantonment Walter, AL, to Mary, Mar. 26, 1862, Fitzpatrick Papers, ADAH; A. G. Jones, Garysburg, NC, to Mother, Oct. 9, 1982, Jones, Garysburg, NC, to Ellick, Oct. 15, 1862, Jones, Garysburg, NC, to Mother, Oct. 31, 1982, Jones Family Papers, SHC-UNC; Fleming Jordan, Goldsboro, NC, to Wife, Apr. 27, 1862, and Jordan, Army of Tennessee, to Wife, July 9, 1864, Jordan Letters, UGA; John Meriwether, Vicksburg, MS, to Wife, Jan. 2, 1863, Mar. 6, 1863, and Meriwether, Lookout Mountain, GA, to Wife, Nov. 17, 1863, Nov. 18, 1863, Meriwether Papers, EU; Thomas J. Moore, Fort Johnson, NC, to Thomas W. Hill, July 17, 1862, Moore, Winchester, VA, to Hill, Sept. 29, 1862, Moore, Kinston, NC, to Hill, Nov. 30, 1862, and Moore, Kinston, NC, to Hill, Jan. 30, 1863, Moore Papers, USC; W. R. Sively, Vicksburg, MS, to Sister, June 6, 1862, Sivley Papers, SHC-UNC; Smith Diary, Nov. 7, 1864, CCCWC, TSLA; D. C. Snyder, Lexington VA, to Wife, Mar. 15, 1865, Snyder Papers, VHS; W. J. J. Webb, Camp, to Father, July 25, 1863, Webb Letters, Leigh, USAMHI; Blomquist and Taylor, *This Cruel War*, 33; Durkin, *John Dooley*, 31, 56, 57, 66; Hubbell, *Confederate Stamps*, 10; Hubbs, *Voices*, 143, 148, 156; Lowe and Hodges, *Letters to Amanda*, 21, 164, 166; Mays, *Let Us Meet in Heaven*, 21, 28, 34, 37, 41, 45, 50, 56, 60, 126, 163, 198, 229, 232, 237; Enoch L. Mitchell, "Letters of Newberry," 54, 77; Osborn, "Letters of Robert Webb Banks," 145, 147, 151, 152; Ryan, "Letters of Cochrane," pt. 2, 59, 60, 147; pt. 5, 281–82, 283, 291; Terrill and Dixon, *History of Stewart County*, 282. See also Brewer, *Confederate Negro*; Daniel, *Army of Tennessee*, 14–15.

23 McMurtrey, *Letters to Lucinda*, 33.

24 Robinson, *Bitter Fruits of Bondage*, 91–93.

25 I. McQueen Auld, Palatka, FL, to Mother, July 1, 1862, Auld Letters, CWMC, USAMHI; Andrew Crawford, Adam's Run, SC, to Mother, Feb. 5, 1865, Crawford Family Papers, USC; Mays, *Let Us Meet in Heaven*, 56, 232;

26 Andrew Crawford, Adam's Run, SC, to Mother, Feb. 5, 1865, Crawford Family Papers, USC.

27 S. W. Farrow, Camp Wright, LA, to Josephine, Apr. 8 and 11, 1863, Farrow Papers, CAH-UT. See also Phillips Fitzpatrick, Dog River, AL, to Mary, June 29, 1862, Fitzpatrick Papers, ADAH; A. H. Jones, Garysburg, NC, to Ellick, Oct. 15, 1862, and Jones, Garysburg, NC, to Mother, Oct. 31, 1982, Jones Family Papers, SHC-UNC; William A. Stephens, Vicksburg, MS, to Susan, Mar. 1863, Stephens Papers, EU; Grantham, "Letters from Hightower," 198.

28 Abel Crawford, New Market, VA, to Mother, Oct. 8, 1864; Crawford, Strasburg, VA, to Mother, Oct. 15, 1864; Crawford, New Market, VA, to Mother, Oct. 29, 1864; Crawford, New Market, VA, to Mother, Nov. 6, 1864 (quotation); Jim Crawford, New Market, VA, to Fannie, Oct. 8, 1864, Crawford Letters, CCCWC, TSLA.

29 Blomquist and Taylor, *This Cruel War*, 33.

30 I. McQueen Auld, Camp Call, FL, to Mamie, July 14, 1862, Auld Letters, CWMC, USAMHI.

31 Thomas J. Moore, Winchester, VA, to Thomas W. Hill, Sept. 29, 1862, Moore Papers, USC. See also John Putnam, Battery Marshall Sullivan, to Companion and Children, Feb. 1865, Putnam Papers, USC.

32 Rice Diary, May 3, 1863, CAH-UT.

33 Hubbs, *Voices*, 174, 212; Gibbs Morgan, Port Hudson, LA, to Mother, Sept. 24, 1862, Morgan Letter, LSU.

34 Here I follow the argument in Levine, *Confederate Emancipation*.

35 Lowe and Hodges, *Letters to Amanda*, 182.

36 James B. Jones, Camp Pegram, VA, to Alexander, Feb. 12, 1864, Jones Family Papers, SHC-UNC. See also Hubbs, *Voices*, 355.

37 Cate, *Two Soldiers*, 16–19.

38 Blomquist and Taylor, *This Cruel War*, 322–33. See also Wallace Diary, Apr. 3, 4, 1865, SHC-UNC.

39 E. R. Willis, Richmond, VA, to Father, Jan. 2, 1865, Willis Family Papers, USC.

40 Battle, *Civil War Letters*, 18. For the numbers of African Americans in uniform, see Hahn, *Nation Under Our Feet*, 91–92.

41 G. H. Burns, Jackson, MS, to Wife, Jan. 8, 1863, Burns Letters, CNMP.

42 Moseley, *Stilwell Letters*, 109.

43 Williamson Diary, Nov. 28, 1863, Leigh, USAMHI.

44 W. R. Sivley, Shurbuta, MS, to Janie, Dec. 9, 1863, Sivley Papers, SHC-UNC; John Crittenden, Dalton, GA, to Bettie, Mar. 29, 1864, Crittenden Papers, AU.

45 Wiley, "This Infernal War," 171.

46 Moseley, *Stilwell Letters*, 109. See Wiley, *Life of Johnny Reb*, 314–15.

47 Cate, *Two Soldiers*, 138, 164.

48 Hubbs, *Voices*, 341; John Crittenden, Gadsden, AL, to Bettie, Oct. 22, 1864, Crittenden Papers, AU.

49 John T. Knight, "the Cow Lands of Sorrow," to Susan Knight, Oct. 15, 1863, Knight Letters, CCCWC, TSLA. See also Leas, "Diary of Burum," 40, CCCWC, TSLA.

50 A. D. Craver, Iuka, MS, to James M. Robertson, Dec. 5, 1864, Craver Letter, Leigh, USAMHI.

51 Charles M. Hurley, Petersburg, VA, to Emma Louise Grant, July 31, 1864, Hurley Papers, CWMC, USAMHI.

52 T. S. McAllister, Petersburg, VA, to Father and Mother, July 31, 1864, McAlister Letter, CWMC, USAMHI. This item is a photocopied clipping of a letter that appeared in the Mar. 20, 1906, *Nicholas County (W.Va.) Chronicle*. See also Edgar Smithwick, Petersburg, VA, to Mother, Aug. 8, 1864, Smithwick Papers, Duke.

53 Ryan, "Letters of Cochrane," pt. 1, 292–93.

54 Leas, "Diary of Burum," 34–35, CCCWC, TSLA; E. B. Coggin, Fredericksburg City, MD, to n.p., Sept. 7, 1862, Coggin Papers, ADAH; F. A. Bleckley, Effingham Co., GA, to n.p., Jan. 20, 1865, Bleckley Letters, Leigh, USAMHI.

55 J. R. Parker, Corinth, MS, to Amanda, May 22, 1862, Parker Letters, CWMC,

USAMHI. See also A. J. Terry, Camp Jackson, VA, to Wife, May 29, 1863, Terry Family Papers, SHC-UNC; W. Y. Mordecai, Bunker Hill, VA, to Mother, Oct. 19, 1862, Mordecai Papers, VHS; R. T. Wood, Atlanta, GA, to Mary & Children, July 12, 1864, Wood Papers, UGA.

56 O. V. Strickland, Dalton, GA, to Mother, Dec. 18, 1863, Strickland Papers, EU.

57 E. A. Penick, Gordonsville, VA, to Son, Mar. 18, 1862, Penick Papers, VHS. See also in the same collection Penick's letters of Apr. 21, 1862 and Sept. 5, 1862.

58 Fleming Jordan, Atlanta, GA, to Wife, July 11, 1864, Jordan Letters, UGA. For the general breakdown of slavery, see for example Hahn, *Nation Under Our Feet*, 14, 62–115; McPherson, *Ordeal by Fire*, 394–96; Robinson, *Bitter Fruits of Bondage*, 178–82.

59 John T. Knight, Arkansas Post, AR, to Susan Knight, Jan. 13, 1862, and Knight, Bayou Bluff, to Susan Knight, Nov. 4, 1863, Knight Letters, CCCWC, TSLA.

60 William H. Barnes, Thibodeaux, LA, to Lizzie, June 26, 1863, Barnes Papers, CAH-UT. See also Newt Bosworth, Fishersville, VA, to Friend, June 28, 1864, Bosworth Family Collection, Leigh, USAMHI.

61 Isaac Walters, Drewry's Bluff, VA, to Wife, Nov. 16, 1862, Coston Papers, SHC-UNC.

62 Fleming Jordan, Atlanta, GA, to Wife, July 18, 1864, Jordan Letters, UGA.

63 Mays, *Let Us Meet in Heaven*, 29, 33, 43, 46, 51, 58, 78, 85, 90, 103, 112, 171, 177, 180, 192, 223 (quotations 29, 46).

64 John Meriwether, Camp Holt, AL, to Wife, July 18, 1862; Meriwether, Mobile, AL, to Wife, Oct. 6, 1862; Meriwether, Camp Forney, AL, to Wife, Nov. 13, 1862; and Meriwether, Vicksburg, MS, to Wife, Feb. 15, 1863, Meriwether Papers, EU. See also Madison Kilpatrick, Camp, to Wife, Aug. 12, 1864, Kilpatrick Letters, AU.

65 Wiley, "This Infernal War," 217.

66 Benjamin W. Lee, Little Rock, AR, to Silas Williams, Dec. 14, 1862, Knight Letters, CCCWC, TSLA.

67 Wiley, "This Infernal War," 194, 196.

68 Battle, *Civil War Letters*, 24.

69 Griffith, *Yours Till Death*, 58.

70 T. L. Camp, Chattanooga, TN, to Mary, Nov. 22, 1863, Camp Family Papers, EU; J. F. Coghill, Fredericksburg, VA, to Pappy, Ma, and Mit, Jan. 25, 1863, Coghill Letters, SHC-UNC; J. M. Davidson, Shelbyville, TN, to Julia, Jan. 13, 1863, Davidson Papers, EU; Henry Mowrer, Petersburg, VA, to Wife, Jan. 8, 1865, Mowrer Papers, CWMC, USAMHI; Blomquist and Taylor, *This Cruel War*, 170.

71 Amon W. Updike, New Kent County, VA, to Sister, Apr. 30, 1864, Updike Letters, CWMC, USAMHI.

72 Griffith, *Yours Till Death*, 2, 3, 19, 22, 40, 45, 47, 57, 64, 73, 86, 87, 88, 89, 91, 93, 96, 97, 98, 101, 127 (quotations 93, 127).

73 Wiley, "This Infernal War," 173, 186; B. Mason, Montgomery, AL, to Nancy, Apr. 2, 1862, Mason Letters, Leigh, USAMHI.

74 Holland, *Keep All My Letters*, 43, 52, 55, 56, 61, 65, 68, 71, 72, 74, 76, 90, 92, 94.

CHAPTER 3

1   H. W. Robinson, "To the Girl I Love," Robinson Letters, EU. In a note, Bell Wiley suggests that Robinson may have been a conscript. See also 42nd Georgia, http://www.42ndgeorgia.com (accessed Oct. 21, 2007).

2   H. W. Robinson, Beans Station, TN, to Wife, July 28, 1862, Robinson Letters, EU.

3   Barton, *Goodmen*, 3–4; Carmichael, *Last Generation*, 10–15, 95–96; Faust, *Mothers of Invention*, 9–29, 223; Linderman, *Embattled Courage*, 7–110; McPherson, *For Cause and Comrades*, 131–41; Reid Mitchell, *Civil War Soldiers*, 67–68, 77, 84–85, 177–78; Reid Mitchell, *Vacant Chair*; Rable, *Civil Wars*, 31–49; Robertson, *Soldiers Blue and Gray*, 13–14, 102–21; Whites, *Crisis in Gender*, 5–6, 15–63; Wiley, *Life of Johnny Reb*, 209–10, 270–85. McCurry, *Masters of Small Worlds*, 72–75, 268–69, denies that Southern yeoman households were influenced by Northern, middle-class notions of domesticity but reaffirms the role of women as symbols during the secession crisis.

4   Jimerson, *Private Civil War*, 24–26; McPherson, *For Cause and Comrades*, 134–35; Wiley, *Life of Johnny Reb*, 167, 216, 270–71 (quotation 270); Robertson, *Soldiers Blue and Gray*, 13–14, 102–21; Linderman, *Embattled Courage*, 80–98 (quotation 87); Sheehan-Dean, *Confederates at War*, 58–60.

5   Reid Mitchell, *Vacant Chair*, 3–69, 71–87, 115–59.

6   Ibid., 160–66.

7   Manning, *This Cruel War*, 11–12, 35–38, 57–67, 105–6, 110, 168, 202–3, 218–19.

8   Berry, *All That Makes a Man* (quotations 183, 192). For a somewhat different view that focuses on young elites and devoted Confederates, see Carmichael, *Last Generation*.

9   Glatthaar, *General Lee's Army*, 203; W. H. Franklin, Chatham, VA, to Brother, Feb. 12, 1862, Franklin Correspondence, Duke.

10 Wiley, *"This Infernal War,"* 203, 209, (quotation 203). See also Hubbs, *Voices*, 117, 177.

11 Haynes, *Field Diary*, 11.

12 I. M. Auld, Augusta, GA, to Mother, Aug. 8, 1862, Auld Letters, CWMC, USAMHI; Marion Coiner, Camp, to Sister, Mar. 20, 1864, Coiner Family Papers, VHS; "Diary of a Virginia Cavalry Man," 210; Rice Diary, May 3, 7, 1863, CAH-UT; T. J. Rounsaville, Camp Hope, AR, to Niece, Sept. 14, 1864, Rounsaville Letters, CWMC, USAMHI; Smith, *Here's Yer Mule*, 13, 16, 17; Wallace Diary #3059-z, 25, 75, 76, 88, SHC-UNC; Phillips, *Diehard Rebels*, 97–98.

13 Williamson Diary, Dec. 4, 1863, Box 28, Leigh, USAMHI.

14 William H. Barnes, Thibodeaux, LA, to Lizzie, June 26, 1863, Barnes Papers, CAH-UT.

15 Durkin, *John Dooley*, 14–15. For a trans-Mississippi example, see Wallace Diary #3059-z, 25, SHC-UNC.

16 Moseley, *Stilwell Letters*, 39–40.

17 Eaton Diary, 7, 9, 10, SHC-UNC; Hubbell, *Confederate Stamps*, 11. See also Hubbs, *Voices*, 178–79.

18 Mellon, "Florida Soldier," 258. As late as February 1865, Thomas Key drew strength from women in Columbus, Georgia, who greeted his arriving battery with food and drink. See Cate, *Two Soldiers*, 186.

19 John Crittenden, Florence, AL, to Bettie, Oct. 31, 1864, Crittenden Papers, AU.

20 Lowe and Hodges, *Letters to Amanda*, 62. See also Cawthon, "Letters of a Private," 538.

21 Cash and Howorth, *My Dear Nellie*, 77.

22 McMurtrey, *Letters to Lucinda*, 2.

23 D. C. Snyder, Lexington, VA, to Wife, Mar. 15, 1865, Snyder Papers, VHS.

24 Cate, *Two Soldiers*, 20, 26–27. For similar complaints, see Wiley, *"This Infernal War,"* 368.

25 Newt Bosworth, Camp, to Pa, Apr. 15, Sept. 8, 1863, Bosworth Family Collection, Leigh, USAMHI.

26 E. W. Treadwell, Shelbyville, TN, to Mattie, Apr. 27, 1863, Treadwell Letters, ADAH.

27 John French White, City Point, VA, to Wife, May 16, 1863, White Papers, VHS.

28 Wiley, *"This Infernal War,"* 249.

29 Berry, *All That Makes a Man*, 46–47, 83–85, 114–18; Faust, *James Henry Hammond*, 58–65; Faust, *Mothers of Invention*, 139–41, 145–52; Ott, *Confederate Daughters*, 26–30, 100–116; Rable, *Civil Wars*, 51–54, 192–94.

30 Northen, *All Right Let Them Come*, 41, 42, 55–59, 66, 77, 79, 86, 92 (quotations 55, 56, 58, 66, 86, 92). A "grass widow" was a married woman whose husband was away, either in the army or due to a more permanent separation.

31 William D. Alexander Diary, vol. 2, 12, 63, 67, SHC-UNC; Marion Coiner, Headquarters, to Sister, Feb. 6, 1864, Coiner Family Papers, VHS; Auvergne D'Antignac, Frederick Hall, VA, to Mary, Aug. 22, n.d., D'Antignac Letter, CWMC, USAMHI; J. T. Nobles and W. J. Nobles, Pocatiligo, SC, to James A. Nobles, Nancy Nobles, Becca Nobles, and Mattie Nobles, Apr. 23, 1862, and J. T. Nobles and W. J. Nobles, Pocatiligo, SC, to Sister, Apr. 23, 1862, Nobles Papers, USC; Pate, *This Evil War*, 199–200; T. T. Raines, Camp Pender, VA, to Ma, Oct. 7, 1863, Raines Letter, Leigh, USAMHI; W. R. Sivley, Shurbuta, MS, to Sister, Sept. 20, Oct. 21, 1863, Jan. 27, 1864, Sivley Papers, SHC-UNC.

32 Johnson Webb, Ft. Gaines, AL, to Father & Mother, Mar. 22, 1863, Webb Letters, Leigh, USAMHI; W. R. Sivley, to Jennie, Jan. 24, Feb. 8, Mar. 22, 1865, Sivley Papers, SHC-UNC. See also Sanders, "Letters of a Confederate Soldier," 1238, 1239; Wynne and Taylor, *This War So Horrible*, 36; Faust, *Mothers of Invention*, 150–51; Barber, "'White Wings of Eros,'" 119–32; Ott, *Confederate Daughters*, 26–30, 100–116. Anya Jabour suggests that young Confederate women were no more interested in wartime marriage than the men were. See her *Scarlett's Sisters*, 270–80.

33 Mellon, "Florida Soldier," 264. See also Rable, *Civil Wars*, 193–94.

34 Wiley, *Life of Johnny Reb*, 51–58. See also Robertson, *Soldiers Blue and Gray*, 116–21.

35 Robert Emmet Corry, Corinth, MS, to Wife, June 17, 1864, Corry Confederate Collection, AU.

36 Lowe and Hodges, *Letters to Amanda*, 79; Mays, *Let Us Meet in Heaven*, 211. See also Cash and Howorth, *My Dear Nellie*, 168–69, 194; Cate, *Two Soldiers*, 191; John S.

Meriwether, Eufaula, AL, Mar. 20, 29, Apr. 8, 1864, Meriwether Papers, EU; Robert A. Williams, Chattanooga, TN, to Mittie Williams, Aug. 23, 1863, Williams Letters, ADAH.

37 Fleming Jordan, Griffin, GA, to Wife, Mar. 29, 1862, Jordan, Goldsboro, NC, to Wife, Apr. 17, 18, 1862, Jordan Letters, UGA.

38 Cash and Howorth, *My Dear Nellie*, 168–69, 194; Rable, *Civil Wars*, 59–61; John S. Meriwether, Eufala, AL, to Alice, Apr. 8, 1864, Meriwether Papers, EU.

39 H. W. Robinson, Beans Station, TN, to Wife, Aug. 3, 1862, Robinson Letters, EU.

40 Cash and Howorth, *My Dear Nellie*, 168–69; 194; Rable, *Civil Wars*, 59–61.

41 Robert Bates, Henrico Co., VA, to Wife, May 20, 1862, Bates Letter, Leigh, USAMHI; Battle, *Civil War Letters*, 20; John T. Beggs, n.p., to Ginnie, [Apr.–June. 1862], Beggs and Janssen Family Papers, SHC-UNC; John W. Bell, n.p., to Nannie, June 16, 1862, Bell Letters, CMM, LSU; Blomquist and Taylor, *This Cruel War*, 2, 11, 17, 20, 25, 28, 114; G. H. Burns to Wife, May 18, June 22 , July 26, Aug. 9, 16, 1863, Burns Letters, CNMP; Cash and Howorth, *My Dear Nellie*, 64, 66, 67, 72, 76, 81–84; Cawthon, "Letters of a Private," 533; E. B. Coggin to Wife, July 14, 20, 23, Aug. 13, Dec. 21, 1862, Coggin Papers, ADAH; Isaac Walters, Petersburg, to Wife, May 31, 1862, Costen Papers, SHC-UNC; Robert Dickinson, Charleston, SC, to Amanda, June 23, 1862, Dickinson Papers, USC; S. W. Farrow, Camp Waterhouse, TX, to Josephine, July 28, 1862, and Farrow, Camp Josephine McDaniel, TX, to Josephine, Sept. 20, 1862, Farrow Papers, CAH-UT; Lee Faulkner, Galveston, TX, to Wife, Nov. 12, 1862, Faulkner and Wilson Papers, CAH-UT; Phillips Fitzpatrick, Dog River, AL, to Mary, Mar. 23, 1862, and Fitzpatrick, Cantonment Walter, AL, to Mary, Mar. 26, 1862, Fitzpatrick Papers, ADAH; J. C. Franklin, Richmond, VA, to Wife, June 23, 1862, Franklin Correspondence, Duke; Griffith, *Yours Till Death*, 2, 3, 5, 7, 9, 11, 12, 14, 35; J. W. Griffin, Richmond, VA, to Wife, July 6, 1862, and Griffin, n.p., to Wife, Aug. 23, 1862, Griffin Papers, Duke; Hatley and Huffman, *Letters of William F. Wagner*, 9, 10, 13, 19, 21–22, 24; Holland, *Keep All My Letters*, 27, 28, 30, 31, 42, 54, 55; Jesse C. Knight, Camp Boone, GA, to Wife, May 22, 1862, and Knight, Chatham County, GA, to Wife, June 18, 1862, Knight Family Papers, UGA; John T. Knight, Washington, AR, to Susan Knight, Oct. 1, 1862, Knight Letters, CCCWC, TSLA; Lanning Diary, 1–3, 12, ADAH; Charles, Richmond, VA, to Dr. Lee, Lee Papers, Duke; Lowe and Hodges, *Letters to Amanda*, 12, 14, 20, 27, 29, 59, 33, 39, 47, 51; J. R. Manson, Fredericksburg, VA, to Charlotte, July 12, 1862, Manson Diary and Letters, CWMC, USAMHI; McLaughlin, *Cherished Letters of Hendricks*, 25, 27, 32, 35, 38; McMurtrey, *Letters to Lucinda*, 1, 5; John Meriwether, Camp Holt, to Wife, June 13, 1862, and Meriwether, Mobile, AL, to Wife, Oct. 19, 1862, Meriwether Papers, EU; Moseley, *Stilwell Letters*, 17, 25, 27, 28, 49, 52, 58, 77, 103, 112; Elijah M. Odom, n.p., to Sarah F. Odom, Mar. 25, 1862, Odom Letters, MDAH; E. A. Penick, [Richmond, VA], to Mary, Mar. 11, 162, Penick Papers, VHS; C. D. Sides, Fredericksburg, VA, to Wife, Dec. 25, 1863, Sides Letters, CWMC, USAMHI; Smith, *Here's Yer Mule*, 23–24; William A. Stephens, Knoxville, TN, to Susan, July 13, 1862, Stephens Papers, EU; B. F. Tamplin, Grimes Co., TX, to Retincia, Mar. 24, 1862, Tamplin Letters, CMM, LSU; M. Thornton, Loachapoka, AL, to Wife, Apr. 30, 1862, Warrick Papers, ADAH; John Thurman,

Memphis, TN, to Wife, Mar. 17, 1862, Thurman Papers, SHC-UNC; John William Watson, n.p., to Wife, Oct. 5, 1862, Watson Family Papers, VHS; John French White, Richmond, VA, to Wife, May 19, 1862, White Papers, VHS; J. A. Wilson, Abbeville, MS, to Lizzie, Nov. 12, 1862, and Wilson, Camp Sloan, MS, to Lizzie, Nov. 22, 1862, Wilson Letters, MDAH; Wiley, "This Infernal War," 28, 52, 57, 59, 61, 64, 79, 80, 92, 95, 96, 106, 116, 121.

42 "My beloved is unto me as a cluster of camphire in the vineyards of Engedi. Behold, thou art fair, my love; behold, thou art fair; thou hast doves' eyes. Behold, thou art fair, my beloved, yea, pleasant: also our bed is green." William H. Barnes, Camp Terrell, to Lizzie, Nov. 2, 1862, Barnes Papers, CAH-UT.

43 William P. Cline, Camp, to M. C. Cline, Apr. 19, 28, 1862, Cline Papers, SHC-UNC.

44 Ownby, "Patriarchy in the World," 229–34; Marten, *Children's Civil War*, 69; M. Thornton, Loachapoka, AL, to Wife, Apr. 30, 1862, Warrick Papers, ADAH.

45 E. A. Penick, [Richmond], to Mary, Mar. 11, 16, 1862, Penick Papers, VHS.

46 Cawthon, "Letters of a Private," 538; J. M. Davidson, Louden, TN, to Julia, Dec. 24, 1862, Feb. 14, 1863, Davidson Papers, EU; Durkin, *John Dooley*, 82; A. L. Galloway, n.P., to Eliza, July 1, 1862, Galloway Letters, AU; Grantham. ed., "Letters from Hightower," 180; Harley and Zimmerman, *Fighting 57th*, 21, 22; J. H. Lee, n.p., to Wife, Dec. 25, 1862, Lee Letters, EU; Lowe and Hodges, *Letters to Amanda*, 41; Mitchell, "Letters of Newberry," 54; F. Niebuhr, Grenada, to Parents and Brothers and Sisters, n.d., Niebuhr Papers, CAH-UT; John Putnam, Battery Michael Sullivan, to Wife and Children, Dec. 24, 1864, Putnam Papers, USC; Pharis Shearer, Estill Springs, to Jennie, Dec. 3, 1862, Sivley Papers, SHC-UNC.

47 Phillips Fitzpatrick, Fort Gaines, to Mary, June 9, 1864, Fitzpatrick Papers, ADAH.

48 McMurtrey, *Letters to Lucinda*, 5.

49 Sheehan-Dean, *Why Confederates Fought*, 2, 27–28, 59–60, 133–37 (quotation 2).

50 Harvey Bailey, Asheville, NC, to Wife and Children, May 6, 1864, Bailey Letters, CWMC, USAMHI; Blomquist and Taylor, *This Cruel War*, 187, 211, 222, 224, 263, 274, 274, 311; Cash and Howorth, *My Dear Nellie*, 142, 147, 148, 156, 168, 194; Cate, *Two Soldiers*, 29; W. Duncan Cole, Mobile, AL, to Wife, June 21, 1863, Cole Letters, CWMC, USAMHI; E. B. Coggin, Bunker Hill, VA, to Wife, July 19, 1863, and Coggin, Culpeper Court House, VA, to Wife, July 27, 1863; Coggin Papers, ADAH; John F. Davenport, Clinton, TN, to Wife, Dec, 22, 1863, Davenport Letters, ADAH; J. M. Davidson, Shelbyville, TN, to Wife, Feb. 14, 1863, Davidson Papers, EU; D. M. Denney, Atlanta, GA, to Sinai and Children, Aug. 24. 1864, Denney Family Papers, AU; A. J. Edge, Enterprise, MS, to Wife, June 10, 1863, and Edge, Dalton, GA, to Wife, Mar. 12, 1864, Andrew J. Edge Papers MSS 346 (microfilm), EU; E. K. Flournoy, Vicksburg, MS, to Wife, Mar. 14, 27, Apr. 25, 1863, and Flournoy, Petersburg, VA, to Wife, July 15, 1863, Flournoy Letters, ADAH; James P. Garrison, Fredericksburg, VA, to Wife, Mar. 3, 1863, Garrison Papers, EU; G. W. Giles, Meridian, MS, to Wife, May 3, 1863, Giles Letters, CMM, LSU; Griffith, *Yours Till Death*, 44, 47, 62, 76, 92, 96, 97; Holland, *Keep All My Letters*, 77, 82, 92, 98, 106–7; B. R. Jeffares, Fields Hospital, to B. R. H. Jeffares, Dec. 3, 1864, Newell Family Papers, AU; John T. Knight, Little Rock, AR, to Susan Knight, Jan. 1, 1863, and Knight, Pine

Bluff, AR, to Wife, Jan, 31, 1863, Knight Letters, CCCWC, TSLA; W. H. H. Lee, Meridian, MS, to Wife, May 15, 1863, W. H. H. Lee, Yazoo City, MS, to Wife, June 10, 1863, Lee Papers, USC; Lowe and Hodges, *Letters to Amanda*, 47, 51, 52, 62, 84, 85, 109, 126, 129; Johnston, "Letters of Barnes," 91; J. R. Manson, Fredericksburg, VA, to Charlotte, May 17, 1863, Manson Diary and Letters, CWMC, USAMHI; McLaughlin, *Cherished Letters*, 39, 41, 51, 61; McMurtrey, *Letters to Lucinda*, 28, 36, 38, 40; Moseley, *Stilwell Letters*, 94, 108, 112; Henry Neal, Camp Chester, to Wife, Jan. 1, 8, Feb. 5, 1865, Neal, n.p., to Wife, Mar. 19, 1865, Neal Papers, VHS; J. B. Sanders, Vicksburg, MS, to Elizabeth Sanders, July 18, 1863, Sanders Papers, MDAH; D. C. Snyder, Swoope's Depot, to Wife, Jan. 12, Feb. 13, Mar. 15, 1865, Snyder Papers, VHS; M. R. Norman, Saltville, VA, to Elisabeth Norman, Apr. 8, 1863, Tiedeken Papers, VHS; Thomas Warrick, Tennessee, to Wife, Apr. 8, 1863, and Warrick, Shelbyville, TN, to Wife, May 18, 1863, Warrick Papers, ADAH; John French White, Chaffin's Farm, VA, to Wife, Nov, 14, Dec. 25, 1863, White Papers, VHS; Wiley, *"This Infernal War,"* 208, 212, 225, 230, 236, 259, 264–69, 270, 306, 428, 444.

51 Such complaints are ubiquitous. For examples, see Cash and Howorth, *My Dear Nellie*, 168–69, 231, 235; E. K. Flournoy, Petersburg, VA, to Wife, July 15, 1863, Flournoy Letters, ADAH; Griffith, *Yours Till Death*, 97; Holland, *Keep All My Letters*, 65, 66, 92; John T. Knight, Pine Bluff, AR, to Susan Knight, Jan. 31, 1863, and Knight, Bayou Deglaze, to Susan Knight, Dec. 28, 1863, Knight Letters, CCCWC, TSLA; Lanning Diary, 3; ADAH; Lowe and Hodges, *Letters to Amanda*, 109; Moseley, *Stilwell Letters*, 17, 27, 103, 112, 241, 245; Elijah M. Odom, Jackson, MS, to Sarah F. Odom, Jan. 1, 11, 16, Feb. 2, 1863, Odom Papers, MDAH; Thomas Warrick, Tennessee, to Wife, Apr. 8, 1863, and Warrick, Shelbyville, TN, to Wife, June 23, 1863, Warrick Papers, ADAH; John William Watson, n.p., to Wife, n.d., Watson Family Papers, VHS; John French White, Chaffin's Farm, VA, to Wife, Feb. 16, 1864, White Papers, VHS; Wiley, *"This Infernal War,"* 292; R. F. Yeager, Camden, AR, to Mattie, Mar. 17, 1864, Yeager Letters, UAR.

A few soldiers wrote similar letters to siblings and parents. See for example George H. Chatfield, n.p., to Mother, Apr. 12, 1864, Chatfield Letters, CWMC, USAMHI; J. D. Joyner, Camp Gregg, VA, to Mother, Apr. 15, 1863, Joyner Family Papers, SHC-UNC; W. H. Robertson, Livingston, AL, to parents, May 29, 1864, and Robertson, Gainesville, AL, to Sisters, May 10 [1864?], Robertson Papers, MDAH; J. D. Stapp, Petersburg, VA, to Mother, Jan. 29, 1864, Stapp Letters, VHS. See also McPherson, *For Cause and Comrades*, 132–35.

52 John S. Meriwether, Vicksburg, MS, to Wife, Jan. 24, 1863, Meriwether Papers, EU.

53 J. A. Wilson, Camp Sloan, to Lizzie, Nov. 22, 1862, Feb. 25, 1863, Wilson Letters, MDAH; Wiley, *"This Infernal War,"* 212, 215, 216, 225, 230, 234, 255, 259, 264, 270, 306, 328, 334, 343, 360.

54 E. W. Treadwell, Shelbyville, TN, to Wife, Apr. 7, 16, 27, 1863, Treadwell Letters, ADAH.

55 Johnston, *Letters to Lucinda*, 28, 40.

56 Moseley, *Stilwell Letters*, 33, 94, 103, 108–11, 128, 175, 213. In September, Stilwell added an odd, cruel note. Having received her photograph, he responded to Molly

that you "don't look like you did when I left. If it looks like you, you have broke very fast. I fear that you are not cheerful enough, you must not grow old and get ugly." See also Mays, *Let Us Meet in Heaven*, 95.

57 Blomquist and Taylor, *This Cruel War*, 237, 240, 245, 256–57; Cash and Howorth, *My Dear Nellie*, 64, 66, 67, 72, 131–32; Robert Emmet Corry, Columbus, MS, to Wife, July 25, 1864, Corry Confederate Collection, AU; Griffith, *Yours Til Death*, 92, 94; Harley and Zimmerman, *Fighting 57th*, 22; Lanning Diary, 12, 19, 22, ADAH; John Meriwether, Lookout Mountain, GA, to Wife, Nov. 13, 1863, Meriwether Papers, EU; Wiley, *"This Infernal War,"* 392, 411, 412–13, 418; J. C. Williams, Chattahoochee, to Sister, July 14, 1864, Williams Papers, AU.

58 Cawthon, "Letters of a Private," 542–43.

59 Marten, *Children's Civil War*, 68–71, 87–93.

60 J. W. Griffin, n.p., to Wife, July 15, 1862, J. W. Griffin Papers, Duke; William A. Stephens, Knoxville, TN, to Susan, July 13, 1862, Stephens Papers, EU.

61 Harvey Bailey, Asheville, NC, to Aldecha Bailey, Apr. 28, 1864, Bailey Letters, CWMC, USAMHI; Jones and Martin, *The Gentle Rebel*, 96–97. A. G. Jones sent orders home to his brother to train his dogs to run rabbits and hunt squirrels. See Jones, Garysburg, NC, to Ellick, Oct. 15, 1862, Jones Family Papers, SHC-UNC.

62 James A. Wilson, Meridian, MS, to Son, Dec. 15, 1864, Wilson Letter, CWMC, USAMHI.

63 W. Duncan Cole, Camp, to Cornelia, Apr. 13, 1864, Cole Letters, CWMC, USAMHI.

64 Blomquist and Taylor, *This Cruel War*, 231; Robert Dickinson, Charleston, SC, to Amanda, June 23, 1862, Dickinson Papers, USC; Madison Kilpatrick, Griffin, GA, to Wife, Oct. 28, 1864, Kilpatrick Letters, AU; Lowe and Hodges, *Letters to Amanda*, 29, 112; John Meriwether, n.p., to Wife, Sept. 22, 1862, Meriwether Papers, EU; R. E. Mobley, Petersburg, VA, to Bettie, Jan. 1, 1865, Mobley Diary and Letters, Box 24, Leigh, USAMHI; John W. Bell, n.p., to Nannie, June 16, 1862, Bell Letters, CMM, LSU; J. W. Tindall, Mt. Pleasant, to Wife, May 20, 1864, Tindall Papers, USC; J. C. Williams, Camp Gordon, GA, to Wife, Mar. 29, 1863, Williams Papers, AU.

65 Griffith, *Yours Till Death*, 54; Holland, *Keep All My Letters*, 67; Lowe and Hodges, *Letters to Amanda*, 14, 16, 26, 80 (quotations 16, 26).

66 J. C. Williams, Camp Gordon, GA, to Wife, Mar. 29, 1863, Williams Papers, AU.

67 J. W. Griffin, Richmond, VA, to Wife, Oct. 9, 1863, Griffin Papers, Duke; William A. Stephens, Knoxville, TN, to Susan, Dec. 27, 1863, Stephens Papers, EU; Marten, *Children's Civil War*, 93–100.

68 Blomquist and Taylor, *This Cruel War*, 324.

69 John Meriwether, n.p., to Wife, Sept. 22, 1862, Meriwether Papers, EU.

70 Wiley, *"This Infernal War,"* 28, 38, 43, 49, 57, 64, 76, 121, 126 (quotations 28, 76).

71 Ibid., 130, 133, 136, 142, 145, 147, 152, 156, 167, 172, 202, 208, 218, 243, 252, 259, 302, 306, 333, 337 (quotations 130, 145, 152, 172, 208). See also Marten's comments on Fay in *Children's Civil War*, 73.

72 Wiley, *"This Infernal War,"* 142, 208, 218, 252, 259, 302, 306, 337, 400, 425 (quotations 218, 252).

73 Marten, *Children's Civil War*, 73–74; Cash and Howorth, *My Dear Nellie*, 72, 131–32;

Griffith, *Yours Till Death*, 13, 32 (quotation 32); Schantz, *Awaiting the Heavenly Country*, 11–13.

74 McCurry, *Masters of Small Worlds*. See also Carmichael, *The Last Generation*, 47–48; Manning, *This Cruel War*, 29–39. For yeomen and their desire for economic independence, see also Hahn, *Roots of Southern Populism*.

75 Four works that do touch on this dimension are Cashin, "'Since the War Broke Out,'" 200–12; Faust, *Mothers of Invention*, 34–35, 51–52, 56–57, 121–23; Laskin, "Good Old Rebels," 336–44; and Rable, *Civil Wars*, 50–51, 96–99, 112–15. For a different argument that stressed a growing fusion of family and national concerns, see Sheehan-Dean, *Why Confederates Fought*, 135–36.

76 Robert Bates, Henrico County, VA, to Wife, May 20, 1862, Bates Letter, Leigh, USAMHI; John W. Bell, n.p., to Nannie, June 16, 1862, Bell Letters, CMM, LSU; Blomquist and Taylor, *This Cruel War*, 2, 3, 8, 12, 17, 21, 28, 70, 105, 135; William P. Cline, Wake County Camp, to Mary C. Cline, Apr. 28, 1862, Cline, Goldsboro, NC, to Mary C. Cline, May 9, 1862, and Cline, Petersburg, VA, to Mary C. Cline, July 12, Aug. 10, 1862, Cline Papers, SHC-UNC; E. B. Coggin, Front Royal, VA, to Wife, Dec. 21, 1862, Coggin Papers, ADAH; I. Walters, Petersburg, VA, to Wife, May 31, 1862, Costen Papers, SHC-UNC; Robert Dickinson, Charleston, SC, to Amanda, June 23, 1862, Dickinson Papers, USC; C. D. Epps. Whitefield County, to Catherine Epps, Aug. 10, 1862, and Epps, Cumberland Gap, to Wife, Oct. 25, 1862, Epps Papers, SHC-UNC; Phillips Fitzpatrick, Dog River, to Mary, Mar. 23, Apr. 13, 1862, Fitzpatrick Papers, ADAH; J. W. Griffin, Richmond, VA, to Wife, July 6, 1862, Griffin Papers, Duke; Griffith, *Yours Till Death*, 1, 2, 3, 5, 8, 12; Harley and Zimmerman, *Fighting 57th*, 16, 19, 20, 24; Hatley and Huffman, *Letters of Wagner*, 10, 13, 20–22; John H. Hundley, Gordonsville, VA, to Sally Hundley, Sept. 30, 1862, Hundley Family Papers, SHC-UNC; Johnston, "Letters of Barnes," 79–80, 88, 89, 90; Johnston, *Letters to Lucinda*, 3; 7, 14, 17; Jesse C. Knight, Chatham County, GA, to Wife, June 30, 1862, and Knight, Northern VA, to Wife, Oct. 24, 1862, Knight Family Papers, UGA; Miles M. Lewis, Falling Creek, VA, to Amy M. Lewis, Aug. 5, 1862, Lewis Papers, CWMC, USAMHI; Lowe and Hodges, *Letters to Amanda*, 12, 14, 20, 21; J. R. Manson, Falling Creek, to Charlotte, July 12, 1862, Manson Diary and Letters, CWMC, USAMHI; John Meriwether, Mobile, AL, to Wife, July 22, 1862, Meriwether Papers, EU; Elijah M. Odom, n.p., to Sarah F. Odom, Mar. 25, 27, 1862; Odom Letters, MDAH; E. A. Penick, n.p., to Wife, Aug. 29, 1862, Penick Papers, VHS; H. W. Robinson, Cumberland Gap, TN, to Wife,, June 7, 1862, Robinson Letters, EU; John M. Smith, Grenada, MS, to Teresa A. Smith, Dec. 26, 1862, Smith Letter, CWMC, USAMHI; Moseley, *Stilwell Letters*, 27, 28, 64; Thomas Warrick, Tupelo, MS, to Wife, June 13, 1862, and Warrick, Hamilton County, TN, to Wife, Aug. 11, 17, Sept. 10, Warrick Papers, ADAH; Wiley, "*This Infernal War*," 64, 109, 142, 168. A few men wrote parents and siblings with similar advice, see for example Mitchell, "Letters of Newberry," 49, 50, 51, 52–53.

77 Battle, *Civil War Letters*, 13.

78 William H. Barnes, Camp Terrill, to Lizzie, Sept. 24, Oct. 30, 1862, Barnes Papers, CAH-UT; Blomquist and Taylor, *This Cruel War*, 46, 58, 88, 91, 96, 110, 135; Lowe

and Hodges, *Letters to Amanda*, 33; Johnston, *Letters to Lucinda*, 8, 9; Moseley, *Stilwell Letters*, 43. For a similar letter to a brother, J. D. Padgett, Coles Island, to Brother, May 3, 1862, J. D. Padgett Papers, USC.; J. A. Patton, Wayside Hospital, to Wife, Nov. 27, 1862, Patton Letters, EU.

79 Battle, *Civil War Letters*, 13; William P. Cline, Wake County Camp, to Father in Law, Apr. 14, 1862, and Cline, Goldsboro, NC, to M. C. Cline, May 9, 1862, Cline Papers, SHC-UNC; J. F. Coghill, Yorktown, VA, to M. T., Apr. 16, 1862, Coghill Letters, SHC-UNC; I. Walters, Drewry's Bluff, VA, to Wife, Nov. 3, 1862, Costen Papers, SHC-UNC; C. D. Epps, Whitefield County, to Catherine Epps, Aug. 10, 1862, Epps Papers, SHC-UNC; George K. Evans, Hanover Hospital, to Friend, Aug. 11, 1862, and Evans, Hanover Hospital, to B. Shepard, Sept. 2, 1862, Evans Letters, Duke; J. R. Manson, Falling Creek, to Charlotte, July 12, 1862, Manson Diary and Letters, CWMC, USAMHI; John Meriwether, Camp Holt, to Wife, June 13, 1862, Meriwether Papers, EU; E. A. Penick, Drewry's Bluff, VA, to Mary & Children, July 31, 1862, Penick Papers, VHS; Moseley, *Stilwell Letters*, 28; I. Walters, Drewry's Bluff, VA, to Bosom Companion, Jan. 26, 1863, Costen Papers, SHC-UNC; Wiley, *"This Infernal War,"* 67, 109.

80 Mays, *Let Us Meet in Heaven*, 22, 28, 33, 39, 45, 51, 54, 56, 59, 65, 85, 86, 90, 93, 98, 102, 112, 117, 118, 126, 128, 138, 141, 143, 144, 151, 153, 163, 167, 172.

81 William P. Cline, Richmond, VA, to Mary C. Cline, Aug. 24, 1862, Cline Papers #5019-z, SHC-UNC; B. F. Henderson, n.p., to Jane, Nov. 28, 1862, Henderson Letters, ADAH;

82 J. W. Griffin, Richmond, VA, to Wife, Oct. 9, 1863, Griffin Papers, Duke.

83 Jesse C. Knight, Richmond, VA, to Wife, July 25, 1862, Knight Family Papers, UGA.

84 Blomquist and Taylor, *This Cruel War*, 149, 159, 196; D. W. Chenault, Albany, KY, to Brother, Mar. 11, 1863, Chenault Letters, CWMC, USAMHI; E. B. Coggin, Rapidan Station, VA, to Wife, May 29, 1863, Coggin Papers, ADAH; John F. Davenport, Clinton, TN, to Wife, Dec. 22, 1863, Davenport Letters, ADAH; A. J. Edge, Vicksburg, MS, to Wife, Feb. 20, Mar. 27, Apr. 5, 1863, Edge Papers, EU; C. D. Epps, Louden, TN, to Wife, Jan. 30, 1863; Epps Papers, SHC-UNC; E. K. Flournoy, Vicksburg, MS, to Wife, Mar. 14, 27, Apr. 2, 15, 1863, Flournoy Letters, ADAH; Theophilis Frank, Orange Court House, VA, to Wife, Nov. 22, 1863, Frank Family Letters, SHC-UNC; Griffith, *Yours Till Death*, 56, 71, 79, 90, 94; Harley and Zimmerman, *Fighting 57th*, 80, 100, 127, 128, 142–43; Hatley and Huffman, *Letters of Wagner*, 39, 40, 46; Holland, *Keep All My Letters*, 74, 76, 78, 100, 101, 103, 116; Jones and Martin, *The Gentle Rebel*, 16; Miles M. Lewis, Guniea Station, VA, to Amy M. Lewis, Mar. 21, 1863, Miles M. Lewis Papers, CWMC, USAMHI; Lowe and Hodges, *Letters to Amanda*, 47, 51, 56, 59, 62, 64, 69, 83, 84, 96, 101, 104; J. R. Manson, Fredericksburg, VA, to Charlotte, May 17, 1863, Manson Diary and Letters, CWMC, USAMHI; John Meriwether, Vicksburg, MS, to Wife, Jan. 6, 1863, Meriwether Papers, EU; A. M. Sewell, Vicksburg, MS, to Louisa, Feb. 4, Mar. 28, 1863, and Sewell, Chickamauga, GA, to Louisa, Oct. 17, 1863, Sewell Correspondence, EU; A. E. Shore, Camp Gregg, VA, to Wife & Friends, Feb. 27, Mar. 18, 1863, Shore Letters, EU; Wiley, *"This Infernal War,"* 317.

85 Griffith, *Yours Till Death*, 36.

86 McLaughlin, *Letters of Hendricks*, 67. See also Battle, *Civil War Letters*, 23; J. W. Griffin, Richmond, VA, to Wife, Oct. 9, 1863, J. W. Griffin Papers, Duke; William P. Cline, Goldsboro, NC, to Mary C. Cline, May 9, 1862, Cline Papers, SHC-UNC; Johnston, "Letters of Barnes," 89; Lowe and Hodges, *Letters to Amanda*, 52, 56; H. W. Robinson, Cumberland Gap, TN, to Wife, June 7, 1862, Robinson Letters, EU; Wiley, "*This Infernal War,*" 360.

87 McMurtrey, *Letters to Lucinda*, 22.

88 S. W. Farrow, Camp White, LA, to Josephine, Apr. 8 and 11, 1863, Farrow Papers, CAH-UT.

89 John S. Meriwether, n.p., to Wife, n.d., Meriwether Papers, EU. See also Thomas Warrick, Hamilton County, TN, to Wife, Oct. 20, 1862, Warrick Papers, ADAH

90 John Meriwether, Eufaula, AL, to Wife, Mar. 29, 1864, Meriwether Papers, EU. G. H. Burns, Vicksburg, MS, to Wife, Mar. 25, 1863, Burns Letters, CNMP.

91 James Alexander, Jackson, MS, to Wife and Children, June 7, 1863, Alexander Collection, AU; Battle, *Civil War Letters*, 23; Blomquist and Taylor, *This Cruel War*, 216, 226, 228, 230, 235, 237, 247, 258, 263, 270, 274, 311; Cash and Howorth, *My Dear Nellie*, 156, 171; A. J. Edge, Dalton, GA, to Wife, Feb. 8, 15, Mar. 6, 12, 1864, Edge Papers, EU; Charlie Figgat, New Market, VA, to Wife, Nov. 15, 1864, Figgat Letter, Leigh, USAMHI; W. V. Fleming, Blakely, AL, to Mary S. Fleming, Aug. 22, Oct. 20, 1864, Fleming Correspondence, ADAH; E. K. Flournoy, Dalton, GA, to Wife, Feb. 10, 15, Mar. 1, 1864, and Flournoy, Gadsden, AL, to Wife, Oct. 22, 1864, Flournoy Letters, ADAH; Theophilis Frank, n.p., to Wife, Mar. 9, 16, 24, 1864, Frank Family Letters, SHC-UNC; Griffith, *Yours Till Death*, 36, 114, 123, 126; Harley and Zimmerman, *Fighting 57th*, 248; Jones and Martin, *The Gentle Rebel*, 23–24, 115; Madison Kilpatrick, Griffin, GA, to Wife, Oct. 28, 1864, Kilpatrick Letters, AU; Moses Kirkland, Atlanta, GA, to Wife, June 1, 4, 9, 1864, Kirkland Papers, EU; Philip P. Lewis, Rock Island, IL, to Wife, Feb. 2, 1864, Lewis Letters, CWMC, USAMHI; Lowe and Hodges, *Letters to Amanda*, 111, 116, 121, 122, 126, 128, 136, 139, 156, 162; Mays, *Let Us Meet in Heaven*, 177, 181, 185, 198, 207, 208, 210, 230; McLaughlin, *Letters of Hendricks*, 67; John McLaurin, n.p., to Brother, Jan. 25, 1864, McLaurin Family Papers, SHC-UNC; H. R. Rodgers, Corinth, MS, to Tabitha, Nov. 9, 1864, Rodgers Letters, CWMC, USAMHI; A. M. Sewell, n.p., to Louisa, Apr. 3, 1864, Sewell Correspondence, EU; A. E. Shore, Fairview Hospital, VA, to Wife, Jan. 10, 1864, Shore Letters, EU; William A. Stephens, n.p., to Susan, [Mar. 1864?], and Stephens, Tuscumbia, AL, to Susan, Oct. 31, 1864, Stephens Papers, EU; John Thurman, West Point, MS, to Wife, June 22, 1864, Thurman Papers, SHC-UNC; R. F. Yeager, Camden, AR, to Mattie, Mar. 17, 1864, Yeager Letters, UAR; Faust, *Mothers of Invention*, 121–23, 134–38. Only two similar letters exist for 1865, see R. E. Mobley, Petersburg, VA, to Bettie, Jan. 1, 1865, Mobley Diary and Letters, Leigh, USAMHI; John Thurman, Near C. Railroad, to Wife, Jan. 26, 1865, Thurman Papers, SHC-UNC; R. T. Wood, Atlanta, GA, to Wife & Children, July 15, 23, 1864, Wood Papers, UGA.

92 E. K. Flournoy, Dalton, GA, to Wife, Feb. 10, 1864, Flournoy Letters, ADAH.

CHAPTER 4

1 Osborn, "Letters of Robert Banks," 141–42 (quotations 142).

2 Johnston, "Vinson Confederate Letters," 110. See also J. A. Frierson, Cotide, MS, to Ma, Apr. 18, 1863, Frierson Correspondence, LSU; B. F. Henderson, n.p., to Jane, Sept. 23, 1862, Henderson Papers, ADAH; A. M. Sewell, n.p., to Louisa, Sept. 1863, Sewell Correspondence MSS 340 (microfilm), EU. See also Jimerson, *Private Civil War*, 126–30; Phillips, "Brother's War," 68–69, 71–82.

3 Phillips, "A Brothers War?" 69–71; Reid Mitchell, *Civil War Soldiers*, 24–36; Grimsley, *Hard Hand of War*, 7; Glatthaar, *General's Lee's Army*, 150–55; Wiley, *Life of Johnny Reb*, 15–17, 309–16.

4 Grimsley, *Hard Hand of War*, 1–141; Royster, *The Destructive War*, esp. 79–143. Unlike Grimsley, Royster emphasizes the notion that a desire for a war of destruction from the first characterized Northern civilians. I have suggested elsewhere that Grimsley missed some of the earliest expressions of hard war in Appalachia. See Noe, " 'Exterminating Savages.'"

5 Glatthaar, *General Lee's Army*, 153.

6 Durkin, *John Dooley*, 9, 29, 70.

7 Northen, *All Right Let Them Come*, 53.

8 Smith, *Here's Yer Mule*, 27.

9 G. H. Chatfield, Salem, AL, to Parents, Mar. 16, 1862, Chatfield Letters, CWMC, USAMHI.

10 For "minions," see Moseley, *Stillwell Letters*, 59. For "yankey villians," see J. R. Palmer, Corinth, MS, to Amanda, May 22, 1862, Parker Letters, CWMC, USAMHI. For "vandals," see Edwin Tuttle, Burton's Farm, VA, to Mother, Dec. 23, 1862, Tuttle Letters, EU; and Cash and Howorth, *My Dear Nellie*, 66, 74. For "devils," see Lowe and Hodges, *Letters to Amanda*, 11, 25. See also B. Wylie Scott, Camp, to Ella Merryman, June 5, 1862, Merryman Papers, VHS; Phillips, "A Brothers War?" 72–77.

11 Cash and Howorth, *My Dear Nellie*, 74, 76.

12 E. A. Penick, Bethel Church, VA, to Family, Apr. 19, 1862, Penick Papers, VHS.

13 Moseley, *Stillwell Letters*, 82.

14 John Thurman, Barnsville, MS, to Wife, Apr. 3, 1862; and John Thurman, Monterey, MS, to Wife, Apr. 9, 1862, Thurman Papers, SHC-UNC. See also Wiley, *Life of Johnny Reb*, 310.

15 J. B. Sanders, n.p., to Elisabeth Sanders, Nov. 29, 1862, Sanders Papers, MDAH.

16 Wiley, *"This Infernal War,"* 55, 66, 102, 113, 139, 168, 175, 179, 189.

17 John French White, Richmond, VA, to Wife, May 19, 1862, White Papers, VHS.

18 Lafayette Henderson, n.p., to Jane, Sept. 23, 1862, Henderson Papers, ADAH.

19 Mellon, "Florida Soldier," 246.

20 Grimsley, *Hard Hand of War*, 142–225; Royster, *The Destructive War*, 352–59.

21 Northen, *All Right Let Them Come*, 53. See also D. R. Childers, Chattanooga, TN, to J. W. Palmer, July 22, 1863, Wood Papers, UGA.

22 Samuel Ridley, n.p., to James Ridley, Mar. 6, 1863, Ridley Papers, CCCWC, TSLA.

23 Park, *Letters of the Shibley Brothers*, Mar. 8, 1863.

24 John S. Meriwether, Vicksburg, MS, to Alice, Mar. 15, 1863, Meriwether Papers, EU.

25 Blomquist and Taylor, *This Cruel War*, 174, 173.

26 Edwin E. Rice Diary, May 25, 1863, CAH-UT.

27 Cash and Howorth, *My Dear Nellie*, 121, 134, 142.

28 Wiley, *"This Infernal War,"* 189, 226, 246, 251, 266, 287, 291, 292, 295, 297, 301, 319, 328, 342, 357, 359.

29 Hubbs, *Voices*, 164, 166. Mays, *Let Us Meet in Heaven*, 81–82.

30 John French White, City Point, VA, to Mattie, May 3, 1863, White Papers, VHS.

31 Durkin, *John Dooley*, 93, 96, 98.

32 Lowe and Hodges, *Letters to Amanda*, 11, 25, 100.

33 W. Y. Mordecai, Culpeper Court House, VA, to Mother, Oct. 20, 1863, Mordecai Papers, VHS.

34 G. H. Burns, Dalton, GA, to Wife and Sisters, Feb. 1, 1864, Burns Letters, CNMP.

35 Ben Robertson, Dalton, GA, to Sister, Feb. 28, 1864, Robertson Papers, MDAH. See also John Crittenden, Dalton, GA, to Bettie, Mar. 12, 1864, Crittenden Papers, AU.

36 Harvey Bailey, Asheville, NC, to Aldecha Bailey, Apr. 28, 1864, Bailey Letters, CWMC, USAMHI.

37 Hubbell, *Confederate Stamps*, 12.

38 Thomas J. Moore, Nottoway Bridge, VA, to Thomas J. Hill, Aug. 1, 1864, Moore Papers, USC. See also John Crittenden, [New] Hope Church, GA, to Bettie, May 29, 1864, and Crittenden, Marietta, GA, to Bettie, June 19, 1864, Crittenden Papers, AU; Jones and Martin, *The Gentle Rebel*, 49; Lanning Diary, Sept. 27, 1864, ADAH; J. S. G. McGhea, Harrisonburg, VA, to Flora, Oct. 2, 1864, McGhea Letter, Leigh, USAMHI; P. Retif, St. James Island, SC, to Mama, Sept. 26, 1864, Retif Letters, CMM, LSU; Cate, *Two Soldiers*, 39, 90.

39 Cash and Howorth, *My Dear Nellie*, 172, 185.

40 F. B. Ward, Hanover, VA, to Sister, May 23, 1864, Ward Letters, Leigh, USAMHI; William P. Head, Pineville, LA, to Children, June 4, 1864, Head Letters, CAH-UT; Leas, "Civil War Diary of Burum," CCCWC, TSLA; Horace M. Wade, Bottom's Bridge, VA, to Sister, June 22, 1864, and Wade, Stony Sation, VA, to Sister, July 18, 1864, Wade Letters, Leigh, USAMHI. This was common, see Wiley, *Life of Johnny Reb*, 313.

41 Cate, *Two Soldiers*, 39, 70, 107, 109, 154, 158, 164.

42 William P. Head, Camp Hope, LA, to Children, Aug., 1864, Head Letters, CAH-UT.

43 J. D. Padgett, Bivouac, to Father, July 9, 1864, Padgett Letters, CWMC, USAMHI. See also Phillips, "A Brother's War?" 80–84.

44 J. T. Bleckley, Aiken, SC, to Sister, Mar. 4, 1865; Bleckley Letters, Leigh, USAMHI.

45 John T. Beggs, Corinth, MS, to Sister, Apr. 26, 1862, Beggs and Janssen Family Papers, SHC-UNC. See also Hubbs, *Voices*, 83.

46 S. T. Foster, Arkansas Post, AR, to Mary, Oct. 19, 1862, Foster Letter, Leigh, USAMHI.

47 John French White, Frederick, MD, to Wife, Aug. 1862, White, Winchester, VA, to Mat, Oct. 12, 1862, and White, Camp, to Mat, Dec. 1, 1862, White Papers, VHS.

48 G. W. Giles, Meridian, MS, to Wife, May 3, 1863, Giles Letters, CMM, LSU; Moseley, *Stilwell Letters*, 275; Park, *Letters of the Shibley Brothers*, Jan. 7, Feb. 21,

Mar. 8, 1863; A. M. Sewell, n.p., to Louisa, Sept. 1863, Sewell Correspondence, EU; W. R. Sivley, Shurbuta, MS, to Sister, Oct. 21, 1863, Sivley Papers, SHC-UNC; Wiley, "This Infernal War," 56. For a Virginian, see Thomas T. Hoskins, Orange Court House, VA, to Papa, Hoskins Family Papers, VHS.

49 Cash and Howorth, *My Dear Nellie*, 111, 116, 136 (quotation 136).

50 William P. Head, Camp Green, LA, to Wife, Aug. 12, 1863, Head Papers, CAH-UT.

51 T. L. Camp, Camp, to Mary, May 21, 22, 1864, Camp Family Papers, EU; Cash and Howorth, *My Dear Nellie*, 194, 198; R. B. Jett, Fort Gilmer, VA, to Father and Mother, Oct. 30, 1864, Jett Papers, EU; Lowe and Hodges, *Letters to Amanda*, 187; J. B. Sanders, Pollard, AL, to Elizabeth Sanders, Feb. 18, 1864, and Sanders, n.p., to Elizabeth Sanders, June 15, 1864, Sanders Papers, MDAH; W. R. Sivley, Demopolis, AL, to Sister, Feb. 20, 1864, Sivley Papers, SHC-UNC.

52 Abel Crawford, Petersburg, VA, to Dora Potts, Aug. 26, 1864, Crawford Letters, CCCWC, TSLA.

53 Jimerson, *Private Civil War*, 170–75; Elisabeth Lauterbach Laskin, "Good Old Rebels," 307–11, 330–31; Reid Mitchell, *Civil War Soldiers*, 37–39; Phillips, "A Brothers' War?" 67–84; Robertson, *Soldiers Blue and Gray*, 139–44; Wiley, *Life of Billy Yank*, 350–57; Wiley, *Life of Johnny Reb*, 315–21 (quotation 319). For a contrary view, see Linderman, *Embattled Courage*, 66–71, 236–39. Linderman maintains that mutual suffering outweighed antipathy.

54 Wiley, *Life of Johnny Reb*, 321.

55 Holland, *Keep All My Letters*, 78. See also Blomquist and Taylor, *This Cruel War*, 310.

56 E. B. Coggin, Port Royal, VA, to Wife, Dec. 26, 1862, Coggin Papers, ADAH. See also J. F. Coghill, Rhemanck Ford, VA, to Mit, Sept. 27, 1863, Coghill Letters, SHC-UNC; W. J. Hart, n.p., to Father, June 19, 1862, Hart Brothers Letters, CWMC, USAMHI; Harley and Zimmerman, *Fighting 57th*, 33, 73; J. A. Wilson, Point Leflore, MS, to Lizzie, Mar. 31, 1863, Wilson Letters, MDAH.

57 Thomas J. Moore, Nottoway Bridge, VA, to Thomas W. Hill, Aug. 1, 1864, Moore Papers, USC.

58 John Crittenden, Camp, to Bettie, July. 15, 1864, Crittenden Papers, AU; Mays, *Let Us Meet in Heaven*, 160, 162; Griffith, *Yours Till Death*, 69, 93; Ryan, "Letters of Cochrane, pt. 5, 278

59 J. F. Coghill, Rhemanck Ford, VA, to Mit, Sept. 27, 1863, Coghill Letters, SHC-UNC.

60 E. B. Coggin, Port Royal, VA, to Wife, Dec. 26, 1862, Coggin Papers, ADAH.

61 Enoch L. Mitchell, "Letters of Thomas Jefferson Newberry," 74.

62 Eaton Diary, May 5, 8, 1863, #1807, SHC-UNC; Wynne and Taylor, *This War So Horrible*, 68; E. A. Penick, Louden County, VA, to Wife, Sept. 5, 1862, Penick Papers, VHS. The soldier Williams buried was I. Corlist of the 51st Ohio.

63 I. M. Auld, Fredericksburg, VA, to Mother, May 8, 1863, Auld Letters, CWMC, USAMHI. For a different perspective, see Rice Diary, May 25, 1863, CAH-UT.

64 Park, *Letters of the Shibley Brothers*, Oct. 4, 1862.

65 Haynes, *Field Diary*, 15. See also Griffith, *Yours Till Death*, 2.

66 Hubbs, *Voices*, 325.

67 Cawthon, "Letters of a Private," 544.

68 J. C. Brightman, Tyler, TX, to Mother, Dec. 13, 1864, Brightman Papers, CAH-UT.

69 R. Dickinson, Charleston, to n.p., June 6, 1862, and Dickinson, Charleston, to Amanda, June 23, 1862, Dickinson Papers, USC.

70 Davis Diary, June 4, Sept. 19, 1864, VHS.

71 Haynes, *Field Diary*, 19, 20.

72 Leas, "Diary of Burum," 41, 42, CCCWC, TSLA.

73 John T. Knight, Pine Bluff, AR, to Susan Knight, Jan. 31, 1863, Knight Letters, CCCWC, TSLA; T. J. Rounsaville, Pine Bluff, AR, to Niece, Feb. 8, 1863, Rounsaville Letters, CWMC, USAMHI; J. C. Brightman, Tyler, TX, to Mother, Dec. 13, 1864, Brightman Papers, CAH-UT; Griffith, *Yours Till Death*, 2; Johnston, *Letters to Lucinda*, 2; Mellon, "Florida Soldier," 249; F. Niebuhr, Yazoo River, MS, to Caroline, Feb. 27, Mar. 25, 1863, Niebuhr Papers, CAH-UT.

CHAPTER 5

1 J. H. Lee, Camp College, AL, to Wife, May 29, 1862, and Lee, Camp College, to Father, June 6, 1862, Lee Letters, EU.

2 Moore, *Conscription and Conflict*, 2–6.

3 Ibid., 6–8.

4 This was calculated using Purchasing Power of Money, http://measuringworth .com/calculators/ppowerus (accessed Oct. 10, 2007); and Confederate Inflation Rates (1861–65), http://inflationdata.com/Inflation/Inflation_Rate/Con federateInflation.asp (accessed Oct. 10, 2007).

5 Moore, *Conscription and Conflict*, 9–18; Wiley, *"This Cruel War,"* 168; McPherson, *Ordeal by Fire*, 181–83.

6 McPherson, *For Cause and Comrades*, ix, 6–8, 102–3; Weitz, *More Damning than Slaughter*, 77–78, 106–8; Logue, *To Appomattox and Beyond*, 29; J. H. Lee, Georgia, to Wife, Aug. 12, 1862, and Lee, Dalton, GA, to Wife, Aug. 28, 1862, Lee Letters, EU; Green, *Gracie's Pride*, 251–52, 488–89.

7 Theophilis Frank, n.p., to Wife, Oct. 17, 1863, Frank Family Letters, SHC-UNC.

8 Manning, *This Cruel War*, 4; McPherson, *For Cause and Comrades*, 5.

9 Johnson, *Warriors into Workers*, 11–12, 56, 73–100, 102–4, 112–42; McPherson, *Ordeal by Fire*, 377–78. For other books that discuss Union soldiers fighting for pay, see Bruce, *Harp and the Eagle*; Wilkinson, *Mother*.

10 A. G. Jones, Kinston, NC, to Parents, Jan. 28, 1863, Jones Family Papers, SHC-UNC; Henry Mowrer, n.p., to Wife, July 24, 1863, Mowrer Letters, CWMC, USAMHI. My scattered research in Union army sources hints that money was a stronger incentive to Northern later enlisters, but much more scholarship is required.

11 I. M. Auld, Camp, to Mamie, June 11, 1862, Auld Letters, CWMC, USAMHI; John T. Beggs, Tullahoma, TN, to Sister, Apr. 5, 1863, Beggs and Jannsen Family Papers, SHC-UNC; John Blair Diary (microfilm), Jan. 6, 1863, CCCWC, TSLA; G. H. Burns, Camp McDonald, GA, to Wife, June 14, 1862, Burns Letters, CNMP;

William D. Clover, Sullivan County, TN, to Wife, Sept. 8, 1862, Clover Letters, Leigh, USAMHI; William A. Collins, Petersburg, VA, to Father, July 12, 17, 1862, Collins Papers, SHC-UNC; L. R. Dalton, Malvern Hill, VA, to Par, June 25, 1864, Dalton Letters, Leigh, USAMHI; C. D. Epps, Tunnel Hill, GA, to Catherine Epps, Aug. 3, 10, 1862, Epps Papers, SHC-UNC; E. K. Flournoy, Chickasaw Bayou, MS, to Wife, Mar. 30, 1863, Flournoy Letters, ADAH; Theophilis Frank, n.p., to Wife, Oct. 17, 1863, Frank Family Letters, SHC-UNC; A. L. Galloway, Montgomery, AL, to Wife, May 24, 1862, Armistead L. Galloway Letters, AU; Griffith, *Yours Till Death*, 1; W. A. Gyles, Fort Johnson, SC, to Mother, Feb. 22, 1862, Gyles Papers, USC; Hartley and Zimmerman, *Fighting 57th*, 22, 27; Hatley and Huffman, *Letters of Wagner*, 24; Holland, *Keep All My Letters*, 23, 24, 25, 29, 30, 37, 60, 61, 64; Hubbell, *Confederate Stamps*, 2; A. G. Jones, Kinston, NC, to Parents, Jan. 28, 1863, Jones Family Papers, SHC-UNC; Kees Diary, 1, 2, 20, MDAH; Jesse C. Knight, Chatham County, GA, to Wife, June 18, 1862, Knight Family Papers, UGA; John T. Knight, Washington, AR, to Susan Knight, Oct. 1, 1862, and Knight, Camp Holmes, AR, to Susan Knight, Oct. 19, 1862, Knight Letters, CCCWC, TSLA; Matthew A. Knight, Camp Davies, to Brother, Knight Family Papers, UGA; Lanning Diary, 1, ADAH; J. H. Lee, Camp College, AL, to Wife, May 29, 1862, and Lee, Camp College, to Father, June 6, 1862, Lee Letters, EU; Lowe and Hodges, *Letters to Amanda*, 14; Henry Mowrer, n.p., to Wife, July 24, 1863, Mowrer Letters, CWMC, USAMHI; Elijah M. Odom, Vicksburg, MS, to Sarah F. Odom, July 22, 1862, Odom Letters, MDAH; J. A. Patton, Camp Mangum, NC, to Wife, Apr. 6, 1862, Patton Letters, EU; H. W. Robinson, Cobb County, GA, to Wife and Family, Mar. 25, 26, 1862, Robinson Letters, EU; Ryan, "Letters of Cochrane," pt. 1, 291, 294; Sanders, "Letters of a Soldier," 1232, 1233; C. D. Sides, Fredericksburg, VA, to Wife, Feb. 10, 1862, Sides Letters, CWMC, USAMHI; Thomas Warrick, Loachapoka, AL, to Companion, Mar. 9, 1982, Warrick Papers, ADAH; Wiley, *"This Cruel War,"* 168, 313, 330; J. C. Williams, Thunderbolt, GA, to Honey, Dec. 22, 1862, Williams Letters, AU. The eight men who wrote of sending the bounty home were Brooks, Collins, Epps, Flournoy, Gyles, Kees, John Knight, and Sides. Material within the L. R. Dalton Letters suggest that he was age seventeen at enlistment, not eighteen or nineteen as the census suggests.

12 Holland, *Keep All My Letters*, 61.

13 John T. Beggs, Tullahoma, TN, to Sister, Apr. 5, 1863, Beggs and Jannsen Family Papers, SHC-UNC; C. D. Epps, Tunnel Hill, GA, to Catherine Epps, Aug. 3, 10, 1862, Epps Papers, SHC-UNC; Holland, *Keep All My Letters*, 23, 24, 25, 29, 30, 37, 60, 61, 64; J. H. Lee, Camp College, AL, to Wife, May 29, 1862, and Lee, Camp College, AL, to Father, June 6, 1862, Lee Letters, EU. Elijah M. Odom, Vicksburg, MS, to Sarah F. Odom, July 22, 1862, Odom Letters, MDAH; Thomas Warrick, Loachapoka, AL, to Companion, Mar. 9, 1982, Warrick Papers, ADAH.

14 Ryan, "Letters of Cochrane," pt. 1, 291.

15 Ibid., 294.

16 W. V. Fleming, Mobile, AL, to Wife, May 12, 1862, Fleming Correspondence, ADAH.

17 McPherson, *Ordeal By Fire*, 165, 168, 181–82; Logue, *To Appomattox and Beyond*, 25.

Out of the 647 men she sampled through letters and diaries, Elisabeth Laskin only identified nine conscripts. She also confirmed fifty-eight draftees through a companion study of ten sampled rosters. Yet close study of one company's records that included detailed information on conscription revealed that 44 of 138 men (32 percent) were conscripts. She accordingly suggests that incomplete records coupled with a reluctance to admit being drafted led to many draftees slipping through the documentary cracks. See Elisabeth Lauterbach Laskin, "Good Old Rebels," 22–23.

18 Homer Adams, Notasulga, AL, to Timoleon, Apr. 7, 1863, Adams Family Papers, UAL; John A. Clover, Kinston, NC, to Father & Mother, Apr. 6, 1862, and N. J. Clover, Kinston, NC, to Mother, Apr. 8, 1864, Clover Letters, Leigh, USAMHI; Neill McLaurin, Garysburg, NC, to Brother, Sept. 1, 1862, McLaurin Family Papers, SHC-UNC; W. A. Crouch, Cotton Plant, AR, to Wife, Oct. 13, 26, 1862, Crouch Letters, UAR; Charlotte Waldrop, Little Garden, VA, to Sister, Aug. 3, 1862, Baker Family Papers, VHS; Thomas J. Elliott, Norfolk, VA, to Wife, Apr. 19, 1862, and Elliott, Suffolk, VA, to Wife, Apr. 27, 1862, Elliott Papers, Duke; Elisabeth Lauterbach Laskin, "Good Old Rebels," 110–21.

19 John A. Clover, Kinston, NC, to Father & Mother, Apr. 6, 1862, and N. J. Clover, Kinston, NC, to Mother, Apr. 8, 1864, N. J. Clover Letters, Leigh, USAMHI; Weitz, *More Damning than Slaughter*, 25–33.

20 Homer Adams, Notasulga, AL, to Timoleon, Apr. 7, 1863, Adams Family Papers, UAL; W. A. Crouch, Cotton Plant, to Wife, Oct. 13, 26, 1862, Crouch Letters, UAR.

21 Thomas J. Elliott, Norfolk, VA, to Wife, Apr. 19, 1862, and Elliott, Suffolk, VA, to Wife, Apr. 27, 1862, Elliott Papers, Duke.

22 Hartley and Zimmerman, *Fighting 57th*, 143.

23 H. C. Harris, Mobile, AL, to Sister, Nov. 2, 1862, Harris Letter, UAL.

24 M. McBride, Cypress Creek, NC, to Son, July 26, 1862, and A. D. McBride, North Carolina, to Wife, Aug. 16, 1862, McBride Family Papers, SHC-UNC. See also H. W. Robinson, Cobb County, GA, to Wife and Family, Mar. 25, 26, 1862, Robinson Letters, EU.

25 W. P. Farnsworth, Atlanta, GA, to Brother, Mar. 30, 1863, Farnsworth Family Letters, CAH-UT.

26 Joseph D. Joyner, Franklinton, NC, to Papa, Feb. 10, 1862, Joyner Family Papers, SHC-UNC.

27 Glatthaar, *General Lee's Army*, 401, 403–7; McPherson, *For Cause and Comrades*, 8–9, 116.

28 W. Y. Mordecai, Hamilton's Crossing, VA, to Mother, June 1, 1863, Mordecai Papers, VHS; E. W. Treadwell, Shelbyville, TN, to Wife, Apr. 29, 1863, Treadwell Letters, ADAH; Wiley, *"This Cruel War,"* 36, 109, 224.

29 Holland, *Keep All My Letters*, 99.

30 William P. Cline, Fredericksburg, VA, to Mary C. Cline, Aug. 15, 1863, Cline Papers #5019-z, SHC-UNC; A. G. Jones, Culpeper County, VA, to Brother, Sept. 4, 1863, Jones Family Paper, SHC-UNC. Cline spelled the man's name "Mark huit"; I extrapolated "Hewitt." See also Moseley, *Stilwell Letters*, 33.

31 Cash and Howorth, *My Dear Nellie*, 133.

32 J. R. Manson, Falling Creek, VA, to Mother, July 27, 1862, Manson Diary and Letters, CWMC, USAMHI.

33 E. W. Treadwell, Shelbyville, TN, to Wife, Apr. 29, 1863, Treadwell Letters, ADAH.

34 William A. Collins, Petersburg, VA, to Henry Collins, July 10, 1862, Collins Papers, SHC-UNC.

35 C. W. Bunker, Camp East Tennessee, TN, to Sister, Nov. 11, 1863, Bunker Papers, SHC-UNC; Moseley, *Stilwell Letters*, 33, 42; Cash and Howorth, *My Dear Nellie*, 144, 148; Ryan, "Letters of Cochrane," pt. 2, 64–65.

36 Moore, *Conscription and Conflict*, 27–32; Fay, "*This Infernal War*," 137–38.

37 J. R. Manson, Falling Creek Camp, VA, to Mother, Aug. 9, 1862, Manson Diary and Letters, CWMC, USAMHI; McPherson, *For Cause and Comrades*, 116, 142–43, 168.

38 Moore, *Conscription and Conflict*, 27–36; McPherson, *Ordeal by Fire*, 181–83; Wiley, *Life of Johnny Reb*, 125–27.

39 Moore, *Conscription and Conflict*, 36–51; Logue, *To Appomattox and Beyond*, 25; Wiley, *Life of Johnny Reb*, 126.

40 Marion Coiner, Head Quarters, to Mary Coiner, Feb. 21, 1864, Coiner Family Papers, VHS; J. C. Brightman, Stafford's Point, TX, to Mother, May 29, 1865, Brightman Papers, CAH-UT; "Some Confederate Letters," 565.

41 Affidavits, Bailey Family Papers, VHS; Malvina Ashby, n.p., to Hugh M. Nelson, Mar. 22, 1862, and James H. Bartlett, n.p., to Hugh M. Nelson, Mar. 22, 1862, Nelson Letters, Leigh, USAMHI.

42 The significance of these figures is admittedly unclear, for we lack any sense of how many soldiers in the general population of Confederate soldiers attempted to secure substitutes. More research is needed.

43 Phillips Fitzpatrick, Cantonment Walter, AL, to Mary, Mar. 26, 1862, and Fitzpatrick, Dog River, to Mary, May 21, 1862, Fitzpatrick Papers, ADAH. See also Noe, "Alabama," 182–84.

44 Phillips Fitzpatrick, Cantonment Walter, AL, to Mary, May 21, June 9, 12, 22, and Fitzpatrick, Dog River, AL, to Maj. H. Elmore, June 24, 1862, Fitzpatrick Papers, ADAH.

45 Phillips Fitzpatrick, Cantonment Walter, AL, to Mary, June 28, 29, July 6, 1862, Fitzpatrick Papers, ADAH.

46 Affidavits, Bailey Family Papers, VHS; W. Duncan Cole, Mobile, AL, to Wife, June 21, 1862, Cole Letters, CWMC, USAMHI; Lafayette Henderson, n.p., to Jane, Nov. 28, 1862, Henderson Letters, ADAH; Moseley, *Stillwell Letters*, 25; Glatthaar, *General Lee's Army*, 399–400.

47 H. E. Neal, Camp Wyatt, VA, to Dearest, Sept. 11, 1862, and Neal, n.p., to Wife, Mar. 19, 1865, Neal Papers, VHS; Fleming Jordan, Griffin, GA, to Wife, Mar. 12, 1862, Jordan Letters, UGA; H. C. Harris, Mobile, AL, to Sister, Nov. 2, 1862, Harris Letter, UAL.

48 C. D. Epps, Tunnel Hill, GA, to Catherine Epps, Aug. 3, 1862, and Epps, Camp Smith, GA, to Wife and Children, n.d., Epps Papers, SHC-UNC; Elijah M. Odom, Vicksburg, MS, to Sarah F. Odom, Apr. 15, 1862, Odom Letters, MDAH; Typescript Autobiography, Snyder Papers, VHS.

49 J. A. Wilson, Tupelo Station, MS, to Lizzie, June 11, 1862, Wilson Letters, MDAH.

50 Blomquist and Taylor, *This Cruel War*, 52, 54, 57, 59, 62, 65, 70, 71, 74, 85, 87 (quotations 52, 57, 74, 85).

51 Wiley, *"This Infernal War,"* 56, 58, 61, 69, 84–85, 87, 88, 90–91, 96, 97, 99 (quotations 56, 96, 97).

52 Ibid., 101–3, 106, 109, 114, 118, 125, 129, 137–38, 141, 144 (quotation 101).

53 S. M. Baker, Madison Court House, VA, to Mary. A. Baker, Nov. 22, 1863, and Mary A. Baker, Burnett's, VA, to Son, Jan. 12, Apr. 30, 1863, Baker Family Papers, VHS.

54 Thomas J. Moore, Kinston, NC, to Sister, Nov. 19, 1862, and Moore, Charleston, SC, to Thomas W. Hill, Apr. 29, 1863, Moore Papers, USC.

55 John Blair Diary, Mar. 23, 24, 26, 1863, CCCWC, TSLA; James Montgomery Lanning Diary, Mar. 11, 1863, ADAH.; J. C. Williams, Camp Gordon, GA, to Wife, Mar. 25, 1863, Williams Papers, AU.

56 A. E. Shore, Camp Gregg, VA, to Wife & Friends, Feb. 27, Mar. 29, 1863, Shore Letters, EU.

57 J. A. Patton, n.p., to Wife, Feb. 18, 1863, Patton Letters, EU; J. A. Wilson, Vicksburg, MS, to Lizzie, May 6, 1863, Wilson Letters, MDAH.

58 Enoch L. Mitchell, "Civil War Letters," 61, 62, 63, 64, 65, 67, 69, 70.

59 M. R. Norman, Camp Saltville, VA, to Better Norman, June 21, 1863, Tiedeken Papers, VHS.

60 Griffith, *Yours Till Death*, 79, 81, 90, 91, 96, 97. See also William A. Stephens, Dalton, GA, to Susan, Dec. 18, 1863, Stephens Papers, EU.

61 George H. Chatfield, Haynes Landing, MS, to Mother, Apr. 15, 1863, Chatfield Letters, CWMC, USAMHI; A. H. Crawford, Pollard, AL, to Dora Potts, Dec. 5, 1863, Crawford Letters, CCCWC, TSLA. See also G. H. Burns, Dalton, GA, to Wife and Sisters, Feb. 1, 1864, Burns Letters, CNMP; J. W. Tindall, Mt. Pleasant, to Wife, Nov. 17, 1863, J. W. Tindall Papers, USC.

62 A. M. Sewell, Camp, to Louisa, Feb. 19, 21, Mar. 6, 1864, Sewell Correspondence, EU.

63 S. W. Farrow, Linsport, LA, to Josephine, Dec. 31, 1863, Farrow Papers; J. T. Knight, Marksville, to Mother and Family, Jan. 11, 1864, Knight Letters, CCCWC, TSLA.

64 A. J. Edge, Dalton, GA, to Companion, Mar. 26, 1864, Edge Papers, EU; Blomquist and Taylor, *This Cruel War*, 225; W. H. Tamplin, Marksville, to Tinicia, Feb. 20, 1864, and undated letter, 1864, Tamplin Letters MSS 3015, CMM, LSU.

65 Mays, *Let Us Meet in Heaven*, 71, 80, 168, 169, 173 (quotation 168).

66 For a similar conclusion, see Sheehan-Dean, *Confederates at War*, 143.

CHAPTER 6

1 J. R. Manson, Fredericksburg, VA, to Charlotte, May 17, 1863, Manson Diary and Letters, CWMC, USAMHI.

2 J. R. Manson, Culpeper Court House, VA, to Charlotte, July 30, 1863, Manson Diary and Letters, CWMC, USAMHI.

3 J. R. Manson, Culpeper Court House, VA, to Sister, Nov. 13, 1863, Manson Diary and Letters, CWMC, USAMHI.

4 "A Spiritual Diary: Captain Joseph Richard Manson, 1831–1918, Meherrin Grays, Company I, 12th Virginia Infantry, Mahone's Brigade, Anderson's Division, A. P. Hill's Corps," typescript, (quotations 3, 4, 23) Manson Diary and Letters, CWMC, USAMHI.

5 Jason Phillips, in *Diehard Rebels*, 35, rightly refers to Manson's journal as "one of the most remarkable diaries of the Civil War." Phillips errs, however, in linking Manson to "diehards" who "focused on the thinnest silver linings" (34) to maintain their fighting motivation. Manson in fact hated the war, longed for it to end, equated Davis with Lincoln, and coped by retreating into his Biblical closet to pray.

6 Robertson, *Soldiers Blue and Gray*, 172.

7 Barton, *Goodmen*, 66–75; Carmichael, *Last Generation*, 103–6, 105, 180–81; Daniel, *Army of Tennessee*, 115–25; Faust, *This Republic of Suffering*, 172; Harvey, " 'Yankee Faith' and Southern Redemption," 167–81; McPherson, *For Cause and Comrades*, 63; Reid Mitchell, *Civil War Soldiers*, 173; Noll, *Civil War as a Theological Crisis*, 11–14, 17–25, 31–50; Phillips, *Diehard Rebels*, 13–15; Robertson, *Soldiers Blue and Gray*, 170–71; Stout, *Upon the Altar*; Wiley, *Life of Johnny Reb*, 174; Woodworth, *While God Is Marching On*, 6–89, 117–44. Another essay included in Miller, Stout, and Wilson, *Religion and the American Civil War* disputes the notion that Confederates were more religious than their foes, and asserts they were only more open and expressive with their dramatic revivals. See Reid Mitchell, "Christian Soldiers?" 297–309. The only major work to deal with soldiers' religion specifically, Woodworth, *While God Is Marching On*, argues for no real difference between the two sectional groups, and indeed mixes Confederate and Union soldiers alike in his descriptions of "the Great Revival."

8 McPherson, *For Cause and Comrades*, 63.

9 Barton, *Goodmen*, 24, 25, 66–75; Elisabeth Lauterbach Laskin, "Good Old Rebels," 398–400; Wiley, *Life of Johnny Reb*, 174–85. See also Logue, *To Appomattox and Beyond*, 63; Phillips, *Diehard Rebels*, 11–20; Robertson, *Soldiers Blue and Gray*, 172–76; Sheehan-Dean, *Why Confederates Fought*, 21, 46. Carmichael, *Last Generation*, 181–90, argues that the young officers of the Old South's "last generation" did preserve their piety and drew strength from the belief that their cause also was God's. Meanwhile, Woodworth, *While God Is Marching On*, 117–44, 175–98, acknowledges widespread impiety in early camps, but maintains on the whole that other scholars' recitations of non-Christians within the army on the whole are overstated.

10 Berends, " 'Wholesome Reading," 131–55; Carmichael, *Last Generation*, 151–52, 180, 183–84; Gallagher, *Confederate War*, 52–53; Logue, *To Appomattox and Beyond*, 75–78; Manning, *This Cruel War*, 141–42; McPherson, *For Cause and Comrades*, 63–66, 75–76; Reid Mitchell, "Christian Soldiers?" 298–302, 305–8; Reid Mitchell, *Civil War Soldiers*, 173–74, 185; Phillips, *Diehard Rebels*, 15–17, 20–34; Robertson, *Soldiers Blue and Gray*, 173–88; Sheehan-Dean, *Why Confederates Fought*; 109–10, 130–32; Stout, *Upon the Altar*, 287–92, 354–55; Stout and Grasso, "Civil War, Religion, and

Communications," 318–40; Wiley, *Life of Johnny Reb*, 180–91; Woodworth, *While God Is Marching On*, 27–51, 84–89, 193–255.

11 McPherson, *For Cause and Comrades*, 75.

12 Carmichael, *Last Generation*, 179–80, 188–92; Gallagher, *Confederate War*, 49–52; Manning, *This Cruel War*, 141–45, 217–18; McPherson, *For Cause and Comrades*, 675–76; Reid Mitchell, *Civil War Soldiers*, 173–74, 185; Phillips; *Diehard Rebels*, 28–39; Stout, *Upon the Altar*, 408–11; Woodworth, *While God Is Marching On*, 253–55, 270–86.

13 E. A. Penick, Richmond, VA, to Mary, Mar. 16, 1862, Penick Papers, VHS.

14 William A. Collins, Petersburg, VA, to Rev. J. M. Smith, Aug. 3, 1862, Collins Papers, SHC-UNC.

15 W. J. Peel, Clarksville, AR, to Lizzie, Jan. 21, 1862, Peel Papers, UAR.

16 Smith, *Here's Yer Mule*, 22.

17 F. Niebuhr, Jackson, MS, to Parents and Brothers and Sisters, n.d., Niebuhr Papers, CAH-UT.

18 John Thurman, Barnsville, MS, to Wife, Mar. 26, 1862, Thurman Papers, SHC-UNC. See also F. Niebuhr, Holly Springs, TX, to Parents and Brothers and Sisters, Sept. 2, 1862, Niebuhr Papers, CAH-UT.

19 Battle, *Civil War Letters*, 4. Woodworth, *While God Is Marching On*, 182. See also William A. Collins, Goldsboro, NC, to Father, Mar. 27, May 17, 1862, Collins Papers, SHC-UNC.

20 Kauffman Diary, June 15, 1862, SHC-UNC.

21 William A. Collins, Petersburg, VA, to Sister, June 13, 1862, and Collins, Petersburg, VA, to Revell M. Smith, June 21, 1862, Collins Papers, SHC-UNC. See also T. E. Lee, Richmond, VA, to Wife, July 26, 1862, Lee Letters, UGA; Hubbs, *Voices*, 91, 97.

22 Blomquist and Taylor, *This Cruel War*, 55–56, 60; J. H. Lee, Dalton, GA, to Wife, Aug. 26, 1862, Lee Papers MSS 69; J. A. Wilson, West Point, MS, to Lizzie, May 16, 1862, Wilson Letters, MDAH.

23 Park, *Civil War Letters*, Aug. 30, 1862.

24 Griffith, *Yours Till Death*, 6.

25 G. H. Burns, Camp McDonald, GA, to Wife, May 25, 1862, Burns Letters, CNMP.

26 Jason Phillips suggests that for many soldiers, such exhortations demonstrate a growing gulf between camp and home front, but adds that for others they represent "a shared religion" that "united some Confederates with loved ones." See his *Diehard Rebels*, 23.

27 J. R. Palmer, Corinth, MS, to Amanda, May 13, 1862, Parker Letters, CWMC, USAMHI; Cash and Howorth, *My Dear Nellie*, 54; Jesse C. Knight, Culpeper Court House, VA, to Wife, Sept. 9, 1862, Knight Family Papers, UGA.

28 J. M. Davidson, Knoxville, TN, to Julia, June 14, 1862, Davidson Papers, EU.

29 William S. Lacy, Ashland, VA, to Ma, June 27, 1862, Lacy Papers, SHC-UNC.

30 E. A. Penick, Richmond, VA, to Mary, Mar. 16, 1862, Penick Papers, VHS.

31 Woodworth, *While God Is Marching On*, 11.

32 Elijah M. Odom, Vicksburg, MS, to Sarah F. Odom, July 15, 1862, Odom Letters, MDAH.

33 Wiley, *"This Infernal War,"* 94.

34 Miles W. Lewis, Falling Creek, VA, to Amy M. Lewis, Aug. 5, 1862, Miles W. Lewis Papers, CWMC, USAMHI.

35 Jesse C. Knight, Chatham County, GA, to Wife, June 18, 1862, Knight Family Papers, UGA.

36 Battle, *Civil War Letters,* 11.

37 J. W. Griffin, Richmond, VA, to Wife, Oct. 25, 1862, Griffin Papers, Duke.

38 Cawthon, "Letters of a Private," 534, 535.

39 J. C. Williams, Thunderbolt, GA, to Honey, Dec. 28, 1862, Williams Papers, AU; Cawthon, "Letters of a Private," 539. Moseley, *Stilwell Letters,* 8; Wiley, *"This Infernal War,"* 71; Phillips, *Diehard Rebels,* 21–23; Woodworth, *While God Is Marching On,* 72–77.

40 G. H. Burns, Camp McDonald, GA, to Wife, May 18, 1862, Burns Letters, CNMP. In the same collection, see also Burns's letters of June 28, 1862 and July 16, 1862.

41 E. B. Coggin, Gordonsville, VA, to Wife, July 20, 1862, Coggin Papers, ADAH.

42 Blomquist and Taylor, *This Cruel War,* 18, 29, 33 (quotation 18).

43 Battle, *Civil War Letters,* 7; *Hymns for the Camp,* 14, electronic ed., http://doc south.unc.edu/imls/hymns/hymns.html#hymns14 (accessed Dec. 4, 2007).

44 John French White, Richmond, VA, to Wife, May 19, 1862, White Papers, VHS. See also William P. Cline, Camp Mangum, NC, to M. C. Cline, May 3, 1862, Cline Papers, SHC-UNC; William A. Collins, Camp Mangum, NC, to Father, Mar. 27, 1862, Collins Papers, SHC-UNC; Jesse Lippard, Petersburg, VA, to S. S. Collins, B. L. Collins, and John Collins, July 12, 1862, Collins Papers, SHC-UNC.

45 Wiley, *"This Infernal War,"* 111.

46 John F. Davenport, Tazewell, VA, to Wife, Aug. 20, 1862, Davenport Letters, ADAH.

47 Robert Dickinson, Charleston, SC, to Amanda, June 23, 1862, Dickinson Papers, USC.

48 F. Niebuhr, Holly Springs, MS, to Parents and Brothers and Sisters, Oct. 15, 1862, and Niebuhr, Jackson, MS, to Parents and Brothers and Sisters, n.d., Niebuhr Papers, CAH-UT.

49 William A. Collins, Camp Mangum, NC, to Father, Mar. 27, 1862, Collins Papers, SHC-UNC. See also A. L. Galloway, n.p., to Wife, June 22, 1862, Galloway Letters, AU.

50 Miles W. Lewis, Falling Creek, VA, to Amy M. Lewis, Aug. 5, 1862, Miles W. Lewis Papers, CWMC, USAMHI.

51 E. B. Coggin, Gordonsville, VA, to Wife, July 20, 1862, Coggin Papers, ADAH.

52 Wiley, *"This Infernal War,"* 34.

53 Blomquist and Taylor, *This Cruel War,* 13.

54 Faust, *This Republic of Suffering,* 177–80; Ownby, "Patriarchy," 234–41; McCurry, *Masters of Small Worlds,* 171–76; Paludan, "Religion and the American Civil War," 30–31; Schantz, *Awaiting the Heavenly Country,* 38–69; Woodworth, *While God Is Marching On,* 40–51.

55 G. H. Burns, Bridgeport, AL, to Wife, July 26, 1862, and Burns, Clinton, TN, to Wife, Aug. 9, 1862, Burns Letters, CNMP.

56 A. J. Edge, Camp McDonnell, GA, to Companion, Mar. 28, 1862, Edge Papers, EU. See also E. B. Coggin, Gordonsville, VA, to Wife, July 20, 1862, Coggin Papers, ADAH; A. L. Galloway, n.p., to Eliza, July 1, 1862, and Galloway, Lauderdale Springs, MS, to Wife, Aug. 13, 1862, Galloway Letters, AU; Hatley and Huffman, *Letters of Wagner*, 11; Jesse Lippard, Petersburg, VA, to S. S. Collins, B. L. Collins, and John Collins, July 12, 1862, Collins Papers, SHC-UNC; J. T. Nobles and W. J. Nobles, James Island, SC, to Beloved Ones at Home, June 18, 1862, Nobles Papers, USC.

57 John F. Davenport, Cumberland Gap, to Wife, Sept. 7, 1862, Davenport Letters, ADAH.

58 William P. Cline, Camp Mangum, NC, to M. C. Cline, May 3, 1862, Cline Papers, SHC-UNC. See also Cline's similar letter of June 3, 1862.

59 Holland, *Keep All My Letters*, 34, 63, 69 (quotation 34); Ownby, "Patriarchy," 236–37.

60 Robert Dickinson, Charleston, SC, to Amanda, June 23, 1862, Dickinson Papers, USC.

61 Kennedy Diary, 1–16, SHC-UNC; Thomas Warrick, Tyra, TN, to Wife, Oct. 6, 1862, Warrick Papers, ADAH; Woodworth, *While God Is Marching On*, 193. See also William H. Barnes, Camp Doak, to Lizzie, Oct. 29, 1862, Barnes Papers, CAH-UT; Ryan, "Letters of Cochrane," pt. 3, 145–46; E. R. Willis, Fredericksburg, VA, to Father & Mother, Dec. 18, 1862, Willis Family Papers, USC.

62 J. M. Davidson, Harrodsburg, KY, to Julia, Oct. 12, 1862, and Davidson, Kingston, TN, to Julia, Dec. 19, 1862, Davidson Papers, EU.

63 J. M. Davidson, Harrodsburg, KY, to Julia, Oct. 12, 1862, and Davidson, Kingston, TN, to Julia, Dec. 19, 1862, Davidson Papers, EU. See also G. H. Burns, Vicksburg, MS, to Wife, Apr. 2, 1863, Burns Letters, CNMP; E. K. Flournoy, Chickasaw Bayou, MS, to Wife, Apr. 2, 1863, and Flournoy, Vicksburg, MS, to Wife, Apr. 15, 1863, Flournoy Letters, ADAH; Miles W. Lewis, Guinea Station, VA, to Amy M. Lewis, Mar. 23, 1863, Miles W. Lewis Papers, CWMC, USAMHI; Lowe and Hodges, *Letters to Amanda*, 63; Moseley, *Stilwell Letters*, 38, 40, 52, 66–67, 77, 127, 147; J. C. Williams, Thunderbolt, GA, to Honey, Dec. 22, 1862, and Williams, Camp Gordon, GA, to Wife, Feb. 16, 1863, Williams Papers, AU.

64 John French White, Winchester, VA, to Mat, Oct. 12, 1862, White Papers, VHS.

65 Blomquist and Taylor, *This Cruel War*, 124, 158, 161. See also Isaac Walters, Drewry's Bluff, VA, to Wife, Nov. 3, 1862, Costen Papers, SHC-UNC.

66 Moseley, *Stilwell Letters*, 107, 138–39; Griffith, *Yours Till Death*, 47, 60.

67 Cawthon, "Letters of a Private," 540–41, 542; J. M. Davidson, Shelbyville, TN, to Julia, Feb. 14, 1863, Davidson Papers, EU.

68 Elijah M. Odom, Vicksburg, MS, to Sarah F. Odom, Jan. 11, 26, 1863, Odom Letters, MDAH; G. H. Burns, Vicksburg, MS, to Wife, Apr. 2, 1863, Burns Letters, CNMP; E. K. Flournoy, Vicksburg, MS, to Wife, Apr. 15, 1863, Flournoy Letters, ADAH

69 F. Niebuhr, Yazoo River, MS, to Parents, and Brothers and Sisters, Mar. 5, 1863, Niebuhr Papers, CAH-UT. See also his letter of Jan. 1, 1863.

70 Wiley, *"This Infernal War,"* 222–23, 226, 238, 239. See also Johnston, "Vinson Let-

ters," 105; McLaughlin, *Cherished Letters*; Park, *Civil War Letters*, Feb. 21, Mar. 8, 1863. The Shibleys' version of the psalm reads: "God is our refuge and strength; a powerful help in trouble. Therefore we will not fear though earth change. He quieteth wars to the end of the earth; the bow he breaketh in pieces and cutteth asunder the spear."

71 Lanning Diary, Feb. 8, 1863, ADAH.

72 E. K. Flournoy, Vicksburg, MS, to Wife, Apr. 15, 1863, Flournoy Letters, ADAH. See also Flournoy's letter of Apr. 2, 1863.

73 A. G. Jones, Kinston, NC, to Parents, Jan. 28, 1863, Jones Family Papers, SHC-UNC; John. S. Meriwether, Mobile, AL, to Alice, Oct. 19, 1862, Meriwether Papers, EU; G. H. Burns, Vicksburg, MS, to Wife, Feb. 24, 1863, Burns Letters, CNMP. For similar, contemporary complaints about chaplains, or the lack thereof, see Mellon, "Florida Soldier," 247; Northen, *All Right Let Them Come*, 46, 59; Elijah M. Odom, Vicksburg, MS, to Sarah F. Odom, Mar. 19, 1863, Odom Letters, MDAH. For the diary of a chaplain who only came to the army in March 1863, see DeWitt Diary, CCCWC, TSLA, For openness to other expressions of faith, see Northen, *All Right Let Them Come*, 61, 77.

74 Durkin, *John Dooley*, 54, 58–59.

75 Lowe and Hodges, *Letters to Amanda*, 26, 39.

76 Ibid., 72.

77 Green Diary, June 21, July 26, Aug. 30, 1863, SHC-UNC.

78 J. M. Davidson, Shelbyville, TN, to Julia, May 3, 1863, Davidson Papers, EU.

79 Park, *Civil War Letters*, June 21, 1863.

80 Mellon, "Florida Soldier," 249–50.

81 Moseley, *Stilwell Letters*, 159, 163.

82 James S. Alexander, Jackson, MS, to Wife and Children, June 7, 1863, Alexander Collection, AU; Battle, *Civil War Letters*, 20; William D. Cole, Wartrace, TN, to Cornelia, June 24, 1863, Cole Letters, CWMC, USAMHI; John G. Fowler, n.p., to Sister, June 17, 1863, Lee Papers, USC; Griffith, *Yours Till Death*, 70; Haynes, *Field Diary*, 33; Holland, *Keep All My Letters*, 85; Johnston, "Vinson Letters," 82, 84, 86; Miles W. Lewis, Guinea Station, VA, to Amy M. Lewis, June 1, 1863, Miles W. Lewis Papers, CWMC, USAMHI; W. H. H. Lee, Yazoo City, MS, to Wife, June 10, 1863, Lee Papers, USC; Mays, *Let Us Meet in Heaven*, 86, 112, 121, 122; Moseley, *Stilwell Letters*, 191, 197; Northen, *All Right Let Them Come*, 92; J. B. Sanders, Vicksburg, MS, to Elisabeth Sanders, July 8, 1863, Sanders Papers, MDAH; A. D. Terry, Camp Jackson, to Wife, May 29, 1863, Terry Family Papers, SHC-UNC; W. J. J. Webb. Fredericksburg, VA, to Mother, May 23, 1863, and Webb, n.p., to Mother, July 7, 1863, Webb Letters, Leigh, USAMHI; John French White, City Point, VA, to Mattie, May 3, 1863, White Papers, VHS.

83 A. J. Edge, Enterprise, MS, to Companion, July 10, 1863, Edge Papers, EU

84 S. W. Farrow, Bluff Springs, AR, to Josephine, July 19, 1863, Farrow Papers, CAH-UT.

85 Isaac Barineau, Orange Court House, VA, to Kate Barineau, Aug. 6, 1863, Barineau Collection, CWMC, USAMHI.

86 J. M. Davidson, Meridian, MS, to Julia, Aug. 24, 1863, Davidson Papers MSS

(microfilm), EU. See also Kennedy Diary, 37–58, SHC-UNC; Mays, *Let Us Meet in Heaven*, 133, 140; E. R. Willis, Orange Court House, VA, to Father, Aug. 21, 1863, Willis Family Papers, USC. There were exceptions; see Wiley, *"This Infernal War,"* 333, 337.

87 J. F. Coghill, Orange Court House, VA, to Mit, Sept, 4, 1863, Coghill Letters, SHC-UNC.

88 Moseley, *Stilwell Letters*, 205, 208. See also Hubbs, *Voices*, 197–99.

89 William S. Lacy, Rapidan Station, VA, to Sister, Sept. 23, 1863, Lacy Papers, SHC-UNC.

90 Johnston, "Confederate Letters," 86–87, 88.

91 Allen Shadrick, Gordonsville, VA, to Wife, Sept. 27, 1863, Shadrick Letters, Leigh, USAMHI; T. T. Hoskins, Culpeper Court House, VA, to Papa, Aug. 26, Sept. 2, 1863, and Hoskins, Racoon Ford, VA, to Mama, Oct. 3, 1863, Hoskins Family Papers, VHS.

92 John William Watson, Richmond, VA, to Wife, Sept. 27, Oct. 21, 1863, Watson Family Papers, VHS. For hospital-based revivals in Richmond, see also James C. Franklin, Richmond, VA, to Sister, Sept. 12, 1863, Franklin Correspondence, Duke. See also Hatley and Huffman, *Letters of Wagner*, 55.

93 A. M. Sewell, Chickamauga, TN, to Louisa, Oct. 19, 1863, Sewell Correspondence, EU.

94 G. H. Burns, Chickamauga, TN, to Wife, Oct. 11, 1863, Burns Letters, CNMP.

95 Blomquist and Taylor, *This Cruel War*, 184, 186, 193, 208 (quotations 186, 193).

96 Lanning Diary, 6, 10, 13, 19, ADAH.

97 Edgar Smithwick, Camp, to Mother, Nov. 19, 1863, Smithwick Papers, Duke; Mays, *Let Us Meet in Heaven*, 154, 156.

98 Green Diary, Dec. 10, 1863, SHC-UNC. Woodworth, *While God Is Marching On*, 231–53, depicts a single revival that started in the summer of 1862 and continued to the end of the war.

99 Kennedy Diary, 37–58, SHC-UNC; Cate, *Two Soldiers*, 10–19; W. R. Sivley, Sherbuta, MS, to Janie, Dec. 1, 1863, Sivley Papers, SHC-UNC.

100 J. W. Griffin, Richmond, VA, to Wife, Dec. 25, 1863, Griffin Papers, Duke.

101 Green Diary, Feb. 28, 1864, SHC-UNC. See also Alex Gobbel, Washington, DC, to Prof. B. S. Hedrick, Jan. 5, 1864, Hedrick Letters, UAL; Edgar Smithwick, Camp, to Mother, Feb. 7, 1864, Smithwick Papers, Duke; John William Watson, Staunton, VA, to Wife, Jan. 16, 1864, Watson Family Papers, VHS.

102 G. H. Burns, Dalton, GA, to Wife, Feb. 1, 1864, Burns Letters, CNMP; John Crittenden, Dalton, GA, to Bettie, Mar. 29, 1864, Crittenden Papers, AU; Mosely, *Stilwell Letters*, 244.

103 Wynne and Taylor, *This War So Horrible*, 41, 45–46 (quotations 45–46). See also Blomquist and Taylor, *This Cruel War*, 230, 232, 235, 236, 245. For fast days see Phillips, *Diehard Rebels*, 27–29; Stout and Grasso, "Civil War, Religion, and Communications," 319–20, 325–27, 333–35, 338–39, 343–45.

104 Cate, *Two Soldiers*, 69.

105 Mosely, *Stilwell Letters*, 247. Absalom Burum of Thomas's Legion told a different story. "No preaching," he complained, "we never even had a service last Friday day

of fasting, humiliation & prayer." Burum blamed his chaplain. "Christianity seems to be at a low ebb," he lamented. "Our Chaplain lays about here in camps & seldom ever preaches." See Leas, "Diary of Burum," 34, 35

106 T. L. Camp, Camp, to Mary, Apr. 14, 1864, Camp Family Papers, EU; Cate, *Two Soldiers*, 75, 76, 78; John Crittenden, Camp, to Bettie, Apr. 4, 1864, Crittenden Papers, AU; A. J. Edge, Dalton, GA, to Companion, Apr. 30, 1864, Edge Papers MSS 346, EU; Thomas Warrick, Dalton, GA, to Wife, Apr. 8, 1864, Warrick Papers, ADAH.

107 G. H. Burns, Dalton, GA, to Wife, May 2, 1864, Burns Letters, CNMP.

108 Green Diary, 30, 31, SHC-UNC.

109 Mosely, *Stilwell Letters*, 252, 254.

110 Mays, *Let Us Meet in Heaven*, 206; J. W. Tindall, Mt. Pleasant, to Wife, May 20, 1864, Tindall Papers, USC.

111 John F. Davenport, Bristol, VA, to Wife, Apr. 2, 1864, Davenport Letters, ADAH. For a prisoner, see H. Bradford, Johnson's Island, OH, to Mary, Mar. 20, 1864, Bradford Papers, Florida State University, Tallahassee, Fla.

112 George H. Chatfield, n.p., to Mother, Apr. 12, 1864, Chatfield Letters, CWMC, USAMHI; J. A. Frierson, Roveleve, to Apr. 22, 1864, Frierson Correspondence, LSU; J. B. Sanders, Rome, GA, to Elisabeth Sanders, Apr. 28, May 1, 1864, and Sanders, New Hope Church, GA, to Elisabeth Sanders, May 7, 1864, Sanders Papers, MDAH.

113 Wallace Diary, 71–74 (quotations 71, 74), SHC-UNC.

114 Harvey Bailey, Camp Vance, VA, to Wife and Children, May 17, 1864, Bailey Letters, CWMC, USAMHI; "Letters of Cadenhead," 565; John F. Davenport, Chafin's Bluff, VA, to Wife, June 1, 1864, Davenport Letters, ADAH; Griffith, *Yours Till Death*, 108; R. B. Jett, Saltville, VA, to N. E. Burch, May 29, 1864, Jett Papers, EU.

115 J. W. Tindall, Florence, SC, to Wife, May 25, 1864, Tindall Papers, USC.

116 John Crittenden, Camp, to Bettie, July 15, 1864, Crittenden Papers, AU.

117 Blomquist and Taylor, *This Cruel War*, 271; Cash and Howorth, *My Dear Nellie*, 205; Cate, *Two Soldiers*, 115, 116, 122, 134; Davis Diary, June 12, 13, 1864, VHS; W. V. Fleming, Blakeley, AL, to Mary S. Fleming, Sept. 14, 1864, Fleming Correspondence, ADAH; Theophilis Frank, James River, VA, to Wife, June 24, 1864, Frank Family Letters, SHC-UNC; James E. Green Diary, 39, Green Diary, SHC-UNC; Fleming Jordan, Army of Tennessee, to Wife, July 15, 1864, Jordan Letters, UGA; Kees Diary, 42, MDAH; Lear Diary, Sept. 11, 31, 1864, EU; J. D. Padgett, Bivouac, to Father, July 9, 1864, Padgett Letters, CWMC, USAMHI; W. H. Rucker, Asheville, NC, to Wife, July 27, 1864, Rucker Scrapbook, SHC-UNC; J. B. Sanders, Barnesville, GA, to Elizabeth Sanders, July 13, 1864, and Sanders, Atlanta, GA, to Elizabeth Sanders, Aug. 14, 1864, Sanders Papers, MDAH; A. E. Shore, Chafin's Bluff, VA, to Wife & Family, July 19, 1864, Shore Letters, EU; R. T. Wood, Atlanta, GA, to Wife & Children, July 15, 1864, Wood Papers, UGA.

118 J. H. Lee, Petersburg, VA, to Wife, July 24, 1864, Lee Papers, EU.

119 J. W. Tindall, Frayser's Farm, VA, to Wife, June 16, 1864, Tindall Papers, USC.

120 E. H. Hampton, Chattahoochee River, to Aldecha Bailey, July 14, 1864, Bailey

Letters, CWMC, USAMHI. For a similar reference to "a tie in heaven," see Jones and Martin, *The Gentle Rebel*, 49.

121 Cate, *Two Soldiers*, 134; Moseley, *Stilwell Letters*, 275. See also Alexander Diary, vol. 2, 65, SHC-UNC; Blomquist and Taylor, *This Cruel War*, 299; Marion Coiner, Camp, to Sister, Jan. 2, 1865, Coiner Family Papers, VHS; Abel H. Crawford, New Market, VA, to Dora, Oct. 29, 1864, Crawford Letters, CCCWC, TSLA; Crow, *Diary of a Confederate Soldier*, 117; John P. Dull, New Market, VA, to Giney Dull, Nov. 9, Dec. 22, 1864, Dull Letters, VS; Jones and Martin, *The Gentle Rebel*, 49, 68, 108, 124; Lowe and Hodges, *Letters to Amanda*, 188, 193, 199; Pate, *This Evil War*, 199, 200; John Putnam, Sullivan's Island, SC, to Wife, Dec. 15, 27, 1864, Putnam Papers, USC; D. C. Snyder, Camp, to Wife, Dec. 25, 1865, Snyder Papers, VHS.

122 Cawthon, "Letters of a Private," 545–47 (quotation 545). See also Cate, *Two Soldiers*, 175, 179; John P. Dull, Camp Ewell, VA, to Giney Dull, Feb. 20, 1865, Dull Papers, VS; S. W. Farrow, Camp Macgruder, LA, to Josephine, Jan. 13, 1865, Farrow Papers, CAH-UT. Woodworth, *While God Is Marching On*, 245–46, 252, suggests that interest in religion remained strong, but so few letters from later enlisters exist for the period that it is impossible to say if they should be included.

123 Phillips, *Diehard Rebels*, 30–36; Woodworth, *While God Is Marching On*, 270–86.

124 Wiley, "*This Infernal War*," 443. Fay, as usual, was an exception, see Woodworth, *While God Is Marching On*, 270–86. See also Cate, *Two Soldiers*, 181. For prisoners, see Davis Diary, Apr. 9, 23, May 7, 1865, VHS.

125 Ben Robertson, Marietta, GA, to Sister, June 23, 1864, Robertson Papers, MDAH.

126 Reid Mitchell, *Civil War Soldiers*, 64–71; Newton, "Amazing Grace," *Olney Hymns*.

CHAPTER 7

1 "Our Montgomery Correspondence," *Charleston Mercury*, Apr. 23, 1861, *Chronicles of the Civil War*, http://www.pddoc.com/cw-chronicles/?p=1405 (accessed Jan. 10, 2008); Schulte, "Re: Confederate Units at Pensacola," Florida in the Civil War Message Board, http://history-sites.com/mb/cw/flcwmb/index.cgi?noframes;read=1764 (accessed Jan. 10, 2008); L. H. Mathews, "Our Mess," Part 1, Mathews Poem, Leigh, USAMHI.

2 L. H. Mathews, "Our Mess," Part 1, Mathews Poem, Leigh, USAMHI; Florida 1st Infantry, http://www.psy.fsu.edu/thompson/cw/1-fl-inf/fl-1st-inf.html (accessed Jan. 10, 2008). I was unable to identify Dick or John T.

3 Wolosky, "Poetry and Public Discourse," 176–84.

4 Wynne and Taylor, *This War So Horrible*, 47, 75–76.

5 Wiley, *Life of Johnny Reb*, 18–19, 59–63, 106, 151–73; Robertson, *Soldiers Blue and Gray*, 8, 65, 75–77, 81–101, 224–25; Linderman, *Embattled Courage*, 234–36, 259; McPherson, *For Cause and Comrades*, 86, 89; Logue, *To Appomattox and Beyond*, 51, 60, 61–62. Reid Mitchell wrote of soldiers' fears in *Civil War Soldiers*, 56–75, and of their responses in *Vacant Chair*, 39–54.

6 Lynn, *Bayonets of the Republic*, 163–82; McPherson, *For Cause and Comrades*, 13, 85–91, 209–10n25 (quotation 85). Jason Phillips, in his recent study of "diehard Rebels,"

concurs that camaraderie and ideology were major factors in sustaining at least the most devoted Confederates soldiers, as they helped convince them of their invincibility and ultimate victory. See Phillips, *Diehard Rebels*, 3, 77–79, 80, 88–89, 127.

7 Berry, *All That Makes a Man*, 181–82; Sheehan-Dean, *Why Confederates Fought*, 1–3, 58–60, 87–88, 156–57, 174–75. For a different view, see Carmichael, *Last Generation*, 72–75, 264–65n34.

8 Wiley, *"This Infernal War,"* 72, 74, 75, 86, 93, 110, 141, 175, 201, 204, 337, 390, 429; William S. Lacy, Rapidan Station, VA, to Sister, Sept. 23, 1863 (quotation), and Lacy, Petersburg, VA, to Sister, Nov. 5, 1864, Lacy Papers, SHC-UNC; Andrew Crawford, Adam's Run, VA, to Mother, Feb. 5, 1865, Crawford Family Papers, USC; Thomas J. Moore, Petersburg, VA, to Thomas W. Hill, Jan. 21, 1865, Moore Papers, USC; W. H. Roberston, Livingston, to Sisters, May 29, [1864], Robertson Papers, MDAH.

9 G. H. Burns, Bridgeport, AL, to Wife, Apr. 6, 1863, Burns Letters, CNMP.

10 John Crittenden, [Dalton, GA], to Mother, Mar. 31, 1864, and Crittenden, Atlanta, GA, to Bettie, July 17, 1864, Crittenden Papers, AU.

11 W. J. J. Webb, Camps, to Father, July 25, 1863, Webb Letters, Leigh, USAMHI.

12 Jesse C. Knight, Culpepper Court House, VA, to Wife, Sept. 9, 1862, Knight Family Papers, UGA.

13 William D. Clover, Zollicoffer, TN, to Wife and Children, Apr. 18, 1863, William D. Clover Letters, Leigh, USAMHI; D. M. Denney, Atlanta, GA, to Sinai and Children, Aug. 24, 1864, Denney Family Papers, AU; Durkin, *John Dooley*, 63, 71–72, 82, 88; Phillips Fitzpatrick, Dog River, AL, to Mary, Mar. 23, 1862, Fitzpatrick Papers, ADAH; Theophilis Frank, Orange Court House, VA, to Wife, Dec. 31, 1863, Frank Family Letters, SHC-UNC; A. L. Galloway, Tupelo, MS, to Wife, July 1, 1862, Galloway Letters, AU; Hatley and Huffman, *Letters of Wagner*, 5; A. G. Jones, Garysburg, NC, to Mother, Oct. 9, 31, 1862, Jones Family Papers, SHC-UNC; Jesse C. Knight, Chatham County, GA, to Wife, June 18, 1862, Knight Family Papers, UGA; Enoch L. Mitchell, "Civil War Letters," 51–52; Isaac Walters, Petersburg, VA, to Wife, May 31, 1862, Costen Papers, SHC-UNC; James I. Willis, James Island, SC, to Father and Mother, Oct. 19, 1863, Willis Family Papers, USC; J. A. Wilson, Grenada, MS, to Lizzie, Dec. 25, 1862, Wilson Letters, MDAH.

14 William J. Hart, n.p., to Father, Sept. 8, 1862, Hart Brothers Letters, CWMC, USAMHI. See also James M. Cadwallander Diary, Feb. 2, Sept. 4, 1864, VS; N. J. Clover, Belfield, VA, to Father and Mother, May 14, 1864, N. J. Clover Letters, Book 25, 70–72, Leigh, USAMHI; Northen, *All Right Let Them Come*, 34, 35, 38, 40, 42, 54, 61, 62, 63, 71, 74, 77, 78; Moseley, *Stilwell Letters*, 19, 23, 25, 80, 125, 141, 193; Simmons, "Diary of Clement, 1865," 80–81; John Thurman, Barnsville, MS, to Wife, Mar. 26, 1862, Thurman Papers, SHC-UNC; J. C. Williams, Camp Gordon, GA, to Wife, Feb. 22, 1863, J. C. Williams Papers, AU.

15 E. A. Penick, Orange Court House, VA, to Son, Apr. 6, 1862, and Penick, Yorktown, VA, to Son, Apr. 16, 1862, Penick Papers, VHS. See also A. J. Edge, Alabama River, to Wife, Feb. 11, 14, 1863, and Edge, Vicksburg, MS, to Wife, Feb. 20, Mar. 20, 1863, Edge Papers, EU; Johnston, "Vinson Letters," 110; A. G. Jones, Kinston, NC, to Parents, Jan. 28, 1863, Jones Family Papers, SHC-UNC; Lowe and Hodges, *Letters*

to Amanda, 6, 13, 83, 97, 98, 110, 115, 137, 157; Mays, *Let Us Meet in Heaven,* 95, 97. Marion Hill Fitzpatrick, in Lowe and Hodges, *Letters to Amanda,* 98, 124, 132, 137, 141, described an active Masonic Lodge in his camp during the winter of 1863–64, but I have found no additional indications of fraternal orders.

16 J. R. Manson, Falling Creek, VA, to Charlotte, July 12, 1862, Manson Diary and Letters, CWMC, USAMHI.

17 Johnston, "Vinson Letters," 110.

18 J. A. Frierson, Pleasant Hill, LA, to Ma, Apr. 16, 1864, Frierson Correspondence, LSU.

19 Lear Diary, Aug. 20, 1864, EU. See also Kauffman Diary, Aug. 12, 1862, SHC-UNC.

20 Hubbs, *Voices,* 183. J. F. Coghill, Williamsport, MD, to Pappy, Ma, and Mit, July 9, 1863, Coghill Letters, SHC-UNC.

21 William S. Lacy, Petersburg, VA, to Sister, Nov. 5, 1864, Lacy Papers, SHC-UNC.

22 J. M. Davidson, Harrodsburg, KY, to Julia, Oct. 12, 1862, and Davidson, Shelbyville, TN, to Julia, Jan. 28, 1863, Davidson Papers, EU. "Cousin Bob Vance" was Robert B. Vance, the brother of North Carolina governor Zebulon Vance. See also D. M. Denney, Opelika, Al, to Sinai and Children, Aug. 27, 1864, Denney Family Papers, AU.

23 W. J. Barron, Johnson's Island, OH, to Cousin, Mar. 28, 1865, Taylor Letters, UAL.

24 Griffith, *Yours Till Death,* 11, 12, 47; John G. Fowler, Dalton, GA, to Sister, Dec. 15, 1863, Lee Papers, USC; John Meriwether, Mobile, AL, to Wife, Sept. 12, 24, 1862, Meriwether Papers, EU. See also Bluford Alexander Cameron Diary, May 22, June 14, 1863, Cameron Papers, CAH-UT; Hartley and Zimmerman, *Fighting 57th,* 19, 24, 26, 27, 29, 31, 45; McMurtrey, *Letters to Lucinda,* 1, 3, 17, 22, 25, 35, 38; McLaughlin, *Letters of Hendricks,* 31.

25 Blomquist and Taylor, *This Cruel War,* 260, 290.

26 Bluford Alexander Cameron Diary, May 29, June 12, 1863, Cameron Papers, CAH-UT; Cawthon, "Letters of a Private," 538, 539, 541; J. F. Coghill, Williamsport, MD, to Pappy, Ma and Mit, Jul. 9, 1863, Coghill Letters, SHC-UNC; S. W. Farrow, Camp Waterhouse, TX, to Father and Mother, July 29, 1862, Farrow Papers, CAH-UT; James P. Garrison, Fredericksburg, VA, to Wife, Feb. 7, 9, 1863, Garrison Papers, EU; Johnson, "Letters of Barnes," 82; J. D. Joyner, n.p., to Mother, n.d., Joyner Family Papers, SHC-UNC; Jesse C. Knight, Chatham County, GA, to Wife, June 30, 1862, Knight Family Papers, UGA; Miles W. Lewis, Falling Creek, VA, to Amy M. Lewis, Aug. 5, 1862, Miles W. Lewis Papers, CWMC, USAMHI; John Thurman, Barnsville, to Wife, Mar. 26, 1862, Thurman Papers #5107, SHC-UNC.

27 J. M. Davidson, Kingston, TN, to Julia, Dec. 19, 1862, Davidson Papers, EU.

28 Thomas J. Moore, Manassas, VA, to Sister, Sept. 2, 1862, Moore Papers, USC. See also Hatley and Huffman, *Letters of Wagner,* 38, 44, 45, 47, 51, 52; Pate, *This Evil War,* 184.

29 G. H. Burns, Bridgeport, AL, to Wife, July 26, 1862, Burns Letters, CNMP. See also his letters of Apr. 2 and 6, 1863.

30 S. W. Farrow, Pine Bluff, AR, to Josephine, Feb. 27, 1863, Farrow Papers, CAH-UT.

31 In cases where relationships were not clear, I determined whether the letter writer

assumed that his correspondent at home knew the comrade mentioned. See Battle, *Civil War Letters*, 12, 14; Newt Bosworth, Fisherville, VA, to Friend, Mar. 19, 1864, Bosworth Family Collection, Leigh, USAMHI; C. W. Bunker, Camp, to Sister, Nov. 2, 1863, and Bunker, Davalls Ford, TN, to Sister, Nov. 18, 1863; Bunker Papers, SHC-UNC; Cawthon, "Letters of a Private," 536, 538, 546; William A. Collins, Camp Magnum, NC, to Sister, Mar. 6, 1862, Collins Papers, SHC-UNC; John Crittenden, [Dalton, GA], to Mother, Mar. 31, 1864, Crittenden Papers, AU; D. M. Denney, Atlanta, GA, to Sinai and Children, Aug. 24, 1864, Denney Family Papers, AU; C. D. Epps, Whitfield Co., GA, to Wife, Aug. 10, 1862, Epps Papers, SHC-UNC; S. W. Farrow, Pine Bluff, AR, to Josephine, Feb. 27, 1863, and Farrow, Camp Wright, AR, to Josephine, Apr. 17, 1863, Farrow Papers, CAH-UT; A. L. Galloway, n.p., to Wife, July 1, 1862, Galloway Letters, AU; Grantham, "Letters from Hightower," 185; Griffith, *Yours Till Death*, 51, 55, 63, 64; Hartley and Zimmerman, *Fighting 57th*, 45; Hatley and Huffman, *Letters of Wagner*, 3, 5, 20, 21, 29, 31, 32, 36, 41, 42, 45, 59, 61, 64, 76; J. H. Lee, Cumberland Gap, TN, to Wife, Dec. 22, 1862, Lee Papers, EU; Miles W. Lewis, Falling Creek, VA, to Amy M. Lewis, Aug. 5, 1862, Miles W. Lewis Papers, CWMC, USAMHI; McLaughlin, *Letters of Hendricks*, 21, 30, 36–37; E. A. Penick, Orange Court House, VA, to Son, Apr. 6, 1862, Penick Papers, VHS; B. Wylie Scott, Fort Siler, NC, to Ella Merryman, May 4, 1862, Merryman Papers, VHS; J. B. Sanders, Carsville, GA, to Elisabeth Sanders, May 18, 1864, Sanders Papers, MDAH; William A. Stephens, Blair's Crossroad, TN, to Susan, Aug. 1862, Stephens Papers, EU; O. V. Strickland, Dalton, GA, to Mother, Strickland Papers, EU; H. W. Robinson, Cumberland Gap, TN, to Wife, May 7, 12, 20, 25, June 8, 1862, Robinson Papers, EU; B. F. Tamplin, Grimes Co., TX, to Retincia, Mar. 24, 1862, Tamplin Letters, CMM, LSU; Thomas Warrick, Tupelo, MS, to Wife, June 13, 15, 1862, and Warrick, Shelbyville, TN, to Wife, Jan. 13, Feb. 12, 1863, Warrick Papers, ADAH.

32 G. H. Burns, Vicksburg, MS, to Wife, Feb. 10, 1863, Burns Letters, CNMP; Griffith, *Yours Till Death*, 11. See also John T. Beggs, Corinth, MS, to Sister, Apr. 2, 20, 1862, Beggs and Janssen Family Papers, SHC-UNC; Hatley and Huffman, *Letters of Wagner*, 34–35, 44; Miles M. Lewis, Guniea Station, VA, to Amy M. Lewis, Mar. 21, 1863, Miles W. Lewis Papers, CWMC, USAMHI; John J. Mendenhall, Petersburg, VA, to Mother, Aug. 8, 1862, Mendenhall Letters, CWMC, USAMHI; J. T. Nobles and W. J. Nobles, James Island, SC, to Beloved Ones at Home, June 18, 1862, Nobles Papers, USC; H. R. Rodgers, Florence, AL, to Tabitha, Nov. 13, 1864, Rodgers Letters, CWMC, USAMHI; C. D. Sides, Fredericksburg, VA, to Wife, Feb. 19, 1863, Sides Letters, CWMC, USAMHI.

33 Blomquist and Taylor, *This Cruel War*, 100, 169–70 (quotation 100).

34 Moseley, *Stilwell Letters*, 2, 7, 19, 22, 25, 27, 30, 57, 63, 92, 96, 100, 165, 169, 216, 220–21, 265 (quotations 165, 169).

35 Ibid., 46, 153, 167; Taylor, "53d Ga. Vols," http://www.rootsweb.com/gaspald3/53rd_georgia_volunteers.htm (accessed Feb. 20, 2008).

36 Wiley, *Life of Johnny Reb*, 20–23, 138–39; Robertson, *Soldiers Blue and Gray*, 21–25; Reid Mitchell, *Vacant Chair*, 43–46; McPherson, *For Cause and Comrades*, 82–89;

Lynn, *Bayonets of the Republic*, 171–73. On the power of flags and especially the near mania involved in capturing them, see Bonner, *Colors and Blood*, 88–92, 154–59.

37 William D. Alexander Diary, v. 1, 10, SHC-UNC; John T. Beggs, Tullahoma TN, to Sister, Apr. 5, 1863, Beggs and Janssen Family Papers, SHC-UNC; D. W. Chenault, Albany, KY, to Brother, Mar. 11, 1863, Chenault Letters, CWMC, USAMHI; Hartley and Zimmerman, *Fighting 57th*, 43–44; M. H. Hunter, Fredericksburg, VA, to Father, Dec. 22, 1862, Hunter Papers, USC; J. D. Joyner, Berkeley Co., VA, to Mother, Oct. 11, 1862, Joyner Family Papers, SHC-UNC; Leas, "Diary of Burum," CCCWC, TSLA; Lowe and Hodges, *Letters to Amanda*, 24, 75; J. R. Manson, Falling Creek, VA, to Charlotte, July 12, 1862, Manson Diary and Letters, CWMC, USAMHI; J. B. Sanders, Atlanta, GA, to n.p., Sept. 6, 1864, Sanders Papers, MDAH; Edgar Smithwick, Magnolia, NC, to Mother, Oct. 16, 1863, Smithwick Papers, Duke; John Thurman, Corinth, MS, to Wife, Apr. 16, 1862, Thurman Papers #5107, SHC-UNC; J. W. Tindall, Florence, AL, to Wife, May 25, 1864, Tindall Papers, USC; J. H. Warrick, Corinth, MS, to Brother, Mar. 24, 1862, Warrick Papers, ADAH; John French White, Chafin's Farm, VA, to Wife, Feb. 22, 1864, White Papers, VHS. Samuel Pickens expressed an unwillingness to leave "this old command" for the Signal Corps but never identified the exact command to which he referred. See Hubbs, *Voices*, 211.

38 H. W. Robinson, Cumberland Gap, TN, to Wife, June 1, 1862, Robinson Papers, EU.

39 For companies, see Cash and Howorth, *My Dear Nellie*, 51, 88; William Duncan Cole, Burchard, TN, to Wife, Aug. 28, 1863, Cole Letters, CWMC, USAMHI; Lowe and Hodges, *Letters to Amanda*, 111, 114, 115; J. R. Manson, Falling Creek, VA, to Charlotte, July 12, 1862, Manson Diary and Letters, CWMC, USAMHI; Enoch L. Mitchell, "Letters of Newberry," 70–71, 73; E. A. Penick, Yorktown, VA, to Mary, Apr. 16, 1862, Penick Papers, VHS; Park, *Civil War Letters*, Sept. 30, Oct. 1, 1862; Samuel Ridley to James Ridley, Mar. 6, 1863, Ridley Papers, CCCWC, TSLA; Wiley, *"This Infernal War,"* 27, 29, 123–25, 138, 150, 216.

40 J. A. Patton, Camp Mangum, NC, to Wife, Apr. 10, 1862, Patton Letters, EU.

41 Prokopowicz, *All For the Regiment*, esp. 4–6, 17–34, 185–89.

42 J. D. Joyner, Berkeley Co., VA, to Mother, Oct. 11, 1862, Joyner Family Papers, SHC-UNC. In the same collection, see also Joyner, Camp, to Brother, May 17, 1864. See also William D. Alexander Diary, v. 1, 50, SHC-UNC; Cash and Howorth, *My Dear Nellie*, 209; Lowe and Hodges, *Letters to Amanda*, 24; Ben Robertson, Atlanta, GA, to Sister, July 23, 1864, Robertson Papers, MDAH; Edgar Smithwick, Kenville, NC, to Mother, July 28, 1863, Smithwick Papers, Duke.

43 John T. Beggs, Tullahoma, TN, to Sister, Apr. 5, 1863, Beggs and Janssen Family Papers; SHC-UNC.

44 J. M. Davidson, Vicksburg, MS, to J. M. C. Dunn, July 3, 1863, Davidson Papers, EU. For another negative view, see H. W. Robinson, Cumberland Gap, TN, to Wife, May 20, June 1, 1862, Robinson Papers, EU.

45 J. M. Davidson, Cooper's Iron Works, to J. M. C. Dunn, May 21, 1864, Davidson Papers, EU; John T. Knight, Camp Diometer, AR, to Susan Knight, Dec. 5, 1862,

Knight Letters, CCCWC, TSLA; Cash and Howorth, *My Dear Nellie*, 179–80; Hardy Matthews, Camp, to Sister, May 13, 1863, McLeod Papers, SHC-UNC.

46 Wiley, *Life of Johnny Reb*, 234–43; Brooks, "Popular Sovereignty," 199–218; Linderman, *Embattled Courage*, 43–60; Logue, *To Appomattox and Beyond*, 32, 58–61; McPherson, *For Cause and Comrades*, 53–61; Reid Mitchell, *Vacant Chair*, 28, 39–54, 81–86; Robertson, *Soldiers Blue and Gray*, 122–30.

47 E. A. Penick, Orange Court House, VA, to Wife, Apr. 1, 1862, and Penick, Yorktown, VA, to Wife, Apr. 16, 1862, Penick Papers, VHS; I. M. Auld, Fredericksburg, VA, to Mother, May 15, 1863, Auld Letters, CWMC, USAMHI. For general comments from men who liked their officers without explaining why, see Alexander Diary, vol. 2, Oct. 3, 4, 1864, SHC-UNC; William P. Cline, Richmond, VA, to Mary C. Cline, Aug. 24, 1862, Cline Papers, SHC-UNC; John H. Hundley, Gordonsville, VA, to Wife, Aug. 19, 1862, Hundley Family Papers, SHC-UNC; A. E. Shore, Chafin's Bluff, VA, to Brother & Sister, Aug. 1864, Shore Letters, EU; B. F. Tamplin, Camp Lubbock, TX, to Retinca, May 9, 1862, Tamplin Letters, CMM, LSU; Thomas Warrick, Loachapoka, AL, to Companion, Mar. 9, 1862, Warrick Papers, ADAH.

48 Terrill and Dixon, *History of Stewart County*, 277. See also Durkin, *John Dooley*, 13, 35; Haynes, *Field Diary*, 3; S. W. Farrow, Monroe, LA, to Josephine, July 4, 1863, Farrow Papers, CAH-UT; Hubbs, *Voices*, 151, 169–70; E. A. Penick, Yorktown, VA, to Wife, Apr. 16, 1862, Penick Papers, VHS; J. B. Sanders, Atlanta, GA, to n.p., Sept. 6, 1864, Sanders Papers, MDAH; William A. Stephens, Chattanooga, TN, to Susan, June 30, 1862, Stephens Papers MSS 324 (microfilm), EU; John Thurman, Barnsville, MS, to Wife, Mar. 26, 1862, Thurman, Corinth, MS, to Wife, May 24, 1862, and Thurman, Tupelo, MS, to Wife, May 17, 1864, Thurman Papers, SHC-UNC.

49 William D. Clover, Zollicoffer, TN, to Ann, Dec. 27, 1862, William D. Clover Letters, Leigh, USAMHI; Haynes, *Field Diary*, 13; Griffith, *Yours Til Death*, 39; Jacob Kent Langhorne, Culpeper Court House, VA, to Sister, May 19, 1863; Additional Personal Papers Collection, VS; Lanning Diary, 1, ADAH; Osborn, "Civil War Letters," 145, 152; Ryan, "Letters of Cochrane," pt. 3, 147; Edgar Smithwick, Magnolia, NC, to Mother, Oct. 9, 1863, Smithwick Papers, Duke; E. R. Willis, Fredericksburg, VA, to Father, Mar. 30, 1863, Willis Family Papers, USC; Wynne and Taylor, *This War So Horrible*, 27, 34.

50 S. W. Farrow, Camp Wright, AR, to Josephine, Feb. 26, 1863, Farrow Papers, CAH-UT.

51 John T. Beggs, Camp Walton, TN, to Sister, Mar. 13, 1862, Beggs and Janssen Family Papers, SHC-UNC.

52 Michael Nihill, Chattanooga, TN, to Mother, July 25, 1863, Prime Collection, CWMC, USAMHI.

53 William H. Barnes, n.p., to Lizzie, Nov. 3, 1862, Barnes Papers, CAH-UT; J. S. Meriwether, Columbus, MS, to Wife, Dec. 21, 1862, Meriwether Papers, EU.

54 Blomquist and Taylor, *This Cruel War*, 304. For general negative comments, see E. K. Flournoy, Chickasaw Bayou, to Wife, Apr. 2, 1863, Flournoy Letters, ADAH; Hatley and Huffman, *Letters of Wagner*, 37; Sanders, "Letters of a Soldier," 1239.

55 William D. Clover, Zollicoffer, TN, to Brother, Dec. 19, 1862, Clover Letters, Leigh, USAMHI.

56 John Crittenden, [New] Hope Church, GA, to Bettie, May 31, 1864, Crittenden Papers, AU; Mays, *Let Us Meet in Heaven*, 71, 75; B. F. Tamplin, Grimes Co., TX, to Retinca, Mar. 24, 1862, Tamplin Letters, CMM, LSU; Wynne and Taylor, *This War So Horrible*, 110; Wiley, *"This Infernal War,"* 46. James Calvin Zimmerman, in Hartley and Zimmerman, *Fighting 57th*, 32, specifically praised his colonel for refusing to lead his regiment into action in November 1862.

57 W. J. J. Webb, n.p., to Father, July 25, 1863, Webb Letters, Leigh, USAMHI. See also J. B. Sanders, Atlanta, GA, to n.p., Sept. 6, 1864, Sanders Papers, MDAH.

58 D. C. Snyder, Lexington, VA, to Wife, Mar. 15, 1865, Daniel Cleveland Snyder Papers, VHS. See also Creed Thomas Davis Diary, Dec. 3, 1864, SHC-UNC; J. D. Joyner, Camp, to Mother, Feb. 11, 1864, Joyner Family Papers #4428, SHC-UNC; Griffith, *Yours Till Death*, 50, 62, 73.

59 Hubbs, *Voices*, 341; Park, *Civil War Letters*, Apr. 30, May 2, Aug. 19, 1863; Cash and Howorth, *My Dear Nellie*, 69, 93, 101, 121–22. See also Marion Coiner, Petersburg, VA, to Sister, Sept. 14, 1864, Coiner Family Papers, VHS; Hartley and Zimmerman, *Fighting 57th*, 21, 22; Jesse C. Knight, Chatham County, GA, to Wife, June 18, 1862, Knight Family Papers, UGA; Ryan, "Letters of Cochrane," pt. 1, 290, pt. 3, 148; J. B. Sanders, Atlanta, GA, to n.p., Sept. 6, 1864, Sanders Papers, MDAH; Wiley, *"This Infernal War,"* 34; Wynne and Taylor, *This War So Horrible*, 64, 76, 77.

60 William H. Barnes, Fort Smith, AR, to Lizzie, Nov. 21, 1862, Barnes Papers, CAH-UT.

61 Thomas J. Moore, Winchester, VA, to Sister, Oct. 15, 1862, Moore Papers, USC.

62 Crow, *Diary of a Confederate Soldier*, 25.

63 Wynne and Taylor, *This War So Horrible*, 74. See also S. W. Farrow, Pine Bluff, AR, to Josephine, Feb. 26, 1863, and Farrow, Nachitoches, LA, to Josephine, July 30, 1863, Farrow Papers, CAH-UT; J. W. Griffin, Richmond, VA, to Wife, Oct. 9, 1863, Griffin Papers, Duke; Jesse C. Knight, Chatham County, GA, to Wife, June 18, 1862, Knight Family Papers, UGA; John T. Knight, Washington, AR, to Susan Knight, Oct. 1, 1862, and Knight, Camp Diometer, AR, to Susan Knight, Dec. 5, 1862, Knight Letters, CCCWC, TSLA; J. H. Lee, Camp College, AL, to Father, June 6, 1862, Lee Papers, EU; Mays, *Let Us Meet in Heaven*, 73; Ryan, "Letters of Cochrane," pt. 3, 147; Thomas Warrick, Tenn., to Companion, Apr. 8, 1863, Warrick Papers, ADAH; Wiley, *"This Infernal War,"* 47, 50, 64, 86, 130.

64 A. E. Shore, Camp Gregg, VA, to Wife & Family, Mar. 18, 1863, Shore Letters, EU.

65 Griffith, *Yours Til Death*, 57–58.

66 Alex McNeill, Martinsburg, VA, to Wife, July 15, 1863, McNeill Papers, USC.

67 Wiley, *Life of Johnny Reb*, 234–43; Linderman, *Embattled Courage*, 43–60; McPherson, *For Cause and Comrades*, 53–61.

68 Reid Mitchell, *Civil War Soldiers*, 22; Gallagher, *Confederate War*, 57–59, 63–65, 86–92; Gallagher, *Lee & His Army in Confederate History*; 5–106; Phillips, *Diehard Confederates*, 90–115. See also Carmichael, *Last Generation*, 204–5; Elisabeth Lauterbach Laskin, "Good Old Rebels," 454–78; Rubin, *Shattered Nation*, 18–20, 37–38, 47–49, 82–83; Sheehan-Dean, *Why Confederates Fought*, 69–70.

69 Daniel Adams (1), Patton Anderson (1), P. G. T. Beauregard (4), Henry Benning (1), Braxton Bragg (1), William F. Brantley (1), Goode Bryan (1) Patrick Cleburne (2), Zachariah Deas (1), Jubal Early (2), Richard Ewell (1), Franklin Gardner (1), Samuel Garland (1), John B. Gordon (1), Henry Heth (1), A. P. Hill (2), John Walker Holmes (1), John B. Hood (1) Stonewall Jackson (12), Joseph Johnston (9), Robert E. Lee (10), Stephen D. Lee (1), James Longstreet (2), William W. Loring (1), Mansfield Lovell (1), Lunsford Lomax (1), William Mahone (1), Same Bell Maxey (1), Leonidas Polk (1), Sterling Price (4), James Edward Rains (1), Robert Ransom (1), Paul Semmes (1), M. L. Smith (1), Alexander Stewart (1), J. E. B. Stuart (2), Robert Toombs (2), and Alfred Vaughan (1).

See I. M. Auld, Fredericksburg, VA, to Mother, May 8, 15, 1863, and Auld, Petersburg, VA, to Mother, July 13, 1864, Auld Letters, CWMC, USAMHI; Battle, "Civil War Letters," 12; T. L. Camp, Camp, to Mary, May 21, July 13, 1864, Camp Family Papers, EU; L. J. Carneal, Martinsburg, VA, to Papa, Oct. 15, 1862, Carneal Papers, VHS; Cash and Howorth, *My Dear Nellie*, 184; Cate, *Two Soldiers*, 113, 159–60; E. B. Coggin, Gordonsville, VA, to Wife, July 20, 1862, Coggin Papers, ADAH; Wallace Comer, Kennesaw Mountain, GA, to Mother and Relatives, June 14, 1864, Comer Family Papers, SHC-UNC; Durkin, *John Dooley*, 40, 51, 56, 62–63; A. L. Galloway, Tupelo, MS, to Wife, June 15, 1862, Galloway Letters, AU; F. M. Goodwin, Campbellton, GA, to Susan, July 13, 1864, Goodwin Letter, UGA; Green Diary, SHC-UNC; Haynes, *Field Diary*, 19; Hartley and Zimmerman, *Fighting 57th*, 114–15; Thomas T. Hoskins, Orange Court House, VA, to Papa, May 15, 1863, Hoskins Family Papers, VHS; Hubbell, *Confederate Stamps*, 4; Hubbs, *Voices*, 159, 168, 195, 199, 239, 243; Johnston, "Vinson Letters," 110; A. G. Jones, Rapidan Station, VA, to Father, Oct. 7, 1863, A. G. Jones, Richmond, VA, to Ellick, May 12, 1864, and James B. Jones, n.p., to n.p., [1865], Jones Family Papers, SHC-UNC; Jones and Martin, *The Gentle Rebel*, 4, 27, 43, 46, 63, 71, 105, 114; Fleming Jordan, Camp Georgia, GA, to Wife, June 2, 1864, Jordan, Chattahoochee, to Wife, July 6, 1864, and Jordan, Atlanta, GA, to Wife, July 13, 1864, Jordan Letters, UGA; R. G. Joyner, Yorktown, VA, to Sister, Apr. 20, 1862, Joyner Family Papers, SHC-UNC; Kennedy Diary, 2, 20, 57, SHC-UNC; William S. Lacy, Ashland, VA, to Ma, June 27, 1862, Lacy Papers, SHC-UNC; Lanning Diary, 23, ADAH; Miles M. Lewis, Guinea Station, VA, to Amy M. Lewis, June 2, 1863, Miles W. Lewis Papers, CWMC, USAMHI; Lowe and Hodges, *Letters to Amanda*, 38, 69, 88, 151; Mays, *Let Us Meet in Heaven*, 77; Enoch L. Mitchell, "Letters of Newberry," 47; W. Y. Mordecai, Hamilton Cross Roads, to Mother, May 15, 1863, and Mordecai, Hagerstown, MD, to Mother, July 8, 1863, Mordecai Papers, VHS; Moseley, *Stilwell Letters*, 14–15, 106, 133, 153, 187, Northen, *All Right Let Them Come*, 45, 76, 91; Osborn, "Letters of Banks," 215–16; J. D. Padgett, Kennesaw Mountain, GA, to Father, July 9, 1864, Padgett Letters, CWMC, USAMHI; J. A. Patton, Greenville, NC, to Sister, May 14, 1863, Patton Letters, EU; E. A. Penick, Bethel Church, VA, to Wife, Apr. 19, 1862, Penick Papers, VHS; H. W. Robinson, Vicksburg, MS, to Wife, Jan. 6, 1863, Robinson Papers, EU; J. B. Sanders, Barnesville, GA, to Joseph B. Sanders, July 13, 1864, Sanders Papers, MDAH; Pharris Shearer, Dalton, GA, to Jennie Sivley, Mar. 6, 10,

27, 1864, Sivley Papers, SHC-UNC; Willie Sivley, Raymond, MS, to Jennie, May 14, 1864, and Sivley, Atlanta, GA, to Jennie, May 24, 1864, Sivley Papers, SHC-UNC; J. D. Stapp, Camp Chafins, VA, to Mother, May 31, June 5, 1864, Stapp Letters, VHS; William A. Stephens, Demopolis, AL, to Wife, Oct. 9, 1863, Stephens Papers, EU; Terrill and Dixon, *History of Stewart County*, 287–88; Wallace Diary, 57, 100, SHC-UNC; J. A. Wilson, Vicksburg, MS, to Lizzie, Mar. 2, 1863, Wilson Letters, MDAH; James White, Knoxville, TN, to Father and Mother, Sept. 25, 1862, White Letters, UAL; Wynne and Taylor, *This War So Horrible*, 104.

70 Lowe and Hodges, *Letters to Amanda*, 88, 151.

71 Braxton Bragg (5), Jubal Early (1), John H. Forney (3), Nathan Bedford Forrest (1), Bryan Grimes (1), Henry Heth (1), A. P. Hill (2), D. H. Hill (1), Theophilus Holmes (1), John B. Hood (1), Joseph Johnston (3), James H. Lane (1), Robert E. Lee (1), Stephen D. Lee (1), Arthur M. Manigault (1), Ben McCullough (1), Felix Robertson (1), Earl Van Dorn (2).

See James S. Alexander, Jackson, MS, to Wife & Children, June 21, 1863, Alexander Collection, AU; Black Diary, Jan. 13, 1865, Virginia Military Institute, Lexington, VA; Cash and Howorth, *My Dear Nellie*, 107, 117, 202, 205; D. R. Childers, Chattanooga, TN, to J. W. Palmer, July 22, 1863, Wood Papers, UGA; Marion Coiner, Camp, to Sister, Mar. 20, 1864, Coiner Family Papers, VHS; R. E. Corry, Okolona, MS, to Lizzie, Nov. 25, 1864, Corry, Columbus, MS, to Wife, July 25, 27, 1864, Corry Confederate Collection, AU; J. M. Davidson, Knoxville, TN, to Julia, June 14, 1862, Davidson Papers, ADAH; S. W. Farrow, Camp Macgruder, LA, to Josephine, Jan. 13, 17, 1865, Farrow Papers, CAH-UT; Green Diary, 35, SHC-UNC; Hubbell, *Confederate Stamps*, 4; A. G. Jones, Garysburg, NC, to Ellick, Oct. 9, 1862, Jones Family Papers, SHC-UNC; Fleming Jordan, Goldsboro, NC, to Father, Apr. 12, 1862, and Jordan, Chattahoochee, GA, to Wife, July 6, 1864, Jordan Letters, UGA; Kauffman Diary, May 2, 1862, SHC-UNC; Kennedy Diary, 26, 41, 44, SHC-UNC; Miles M. Lewis, Guinea Station, VA, to Amy M. Lewis, June 2, 1863, Miles W. Lewis Papers, CWMC, USAMHI; McLaughlin, *Cherished Letters*, 31; Mellon, "Florida Soldier," 254; W. Y. Mordecai, Culpeper Court House, VA, to Mother, Oct. 20, 1863, Mordecai Papers, VHS; Osborn, "Civil War Letters," 147–48; W. J. Peel, McCullough, AR, to Father, Mar. 21, 1862, Peel Papers, UAR; Rice Diary, June 11, 1863, CAH-UT; J. B. Rounsaville, Monticello, AR, to Mattie, Sept. 25, 1864, Rounsaville Letters, CWMC, USAMHI; W. J. J. Webb, n.p., to Father, July 7, 1863, Webb Letters, Leigh, USAMHI; Wallace Diary, 40, 50, SHC-UNC; Robert A. Williams, Chattanooga, TN, to Mittie Williams, July 25, 1863, Williams Letters, ADAH; Wynne and Taylor, *This War So Horrible*, 104, 106, 107.

72 J. H. Lee, Camp College, AL, to Wife, June 14, 1862, Lee Papers MSS 69, EU.

73 R. E. Corry, Okolona, MS, to Lizzie, Nov. 25, 1863, Corry Confederate Collection, AU.

74 R. M. Head, Knoxville, TN, to Friend, Dec. 9, 1862, Comer Family Papers, SHC-UNC.

75 Phillips, *Diehard Confederates*, 116–46.

76 For the Trans-Mississippi, see J. C. Brightman, Velasco, TX, to Brother and Sister,

Jan. 1, 1863, Brightman Papers, CAH-UT; William P. Head, Alexandria, LA, to Wife, Oct. 12, 1862, and Head, Camden, AR, to Wife, Oct. 17, 1864, Head Papers, CAH-UT; J. B. Rounsaville, Monticello, AR, to Mattie, Sept. 25, 1864, Rounsaville Letters, CWMC, USAMHI; Wiley, *"This Infernal War,"* 103–4, 105, 107, 110, 1123, 153, 161, 162, 169, 170, 198, 227, 262, 289, 334, 336, 339, 342, 347, 375, 394, 401, 402, 427. For the West, see Cash and Howorth, *My Dear Nellie*, 53, 69, 71, 77, 79, 85, 87, 92, 111–16, 121, 136, 157, 164, 173, 174, 180, 191; William D. Clover, Sullivan Co., TN, to Wife, Sept. 8, 1862, and Clover, Camp Zollicoffer, to Wife, Oct. 16, Dec. 19, 1862, N. J. Clover Letters, Book, Leigh, USAMHI; Lear Diary, May 6, 14, 16, 17, 19, 20, 21, 29, July 22, Oct. 5, 13, 15, 17, 1864, EU; Ryan, "Letters of Cochrane," pt. 2, 63; W. R. Sivley, Camp Mellon, to Sister, July 3, 1862, and Sivley, Demopolis, AL, to Sister, Feb. 25, 1864, Sivley Papers, SHC-UNC. Lear was a prisoner at the time of his writing.

77 Park, *Civil War Letters*, Mar. 1, Aug. 13, 1863.

78 Isaac Walters, Petersburg, VA, to Wife, May 31, 1862, Costen Papers, SHC-UNC; Thomas J. Moore, Nottoway River, VA, to Thomas W. Hill, July 16, 1864, Moore Papers, USC. See also Alexander Diary, vol. 2, 95, SHC-UNC; W. Y. Mordecai, Bunker Hill, VA, to Mother, Oct. 19, 1862, Mordecai Papers, VHS; Hubbs, *Voices*, 211; Moseley, *Stilwell Letters*, 193, 263, 270; Horace Wade, Stony Creek Station, VA, to Sister, July 3, 16, 1864, Wade Letters, Leigh, USAMHI; Samuel Wilson, Petersburg, VA, to Mother and Sister, July 24, 1864, Wilson Letters, Leigh, USAMHI.

79 Cecil-Fronsman, *Common Whites*; Reid Mitchell, *Civil War Soldiers*, 64–71.

CHAPTER 8

1 Wynne and Taylor, *This War So Horrible*, xi–xvii, 1–21, 42–44 (quotations 43, 44).

2 Wiley, *Life of Johnny Reb*, 123–50.

3 Linderman, *Embattled Courage*, 113–265. See also Logue, *To Appomattox and Beyond*, 78–81.

4 Martin, *Desertion of Alabama Troops*; Weitz, *Higher Duty*; Weitz, *More Damning than Slaughter*. See also Glatthaar, *General Lee's Army*, 408–20.

5 Reid Mitchell, *Civil War Soldiers*, 157–83; Manning, *This Cruel War*, 199–212; Phillips, *Diehard Rebels*, 77, 149–76; Sheehan-Dean, *Why Confederates Fought*, 91–96, 145–47, 180–87. See also Glatthaar, *General Lee's Army*, 410–12; Jimerson, *Private Civil War*, 226–37; Lisa Laskin, " 'Not Near So Much Demoralized,' " 91–111; Robertson, *Soldiers Blue and Gray*, 80.

6 McPherson, *For Cause and Comrades*, 138–39, 141, 162, 167–78, 186 (quotations 168, 138);

7 William A. Collins, Camp Mangum, NC, to Father, Mar. 27, 1862, Collins Papers, SHC-UNC.

8 Thomas J. Elliot, Norfolk, VA, to Wife, Apr. 19, 1862, Elliott Papers, Duke; Sanders, "Letters of a Soldier," 1234.

9 Ryan, "Letters of Cochrane," pt. 1, 292.

10 Wiley, *"This Infernal War,"* 40–41; Robert Bates, Henrico, Co., VA, to Wife, May 20, 1862, Bates Letter, Leigh, USAMHI; H. W. Robinson, Cumberland Gap, TN, to

Wife, June 7, 1862, Robinson Papers, EU; E. B. Coggin, Virginia, to Wife, July 23, 1862, Coggin Papers SPR 419, ADAH; A. L. Galloway, Lauderdale Springs, MS, to Wife, Aug. 13, 1862, Galloway Letters, AU; Kauffman Diary, Aug. 19, 1862, SHC-UNC; Moseley, *Stilwell Letters*, 27; E. A. Penick, Richmond, VA, to Wife, Aug. 5, 1862, Penick Papers, VHS.

11 Wiley, *"This Infernal War,"* 32, 34, 51, 55, 60, 70, 77 (quotation 34).

12 G. H. Burns, Camp McDonald, GA, to Wife, June 1, 1862, Burns Letters, CNMP.

13 Cash and Howorth, *My Dear Nellie*, 70.

14 John Thurman, Corinth, MS, to Wife, Apr. 16, 1862, Thurman Papers, SHC-UNC. See also John Crittenden, Saltillo, MS, to Bettie, July 20, 1862, Crittenden Papers, AU. Griffith, *Yours Till Death*, 10; Moseley, *Stilwell Letters*, 55, 83.

15 E. B. Coggin, Petersburg, VA, to Wife, June 20, 1862, Coggin Papers, ADAH. Coggin expressed similar thoughts in letters dated July 20 and July 23, 1862.

16 S. W. Farrow, Camp Waterhouse, TX, to Josephine, July 3, 1862, Farrow Papers, CAH-UT.

17 Moseley, *Stilwell Letters*, 12.

18 G. H. Burns, Clinton, TN, to Wife, Aug. 9, 1862, Burns Letters, CNMP. See also John Crittenden, Harrison's Ferry, TN, to Bettie, Aug. 24, 1864, Crittenden Papers, AU.

19 Osborn, "Civil War Letters," 146–49, (quotation 148).

20 Moseley, *Stilwell Letters*, 47, 83, 84, 85–86. See also Blomquist and Taylor, *This Cruel War*, 105; G. H. Burns, Vicksburg, MS, to Wife, Feb. 10, Apr. 2, 17, 1863, Burns Letters, CNMP; Durkin, *John Dooley*, 34–35; Hartley and Zimmerman, *Fighting 57th*, 22.

21 Cash and Howorth, *My Dear Nellie*, 99, 103, 105. See also John Crittenden, Loachapoka, AL, to Bettie, May 17, 1862, and Crittenden, Tupelo, MS, to Bettie, July 5, 1862, Crittenden Papers, AU; A. L. Galloway, Tupelo, MS, to Eliza, July 5, 1862, Galloway Letters, AU; Wiley, *"This Infernal War,"* 179–81, 189.

22 John H. Hundley, Richmond, VA, to Wife, Dec. 24, 1862, Hundley Family Papers, SHC-UNC.

23 John S. Meriwether, Columbus, MS, to Alice, Dec. 21, 1862, Meriwether Papers, EU.

24 Griffith, *Yours Till Death*, 43, 56.

25 McLaughlin, *Cherished Letters*, 33; A. M. Sewell, Vicksburg, MS, to Louisa, Feb. 4, 1863, Sewell Correspondence, EU.

26 C. D. Sides, Fredericksburg, VA, to Wife, Feb. 10, 19, 1863, Sides Letters, CWMC, USAMHI.

27 D. W. Chenault, Albany, KY, to Brother, Mar. 11, 1863, Chenault Letters, CWMC, USAMHI; W. M. Clover, Greenville, TN, to Ann, May 11, 1863, Clover Letters, Leigh, USAMHI; John Crittenden, Murfreesboro, TN, to Bettie, Dec. 20, 29, 1862, Crittenden Papers, AU; J. A. Frierson, Cotile, LA, to Ma, Apr. 18, 1863, Frierson Correspondence, Mss 4209, LSU; Griffith, *Yours Till Death*, 36, 38–39, 47; William J. Hart, n.p., to Mother and Father, May 19, 1863, Hart Brothers Letters, CWMC, USAMHI; Hartley and Zimmerman, *Fighting 57th*, 47, 57, 58; Hatley and Huffman, *Letters of Wagner*, 37; John H. Hundley, Gordonsville, VA, to Sally Hund-

ley, Sept. 16, 30, 1862, Hundley Family Papers, SHC-UNC; J. T. Knight, Little Rock, AR, to Susan Knight, Jan. 3, 1863, and Knight, Pine Bluff, AR, to Susan Knight, Jan. 31, 1863, Knight Letters, CCCWC, TSLA; McLaughlin, *Cherished Letters*, 28; McMurtrey, *Letters to Lucinda*, 5, 13–14; Enoch L. Mitchell, "Letters of Newberry," 51; Pate, *This Evil War*, 119; J. A. Patton, n.p., to Wife, Oct. 7, 1862, Patton Letters, EU; A. M. Sewell, Bluntsville, to Louisa, Jan. 20, Feb. 22, Mar. 28, 1863, Sewell Correspondence MSS 340 (microfilm), EU; E. W. Treadwell, Shelbyville, TN, to Mattie, Apr. 5, 1863, Treadwell Letters, ADAH; John William Watson, n.p., to Wife, Oct. 5, 1862, Watson Family Papers, VHS; Glatthaar, *General Lee's Army*, 412.

28 William D. Clover, Camp Zollicoffer, TN, to Brother, Dec. 19, 1862, and Clover, Camp Zollicoffer, TN, to Ann, Dec. 27, 1862, Clover Letters, USAMHI.

29 T. J. Rounsaville, Pine Bluff, AR, to Niece, Feb. 23, 1863, Rounsaville Letters, CWMC, USAMHI.

30 J. T. Knight, Pine Bluff, AR, to Susan Knight, Mar. 10, 14, 1863, Knight Letters, CCCWC, TSLA.

31 Park, *Civil War Letters*, Sept. 30, Oct. 1, Nov. 4, 1862. See also M. Hart, Port Hudson, LA, to Nehemiah Williams, Nov. 10, 1862, Hart Letter, CMM, LSU; F. Niebuhr, Rocky Ford, to Parents, and Brothers and Sisters, Nov. 21, 1862, Niebuhr Papers, CAH-UT.

32 J. A. Wilson, Camp Rogers, MS, to Lizzie, Nov. 4, 1862, Wilson Letters, MDAH.

33 G. H. Burns, Murfreesboro, TN, to Wife, Dec. 23, 1862, Burns, Vicksburg, MS, to Wife, Mar. 12, 1863, and Burns, n.p., to Wife, May 2, 1863, Burns Letters, CNMP; John Crittenden, Murfreesboro, TN, to Bettie, Dec. 20, 1862, Crittenden Papers, AU; Durkin, *John Dooley*, 83; J. A. Frierson, Cotile, LA, to Ma, Apr. 18, 1863, Frierson Correspondence, LSU; M. Gillis, Charleston, SC, to Neil, Feb. 16, 1863, Gillis Family Papers, EU; Griffith, *Yours Till Death*, 47, 56, 65; John S. Meriwether, Vicksburg, VA, to Alice, Mar. 6, 1863, Meriwether Papers, EU; Henry Mowrer, Lenoir Co., NC, to Wife, may 15, 1863, Mowrer Papers, CWMC, USAMHI; Northen, *All Right Let Them Come*, 65; A. M. Sewell, Bluntsville, MS, to Louisa, Mar. 28, 1863, Sewell Correspondence, EU. Thomas Warrick, Tennessee, to Wife, Dec. 15, 1862, Warrick Papers, ADAH; A. G. Jones, Kinston, NC, to Ellick, Jan. 10, 1863, Jones Family Papers, SHC-UNC; Wiley, *"This Infernal War,"* 40–41.

34 T. J. Rounsaville, Pine Bluff, AR, to Mother & Sisters, Mar. 22, 1863, Rounsaville Letters, CWMC, USAMHI.

35 S. W. Farrow, Camp Wright, AR, to Josephine, Mar. 13, 1863, Farrow Papers, CAH-UT.

36 C. D. Sides, Fredericksburg, VA, to Wife, Feb. 10, 1863, Sides Letters, CWMC, USAMHI.

37 Blair Diary, Jan. 13–Feb. 1, 1863, TSLA; Blomquist and Taylor, *This Cruel War*, 162, 167, 175, 179, 180; J. C. Brightman, Velasco, TX, to Brother and Sister, Jan. 1, 1863, Brightman Papers, CAH-UT; Bluford Cameron Diary, May 30, 1863, Cameron Papers, CAH-UT; Cash and Howorth, *My Dear Nellie*, 107; Cawthon, "Letters of a Private," 540; Marcus Bearden DeWitt Diary, May 26, 1863, CCCWC, TSLA; Miles M. Lewis, Guinea Station, VA, to A. M. Lewis, Mar. 21, 23, Apr. 6, 1863,

Miles W. Lewis Papers, CWMC, USAMHI; Thrush H. Massey, Charleston, SC, to Brother, Mar. 9, 1863, Williams Correspondence, SHC-UNC; Moseley, *Stilwell Letters*, 99; A. M. Sewell, Vicksburg, MS, to Louisa, Feb. 4, 22, 1863, Sewell Correspondence, EU; Isaac Walters, Drewery's Bluff, VA, to Wife, Nov. 16, 1862, Costen Papers, SHC-UNC; Wiley, *"This Infernal War,"* 185, 193, 198, 199, 206, 207, 211–12, 215, 220–21, 223, 224, 227, 233, 238, 242, 251, 254; J. A. Wilson, Vicksburg, MS, to Lizzie, Feb., 1862, Wilson Letters, MDAH; Phillips, *Diehard Rebels*, 116–121.

38 Johnston, "Letters of Barnes," 81; C. D. Epps, Decatur, GA, to Wife, May 6, 1863, and Epps, Cumberland Gap, TN, to Wife, June 7, 1863, Epps Papers, SHC-UNC; M. R. Norman, Saltville, NC, to Father and Polly, June 11, 1863, Tiedeken Papers, VHS.

39 Griffith, *Yours Till Death*, 65.

40 Cash and Howorth, *My Dear Nellie*, 109. See also Mays, *Let Us Meet in Heaven*, 71, 80; Wiley, *"This Infernal War,"* 252, 256–67.

41 Albright Diary, May 11, July 5, 18, 1863, VHS; William D. Clover, Cumberland Gap, TN, to Ann, July 26, 1863, Clover Letters, Leigh, USAMHI; William Duncan Cole, Chattanooga, TN, to Cornelia, July 28, 1863, Cole Letters, CWMC, USAMHI; Lowe and Hodges, *Letters to Amanda*, 69; Mays, *Let Us Meet in Heaven*, 122; Moseley, *Stilwell Letters*, 171, 189–90; Wiley, *"This Infernal War,"* 262, 266; Glatthaar, *General Lee's Army*, 283–85. One also should note J. C. Williams, Thunderbolt, GA, to Wife, July 12, 1863, Williams Papers, AU. For Williams, expectations of the fall of Charleston began to convince him that the Confederacy could not win the war.

42 J. R. Manson, Culpeper Court House, VA, to Mother, July 30, 1863, Manson Diary and Letters, CWMC, USAMHI. See also E. B. Coggin, Culpeper Court House, VA, to Wife, July 27, 1863, Coggin Papers, ADAH; J. F. Coghill, Orange Court House, VA, to Pappy, Ma and Mit, Aug. 10, 1863, Coghill Letters, SHC-UNC; Green Diary, 14–17, SHC-UNC; Hartley and Zimmerman, *Fighting 57th*, 128, 137, 139, 140, 141, 142, 143, 145, 149; Hatley and Huffman, *Letters of Wagner*, 57, 60, 63, 65, 67, 76; Hubbs, *Voices*, 194, 199; A. G. Jones, Stevensburg, VA, to Parents, Aug. 21, 1863, Jones Family Papers, SHC-UNC; Glatthaar, *General Lee's Army*, 412–13.

43 William P. Cline, Goldsboro, NC, to Mary C. Cline, May 24, 1862, Cline, Richmond, VA, to Mary C. Cline, June 3, 1862, Cline, Petersburg, VA, to Mary C. Cline, Aug. 10, 1862, Cline, Richmond, VA, to Mary C. Cline, June 9, 1863, Cline, Fredericksburg, VA, to Mary C. Cline, Aug. 7, 15, 1863, Cline Papers, SHC-UNC.

44 J. B. Sanders, Vicksburg, MS, to Elisabeth Sanders, July 14, 1863, Sanders Papers, MDAH.

45 Phillips, *Diehard Rebels*, 118–19; J. B. Rounsaville, Monroe, LA, to Family, June 9, 1863, Rounsaville Letters, CWMC, USAMHI. See also J. T. Knight, Raleigh, LA, to Susan Knight, July 11, 1863, and Knight, Camta, LA, to Susan, Aug. 1, 1863, Knight Letters, CCCWC, TSLA; Wallace Diary, 33–34, SHC-UNC; Wiley, *"This Infernal War,"* 286, 290, 294, 300, 313.

46 J. C. Brightman, New Iberia, LA, to Brother, July 18, 1863, Brightman Papers, CAH-UT.

47 S. W. Farrow, Dehli, LA, to Josephine, July 11, 1863, Farrow, Monroe, LA, to Josephine, July 17, 1863, Farrow, Bluff Springs, AR, to Josephine, July 19, 1863, Farrow,

Natchitoches, LA, to Josephine, July 30, 1863, and Farrow, Alexandria, LA, to Josephine, Aug. 6, 1863, Farrow Papers, CAH-UT.

48 J. T. Knight, Clear Creek, LA, to Susan Knight, Aug. 1, 15, 1863, Knight Letters, CCCWC, TSLA.

49 William Duncan Cole, Chattanooga, TN, to Cornelia, July 28, 1863, Cole Letters, CWMC, USAMHI. See also Cash and Howorth, *My Dear Nellie*, 116, 117; J. M. Davidson, Jackson, MS, to Julia, July 9, 1863, and Davidson, Morton Station, MS, to Julia, July 22, 1863, Davidson Papers, EU; Jesse C. Knight, Winchester, VA, to Wife, Sept. 16, 1862, Knight Family Papers, UGA; Moseley, *Stilwell Letters*, 188, 189; Ryan, "Letters of Cochrane," pt. 5, 277.

50 A. J. Edge, Enterprise, MS, to Wife, July 10, 1863, Edge Papers, EU.

51 Phillips, *Diehard Rebels*, 119–21; J. C. Brightman, St. Landry's Parish, LA, to Brother, Aug. 23, 1863, Brightman Papers, CAH-UT; A. E. Shore, Lexington, VA, to Wife & Children & Mother, Aug. 7, 1863, Shore Letters, EU; Kennedy Diary, 17, 39, 40, 41, 47–48, 49, 56, 58, SHC-UNC. See also Newt Bosworth, Camp, to Friends, Sept. 8, 1863, Bosworth Family Collection, Leigh, USAMHI; J. M. Davidson, Meridian, MS, to Julia, Aug. 24, 1863, Davidson Papers, EU; S. W. Farrow, Big Cane, LA, to Josephine, Oct. 8, 1863, Farrow Papers, CAH-UT; Grantham, "Letters from Hightower," 184–85; Griffith, *Yours Till Death*, 80, 83; Hubbs, *Voices*, 194; Johnston, "Letters of Barnes," 84–86; A. G. Jones, Camp Racoon Ford, VA, to Father, Sept. 11, 1863, Jones Family Papers, SHC-UNC; J. D. Joyner, Camp, to Mother, Sept. 26, 1863, and Joyner, Berkeley Co., VA, to Mother, Oct. 11, 1862, Joyner Family Papers, SHC-UNC; J. T. Knight, Clear Creek, LA, to Susan Knight, Aug. 15, 1863, Knight Letters, CCCWC, TSLA; McMurtrey, *Letters to Lucinda*, 33, 35; Moseley, *Stilwell Letters*, 215; Michael Nihill, Chattanooga, TN, to Mother, July 25, 1863, Prime Collection, CWMC, USAMHI; Wiley, *"This Infernal War,"* 313, 323, 332.

52 Moseley, *Stilwell Letters*, 201–3, 204 (quotation 201).

53 William Duncan Cole, Burchard, TN, to Wife, Aug. 28, 1863, Cole Letters, CWMC, USAMHI.

54 Blomquist and Taylor, *This Cruel War*, 186.

55 Abel H. [Crawford], Pollard, AL, to Dora Potts, Oct. 25, 1863, Crawford Letters, CCCWC, TSLA.

56 Ben Robertson, Dalton, GA, to Sister, Jan. 8, 1864, Robertson Papers, MDAH.

57 Robert Emmet Corry, n.p., to Wife, Nov. 17, 1863, Corry Confederate Collection, AU.

58 Holland, *Keep All My Letters*, 109–15; Wallace Diary, 50, 71, SHC-UNC. Wallace reported a similar mutiny the following June. See also A. J. Edge, Dalton, GA, to Wife, Feb. 15, 1864, Edge Papers, EU.

59 Willie Sivley, Demopolis, AL, to Jennie Sivley, Feb. 20, 1864, Sivley Papers, SHC-UNC. See also Cash and Howorth, *My Dear Nellie*, 157–58.

60 S. W. Farrow, Camp, to Josephine, Mar. 29, 1864, Farrow Papers, CAH-UT.

61 A. H. Massey, Petersburg, VA, to Sister, Apr. 28, 1864, Williams Correspondence, SHC-UNC. The exception was Pvt. James Pickens of the 5th Alabama. See Hubbs, *Voices*, 234, 235, 237.

62 Hatley and Huffman, *Letters of Wagner*, 57, 63, 65, 68 (quotation 65).

63 Blomquist and Taylor, *This Cruel War*, 186, 204, 213, 222.

64 Glatthaar found desertion rates in the Army of Northern Virginia that remained high until September 1864, see *General Lee's Army*, 416–17.

65 William A. Stephens, Dalton, GA, to Susan, May 7, 1864, Stephens Papers MSS 324, EU; Albright Diary, Dec. 15, 1863, Jan. 22, 1864, VHS; Blomquist and Taylor, *This Cruel War*, 185, 188, 195, 198, 321, 328–29; Cash and Howorth, *My Dear Nellie*, 103; Cate, *Two Soldiers*, 8–9, 24, 72, 80, 201; Abel Crawford, Petersburg, VA, to Dora, Feb. 20, 1864, Crawford Letters, CCWC, TSLA; John Crittenden, Dalton, GA, to Bettie, Mar. 12, 20, 1864, Crittenden Papers, AU; J. P. Culp, Camp, to Father, Apr. 28, 1864, J. P. Culp Letters, Duke; S. W. Farrow, Linesport, LA, to Josephine, Jan. 18, 1864, Farrow Papers, CAH-UT; E. K. Flournoy, Chickamauga, GA, to Wife, Nov. 1, 1863, Flournoy Letters, ADAH; Theophilis Frank, Orange Court House, VA, to Wife, Jan. 27, 1864, Frank Family Letters, SHC-UNC; Green Diary, 23, SHC-UNC; Griffith, *Yours Till Death*, 80, 83, 94, 98, 102, 103, 105; Jones Diary, 2, Jones Family Papers, SHC-UNC; J. T. Knight, Marksville, LA, to Susan Knight, Jan. 21, 1864, Knight Letters, CCCWMC, TSLA; Lowe and Hodges, *Letters to Amanda*, 109, 196; A. H. Massey, Ivor Station, VA, to Brother, Feb. 6, 1864, Williams Correspondence, SHC-UNC; Thrush H. Massey, Ivor Station, VA, to Brother, Feb. 23, 1864, and Massey, Petersburg, VA, to Brother, Apr. 13, 1864, Williams Correspondence, SHC-UNC; Mays, *Let Us Meet In Heaven*, 156–157; McLaughlin, *Letters of Hendricks*, 68–69; Mellon, "Florida Soldier," 259, 263; Enoch L. Mitchell, "Letters of Newberry," Jan. 21, 1864; Moseley, *Stilwell Letters*, 224, W. H. Robertson, Yazoo City, MS, to Sisters, Apr. 13, [1864?], Robertson Papers, MDAH; J. B. Sanders, Pollard, AL, to Elisabeth Sanders, Feb. 11, 18, 1864, and Sanders, Rome, GA, to Elisabeth Sanders, Apr. 28, 1864, Sanders Papers, MDAH; A. M. Sewell, Dalton, GA, to Louisa, Dec. 21, 1863, Sewell Correspondence, EU; J. G. Smith, Stickneyville, VA, to n.p., Apr. 2, 1864, Smith Letter, Leigh, USAMHI; Edgar Smithwick, Charleston, SC, to Mother, Apr. 16, 1864, Smithwick Papers, Duke; C. D. Sides, Taylorsville, VA, to Wife, Feb. 28, 1864, Sides Letters, CWMC, USAMHI; W. R. Sivley, Shurbuta, MS, to Janie, Dec. 1, 1863, and Sivley, Camp, to Janie, Jan. 27, 1864, Sivley Papers, SHC-UNC; O. V. Strickland, Dalton, GA, to Mother, Dec. 18, 1863, Strickland Papers, EU; Wilbur Thompson, Dalton, GA, to Wife and Children, Mar. 6, 1864, Thompson Letters, Duke; Wallace Diary, 56–57, SHC-UNC; Glatthaar, *General Lee's Army*, 357–59; Wiley, *"This Infernal War,"* 338, 356–57, 362, 369, 383–85, 394.

66 A. E. Shore, Lexington, VA, to Wife & Children & Mother, Feb. 26, 1864, E. H. Shore and E. D. Kiger, Liberty Mills, VA, to Mother and Sister, Mar. 12, 1864, and A. E. Shore, Richmond, VA, to Brother, July 7, 1864, Shore Letters, EU; Hubbs, *Voices*, 255, 263, 267, 269, 273, 279, 291. For a handful of exceptions, see Blomquist and Taylor, *This Cruel War*, 268–69, 275; Cate, *Two Soldiers*, 89, 128–29; J. M. Davidson, Cooper's Iron Works, GA, to Julia, May 21, 1864, and Davidson, Dallas, GA, to Julia, June 4, 1864, Davidson Papers, EU; Davis Diary, Sept. 6, 9, 25, 1864, VHS; F. M. Goodwin, Campbellton, GA, to Susan, July 13, 1864, F. M. Goodwin Confederate Letter, UGA; Griffith, *Yours Till Death*, 107, 113; Fleming Jordan, Army

of Tennessee, to Wife, July 12, 1864, Jordan Letters, UGA; Thrush H. Massey, Petersburg, VA, to Sister, July 13, 1864, Williams Correspondence #4424, SHC-UNC; McLaughlin, *Cherished Letters*, 77; A. J. Newell, Moulton, AL, to Mother, May 5, 1864, Newell Family Papers RG 681, AU; Ben Robertson, Etowah River, GA, to Sister, May 22, 1864, and Robertson, Atlanta, GA, to Sister, July 23, 1864, Robertson Papers, MDAH; J. W. Tindall, Richmond, VA, to Wife, June 7, 13, 1864, Tindall Papers, USC.

67 Ben Robertson, Lovejoy Station, GA, to Sister, Sept. 7, 1864, Robertson Papers, MDAH. See also Cash and Howorth, *My Dear Nellie*, 202–3, 206, 208; Cate, *Two Soldiers*, 128–29; J. M. Davidson, Columbus, GA, to Julia, Sept. 21, 1864, Davidson Papers, EU; John Thurman, West Point, GA, to Wife, Sept. 7, 1864, Thurman Papers, SHC-UNC.

68 Lanning Diary, 5, ADAH. For similar reactions, see Cash and Howorth, *My Dear Nellie*, 213.

69 Alexander Diary, vol. 2, 49, 59, 77, 86, 93, SHC-UNC; Cash and Howorth, *My Dear Nellie*, 203, 208, 210, 211, 218, 219; Cate, *Two Soldiers*, 130, 136; Davis Diary, Sept. 6, 1864, VHS; William R. Hughes, Petersburg, VA, to Wilson P. Pool, Aug. 16, 1864, Hughes Letters, UAL; Charles M. Hurley, Petersburg, VA, to Louise, Nov. 8, 1864, Hurley Letters, CWMC, USAMHI; Johnston, "Vinson Letters," 110; J. L. J. Lear Diary, Aug. 12, 25, 1864, Lear Diary, EU; J. B. Rounsaville, Monticello, AR, to Mattie, Sept. 25, 1864, Rounsaville Letters, CWMC, USAMHI; Wiley, *"This Infernal War,"* 399.

70 Ashley, *Oh for Dixie!*, 86; Madison Kilpatrick, Griffin, GA, to Wife, Oct. 28, 1864, Kilpatrick Letters, AU; Lanning Diary, 8, ADAH; John Putnam, Sullivan's Island, SC, to Nancy, Nov. 13, Dec. 15, 1864, Putnam Papers, USC; H. R. Rogers, Florence, AL, to Tabitha, Nov. 13, 1864, and Rodgers, Columbia, TN, to Tabitha, Nov. 26, 1864, Rodgers Letters, CWMC, USAMHI.

71 Alexander Diary, vol. 2, 119, SHC-UNC; Griffith, *Yours Till Death*, 125–26 (quotation 125). See also Cate, *Two Soldiers*, 170; W. R. Sivley, New Okolona, MS, to Sister, Jan. 9, 1865, Sivley Papers, SHC-UNC.

72 Cawthon, "Letters of a Private," 545.

73 Albright Diary, Feb. 4, 1865, VHS; Blomquist and Taylor, *This Cruel War*, 319; T. L. Camp, Camp, to n.p., Mar. 2, 1865, Camp Family Papers, EU; Cate, *Two Soldiers*, 147, 202, 204; Marion Coiner, Headquarters, to Sister, Feb. 6, 23, 1865, Coiner Family Papers, VHS; R. E. Corry, Pontotoc, MS, to Wife, Nov. 20, 1864, and Corry, Greensboro, AL, to Wife, Apr. 19, 1865, Robert Emmet Corry Confederate Collection, AU; John Crittenden, n.p., to Bettie, Nov. 3, 1864, Crittenden Papers, AU; Davis Diary, Dec. 24, 25, 1864, VHS; John P. Dull, New Market, VA, to Giney, Dec. 1, 1864, Dull Letters, VS; W. T. Fentress, Appomattox Court House, VA, to Provost Marshall, Nov. 1, 1864, Aylett Family Papers, VHS; Hartley and Zimmerman, *Fighting 57th*, 322; Hubbs, *Voices*, 344, 349, 353, 357, 362; James B. Jones, Camp Pegram, VA, to Grandma, Feb. 16, 1865, Jones Family Papers, SHC-UNC; Fleming Jordan, Lovejoy Station GA, to Wife, Nov. 1, 1864, Jordan Letters, UGA; McLaughlin, *Cherished Letters*, 83; R. E. Mobley, Petersburg, VA, to Bettie, Jan. 1, Feb. 4, 1865,

Mobley Diary and Letters, Leigh, USAMHI; Henry Neal, Chester Station, VA, to Wife, Feb. 5, 1865, Neal Papers, VHS; [Albert R. Phillips], Petersburg, VA, to Mr. Dabney, Mr. Phillips, Jan. 27, 1865, Phillips Papers, Duke; John Putnam, Sullivan's Island, SC, to Wife and Children, Dec. 24, 27, 1864, Putnam Papers, USC; W. R. Sivley, New Okolona, MS, to Sister, Jan. 9, 1865, Sivley Papers, SHC-UNC; D. C. Snyder, Swope's Depot, VA, to Wife, Feb. 13, 1865, Snyder Papers, VHS; John Thurman, Okalona, MS, to Sallie, Jan. 8, 1865, Thurman, Huston, MS, to Sallie, Jan. 14, 1865, and Thurman, n.p., to Wife, Mar. 6, 1865, Thurman Papers, SHC-UNC; Amon W. Updike, Chesterfield Co., VA, to Sister, Jan. 17, 1865, and Updike, Henrico Co., VA, to Sister, Mar. 20, 1865, Updike Letters, CWMC, USAMHI; Wallace Diary, 83, 84, SHC-UNC; Wiley, "This Infernal War," 442–46.

74 W. R. Sivley, Raymond, MS, to Sister, Feb. 8, 1865, Sivley Papers, SHC-UNC. See also John Crittenden, Gadsden, AL, to Bettie, Oct. 22, 1864, Crittenden Papers, AU.

75 Cate, *Two Soldiers*, 200.

76 F. A. Bleckley, Thomas Station, GA, to Sarah, Mar. 29, 1865, Bleckley Letters, Leigh, USAMHI.

77 L. R. Dalton, Chester Dist., SC, to Par, Apr. 6, 1865, Dalton Letters, Leigh, USAMHI; Green Diary, 53, SHC-UNC; Kees (Martin Van Buren) Diary, 51–54, MDAH; Alexander Diary, vol. 2, 136, SHC-UNC; W. H. Robertson, Gainesville, AL, to Sisters, May 10, 1865, Robertson Papers, MDAH. See also Hubbs, *Voices*, 344, 345.

78 Tom Grisham, New [?], GA, to Friend, May 8, 1865, Grisham Letter, Leigh, USAMHI.

79 Lee Faulkner, Galveston, TX, to Wife. May 7, 1865, Faulkner and Wilson Papers, CAH-UT.

CHAPTER 9

1 Durkin, *John Dooley* 17–19 (quotation 18).

2 Ibid., 20–22 (quotations 21, 22).

3 Ibid., 22–24 (quotation 23).

4 Ibid., 24–25, 33–38 (quotation 37–38).

5 Ibid., 38–42, 44–48 (quotations 46–47).

6 Lynn, *Bayonets of the Republic*, 35–36; McPherson, *For Cause and Comrades*, 12.

7 Wiley, *Life of Johnny Reb*, 28–35, 68–81; Robertson, *Soldiers Blue and Gray*, 214–28.

8 Linderman, *Embattled Courage*, 17–33, 61–79, 124–33, 139–68, 240–65.

9 Reid Mitchell, *Civil War Soldiers*, 54–83; Reid Mitchell, *Vacant Chair*, 27–28.

10 McPherson, *For Cause and Comrades*, 30–45, 168–78; Hess, *Union Soldier in Battle*, esp. ix–xii, 97–157, 191–98 (quotation 157); Glatthaar, *General Lee's Army*, esp. 320–33. Both Hess and McPherson criticize Linderman's use of published sources as well as his dismissal of ideology, and McPherson further describes *Embattled Courage* as "thesis-driven" (186). Hess meanwhile goes even farther in offering his work as a counterweight to "modern prejudices, ideological faddishness, and a desire for political correctness" (xi).

11 E. A. Penick, Yorktown, VA, to Mary, Apr. 14, 16, 21, 1862, Penick, Bethel Church, VA,

to Family, Apr. 19, 1862, Penick Papers, VHS. See also J. F. Coghill, n.p., to Mit, Apr. 16, 1862, Coghill Letters, SHC-UNC.

12 John Thurman, Monterey, MS, to Wife, Apr. 9, 1862, and Thurman, Corinth, MS, to Wife, Apr. 15, 1862, Thurman Papers, SHC-UNC.

13 William A. Collins, Petersburg, VA, to Father, June 3, 1862, Collins Papers, SHC-UNC. See also John Crittenden, Bardstown, KY, to Bettie, Sept. 28, 1862, Crittenden Papers, AU; Jimmie McCulloch, New Market, VA, to Wife, Aug. 8, 1862, McCulloch Letter, UGA.

14 John T. Beggs, n.p., to [Ginnie], n.d., Beggs and Janssen Family Papers, SHC-UNC. For a similar account from the same unit, Lathrop, "Confederate Artilleryman," 377–78. For a general discussion of such fears, see Hess, Union Soldier in Battle, 96–97; and Glatthaar, General Lee's Army, 320–21.

15 Lowe and Hodges, Letters to Amanda, 17–18, 24–28, 40 (quotation 27). See also L. J. Carneal, Martinsburg, VA, to Papa, Oct. 15, 1862, Carneal Papers, VHS.

16 Wiley, "This Infernal War," 148–52 (quotation 150–51).

17 Moseley, Stilwell Letters, 2, 4.

18 B. Wylie Scott, Stone Bridge, VA, to Ella Merryman, July 9, 1862, Merryman Papers, VHS.

19 I. M. Auld, Winchester, VA, to Mother, Sept. 22, 1862, Auld Letters, CWMC, USAMHI.

20 Examples of illness are nearly ubiquitous in the sources used for this work, but for extended and easily accessed accounts see Blomquist and Taylor, This Cruel War, 7, 12, 17, 19, 25, 33, 38–39, 46, 54, 59, 111, 114, 119, 123, 133, 139, 151, 153, 157, 213, 223, 229, 233, 237, 240, 248, 256, 295, 306, 309; Cash and Howorth, My Dear Nellie, 83, 89, 99, 182, 184, 223; Griffith, Yours Till Death, 5, 7, 11, 12, 14, 15, 23, 24, 29, 40; Lowe and Hodges, Letters to Amanda, 5, 6, 10, 12, 13, 15, 19, 21, 22, 58, 62, 73, 118, 152, 168, 204; McLaughlin, Cherished Letters, 36–38, 42–43, 45–48, 63–64; Moseley, Stilwell Letters, 21, 23, 28, 38, 56, 74, 173, 264, 271; Wiley, "This Infernal War," 28, 38, 49, 54, 60, 67, 70, 73, 82, 92, 101, 108, 113, 121, 128, 176, 181, 190, 211, 222, 319–20, 322, 325, 333, 340, 415. See also Bluford Alexander Cameron Diary, June 15–22, 25, July 4, 1863, Cameron Papers, CAH-UT; A. J. Edge, Marietta, GA, to Mother, Aug. 25, 1862, Edge Papers, EU; Green Diary, 1, 2, 5, 12, 25, 26, 37–39, SHC-UNC; W. J. Hart, n.p., to Father, June 19, 1862, Hart Brothers Letters, CWMC, USAMHI; Fleming Jordan, Atlanta, GA, to Wife, July 23, 1864, Jordan Letters, UGA; William S. Lacy, Ashland, VA, to Ma, June 27, 1862, Lacy Papers, SHC-UNC; Lanning Diary, 7–9, 11, 19, ADAH; A. T. Miller, Strawberry Plains, TN, to Friend and Nephew, July 15, 1863, Miller Family Papers, VHS. For "skulkers" and cowards, see Glatthaar, General Lee's Army, 63–64, 131, 141–42, 166–67, 323–34; Gordon, "I Never Was a Coward"; Hess, Union Soldier in Battle, 84–88; McPherson, For Cause and Comrades, 6–8, 35–36, 78–79, 80, 116.

21 Crow, Diary of a Confederate Soldier, 29; Hartley and Zimmerman, Fighting 57th, 43–44; Haynes, Field Diary, 4, 6; Lowe and Hodges, Letters to Amanda, 17–18; Edwin D. Tuttle, letter fragment, May 1862, Tuttle Letters, EU; Hess, Union Soldier

in Battle, 14–15, 91–93; McPherson, *For Cause and Comrades*, 39–42; Robertson, *Soldiers Blue and Gray*, 216.

22 H. W. Robinson, n.p., to n.p., [June 18, 1862], Robinson Papers, EU.

23 E. A. Penick, Bethel Church, VA, to Family, Apr. 19, 1862, and Penick, Bethel Church, VA, to Wife, Apr. 25, 1862, Penick Papers, VHS.

24 Kauffman Diary, May 8, 9, June 28, 1862, SHC-UNC.

25 James P. Garrison, n.p., to Wife, June 11, 1862, Garrison Papers, EU.

26 Hubbell, *Confederate Stamps*, 3–4 (quotation 3).

27 Grantham, "Letters from Hightower," 176. For a similar reaction, see J. C. Williams, Thunderbolt, GA, to Honry, Dec. 28, 1862, Williams Papers, AU.

28 Moseley, *Stilwell Letters*, 2, 7. See also Grantham, "Letters from Hightower," 178; Stephen M. Mathis, Louden, Tenn., to Father & Mother, Brothers, and Sisters, Nov. 16, 1862, Mathis Letter, CCCWC, TSLA; Hess, *Union Soldier in Battle*, 37–44; Noe, "Jigsaw Puzzles," 239–40.

29 Terrill and Dixon, *History of Stewart County*, 278.

30 Osborn, "Letters of Banks," 147; Wiley, *"This Infernal War,"* 151; Battle, *Civil War Letters*, 8–9; E. B. Coggin, Orange Co., VA, to Wife, Aug. 13, 1862, Coggin Papers, ADAH; Grantham, "Letters from Hightower," 177; Kauffman Diary, May 8, Aug. 9, 10, 1862 (quotation May 9), SHC-UNC; Terrill and Dixon, *History of Stewart County*, 283.

31 John French White, Virginia Side Potomac, to Wife, Sept. 20, 1862, White Papers, VHS.

32 Grantham, "Letters from Hightower," 177.

33 Lowe and Hodges, *Letters to Amanda*, 26.

34 Ibid., 43, 47; Moseley, *Stilwell Letters*, 89. See also Grantham, "Letters from Hightower," 180.

35 Thomas Warrick, Tennessee, to Wife, Jan. 11, 1863, and Warrick, Shelbyville, TN, to Wife, Jan. 13, 1863, Warrick Papers, ADAH. See also J. M. Davidson, Shelbyville, TN, to Julia, Jan. 13, 20, 1863, Davidson Papers, EU; McLaughlin, *Letters of Henderson*, 30. For other fights, see McMurtrey, *Letters to Lucinda*, 10 (Pound Gap, VA).

36 D. Farnsworth, Vicksburg, MS, to Brother, Dec. 28, 1862, Farnsworth Family Letters, CAH-UT; F. Niebuhr, Grenada, MS, to Parents and Brothers and Sisters, Dec. 25, 1862, Niebuhr Papers, CAH-UT; Cash and Howorth, *My Dear Nellie*, 97–99.

37 Cawthon, "Letters of a Private," 538–39; Blomquist and Taylor, *This Cruel War*, 146. See also Sanders, "Letters of a Soldier," 1237–38.

38 H. W. Robinson, Vicksburg, MS, to Wife, Jan. 2, 1863, Robinson Papers, EU. Robinson's "time" came three months later, but because of smallpox.

39 Blair Diary, Jan. 23, 1863, CCCWC, TSLA; D. Farnsworth, Vicksburg, MS, to Brother, Feb. 22, Mar. 22, Apr. 18, 1863, Farnsworth Family Letters, CAH-UT.

40 Rice Diary, May 17–22, 1863 (quotations May 19, May 22), CAH-UT.

41 Hubbell, *Confederate Stamps*, 8–9; I. M. Auld, Fredericksburg, VA, to Mother, Brothers and Sisters, May 8, 1863, Auld Letters, CWMC, USAMHI; Wiley, *Life of Johnny Reb*, 78–79.

42 Green Diary, 33, SHC-UNC.

43 W. J. J. Webb, Fredericksburg, VA, to Mother, May 23, 1863, Webb Letters, Leigh, USAMHI.

44 Moseley, *Stilwell Letters*, 151.

45 T. T. Hoskins, Culpeper, VA, to Papa, June 10, 1863, Hoskins Family Papers, VHS.

46 Green Diary, 9, SHC-UNC.

47 Moseley, *Stilwell Letters*, 184. See also J. F. Coghill, Williamsport, MD, to Pappy, Ma and Mit, July 9, 1863, Coghill Letters, SHC-UNC.

48 W. Y. Mordecai, Hagerstown, MD, to Mother, July 8, 1863, Mordecai Papers, VHS.

49 J. D. Joyner, Orange Court House, VA, to Mother, Aug. 12, 1863, Joyner Family Papers #4428, SHC-UNC. See also "'Aftermath of Gettysburg,'" http://www.mind spring.com/nixnox/english.html (accessed May 6, 2008).

50 Mellon, "Florida Soldier," 254–55.

51 Park, *Civil War Letters*, July 23, 1863.

52 Griffith, *Yours Till Death*, 71–72, 82–84 (quotation 84). See also William H. Barnes, Thibodeaux, LA, to Lizzie, June 26, 1863, Barnes Papers, CAH-UT; J. C. Brightman, St. Landry's Parish, LA, to Brother, Aug. 23, 1863, Brightman Papers, CAH-UT; Bluford Alexander Cameron Diary, June 15–17, 1863, Cameron Papers, CAH-UT; John F. Davenport, Chattanooga, TN, to Wife, Sept. 26, 1863, Davenport Letters, ADAH; John T. Knight, "the Cow Lands of Sorrow," to Susan Knight, Oct. 15, 1863, Knight Letters, CCCWC, TSLA.

53 Blomquist and Taylor, *This Cruel War*, 199–202 (quotation 202). See also T. P. Whitby, Missionary Ridge, TN, to Father, Nov. 25, 1863, Whitby Papers, AU.

54 Wynne and Taylor, *This War So Horrible*, 30.

55 Pate, *This Evil War*, 183.

56 J. C. Stone, Camp, to Fannie, May 17, 1864, Stone Letter, CWMC, USAMHI. See also D. A. Chesternut, Hanover Junction, VA, to Sister, May 26, 1864, Chester-nut Letter, Leigh, USAMHI; J. B. Sanders, New Hope Church, GA, to Elisabeth Sanders, May [27], 1864, Sanders Papers, MDAH.

57 C. B. Watson, Orange Court House, VA, to Father, May 4, 1864, Watson and Morris Family Correspondence, SHC-UNC.

58 Griffith, *Yours Till Death*, 105; Lowe and Hodges, *Letters to Amanda*, 134, 142; Thomas Warrick, Dalton, GA, to Wife, May 1, 1864, Warrick Papers, ADAH.

59 N. J. Clover, Belfield, VA, to Father and Mother, May 14, 1864, N. J. Clover Letters, Book 25, 70–72, Leigh, USAMHI; Wallace Comer, Dallas, GA, to Sister, June 1, 1864, and Comer, Kennesaw Mountain, GA, to Mother and Relatives, June 14, 1864, Comer Family Papers, SHC-UNC; Mays, *Let Us Meet in Heaven*, 219–25, 242, 253, 259–60 (quotations 219, 220, 225).

60 Davis Diary, May 7–19, 1864 (quotations May 13, 14, 17), VHS.

61 Wynne and Taylor, *This War So Horrible*, 83.

62 Harvey Bailey, Covington, GA, to Wife and Children, June 20, 1864, Bailey Letters, CWMC, USAMHI; Wallace Comer, Kennesaw Mountain, GA, to Mother and Relatives, June 14, 1864, Comer Family Papers, SHC-UNC; E. K. Flournoy, Camp, to Wife, May 22, June 13, 1864, Flournoy, Marietta, GA, to Wife, June 25, 1864, and

Flournoy, Chattahoochee River, GA, to Wife, July 5, 1864, Flournoy Letters, ADAH; Griffith, *Yours Till Death*, 106–7, 112, 113; Moses Kirkland, Camp Chattahoochee, to Lydia, July 2, 1864, Kirkland Papers MSS 348, EU; Enoch L. Mitchell, "Letters of Newberry," 78–79; J. W. Tindall, Army, to Wife, June 6, 1864, J. W. Tindall Papers, USC; Hess, *Union Soldier in Battle*, 64–72; Glatthaar, *General Lee's Army*, 421–72.

63 Robert A. Williams, Marietta, GA, to Mittie Williams, July 2, 1864, Williams Letters, ADAH.

64 Fleming Jordan, Army of Tennessee, to Wife, July 9, 11, 1864, Jordan Letters, UGA.

65 William R. Hughes, Petersburg, VA, to Wife, Aug. 3, 1864, Hughes Letters, UAL. See also John J. Mendenhall, Petersburg, VA, to Mother, Aug. 29, 1864, Mendenhall Letters, CWMC, USAMHI; R. B. Jett, Fort Gilmer, VA, to Mr. Roseborough Evins, Dec. 1, 1864, Jett Papers MS 57, EU.

66 Lowe and Hodges, *Letters to Amanda*, 173, 196, 204 (quotation 196).

67 H. R Rodgers, Nashville, TN, to Wife and Children, Dec. 6, 1864, Rodgers Letters, CWMC, USAMHI. See also Lanning Diary, 15, 21, 24, EU; William A. Stephens, Nashville, TN, to Susan, Dec. 6, 1864, Stephens Papers, EU.

68 Freeman, *R. E. Lee*, vol. 4, 154–55.

69 Matthew 26:41.

WORKS CITED

PRIMARY SOURCES
Manuscript Collections
Alabama Department of Archives and History, Montgomery
  Ebenezer B. Coggin Papers SPR 419
  John F. Davenport Letters SPR 426
  Phillips Fitzpatrick Papers SPR 421
  W. V. Fleming Correspondence SPR 509
  Elijah K. Flournoy Letters SPR 511
  Benjamin Franklin Lafayette Henderson Letters
  James Montgomery Lanning Diary
  E. W. Treadwell Letters SPR 438
  Thomas Warrick Papers SPR 420

Robert A. Williams Letters SPR 109

Auburn University, Special Collections, Auburn, AL
    James S. Alexander Collection RG 926
    Robert Emmet Corry Confederate Collection RG 84
    John Crittenden Papers RG 765
    Denney Family Papers RG 209
    Armistead L. Galloway Letters Collection 780
    B. R. H. Jeffares Letter RG 133
    Madison Kilpatrick Letters RG 31
    Newell Family Papers RG 681
    Thomas Porter Whitby Papers RG 63
    J. C. Williams Papers RG 866

Chickamauga National Military Park, Fort Oglethorpe, GA
    G. H. Burns Letters

Duke University, Special Collections, Durham, NC
    J. P. Culp Letters
    Thomas J. Elliott Papers
    George K. Evans Letters
    James C. Franklin Correspondence
    J. W. Griffin Papers
    Doctor Lee Papers
    R. H. Lee Papers
    Albert R. Phillips Papers
    Edgar Smithwick Papers
    Wilbur Thompson Letters

Emory University, Manuscripts, Archives, and Rare Book Library, Atlanta, GA
    Camp Family Papers MSS 141
    John Mitchell Davidson Papers (microfilm)
    Andrew J. Edge Papers MSS 346 (microfilm)
    James P. Garrison Papers MSS 409
    Gillis Family Papers MSS 300 (microfilm)
    Moses J. Kirkland Papers MSS 348 (microfilm)
    Richard Burch Jett Papers MS 57
    J. L. J. Lear Diary MSS 353 (microfilm)
    James H. Lee Papers MSS 69
    John Samuel Meriwether Papers MSS 253
    James A. Patton Letters MS 76
    Henry W. Robinson Papers MSS 392 (microfilm)
    Aaron M. Sewell Correspondence MSS 340 (microfilm)
    Augustin E. Shore Letters MSS 56
    William A. Stephens Papers MSS 324 (microfilm)
    Oliver V. Strickland Papers MSS 303
    Edwin D. Tuttle Letters MSS 318

Florida State University, Special Collections, Tallahassee
    H. Bradford Civil War Papers
Louisiana State University, Special Collections, Baton Rouge
    John W. Bell Letters MSS 771 (microfilm)
    Jacob Alison Frierson Correspondence, Mss 4209
    G. W. Giles Letters Mss 2133 (microfilm)
    M. Hart Letter, Mss 4553 (microfilm)
    Henry Gibbs Morgan Letter Mss 2035
    P. Retif Letters Mss 3365
    William H. Tamplin Letters, Mss 3015 (microfilm)
Mississippi Department of Archives and History, Jackson
    Kees (Martin Van Buren) Diary
    Odom (Elijah) Letters
    Robertson (William and Ben) Papers
    Sanders (J. B.) Papers
    Wilson (John A.) Letters
Tennessee State Library and Archives, Nashville
    Confederate Collection, Civil War Collection
        Marcus Bearden DeWitt Diary
        John Blair Diary (microfilm)
        Abel H. Crawford Letters (microfilm)
        John Thomas Knight Letters (microfilm)
        Judy H. Leas, "The Civil War Diary of Absalom Joshua Burum"
        Stephen M. Mathis Letter
        Samuel Jones Ridley Papers
        William Austin Smith Diary (microfilm)
United States Army Military History Institute, Carlisle, PA
    Civil War Miscellaneous Collection
        Isaac McQueen Auld Letters
        Harvey Bailey Letters
        Ann Barineau Collection
        George Heil Chatfield Letters
        D. W. Chenault Letters
        William D. Cole Letters
        Auvergne D'Antignac Letter
        Hart Brothers Letters
        Charles Meriweather Hurley Letters
        Miles W. Lewis Papers
        Philip P. Lewis Letters
        Joseph Richard Manson Diary and Letters
        T. S. McAlister Letter
        John J. Mendenhall Letters
        Henry Mowrer Papers

James D. Padgett Letters
Jacob Riley Parker Letters
John Prime Collection
Hugh Ross Rodgers Letters
James B. and Thomas J. Rounsaville Letters
Charles D. Sides Letters
John M. Smith Letter
James C. Stone Letter
Amon Updike Letters
James A. Wilson Letter
Lewis Leigh Collection
Robert Bates Letter, Book 19, 70
F. A. Bleckley Letters, Box 31
Bosworth Family Collection, Box 43
D. A. Chesternut Letter, Box 54
N. J. Clover Letters, Book 25, 70–72
William D. Clover Letters, Book 25, 48–69
A. D. Craver Letter, Box 54
L. R. Dalton Letters, Book 32, 31–49
Charles Miles Figgat Letter, Box 28
Samuel E. Foster Letter, Book 50, 46
Thomas Grisham Letter, Box 54
Benjamin Mason Letters, Book 8, 20–24
L. H. Mathews Poem
J. S. G. McGhea Letter, Book 50, 14
Radford Eugene Mobley Diary and Letters, Box 24
Hugh and Washington Nelson Letters, Book 2, 24–27
T. T. Raines Letter, Book 17, 20
W. N. Rose Letter, Book 19, 80
Allen Shadrick Letters, Box 51
J. G. Smith Letter, Book 25, 85
Horace M. Wade Letters, Book 33A
W. Johnson J. Webb Letters, Book 32, 4, 6–21
Samuel Wilson Letters, Box 54
University of Alabama, W. S. Hoole Special Collections Library, Tuscaloosa
Adams Family Papers
H. C. Harris Letter
Benjamin Sherwood Hedrick Letters
William R. Hughes Letters
Thomas Jones Taylor Letters
Lt. James White Letters
University of Arkansas, Special Collections, Fayetteville
W. A. Crouch Letters

John Wilson Peel Papers

R. F. Yeager Letters

University of Georgia, Hargrett Rare Book and Manuscript Library, Athens

Thomas Ely Lee Letters MS 2882

F. M. Goodwin Confederate Letter MS 1008

Fleming Jordan Letters MS 826

Knight Family Papers MS 528

Jimmie McCulloch Letter MS 2669

Robert T. Wood Papers MS 637

University of North Carolina, Southern Historical Collection, Chapel Hill

William D. Alexander Diaries #2478

Beggs and Janssen Family Papers #4821

Christopher Wren Bunker Papers #4822-z

William Pinkney Cline Papers #5019-z

John Fuller Coghill Letters #1724-z

William A. Collins Papers #5095-z

Comer Family Papers #167-z

Lucy S. Costen Papers #3582-z

Samuel W. Eaton Diary and Letters #1807

C. D. Epps Papers #5018-z

Frank Family Letters #3980-z

James E. Green Diary #2678

Hundley Family Papers #4971-z

Jones Family Papers #2884

Joyner Family Papers #4428

Joseph Fant Kauffman Diary, #3110

Francis Milton Kennedy Diary, M-3008

Drury Lacy Papers #3641

McLaurin Family Papers #358-z

Neil McLeod Papers #4150-z

Adin L. Rucker Scrapbook M-1367

Jane Sivley Papers #1891-z

Terry Family Papers #1448-z

John Thurman and Sallie Ecklin Thurman Papers #5107

James T. Wallace Diary #3059-z

Watson and Morris Family Correspondence #5150-z

Fatima M. Williams and William T. Williams Correspondence #4424

University of South Carolina, Caroliniana Library, Columbia

J. T. Bleckley Letter

Crawford Family Papers

Robert Dickinson Papers

William Alfred Gyles Papers

Miles H. Hunter Papers

William Henry Harrison Lee Papers
Alex McNeill Papers
Thomas John Moore Papers
J. T. and William Nobles Papers
J. D. Padgett Papers
John Putnam Papers
James Ramsey Papers
J. W. Tindall Papers
Willis Family Papers
University of Texas at Austin, Center for American History, Austin
Barnes (William H.) Papers
Brightman (John Claver) Papers
Cameron (Bluford Alexander) Papers
Farnsworth Family Letters
Farrow (Sam W.) Papers
Faulkner (Lee) and Johnaphene S. Wilson Papers
Head (William P.) Papers
Niebuhr (Friedrich Heinrich) Papers
Rice (Edwin E.) Diary
Virginia Historical Society, Richmond
James W. Albright Diary
Aylett Family Papers
Bailey Family Papers
Baker Family Papers
Lafayette J. Carneal Papers
Coiner Family Papers
Creed Thomas Davis Diary
Hoskins Family Papers
Ella Merryman Papers
Miller Family Papers
William Young Mordecai Papers
Henry Edward Neal Papers
Edwin Anderson Penick Papers
Daniel Cleveland Snyder Papers
Joseph D. Stapp Letters
Donald Tiedeken Papers
Watson Family Papers (microfilm)
John French White Papers (microfilm)
Virginia Military Institute, Lexington
William J. Black Diary #015

Books
Allan, Francis D. *Allan's Lone Star Ballads: A Collection of Southern Patriotic Songs Made During Confederate Times.* New York: Burt Franklin, 1874.

Ashley, Joe and Lavon, eds. *Oh for Dixie! The Civil War Record and Diary of Capt. William V. Davis, 30th Mississippi Infantry, C.S.A.* Colorado Springs: Standing Pine Press, 2001.

Battle, John D., ed. *Civil War Letters by Jesse Sumner Battle and James Norman Adams.* Cleveland: Halle Park Press, 1979.

Blomquist, Ann K., and Robert A. Taylor, eds. *This Cruel War: The Civil War Letters of Grant and Malinda Taylor, 1862–1865.* Macon, GA: Mercer University Press, 2000.

Cash, William M., and Lucy Somerville Howorth, eds. *My Dear Nellie: The Civil War Letters of William L. Nugent to Eleanor Smith Nugent.* Jackson: University Press of Mississippi, 1977.

Cate, Wirt Armistead, ed. *Two Soldiers: The Campaign Diaries of Thomas J. Key, C.S.A., December 7-1863–May 17, 1865, and Robert J. Campbell, U.S.A., January 1, 1864–July 21, 1864.* Chapel Hill: University of North Carolina Press, 1938.

Crow, Mattie Lou Teague, ed. *The Diary of a Confederate Soldier: John Washington Inzer, 1834–1928.* Huntsville, AL: Strode, 1977.

Durkin, Joseph T., S.J., ed. *John Dooley: Confederate Soldier. His War Journal.* Foreword by Douglas Southall Freeman. Washington, DC: Georgetown University Press, 1945.

Griffith, Lucille, ed. *Yours Till Death: Civil War Letters of John W. Cotton.* University: University of Alabama Press, 1951.

Hartley, William R., III, and David J. Zimmerman, eds. *The Fighting 57th North Carolina: The Life and Letters of James Calvin Zimmerman.* N.p.: n.p., 2006.

Hatley, Joe M., and Linda B. Huffman. *Letters of William F. Wagner, Confederate Soldier.* Wendell, NC: Broadfoot, 1983.

Haynes, Draughton Smith. *The Field Diary of a Confederate Soldier, Draughton Smith Haynes.* Darien, GA: Ashantilly Press, 1963.

Holland, Katherine S., ed. *Keep All My Letters: The Civil War Letters of Richard Henry Brooks, 51st Georgia Infantry.* Macon, GA: Mercer University Press, 2003.

Hubbell, Raynor. *Confederate Stamps, Old Letters, and History.* Griffin, CA: N.p., n.d.

Jones, Mary Miles, and Leslie Jones Martin, eds. *The Gentle Rebel: The Civil War Letters of 1st Lt. William Harvey Berryhill, Co. D, 43rd Regiment, Mississippi Volunteers.* Yazoo City, MS: Sassafras Press, 1982.

Lowe, Jeffrey C., and Sam Hodges, eds. *Letters to Amanda: The Civil War Letters of Marion Hill Fitzpatrick, Army of Northern Virginia.* Macon, GA: Mercer University Press, 1998.

Mays, Thomas D., ed. *Let Us Meet in Heaven: The Civil War Letters of James Michael Barr, 5th South Carolina Cavalry.* Abilene, TX: McWhiney Foundation, 2001.

McLaughlin, Josie Armstrong, comp. *Cherished Letters of Thomas Wayman Hendricks.* Birmingham: Birmingham Publishing, 1947.

McMurtrey, J. A. *Letters to Lucinda, 1862–1864.* Compiled by Mary Frances Honea Johnston. Huntsville, AL: Mrs. J. H. Johnston, 1985.

Moseley, Ronald H., ed. *The Stilwell Letters: A Georgian in Longstreet's Corps, Army of Northern Virginia.* Foreword by Herman Hattaway. Macon, GA: Mercer University Press, 2002.

Newton, John, and William Cowper. *Olney Hymns. In Three Books.* London: W. Oliver, 1779.

Northen, Charles Swift, III, ed. *All Right Let Them Come: The Civil War Diary of an East Tennessee Confederate.* Voices of the Civil War Series. Knoxville: University of Tennessee Press, 2003.

Park, Ruie Ann Smith, comp. and ed. *The Civil War Letters of the Shibley Brothers, Wm. H. H. and John S., to Their Dear Parents in Van Buren, Arkansas.* Fayetteville, AR: Washington County Historical Society, 1963.

Russell, William Howard. *My Diary North and South.* Ed. by Eugene H. Berwanger. New York: Alfred A. Knopf, 1988.

Smith, Thomas C. *Here's Yer Mule: The Diary of Thomas C. Smith, 3rd Sergeant, Company 'G,' Wood's Regiment, 32nd Texas Cavalry, C.S.A., March 30, 1862–December 31, 1862.* Waco, TX: Little Texas Press, 1958.

Wiley, Bell Irvin, ed. *"This Infernal War": The Confederate Letters of Sgt. Edwin H. Fay.* Austin: University of Texas Press, 1958.

Wynne, Lewis N., and Robert A. Taylor, eds. *This War So Horrible: The Civil War Diary of Hiram Smith Williams.* Tuscaloosa: University of Alabama Press, 1993.

Articles

Cawthon, John A., ed. "Letters of a North Louisiana Private to His Wife, 1862–1865." *Mississippi Valley Historical Review* 30 (Mar. 1944): 533–50.

"The Diary of a Virginia Cavalry Man, 1863–64," *Historical Magazine,* ser. 3, 2 (1873): 210–15.

Grantham, Dewey W., ed. "Letters from H. J. Hightower, A Confederate Soldier, 1862–1864." *Georgia Historical Quarterly* 40 (1956): 174–89.

Johnston, Hugh Buckner, ed. "The Confederate Letters of Ruffin Barnes of Wilson County." *North Carolina Historical Review* 31 (1954): 75–99.

——. "The Vinson Confederate Letters." *North Carolina Historical Review* 25 (1948): 100–110.

Lathrop, Barnes F. "A Confederate Artilleryman at Shiloh." *Civil War History* (1962): 373–85.

Mellon, Knox, Jr., ed. "A Florida Soldier in the Army of Northern Virginia: The Hosford Letters." *Florida Historical Quarterly* 46 (Jan. 1968): 243–71.

Mitchell, Enoch L., ed. "The Civil War Letters of Thomas Jefferson Newberry." *Journal of Mississippi History* 10 (1948): 44–80.

Osborn, George C. "Civil War Letters of Robert W. Banks: Atlanta Campaign." *Georgia Historical Quarterly* 27 (1943): 208–16.

——. "The Civil War Letters of Robert Webb Banks." *Journal of Mississippi History* 5 (1943): 141–54.

Pate, James P., ed. *When This Evil War Is Over: The Correspondence of the Francis Family 1860–65.* Tuscaloosa: University of Alabama Press, 2006.

Ryan, Harriet Fitts, arranger. "The Letters of Harden Perkins Cochrane, 1862–1864, part 1." *Alabama Review* 7 (Oct. 1954): 277–94.

——. "The Letters of Harden Perkins Cochrane, 1862–1864, part 2." *Alabama Review* 8 (Jan. 1955): 55–70.

——. "The Letters of Harden Perkins Cochrane, 1862–1865, part 5." *Alabama Review* 8 (Oct. 1955): 277–90.

Sanders, Mary Elizabeth, ed. "Letters of a Confederate Soldier, 1862–1863." *Louisiana Historical Quarterly* 29 (1946): 1229–40.

Simmons, Slann L. C., ed. "Diary of Abram W. Clement, 1865." *South Carolina Historical Magazine* 59 (1958): 78–83.

"Some Confederate Letters of I. B. Cadenhead, Co. H, 34th Alabama Infantry Regiment." *Alabama Historical Quarterly* 18 (1956): 564–71.

Electronic and Microfilm Sources

Glatthaar, Joseph T., ed. *Confederate Military Manuscripts, Series B, Holdings of Louisiana State University*. Lanham, MD: University Publications of America, 1996.

The Valley of the Shadow. Additional Personal Papers Collection. James M. Cadwallander Diary; John and Giney Dull Letters. http://valley.vcdh.virginia.edu/. Accessed Dec. 15, 2007.

SECONDARY SOURCES
Books

Anderson, Paul Christopher. *Blood Image: Turner Ashby in the Civil War and the Southern Mind*. Baton Rouge: Louisiana State University Press, 2002.

Barrow, Charles Kelly, J. H. Segars, and R. B. Rosenburg., eds. *Forgotten Confederates: An Anthology about Black Confederates*. Journal of Confederate History Series 14. Murfreesboro, TN: Southern Heritage Press, 1995.

Barton, Michael. *Goodmen: The Character of Civil War Soldiers*. University Park: Pennsylvania State University Press, 1981.

Beringer, Richard E., et al. *Why the South Lost the Civil War*. Athens: University of Georgia Press, 1986.

Berlin, Ira. *Many Thousands Gone: The First Two Centuries of Slavery in America*. Cambridge: Harvard University Press, 1998.

Berry, Stephen W., III. *All That Makes a Man: Love and Ambition in the Civil War South*. New York: Oxford University Press, 2003.

Bode, Frederick A., and Donald E. Ginter. *Farm Tenancy and the Census in Antebellum Georgia*. Athens: University of Georgia Press, 1986.

Bonner, Robert E. *Colors and Blood: Flag Passions of the Confederate South*. Princeton: Princeton University Press, 2002.

Brewer, James H. *The Confederate Negro*. Durham, N.C.: Duke University Press, 1969.

Bruce, Dickson D., Jr. *Violence and Culture in the Antebellum South*. Austin: University of Texas Press, 1979.

Bruce, Susannah Ural. *The Harp and the Eagle: Irish-American Volunteers and the Union Army, 1861–1865*. New York: New York University Press, 2006.

Carmichael, Peter S. *The Last Generation: Young Virginians in Peace, War, and Reunion.* Chapel Hill: University of North Carolina Press, 2005.

Cecil-Fronsman, Bill. *Common Whites: Class and Culture in Antebellum North Carolina.* Lexington: University Press of Kentucky, 1992.

Clinton, Catherine, ed. *Southern Families at War: Loyalty and Conflict in the Civil War South.* New York: Oxford University Press, 2000.

Clinton, Catherine, and Nina Silber, eds. *Divided Houses: Gender and the Civil War.* New York: Oxford University Press, 1992.

Daniel, Larry J. *Soldiering in the Army of Tennessee.* Chapel Hill: University of North Carolina Press, 1991.

Donald, David Herbert. *Lincoln.* New York: Simon & Schuster, 1995.

Escott, Paul D. *After Secession: Jefferson Davis and the Failure of Confederate Nationalism.* Baton Rouge: Louisiana State University Press, 1978.

Faust, Drew Gilpin. *The Creation of Confederate Nationalism: Ideology and Identity in the Civil War South.* Baton Rouge: Louisiana State University Press, 1988.

——. *James Henry Hammond and the Old South: A Design for Mastery.* Baton Rouge: Louisiana State University Press, 1982.

——. *Mothers of Invention: Women in the Slaveholding South in the American Civil War.* New York: Vintage Books, 1997.

——. *This Republic of Suffering: Death and the American Civil War.* New York: Alfred A. Knopf, 2008.

Freeman, Douglas Southall. *R. E. Lee: A Biography.* 4 vols. New York: Charles Scribner's Sons, 1942–44.

Gallagher, Gary W. *The Confederate War.* Cambridge: Harvard University Press, 1997.

——. *Lee and His Army in Confederate History.* Chapel Hill: University of North Carolina Press, 2001.

Glatthaar, Joseph T. *General Lee's Army: From Victory to Collapse.* New York: Free Press, 2008.

Gordon, Lesley Jill. *"I Never Was a Coward": Questions of Bravery in a Civil War Regiment.* Frank L. Klement Lecture Series: Alternative Views of the Sectional Conflict. Milwaukee: Marquette University Press, 2006.

Green, Arthur E. *Gracie's Pride: The 43rd Alabama Infantry Volunteers.* Shippensburg, PA: Burd Street Press, 2001.

Greenberg, Kenneth S. *Honor and Slavery: Lies, Duels, Noses, Masks, Dressing as a Woman, Gifts, Strangers, Humanitarianism, Death, Slave Rebellions, the Proslavery Argument, Baseball, Hunting, and Gambling in the Old South.* Princeton: Princeton University Press, 1996.

Grimsley, Mark. *The Hard Hand of War: Union Military Policy toward Southern Civilians.* Cambridge: Cambridge University Press, 1995.

Hahn, Steven. *A Nation Under Our Feet: Black Political Struggles in the Rural South From Slavery to the Great Migration.* Cambridge: Harvard University Press, 2003.

——. *The Roots of Southern Populism: Yeoman Farmers and the Transformation of the Georgia Upcountry, 1850–1890* (New York: Oxford University Press, 1983).

Hess, Earl J. *Liberty, Virtue, and Progress: Northerners and Their War for the Union.* New York: New York University Press, 1988.

——. *The Union Soldier in Battle: Enduring the Ordeal of Combat.* Lawrence: University Press of Kansas, 1997.

Jabour, Anya. *Scarlett's Sisters: Young Women in the Old South.* Chapel Hill: University of North Carolina Press, 2007.

Jimerson, Randall C. *The Private Civil War: Popular Thought During the Sectional Conflict.* Baton Rouge: Louisiana State University Press, 1988.

Johnson, Russell L. *Warriors into Workers: The Civil War and the Formation of Urban-Industrial Society in a Northern City.* New York: Fordham University Press, 2003.

Jordan, Ervin L., Jr. *Black Confederates and Afro-Yankees in Civil War Virginia.* Charlottesville: University Press of Virginia, 1995.

Levine, Bruce. *Confederate Emancipation: Southern Plans to Free and Arm Slaves during the Civil War.* New York: Oxford University Press, 2006.

Linderman, Gerald. *Embattled Courage: The Experience of Combat in the American Civil War.* New York: Free Press, 1987.

Logue, Larry M. *To Appomattox and Beyond: The Civil War Soldier in War and Peace.* Chicago: Ivan R. Dee, 1996.

Lowe, Richard. *Walker's Texas Division, C.S.A.: Greyhounds of the Trans-Mississippi.* Baton Rouge: Louisiana State University Press, 2004.

Lynn, John A. *The Bayonets of the Republic: Motivation and Tactics in the Army of Revolutionary France, 1791–94.* 1984; reprint ed., Boulder, CO: Westview, 1996.

Manning, Chandra. *What This Cruel War Was Over: Soldiers, Slavery, and the Civil War.* New York: Alfred A. Knopf, 2007.

Marten, James. *The Children's Civil War.* Chapel Hill: University of North Carolina Press, 1998.

Martin, Bessie. *Desertion of Alabama Troops from the Confederate Army: A Study in Sectionalism.* New York: AMI, 1966.

McCardell, John. *The Idea of a Southern Nation: Southern Nationalists and Southern Nationalism, 1830–1860.* New York: W. W. Norton, 1979.

McCurry, Stephanie. *Masters of Small Worlds: Yeoman Households, Gender Relations, & the Political Culture of the Antebellum South Carolina Low Country.* New York: Oxford University Press, 1995.

McPherson, James M. *For Cause and Comrades: Why Men Fought in the Civil War.* New York: Oxford University Press, 1997.

——. *Ordeal by Fire: The Civil War and Reconstruction.* New York: Alfred A. Knopf, 1982.

——. *What They Fought For, 1861–1865.* Baton Rouge: Louisiana State University Press, 1994.

Miller, Randall M., Harry S. Stout, and Charles Reagan Wilson, eds. *Religion and the American Civil War.* New York: Oxford University Press, 1998.

Mitchell, Reid. *Civil War Soldiers: Their Expectations and Their Experiences.* New York: Touchstone, 1988.

——. *The Vacant Chair: The Northern Soldier Leaves Home*. New York: Oxford University Press, 1993.

Moore, Albert Burton. *Conscription and Conflict in the Confederacy*. New York: Macmillan, 1924.

Noll, Mark A. *The Civil War as a Theological Crisis*. Chapel Hill: University of North Carolina Press, 2006.

Olsen, Christopher J. *Political Culture and Secession in Mississippi: Masculinity, Honor, and the Antiparty Tradition, 1830–1860*. New York: Oxford University Press, 2000.

Ott, Victoria E. *Confederate Daughters: Coming of Age during the Civil War*. Carbondale: Southern Illinois University Press, 2008.

Phillips, Jason. *Diehard Rebels: The Confederates Culture of Invincibility*. Athens: University of Georgia Press, 2007.

Prokopowicz, Gerald J. *All for the Regiment: The Army of the Ohio, 1861–1862*. Chapel Hill: University of North Carolina Press, 2001.

Rable, George C. *Civil Wars: Women and the Crisis of Confederate Nationalism*. Urbana: University of Illinois Press, 1989.

Robertson, James I., Jr. *Soldiers Blue and Gray*. Columbia: University of South Carolina Press, 1988.

Robinson, Armstead L. *Bitter Fruits of Bondage: The Demise of Slavery and the Collapse of the Confederacy, 1861–1865*. Charlottesville: University of Virginia Press, 2005.

Royster, Charles. *The Destructive War: William Tecumseh Sherman, Stonewall Jackson, and the Americans*. New York: Random House, 1991.

Sanders, Charles W., Jr. *While in the Hands of the Enemy: Military Prisons of the Civil War*. Baton Rouge: Louisiana State University Press, 2005.

Schantz, Mark S. *Awaiting the Heavenly Country: The Civil War and America's Culture of Death*. Ithaca, NY: Cornell University Press, 2008.

Sheehan-Dean, Aaron, ed., *The View from the Ground: Experiences of Civil War Soldiers*. Lexington: University Press of Kentucky, 2007.

——. *Why Confederates Fought: Family and Nation in Civil War Virginia*. Chapel Hill: University of North Carolina Press, 2007.

Stampp, Kenneth M. *The Imperiled Union: Essays on the Background of the Civil War*. New York: Oxford University Press, 1980.

Stout, Harry S. *Upon the Altar of the Nation: A Moral History of the American Civil War*. New York: Viking, 2006.

Terrill, Helen Eliza, and Sara Robertson Dixon, eds. *History of Stewart County, Georgia*. Columbus, GA: Columbus Office Supply, 1958.

Thomas, Emory M. *The Confederacy as a Revolutionary Experience*. Englewood Cliffs, NJ: Prentice Hall, 1971.

——. *The Confederate Nation: 1861–1865*. New York: Harper & Row, 1979.

Weitz, Mark A. *A Higher Duty: Desertion among Georgia Troops during the Civil War*. Lincoln: University of Nebraska Press, 2000.

——. *More Damning than Slaughter: Desertion in the Confederate Army*. Lincoln: University of Nebraska Press, 2005.

Whites, LeeAnn. *The Civil War as a Crisis in Gender: Augusta, Georgia, 1860–1890.* Athens: University of Georgia Press, 1995.

Wiley, Bell Irvin. *The Life of Billy Yank: The Common Soldier of the Union.* Indianapolis: Bobbs-Merrill, 1952.

———. *The Life of Johnny Reb: The Common Soldier of the Confederacy.* Indianapolis: Bobbs-Merrill, 1943.

Wilkinson, Warren. *Mother, May You Never See the Sights I Have Seen: The Fifty-seventh Massachusetts Veteran Volunteers in the Last Year of the Civil War.* Foreword by Emory M. Thomas. New York: Quill, 1990.

Williams, David. *A People's History of the Civil War: Struggles for the Meaning of Freedom.* New York: New Press, 2005.

———. *Rich Man's War: Class, Caste, and Confederate Defeat in the Lower Chattahoochee Valley.* Athens: University of Georgia Press, 1998.

Williams, David, Teresa Crisp Williams, and David Carlson. *Plain Folk in a Rich Man's War: Class and Dissent in Confederate Georgia.* Gainesville: University Press of Florida, 2002.

Woodworth, Steven E. *While God Is Marching On: The Religious World of Civil War Soldiers.* Lawrence: University Press of Kansas, 2001.

Wyatt-Brown, Bertram. *Southern Honor: Ethics and Behavior in the Old South.* New York: Oxford University Press, 1982.

Articles and Essays

Austerman, Wayne R. "The Black Confederates." In *Forgotten Confederates: An Anthology About Black Confederates,* edited by Charles Kelly Barrow, J. H. Segars, and R. B. Rosenburg, 37–49. Journal of Confederate History Series 14. Murfreesboro, TN: Southern Heritage Press, 1995.

Barber, E. Susan. " 'The White Wings of Eros': Courtship and Marriage in Confederate Richmond." In *Southern Families at War: Loyalty and Conflict in the Civil War South,* edited by Catherine Clinton, 119–32. New York: Oxford University Press, 2000.

Berends, Kurt O. " 'Wholesome Reading Purifies and Elevates the Man': The Religious Military Press in the Confederacy." In *Religion and the American Civil War,* edited by Randall M. Miller, Harry S. Stout, and Charles Reagen Wilson, 131–55. New York: Oxford University Press, 1998.

Brooks, Charles E. "Popular Sovereignty in the Confederate Army: The Case of Colonel John Marshall and the Fourth Texas Infantry Regiment." In *The View From the Ground: Experiences of Civil War Soldiers,* edited by Aaron Sheehan-Dean, 199–225. Lexington: University Press of Kentucky, 2007.

Cashin, Joan. " 'Since the War Broke Out': The Marriage of Kate and William McClure." In *Divided Houses: Gender and the Civil War,* edited by Catherine Clinton and Nina Silber, 200–12. New York: Oxford University Press, 1992.

Channing, Steven A. "Slavery and Confederate Nationalism." In *From the Old South to the New: Essays on the Transitional South,* edited by Walter J. Fraser Jr. and Winfred B. Moore Jr., 219–26. Westport, CT: Greenwood Press, 1981.

Dollar, Kent T. " 'Strangers in a Strange Land': Christian Soldiers in the Early Months of the Civil War." In *The View from the Ground: Experiences of Civil War Soldiers*, edited by Aaron Sheehan-Dean, 145–70. Lexington: University Press of Kentucky, 2007.

Escott, Paul. "The Failure of Confederate Nationalism: The Old South's Class System in the Crucible of War." In *The Old South in the Crucible of War*, edited by Harry P. Owens and James J. Cooke, 15–28. Jackson: University Press of Mississippi, 1983.

Glatthaar, Joseph T. "Afterword." In *The View From the Ground: Experiences of Civil War Soldiers*, edited by Aaron Sheehan-Dean, 249–54. Lexington: University Press of Kentucky, 2007.

Harper, Charles W. "Black Loyalty Under the Confederacy." In *Forgotten Confederates: An Anthology About Black Confederates*, edited by Charles Kelly Barrow, J. H. Segars, and R. B. Rosenburg, 7–28. Journal of Confederate History Series 14. Murfreesboro, TN: Southern Heritage Press, 1995.

Harvey, Paul. " 'Yankee Faith' and Southern Redemption: White Southern Baptist Ministers, 1850–1890." In *Religion and the American Civil War*, edited by Randall M. Miller, Harry S. Stout, and Charles Reagen Wilson, 167–86. New York: Oxford University Press, 1998.

Laskin, Lisa. " 'The Army is Not Near So Much Demoralized as the Country Is': Soldiers in the Army of Northern Virginia and the Confederate Home Front." In *The View from the Ground: Experiences of Civil War Soldiers*, edited by Aaron Sheehan-Dean, 91–120. Lexington: University Press of Kentucky, 2007.

Mitchell, Reid. "Christian Soldiers? Perfecting the Confederacy." In *Religion and the American Civil War*, edited by Randall M. Miller, Harry S. Stout, and Charles Reagen Wilson, 297–309. New York: Oxford University Press, 1998.

Noe, Kenneth W. " 'Alabama, We Will Fight for Thee': The Initial Motivations of Later-Enlisting Confederates." *Alabama Review* 62 (July 2009): 163–89.

——. " 'Battle Against the Traitors': Unionist Middle Tennesseans in the Ninth Kentucky Infantry and What They Fought For." In *Sister States, Enemy States: The Civil War in Kentucky and Tennessee*, edited by Kent Dollar, Larry H. Whiteaker, and W. Calvin Dickinson, 123–39. Lexington: University Press of Kentucky, 2009.

——. " 'Exterminating Savages': The Union Army and Mountain Guerrillas in Southern West Virginia, 1861–1862." In *The Civil War in Appalachia: Collected Essays*, edited by Kenneth W. Noe and Shannon H. Wilson, 104–30. Knoxville: University of Tennessee Press, 1997.

——. "Jigsaw Puzzles, Mosaics, and Civil War Battle Narratives." *Civil War History* 53 (Sept. 2007): 236–43.

Olsen, Otto H. "Historians and the Extent of Slave Ownership in the Southern United States." Reprint ed., *Civil War History* 50 (Dec. 2004): 401–17.

Ownby, Ted. "Patriarchy in the World Where There is No Parting: Power Relations in the Confederate Heaven." In *Southern Families at War: Loyalty and Conflict in the Civil War South*, edited by Catherine Clinton, 229–44. New York: Oxford University Press, 2000.

Paludan, Philip Shaw. "Religion and the American Civil War." In *Religion and the American Civil War*, edited by Randall M. Miller, Harry S. Stout, and Charles Reagen Wilson, 21–40. New York: Oxford University Press, 1998.

Phillips, Jason. "A Brothers' War? Exploring Confederate Perceptions of the Enemy." In *The View from the Ground: Experiences of Civil War Soldiers*, edited by Aaron Sheehan-Dean, 67–90. Lexington: University Press of Kentucky, 2007.

Potter, David M. "The Historian's Use of Nationalism and Vice Versa." In *The South and the Sectional Conflict*, 34–83. Baton Rouge: Louisiana State University Press, 1968.

Powell, Lawrence N., and Michael S. Wayne. "Self-Interest and the Decline of Confederate Nationalism." In *The Old South in the Crucible of War*, edited by Harry P. Owens and James J. Cooke, 29–45. Jackson: University Press of Mississippi, 1983.

Rolfs, David W. "The Religious Compromises and Conflicts of Northern Soldiers." In *The View from the Ground: Experiences of Civil War Soldiers*, edited by Aaron Sheehan-Dean, 121–44. Lexington: University Press of Kentucky, 2007.

Rollins, Richard. "Black Southerners in Gray." In *Black Southerners in Gray: Essays on Afro-Americans in Confederate Armies*, edited by Richard Rollins, 1–35. Journal of Confederate History Series 11. Murfreesboro, TN: Southern Heritage Press, 1994.

Sheehan-Dean, Aaron. "The Blue and Gray in Black and White." In *The View from the Ground: Experiences of Civil War Soldiers*, edited by Aaron Sheehan-Dean, 9–30. Lexington: University Press of Kentucky, 2007.

Stout, Harry S., and Christopher Grasso. "Civil War, Religion, and Communications: The Case of Richmond." In *Religion and the American Civil War*, edited by Randall M. Miller, Harry S. Stout, and Charles Reagen Wilson, 313–59. New York: Oxford University Press, 1998.

Thomas, Emory. "Reckoning with Rebels." In *The Old South in the Crucible of War*, edited by Harry P. Owens and James J. Cooke, 3–14. Jackson: University Press of Mississippi, 1983.

Wolosky, Shira. "Poetry and Public Discourse, 1820–1910." In *The Cambridge History of American Literature*, vol. 4 of *Nineteenth-century Poetry, 1800–1910*, edited by Sacvan Bercovitch, 145–480. Cambridge: Cambridge University Press, 2004.

Dissertations, Theses, Unpublished Papers

Glatthaar, Joseph T. "Roundtable Discussion: The State of Civil War Military History." Society of Civil War Historians Meeting, Philadelphia, PA, June 16, 2008.

——. "Why They Fought: Soldiers and Civilians of the Civil War Era." Paper presented at the Civil War and American Memory Symposium, Washington, DC, Nov. 13, 2001.

Laskin, Elisabeth Lauterbach. "Good Old Rebels: Soldiering in the Army of Northern Virginia, 1862–1865." Ph.D diss., Harvard University, 2003.

Manning, Chandra Miller. "What This Cruel War Was Over: Why Union and Confederate Soldiers Thought They Were Fighting the Civil War." Ph.D. diss., Harvard University, 2003.

Electronic Sources

" 'Aftermath of Gettysburg': Letters of John J. English." http://www.mindspring.com/ nixnox/english.html. Accessed May 6, 2008.

Ancestry.com.

Civil War Soldiers and Sailors System, http://www.itd.nps.gov/cwss/. Accessed Aug. 10–18, 2008.

The Civil War in American Memory. *Library of Congress Information Bulletin* 61 (December 2002). http://www.loc.gov/loc/lcib/0212/civilwar.html. Accessed May 1, 2007.

Confederate Inflation Rates (1861–65), http://inflationdata.com/Inflation/Inflation _Rate/ConfederateInflation.asp. Accessed Oct. 10, 2007.

"Drury Lacy," Davidson Encyclopedia, http://library.davidson.edu/archives/ency/ lacyd.asp.

"The 53d Ga. Vols. A Brief Sketch of Its Valiant Record Fighting All Through The War—A Call for a Reunion of the Survivors." *Griffin (Ga.) Daily News*, n.d., http:// www.rootsweb.com/gaspald3/53rd_georgia_volunteers.htm. Accessed July 5, 2007.

Florida 1st Infantry. http://www.psy.fsu.edu/thompson/cw/1-fl-inf/fl-1st-inf.html. Accessed Jan. 10, 2008.

42nd Georgia. http://www.42ndgeorgia.com. Accessed Oct. 21, 2007.

Hymns For the Camp. 2nd rev. ed. Raleigh: Strother & Marcom, 1862. Electronic ed. http://docsouth.unc.edu/imls/hymns/hymns.html#hymns14. Accessed Dec. 4, 2007.

"Our Montgomery Correspondence." *Charleston Mercury*, Apr. 23, 1861. "Chronicles of the Civil War," http://www.pddoc.com/cw-chronicles/?p=1405. Accessed Jan. 10, 2008.

Purchasing Power of Money in the United States from 1774 to 2006, http:// measuringworth.com/calculators/ppowerus. Accessed Oct. 10, 2007.

Schulte, Henry. "Re: Confederate Units at Pensacola," Florida in the Civil War Message Board, http://history-sites.com/mb/cw/flcwmb/index.cgi?noframes;read =1764. Accessed Jan. 10, 2008.

Taylor, W. L. "The 53d Ga. Vols., A Brief Sketch of Its Valiant Record, Fighting All Through The War—A Call for a Reunion of the Survivors." *Griffin (Ga.) Daily News.* http://www.rootsweb.com/gaspald3/53rd_georgia_volunteers.htm. Accessed Feb. 20, 2008.

Twenty-Eight Alabama Infantry Regiment. http://www.archives.state.al.us/referenc/ alamilor/28thinf.html.

INDEX

Albright, James W., 214

Alexander, James S., 214

Alexander, William D., 189, 214

Alexandria, La., 101

Allison, Jonathan, 214

Alspaugh, G. L., 38, 175, 214

American Revolution, 5, 25, 31, 34, 203

Anderson, Patton, 167, 274 (n. 69)

Anderson, Paul Christopher, 4

Anthony, Oliver Preston, 165

Antietam, Battle of, 28, 160, 177, 182, 193, 197, 199

Appomattox, Va., 189, 209, 210

Arkansas Post, Ark., 56

Arkansas troops: 1st Cavalry, 108; 1st Mounted Rifles, 131; 3rd Infantry, 179; 22nd Infantry, 101, 132, 165, 168

Army of Northern Virginia, 9, 32, 47, 141, 160, 202, 209, 214; and morale, 180, 181, 183–86; as symbol, 26, 168

Army of Tennessee, 119, 145, 146, 172, 183–86

Army of the Tennessee, 93

Arnold, Mrs. (Beverley, Va.), 71

Arthur, R. Admire, 214

Ashby, George, 114, 214

Atlanta, Ga., 150, 158, 173

Atlanta campaign, 96, 148, 206–7

Auld, I. M., 50, 100, 164, 197–98, 202, 214, 225

Aylett, William R., 214

Bailey, Harvey, 78–79, 96, 148, 214

Baker, Alpheus, 52

Baker, Samuel, 109, 118, 214, 225

Baltimore, Md., 169

Banks, Nathaniel, 185

Banks, Robert W., 8, 87, 88, 177, 214, 225

Baptists, 128, 132, 134, 139

Barber, Susan, 72

Barineau, Isaac, 143, 214

Barnes, Ruffin, 144, 181, 214, 225

Barnes, William H., 56, 68, 74, 164, 165, 214

Barr, Henry, 56–57, 83

Barr, James M., 73, 95, 100, 119–22, 147, 205, 214; and ideology, 28–29, 30, 33, 34, 36; and slavery, 30, 49, 56–57, 225; wife and farm, 83, 85

Barr, Rebecca, 56, 83

Barron, W. J., 158, 214

Barrow, James H., 214

Bartlett, James, 114

Barton, Michael, 3–4, 39

Bates, Robert, 214

Battle, Jesse S., 52–53, 57–58, 131–32, 134, 135, 214, 225

Battle, John S., 82

Beauregard, P. G. T., 274 (n. 69)

Beggs, Ginnie, 97, 196

Beggs, John T., 39, 97, 162, 164, 196–97, 214

Bell, John W., 214, 225

Bell, William R., 214

Benning, Henry, 274 (n. 69)

Bernard, George, 157

Berry, Stephen W., 4, 26, 67, 156, 236 (n. 69)

Berryhill, William H., 214

Bill (J. M. Barr's slave), 56–57, 83

Bill (Meriwether's slave), 57

Bird, John, 110

Black, William J., 214

Blair, John, 118, 214

Blakley, W. L., 214

Bleckley, F. A., 55, 189, 215

Bleckley, J. T., 97, 215

"Bonnie Blue Flag" (song), 1, 2, 9, 69, 232 (n. 1)

Boston, Mass., 30

Bosworth, Newt, 71, 215

Bounties, 11, 103–5, 106–8, 121, 175, 178, 209

Bradford, H., 215

Bragg, Braxton, 23, 113, 119, 167, 168, 183, 204, 274 (n. 69), 275 (n. 71)

Brandy Station, Battle of, 202–3

Brantley, William F., 274 (n. 69)

Brightman, J. C., 101, 102, 114, 183, 215

Bristoe Station, Battle of, 203

Brooks, Richard H., 9, 58–59, 79, 99, 107, 110, 137, 215, 225, 256 (n. 11)

Brown, John, 45

Browning, John K., 215, 225

Bryan, Goode, 274 (n. 69)

Buell, Don Carlos, 90

Bull Run. *See* Manassas

Bunker, C. W., 112, 214

Bunker, Eng, 112

Bureau of Conscription, 113, 173

Burnett (51st Georgia), 157

Burns, G. H., 33–34, 35, 53, 84, 95–96, 176, 177, 215; and camaraderie, 156, 159; and religion, 132, 134, 137, 141, 145, 146, 147

Burns, Robert, 72

Burrell (Comer's slave), 42–44

Burum, Absalom, 55, 96, 101, 215, 225

Butler, Benjamin, 90, 95

Cadenhead, I. B., 114, 215

Cadwallander, James M., 215

Camaraderie, 11, 12, 153–61

Cameron, Bluford, 215

Camp, T. L., 48, 58, 215

Campbellites, 138

Camp Douglas, Ill., 207

Camp Ford, Tex., 101

Camp Lee, 132

Camp Winn, Ala., 21

Capehart, William R., 215, 225

Carmichael, Peter S., 26

Carneal, Lafayette, 215, 225

Castle Thunder, 111, 182

Catholicism, 23, 132, 141, 179

Chancellorsville, Battle of, 95, 100, 125, 160, 181

Chapman, William H., 53

Charleston, S.C., 2, 188

Chatfield, George, 91, 215, 225

Chatfield, Willie, 91

Chattanooga, Tenn., 187, 204

Chenault, David W., 215, 225

Chenoweth, Jane, 71

Chesternut, D. A., 215

Chickamauga, Battle of, 145, 190

Chickasaw Bluffs, Battle of, 201

Childers, David R., 215, 225

Cleburne, Patrick R., 50–52, 167, 274 (n. 69)

Clement, Abram W., 215

Cline, William P., 74, 110, 111 (ill.), 137, 182, 190, 215

Clover, John, 108, 109, 215

Clover, N. J., 108, 109, 205, 215

Clover, William, 164, 178, 215

Cochrane, Harden P., 21–23, 49, 54–55, 87, 100, 107, 112, 175, 215, 225

Coggin, E. B., 55, 99, 100, 134–35, 176, 215

Coghill, J. F., 27, 35, 36, 58, 100, 144, 158, 215

Coiner, George M., 114, 215, 225

Cole, William D., 79, 116, 183, 215, 225

Collins, William A., 112, 130–31, 132, 136, 175, 196, 215, 256 (n. 11)

Columbus, Miss., 87

Comer, J. Wallace, 42–44, 205

Confederate troops: 10th Cavalry, 58

Conscription, 2, 6, 7, 37, 106, 108–12, 114, 117, 121, 175, 209, 232 (n. 5), 257 (n. 17); acts and policies, 11, 28–29, 105; Bureau of, 173; resistance to, 24

Copland, William, 215

Corbin, Henry, 225

Corinth, Miss., 176; Battle of, 197

Corlist, I., 254 (n. 62)

Corpus Christi, Tex., 97

Corry, Robert Emmet, 73, 168, 185, 215

Cotton, John W., 35, 58, 100, 119, 159, 164, 166, 204, 215; and family, 79, 81, 84, 158; and morale, 181, 188

Cowardice, 198, 209

Crater, The, 54, 97, 106, 207

Craver, A. D., 49–50, 54, 98, 119, 216

Crawford, Andrew, 49, 216, 225

Crawford, George, 39

Lacy, Drury, 37, 218, 226

Lacy, Singleton, 218, 226

Lacy, William S., 37–38, 110, 133, 144, 156, 158, 218, 226

LaGrange, Battle of, 197

Lambeth, Joseph H., 218

Lane, James Henry, 118, 184, 275 (n. 71)

Langhorne, Jacob K., 218, 226

Lanier, John M. P., 218

Lanning, James M., 107, 118, 141, 145, 187, 218, 226

Laskin, Elisabeth Lauterbach, 32, 39, 46–47, 108, 129, 167, 238 (n. 64), 257 (n. 17)

Later enlisters: and African American soldiers, 50–55, 59–60; and age, 14–15; and bounties, 11, 103–5, 106–8, 121, 175, 178, 209, 255 (n. 10), 256 (n. 11); and camaraderie, 12, 153–61, 174; and camp revivals, 127, 129–30, 138–50; and combat, 191–209; and conscription, 11, 37, 105, 106, 108–12, 114, 117, 121, 173, 175, 209, 257 (n. 17); defined, 13; and demographics, 14–18; and desertion, 169, 173–76, 178–87, 190; and duty to enlist, 38, 209; and Emancipation Proclamation, 10, 35, 52–53; and enlistment for pay, 11, 103–8; and enslaved body servants, 42–44, 48–50; and esprit de corps, 11; and families in occupied areas, 97–98; as fathers, 67, 77–81; and federal tyranny, 34–35; and fraternization, 98–102; and hatred of enemy, 11, 60, 86–102, 174; and health, 198, 210; and honor, 38–39, 209; and ideology, 10, 21–23, 26–37, 209; ignored in scholarly literature, 7–8; and independence, 31–37, 203; and infidelity, 64, 72–74; insufficient numbers of, 201; and irreligious camps, 129, 130–33; and liberty, 36, 37, 172, 209; and Abraham Lincoln, 34–35; and love for wives, 63–65, 74–76; and messes, 12, 153–59, 160; and mutiny, 178–79; and nationalism, 23–31, 36, 37, 128; and officers, 163–69, 176; and peer pressure, 37; and primary group cohesion, 12, 155, 160; and reasons not to enlist, 7–9, 37; and religion, 125–51, 173, 174, 175, 188, 200, 264 (n. 73), 265–66 (n. 105), 267 (n. 122); and romance, 71–73; and rumors, 168–69, 174; and slavery, 10, 16, 18, 40, 47–60, 81–86, 125, 209; and states' rights, 36, 37; and subjugation, 35–37, 209; and substitution, 1, 105, 112–21, 175, 258 (n. 42); and unit pride, 11, 160–63; and war weariness, 171–90; and women, 10, 63–86, 129

Lawson, Madison, 218, 226

Leah (Meriwether's slave), 57

Lear, J. L. J., 157, 218, 226

Lee, Benjamin W., 57, 218, 226

Lee, J. H., 103–4, 105–6, 107, 132, 148, 167–68, 219

Lee, R. H., 36, 219

Lee, Robert E., 9, 26, 33, 92, 181, 186, 204, 209, 275 (n. 71); battles and campaigns, 192–93, 202, 203, 205; praised, 166–68, 182, 274 (n. 69)

Lee, Stephen D., 187, 274 (n. 69), 275 (n. 71)

Lee, Thomas E., 219

Lee, William H. H., 219

Leet, Edwin, 219

Levine, Bruce, 51

Lewis, Mary, 133

Lewis, Miles, 133, 136, 219

Lewis, Phillip, 219

Liberty, 5, 9, 10, 28, 31–32, 36, 40, 46, 172, 209

Lincoln, Abraham, 1, 23, 35, 67, 89, 180, 188, 189, 201

Linderman, Gerald, 4, 7, 29, 38, 39, 66, 99, 155, 173–74, 194; and battle, 194, 196, 283 (n. 10)

Lippard, Jesse, 219

Little Rock, Ark., 142

Logue, Larry M., 4, 108

Shelby Springs, Ala., 21

Shelton, Harriet Elisabeth, 64

Sheridan, Phillip, 93

Sherman, William Tecumseh, 53, 93, 96, 185, 188, 210

Shibley, John S., 94, 101, 132, 141, 142, 165, 168, 179, 204, 221

Shibley, William H. H., 94, 101, 132, 141, 142, 168, 179, 204, 221

Shiloh, Battle of, 21–22, 23, 27, 33, 87, 92, 196

Shore, A. E., 118, 166, 184, 187, 221

Shore, Edward H., 221

Shreveport, La., 76

Sides, C. D., 178, 180, 221, 256 (n. 11)

Sims, William H., 221, 227

Sivley, Willie, 26, 36, 53, 185, 188–89, 221, 227

Slavery, 4–5, 10, 16, 40, 48, 57, 125, 209; body servants and camp laborers, 42–44, 48–50; breakdown of, 55–57; and enlistment, 5–6, 10, 44–48; rental and sale, 57–59

Smith, J. G., 221

Smith, John M., 221

Smith, M. L., 274 (n. 69)

Smith, Thomas, 26, 33, 48, 91, 131, 221

Smith, William, 221, 227

Smithson, William B., 221

Smithwick, Edgar, 221

Snider, William E., 221

Snyder, D. C., 49, 70, 116, 149, 165, 221, 227

South Carolina College, 118

South Carolina troops: 5th Cavalry, 29, 49, 147; 3rd Infantry, 36, 52; 16th Infantry, 158; 18th Infantry, 118, 159; 20th Infantry, 147; 21st Infantry, 101, 135; 24th Infantry, 97; Hampton's Legion, 106, 189; Holcomb's Legion, 50, 96; militia, 28–29

South Mountain, Battle of, 191–92

Spotsylvania Court House, Battle of, 187, 205

Stapp, Joseph D., 221, 227

States' rights, 10, 24, 36, 37, 40, 236 (n. 36), 238 (n. 64)

Stephen (Moore's slave), 50

Stephens, Alexander, 188

Stephens, William A., 79, 187, 221, 227

Stevenson, Carter L., 161

Stewart, Alexander P., 171, 274 (n. 69)

Stewart, Rial, 158

Stilwell, Molly, 34, 77–78, 247–48 (n. 56)

Stilwell, William Ross, 33, 34, 53, 92, 112, 116, 177, 181, 184, 221; and battle, 197, 199, 200, 202; and family, 30, 77, 159, 160, 176; and nationalism, 27–28, 30; and religion, 30, 139, 142, 144, 146–47, 149; and women, 69, 71, 247–48 (n. 56)

Stone, J. C., 205, 221, 227

Stones River, Battle of. *See* Murfreesboro, Battle of

Stoutmire, Jacob, 221

Strickland, O. V., 55, 221, 227

Stuart, J. E. B., 166, 274 (n. 69)

Subjugation, 5, 10, 32, 35–36, 37, 40, 209

Substitution, 2, 6, 7, 11, 39, 105, 112–21, 175, 258 (n. 42)

Swett, Charles, 51–52

Tamplin, B. F., 38, 221, 227

Tamplin, W. H., 119, 221, 227

Taylor, Grant, 35, 36, 52, 94, 164, 185, 186, 188, 221; and battle, 201, 204; and family, 78–80, 158; and farm, 82, 85; and neighbors in other regiments, 159, 160; and religion, 132, 135, 136, 139, 145; and slavery, 50, 58, 227; and substitution, 116–17, 119

Taylor, Malinda, 117

Taylor, Richard, 189

Teer, Ide, 158

Tennessee troops: 1st Artillery, 157, 162; McClung's Battery, 118; 3rd Cavalry, 27, 131, 176, 196; 8th Infantry, 35, 60th Infantry, 71, 91, 93; 1st Middle Tennessee Battalion, 94

Wilderness, Battle of the, 111, 182, 190

Wiley Bell I., 7–8, 29, 66, 73, 89, 99, 155, 161, 163, 190, 193–94, 202; and ideology, 3, 26, 31; and reasons for enlistment, 3, 4, 6, 7; and slavery, 44–45; and war weariness, 173, 174

Williams, C. W., 222

Williams, David, 5, 46

Williams, Hiram Smith, 100, 146, 154, 165, 222; and battle, 204, 206; and war weariness, 171–73, 211

Williams, James I., 222, 227

Williams, J. C., 79, 48, 134, 222

Williams, R. C., 110

Williams, Robert A., 206, 222, 227

Williamson, James, 53, 68, 222

Willis, Erastus, 36, 52

Wilson, James A., 16, 79, 118, 132, 222, 227

Wilson, John, 76, 79, 222

Wilson, Samuel, 222, 227

Wimberly, F. D., 42

Women, 2, 10, 63–86, 244 (n. 32); as sustaining motivators, 65–66, 68–71, 243 (n. 3)

Wood, Dallas, 222

Wood, Robert, 222, 227

Woodworth, Stephen E., 129, 131

Woolwine, C. R., 223

Yager, Richard F., 223

Yorktown, Battle of, 33, 195

Zimmerman, James Calvin, 48, 109, 223